Praise for *Wrapped in a Holy Flame*

"Stories speak to the heart of what it is to be human, and these stories help us understand what it is to be divine. Reb Zalman's spiritual insight and clarity make this collection of teachings and tales a powerful and transformative gateway to God and godliness."

—RABBI RAMI M. SHAPIRO, author,
Minyan: Ten Principles for Living a Life of Integrity
and *The Way of Solomon*

"This latest of Zalman's gifts to the Jewish world is by far the most clear, accessible, and authentic explanation of classical Hasidic teachings and their timely relevance. Reb Zalman zaps us with notions so fresh and ripe for our paradigm that they smack of the long-lost aboriginal life-wisdom that birthed the Jewish people and its ever-dynamic ideology to begin with."

—RABBI GERSHON WINKLER, author,
Magic of the Ordinary: Recovering the Shamanic in Judaism

"*Wrapped in a Holy Flame* offers readers a clear philosophical foundation for the connection between traditional Hasidism and new developments in Jewish mysticism today as taught by Rabbi Zalman Schachter-Shalomi. As a well-known teacher of Kabbalah who is also strongly grounded in the Hasidic world, he and his student Nataniel Miles-Yepez make a strong case for the neo-Hasidic underpinnings of the growing Jewish renewal movement."

—RABBI DAVID COOPER, author,
God Is a Verb and *A Heart of Stillness*

"Rabbi Zalman Schachter-Shalomi is at the forefront of everything new and alive in Judaism. He is the Renewer of the Generation. *Wrapped in a Holy Flame* presents profound teachings and stories of the Hasidic masters in a form suited to our time and our modern sensibilities. Reb Zalman is the chief cupbearer at our mystic banquet, offering aged wine in new flasks, wine sweet to the taste of those thirsty for Jewish spiritual wisdom."

—MAGGID YITZHAK BUXBAUM, author,
Jewish Spiritual Practices

WRAPPED IN A HOLY FLAME

Teachings and Tales of the Hasidic Masters

Rabbi Zalman Schachter-Shalomi

o

Edited by

Nataniel M. Miles-Yepez

An Arthur Kurzweil Book

JOSSEY-BASS
A Wiley Imprint
www.josseybass.com

Jossey-Bass books and products are available through most bookstores. To contact Jossey-
Bass directly, call our Customer Care Department within the United States at (800) 956-
7739, outside the United States at (317) 572-3986, or fax (317) 572-4002.

Jossey-Bass also publishes its books in a variety of electronic formats. Some content that
appears in print may not be available in electronic books.

Library of Congress Cataloging-in-Publication Data
Schachter-Shalomi, Zalman, date.
   Wrapped in a holy flame : teachings and tales of the Hasidic masters /
Zalman Schachter-Shalomi ; edited by Nataniel M. Miles-Yepez.—1st ed.
      p. cm.
Includes bibliographical references and index.
   ISBN 0-7879-6573-1
   1. Hasidism. 2. Hasidim—Biography. 3. Hasidim—Legends. 4. Habad.
5. Shneur Zalman, of Lyady, 1745–1813. Liokuote amarim. I.
Miles-Yepez, Nataniel M. II. Title.
   BM198.2 .S33 2003
   296.8'332—dc21   2002154074

Printed in the United States of America
FIRST EDITION
HB Printing 10 9 8 7 6 5 4 3 2 1

CONTENTS

ACKNOWLEDGMENTS

THIS WORK is largely based on a series of lectures given in Boulder, Colorado, at the Naropa Institute in the spring of 1998, highlighting the teachings of a small selection of Hasidic masters. At that time, I held the World Wisdom Chair in Naropa's Department of Religious Studies. The students in these classes represented a wide variety of backgrounds and religious affiliations. Naropa is known for its strong contemplative and psychological emphasis, and this is reflected in the direction many of the lectures took in response to the needs and questions of the students. For much the same reason, some of the material reflects the concerns of feminism and triumphalism. I am indebted to the students of this class for their contribution to this work. In many ways, it belongs to them. My teaching assistant was Rabbi Shoshana Devorah, who deserves much thanks for her part in guiding the students. And thanks to Doug MacLean, who was responsible for recording my lectures.

The material of the book was also supplemented by various articles and recordings made before and after the 1998 lectures at Naropa. Some of these come from the time when I was affiliated with the Lubavitcher Hasidim, and others were made with the editor especially for this book. All of the Hasidic teachings in this work, with the exception of Reb Shlomo's pieces, are my own original translations. My gratitude goes to Rebbetzin Neilah Carlebach for permission to reprint "A Vision of Peace and Harmony." For assisting in culling this material and facilitating various appointments, I thank my secretary, Mary Fulton.

Nataniel Miles-Yepez wrote the biographies (except for the Chabad biographies), coauthored "Dancing from the Infirmary: The Maggid of Koznitz," and wrote most of the notes. Rabbi Arthur Green prepared the first version of "What Reb Nachman Knew." Jennifer Miles transcribed portions of the manuscript and was wonderfully tolerant of its editor throughout the long process. Nicholas Isaac Phares must also be thanked for his research efforts and good humor.

I would also like to thank my friends Arthur Kurzweil and Alan Rinzler of Jossey-Bass for their enthusiastic support for this book.

Z.M.S.-S.

DEDICATION

"This being will not take advantage of another in any way;
this being will not wrong anyone in the world;
this being will become holy in the Holiness of the Lord;
this being will cleave forever (to the Lord);
this being will become wrapped
in a holy flame during prayers. . . ."

—Reb Hillel Zeitlin

To the memory of
Reb Yosef Yitzhak Schneersohn, the Sixth Lubavitcher Rebbe;
Reb Menachem Mendel Schneerson, the Seventh Lubavitcher Rebbe;
Reb Shlomo Halberstam, the Bobover Rebbe;
Reb Gedaliah Kenig of S'fat;
Reb Shalom Noach Brazovsky, the Slonimer Rebbe;
Reb Arele Roth;
and Reb Abraham Joshua Heschel of New York,
peace be upon them.
To Reb Kalonymous Kalmisch Shapira of Piasetzna
and Reb Hillel Zeitlin,
may their sacrifice be remembered.

—Zalman Meshullam Schachter-Shalomi

For my beloved abuelita, Margarita, peace be upon her,
and the Navarros, who have so long waited for this aliyah.

—Nataniel M. Miles-Yepez

AUTHOR'S PREFACE

MOST OF THE TIME when people talk about Hasidism, depending on who is telling the story, there usually seems to be a hidden agenda. For instance, there are people who will tell a Hasidic tale in the hopes that this will inspire you to become a restorationist, so that we can go back to the old "tried and true" ways of observing Jewish Law. There are others who will tell Hasidic tales, wanting to show you how the Hasidim liberated us from Jewish Law, because there are also all kinds of tales that point in that direction. Neither of these agendas has anything to do with my intent.

Years ago, when I read William James's *Varieties of Religious Experience* and Aldous Huxley's *Perennial Philosophy,* wonderful books, I found to my disappointment that neither had much in the way of Jewish voices or Jewish mystical analogues to other mystical traditions. There was a real ache in my heart that Hasidism was not represented in these great collections. And it troubled me that this aspect of what the internal world of a Hasid was was not available in English in a way that people could easily access.

There is an element in which Christianity provided an early form of that same mode that Hasidism brought out. Hasidim tell how Reb Mendel of Kotzk, when someone came to him to vilify a certain ritual slaughterer for some triviality, the Kotzker shouted at him, "Why are you so worried about what goes into the mouth and not about what comes out of the mouth!" Now, I don't believe the Kotzker had read the New Testament and was quoting Jesus there. Nevertheless, the same teaching is represented. On the other hand, Sholem Asch, in his novels *The Nazarene* and *The Apostle,* wishes to make Jesus accessible to Jews in Yiddish, so he describes him almost like a Hasidic personality. So there was this wonderful quality that was available in Hasidism, and it was largely hidden from the world. For this alone, it would be well worth bringing out this collection of talks that I gave to a broad range of students in recent years. But my intention here was a different one.

There is a need for people to move into the heart of a tradition. You are certainly aware that there are people only on the outside of Buddhism, Hinduism, Christianity, and other religions. And now there are some people who are penetrating to the inside and finding the Christian mystics,

Vedanta, and Vajrayana, because this has been made available and accessible to people. And so I felt there was a need for people to know about the interior life that Hasidism could produce and has produced for many people.

Not everything in this book, my own rendering of these teachings, would have been acceptable to these Hasidic masters in their time, but I do believe that from the perspective of our time, they would be satisfied with my rendition. By and large, this comes not only from my having lived as a Hasid in the Chabad Hasidic lineage but also from having visited the different Rebbes and from studying the teachings of different groups. And so now, when I approach a Hasidic text of insight and meditation, a teaching, or a Hasidic tale, I measure it according to my emotional reaction: does it inspire me, does it open me to something deeper, does it make my soul bigger rather than smaller? I have the feeling that there are already enough religious texts that make your soul smaller, and I had no intention of adding to them by translating them.

Martin Buber also felt that he wanted to bring Hasidism to the Western world, and he did make a great contribution in this regard, except that he got it largely from books and hadn't been involved in *davvenen* and singing the Hasidic melodies. And, I believe, neither did Gershom Scholem get it quite right in his controversy with Buber over this issue. Scholem felt that the essence of a Hasidic master was found in his teaching, whereas Buber felt that the essence was in the tales. I, on the other hand, feel that neither the teachings nor the tales are quite enough to get the essence; one must also learn the melodies (*niggunim*) and modes of prayer of the masters, which are quite unique. So I gave myself over to learning these melodies and the modes of prayer of the various Hasidim, in addition to the tales and teachings.

Thus I present here one person's distillation of the Hasidic inner world, a person who is also aware of the inner worlds of other religious paths and who also believes in a generic spirituality that pervades all spiritual paths, from Shamanism to Judaism. It is my hope that the reader will enjoy and appreciate the reading of this book and will give credit to Nataniel Miles-Yepez for gathering this material together and shaping it in to a readable whole.

Boulder, Colorado   ZALMAN MESHULLAM SCHACHTER-SHALOMI
27 Adar, the Yahrzeit
of Rebbetzin Malkah of Belz

EDITOR'S PREFACE

WRAPPED IN A HOLY FLAME is not a book of rigorous linear teaching or even equally representative of all the Hasidic masters it treats, for it evolved from the dynamic and organic teaching process, a process that is ever ready to turn aside in curiosity, to explain a difficult concept, and to follow the true course of inspiration. By far the most thoroughly discussed teaching in the book is that of the Chabad school of thought. And this is due not only to its profound influence on the Hasidic world and its rigorous philosophy but also because it is the Hasidic home in which the author lived for much of his life. From this perspective, its strong emphasis is, I believe, justified and even a service to the reader.

In the lengthy preparation of this book, the holy souls of these *tzaddikim* have spoken to me a timeless and placeless message of the renewal of the spirit, which I hope is communicated across these pages. For me, this book has truly been a labor of learning as well as love. And as much as this feeling is due to the those holy beings, at least as much is due to its author, whose extraordinary energy and brilliance give this book its vitality. Thank you, Reb Zalman.

For the reader, I have but one piece of advice, which comes from the great Hasidic master, Reb Abraham Joshua Heschel of Apt: "Awaken your heart, and put your mind to it!"

Boulder, Colorado
January 2003

NATANIEL M. MILES-YEPEZ

NOTE TO THE READER

GENDERED LANGUAGE is still a problem in our world, and the difficulty remains around using masculine or feminine personal pronouns with regard to God and entities of nonspecific gender. Throughout this book, masculine language has largely been maintained in traditional contexts, while most others present God in nonspecific terms, except in particular cases where the Divine Feminine or Divine Masculine is clearly being referenced. Please be aware that the great works of the Hebrew sages were written at a time when masculine language was understood to encompass the feminine, and God in the Jewish tradition has always been acknowledged as having both masculine and feminine traits.

WRAPPED IN A HOLY FLAME

A RENAISSANCE
OF PIETY

THE TEACHINGS OF HASIDISM
AND THE SHIFTING PARADIGM

HASIDIC TRADITION[1] has it that the Jewish people were completely exhausted and faint, left without energy, after being ravaged by the external catastrophe of Chmielnicki[2] and his hordes, and the internal catastrophe brought about by the failed Messiahs, Shabbetai Tzvi and Jacob Frank.[3] The well of inspiration had dried up and with it all direct contact with the Almighty. Coupled with this poverty of the spirit, the Torah intelligentsia had drawn a serious distinction between themselves and those on a lower level of intellectual attainment. Thus it is commonly said, "Israel would not have had the strength to survive and live up to the days of the Messiah had not God taken some of the light of the Messiah and focused it in the soul of the Ba'al Shem Tov, whom He sent to succor Israel."

Rabbi Israel Ba'al Shem Tov, the holy master and teacher, through whom the lifeline to the firsthand experiences of Torah realities was reestablished, was born in 1698 (5458 on the Hebrew calendar), lived sixty-two years, and passed on the first day of Shavuot in the year 1760 (5520). He left no books, though there are some letters of his extant.[4] His influence, then, was immediate. The change he brought about in his environment and in the people around him was direct and seminal. His life and teaching brought about an explosion of spirituality that was ultimately to dot the map of Eastern Europe; towns in Poland, Hungary, Czechoslovakia, Rumania, Russia, Lithuania, and Latvia would become synonymous with the "who's who" of the Hasidic world. Who would have even noticed little towns like Medzibozh, Bratzlav, and Lubavitch, had they not become identified with important leaders of the Hasidic movement?

What was it that marked the teaching of the Ba'al Shem Tov? Perhaps more than anything else, it was the quality of *mamash*, "so-beingness," with which he approached the central issues of Judaism. The whole world is *truly* filled with God's glory, and everyone can *truly* approach that God. What good is there in believing in a deity of whom one can only say, "God once created this world and has since then been deaf, dumb, and blind to us"? Every leaf driven by the wind rolls through the grass by specific design of God who creates it. For the Ba'al Shem Tov, there are no accidents. A tinker asking for things to mend is the voice of Providence asking humankind to repent. Fervor in the "heart afire" views God even behind the apparent eclipse, whereas a bitter detachment turns even the most fluid water of revelation into hard, frozen objects of idolatry. The poor can truly pray to God Who Is Poor.

The fervor of preaching was not enough for the Ba'al Shem Tov. Many before him had talked of what was needed but never managed to show how achieving it could be done. The Ba'al Shem Tov, in a conscious ascent to the high celestial regions, visiting the mansions of the Messiah, asked the Messiah, "When will my master come?" to which the Messiah replied, "In this you will know; when your teachings are published and become manifest in the world and your sources spread outward, and that which I have taught you, and which you have attained, when even they will be able to effect such unifications and such ascendances as you do."[5] This, then, was the mission of the Ba'al Shem Tov, to make the innermost wellsprings available to those on the "outside." Like God's promise to Abraham: "*Ufaratzta*—And you will burst forth westward, eastward, to the north, and to the south." The Messiah's promise to the Ba'al Shem Tov became a rallying cry of the Hasidim.

There is no way to fully estimate the impact of the Ba'al Shem Tov. There is no Jewish institution today, no matter how deviant from the norms of Judaism, that can claim to have been unaffected by Hasidism. The Ba'al Shem Tov was a genius in generating *pure joy, pure will*. As he said to one who came to attack him and remained as a disciple, "It is not that you cannot believe; it is that you do not *will* to believe." This is the legacy of the Ba'al Shem Tov and Hasidism.

Hasidism and Existentialism

The Hasidic writings of Martin Buber and Abraham Joshua Heschel[6] have led some people to wonder if there is a connection between Hasidism and existentialism. The answer to that question depends on when it is raised. If it was asked in 1951 or 1952, you would have gotten a resounding yes from all sides. That was when existentialism was most influential. And one of the statements that the existentialists were making then was that *existence* is prior to *essence*. In other words, it isn't "I think, therefore I am," but rather "I am, therefore I think." This emphasis makes a difference.

The other factor is that a certain and increasing amount of consciousness, awareness, had set in. It is a strange phenomenon, because living in the middle of it, you don't notice it so much. In this sense, we are like the frog in the kettle. If you take a frog and you drop it in hot water, it jumps out right away. If you put cold water in the kettle, and you heat it up slowly, it'll keep on swimming in there until it's cooked. We don't notice the shifts that happen to us over time because they are almost imperceptible. It takes a certain kind of consciousness to notice the shifts. What psychedelics did, for instance, was speed up the mind so that you were able to notice the shifts more clearly. One of the shifts that happened with existentialism was a recognition of something that Jean Paul Sartre[7] pointed out, "I cannot take a moral holiday." With every decision that I make, I have to handle all of the repercussions of that decision. And from that predicament—the word *predicament* was very strong in existentialism—"there was no exit." Notice the connection between "no exit" and the word *nausea*, which were the titles of Sartre's books. It almost suggests that life makes you sick, that it isn't fun, and that there is no exit from that. That is the atheist existentialist position.

There were also some theistic, religious existentialists who said, "How do I know there is a God? Because I base my life on it. The fact that I decide, that I commit myself to a life with God makes God present." What was interesting about this was that it was a prelude for Peter L. Berger, a sociologist, who was saying, "While you may not have a proof from philosophy about the existence of God, God is a sociological phenomenon. The more people believe in God, the more God is present in the world." And if I take this still further, into morphogenetic fields, we are then making God great and increasing the "God-field." The more people make deposits of belief, if you will, the more the God-field grows. So the religious existentialist began in the same vein as Sartre and Camus,[8] except that this existentialist was coming from a place that says, "My commitment to God makes God present." From there, it is but a step to the "I and Thou" of Buber.[9]

For a long while, the people who were writing the Neo-Hasidic material adopted the language of existentialism. Reconstructionists did the same. If you go into the back issues of *Reconstructionist* magazine, after Mordecai Kaplan had stopped writing for it, Milton Steinberg and Richard Rubenstein[10] were also using the language of existentialism quite strongly.

Hasidism and Neo-Hasidism[11]

When Buber and others were writing about Hasidism, there were many premature obituaries being published about the once great Hasidic movement, announcing its decay and demise. The Hasidism, once defined as a pietist reform or a revolt of the unlettered, is today usually dubbed "Ultra-Orthodox." Like many of the resurgent orthodoxies of our time, it also acquired a hyphenated *Neo*-prefixed school. Abraham Joshua Heschel and Martin Buber have often been defined as Neo-Hasidic thinkers. Buber, in particular and in large measure, is responsible for much of our present interest in Hasidism. His translations, retellings of Hasidic tales, and studies in comparative mysticism have added immeasurably to the West's familiarity with Hasidism. Buber's own development led him from his earlier "ecstatic" and "unitive" period to his later "I-Thou" period. At about the same time, Reb Shalom Dov Baer Schneersohn wrote *Kuntres HaT'fillah*, a treatise on prayer dealing with unitive contemplation. It was an era when many a Hasid and many a *yeshiva* student in Lubavitch experienced the beholding of the living God. However, Buber was likely not aware of this, never being a Hasid immersed in the type of *agape* community he later celebrated. For reasons that seemed imperative to him at the time, illustrated in his introductory essay to *Pointing the Way,* Buber changed his views to a dialogical approach, as he framed it. The unitive experience is not given to many people. We live in a world in which the monistic way seems unreal and in which the dualistic way is the real dimension of living. But the dualistic way, too, does not lend itself to a fulfilled life. Thus the step from the dualistic to the dialogical way was necessary for Buber. When Nietzsche said, "God is dead," he was of course referring to the "It" to which God had been reduced, since for Nietzsche, the living God had ceased to live among us. The infinite "It" of God is meaningless for all those who cannot attain to *unio mystica,* mystical union. Buber's insight into the God who can be met and "Thou-ed" (addressed in the second person) is very helpful, especially when we realize how seldom one finds oneself in the relationship that is occasioned by the *primary word* (I-Thou). Suddenly, God is no longer dead: God is in hiding, eclipsed. That One "comes where He is let in." To Buber, this saying of the Kotzker Rebbe means that God is available where humankind is ready to engage, or to be engaged, in dialogue.

But for Buber, there is no *conversation* in this dialogue. There is only a confrontation. God does not say "do this" or "do that," "become this" or "become that." The dialogue is wordless. It is possible that Buber was afraid that the "word" would become "flesh," leaving only a nondialogical *halakha,* or law. This seems to be the point in his correspondence with his friend, the philosopher Franz Rosenzweig. "God is not a lawgiver, and therefore the law has no universal validity for me." However, the problems encountered in the unitive decidedly remain in the dialogical realm, though humans very seldom live in the dialogical universe. The objective, "Itty" universe awaits us. Buber gave not bread but stones to the one who lives in the "Itty" world. True, the model of meeting others is always in Buber's mind. One can confront the other by yielding to that one's "It" the inherence of an unconditioned "Thou." But a person can do only one thing at a time. When facing the "It" of another, one can yield that person a "Thou." When facing the "It" of God, one cannot yield God a "Thou." We become so absorbed in the process of conceptualizing God's "It" that we cannot meet "It" as "Thou." Yet is not God notorious for *not* providing us with an "It"? "Take heed, for ye saw no image."

The scholastics had it better. Man is actual and potential. The actual in Man is yielded to the person; the potential in Man is confronted as an "It." But God, being pure actuality, is granted self-existence, *aseity* of being. Thus the One is not eclipsed but can be met. Man, in this case, does not have to project *and* meet at the same time. And so *das Zwischenmenschliche* (the interhuman), despite its attraction, cannot really serve as the only good model for the relationship between us and God. Buber's reduction of one Hasidic idea into a miniature system was not Hasidism. The latter is organic, having been created by the striving of more than *one.* It is rich with many coordinates. The Kotzker Rebbe would say, "If I am I because I am I, and you are you because you are you, then I *am* I, and you *are* you. But if I am I because you are you, and you are you because I am I, then I am *not* I, and you are *not* you." And this is only one of the infinite coordinates of God. Buber felt that he had to reject the "gnostic" coordinates, as he argues against Jung, but in Hasidism, there is room for the Immanent (*M'malleh Kol Almin*) as well as the Transcendent (*Sovev Kol Almin*) in the shadow of the Infinite (*Ain Sof*).

Abraham Joshua Heschel corrected this in some measure. He added the coordinates of time-space. God, *YHVH*, numerically equivalent to twenty-six, becomes Time in the twenty-six hours of the Sabbath (the Sabbath begins earlier and ends later than the ordinary day). God is incarnated in the twenty-six hours of the Sabbath of Sabbaths, Yom Kippur. Then God is available. Whoever enters the "palace of Time" from the world of space is in God. The time of prayer each day is a miniature Sabbath, where the Father and the child can meet in the intimacy of the private domain. Admittedly, Heschel goes beyond Buber. Heschel employs many Hebrew terms and allows conceptually Jewish associations to be formed. Furthermore, Heschel adds an everyday coordinate, in terms of a *"God-me"* relationship. God is the center of the universe, yet to every human it is her or his own *I*. However—and this is the great contribution of Heschel—in the moment of "radical amazement," I discover that I am only a *me*. Thus do I become aware that God, the Ground of All and the Center of All, deigns to be and see *me*. This is so because I have availed myself of the opportunity of "making myself visible to God." By intending to be seen, by praying, I make myself visible to God. This begets the emotional response of respect (*Yir'ah*). It is a looking-back, being startled by an awareness that I am being seen: retrospect. From this moment on, I find myself in a *situation*. This mode of thinking is altogether different. The human being is obligated when in the situational predicament of being seen. This is not true for the mere conceptual assent to the *idea* of being seen.

In Heschel's thinking, there is room for coordinates like "faith," "prayer" (liturgical and spontaneous), "revelation," and *halakha* that I am "responsible for" and "answerable to." God *sees* me, and I am amazed. God, the only *real* Center and pronominal Subject, reveals and decrees, and I (not as a subject but as the object of God) cannot help but reply, *"Na'aseh V'Nishma"* ("I shall do and I shall obey"), and begin to act. "My problem is not whether my soul has attained salvation. My problem is what is the next *mitzvah* that God wants me to do." Having been seen, my *me* is hooked, committed. Yet where can my *me* commune with the One? I can meet God whenever God becomes a *Thou* in time, and my *me* becomes an *I*. Then God can tell me what God demands of *me*. This is revelation. I can make my splintered self visible to God, and God can mend and fulfill it. This is prayer. Prayer and revelation go hand in hand, depending on whether at this moment I am praying *out* (praying myself out to God) in petition or praying God in to me, in the revelation of liturgy or the revelation of Torah. Heschel is not afraid that the word will become flesh. He wants it to become incarnate, not in *space*, but in *time*.

However, for the Hasid, Heschel, once a Hasid too, is self-limiting. He has incorporated only such traditional coordinates as he needs. There are still difficulties in store for those who want to proceed from his system and become what the God to Whom *they* have made themselves visible wants them to be. Heschel may have recovered for us "the question to which the Torah is the answer." Nevertheless, now that we know that "the Torah is God's anthropology, not our theology," now that we know *what God would have us become,* we still need competent direction and guidance. In short, the Hasid says, "We need a Rebbe."

We cannot become Hasidim from Buber and Heschel. As wife implies husband, and as child implies father, so the term *Hasid,* in its traditional context, implies a living and continuous relationship with a Rebbe. In Hasidic parlance, one is *a Rebben's a Hasid* (a Rebbe's Hasid) as one might be in Yiddish *a tatten's a kind* (a father's child). And one cannot claim exemption from this relationship by pointing to the example of the Bratzlaver Hasidim, despite the fact that their Rebbe, Reb Nachman, entered the Supersubstantial roughly two hundred years ago. He is *still* their Rebbe, and to his Hasidim it matters little whether he is on this plane or not. Bratzlaver Hasidim are certain that he presides over their prayer, seated in his chair, the very same one in which he sat while in the flesh. Yet there are those who claim to be Hasidim though they have no Rebbe. The traditional Hasid, paraphrasing Theodor Gaster, would say, "If a Hellenist is not a Greek and a Judaist is not a Jew, then a Hasidist is not a Hasid, and a Neo-Hasid is only a Hasidist."

The traditional world of the Hasid has many other coordinates, all of which define his Hasid-ing and his Rebbe's Rebbe-ing. The cosmology and psychology of the Hasid's world are larger than those of either Buber or Heschel. Its morals and ethics embrace the unconscious.

God is both Person and Nonperson for the Hasid. God becomes Person by emanating the world of *Atzilut,* in which God assumes intellect and emotions in order to become known to Man. God is Absolute and unrelating Infinite (*Ain Sof*) before the Contraction (*Tzimtzum*) of God's Light. *Before* is not a temporal but a *present-eternal* state. God's Light is and is not identical with the *Ain Sof,* just as the sunlight is and is not identical with the sun. In the lower worlds, in "creation," God's Presence is the *Shekhinah.* Here on earth, the *Shekhinah,* the Divine Spouse, Who is our Divine Mother, is in Exile, just as in the world of *Atzilut* our Divine Father is in Exile. The *Shekhinah* is held prisoner in innumerable little sparks, awaiting redemption at our hand. Whenever a *minyan* is convened where She is, "She radiates so powerfully that an angel, even from the highest of angelic hierarchies, would be annihilated."

This is the world where the deistic truth is learned: "There is none comparable to Thee, O Lord our God, in this world." In the spiritual universes of Creation, Formation, and Function, the theistic truth is made manifest: "There is none beside Thee, O our King, in the life of the world to come." The truth of pantheism waits for the days of the Messiah to be demonstrated: "Nothing but Thou exists, O our Redeemer, in the days of the Messiah." Then the level of *Atzilut,* in which God, as Person, is each human's attainment, will be made manifest, fulfilling God as the water covers the sea. The final Parousia of the Impersonal Infinite is to be demonstrated at the resurrection of the dead: "There is none like Thee, O our Savior, at the resurrection of the dead."

All of these are equally true for the traditional Hasid, depending on the level of attainment. Hasidim see themselves reincarnated again and again. If they are to progress, they need the help and the guidance of a Rebbe. The Rebbe knows the purpose of the Hasid's present incarnation, as well as the levels and rungs, the advances and setbacks experienced in previous ones.

For the Hasid, there is no point in arguing whether the Way of Torah is greater than the Way of Service (*Avodah*) or the Way of Deeds of Lovingkindness (*Gemillut Chasadim*). This depends entirely on the root of the Hasid's soul. We say, "Our God and God of our parents" because we, in our lives, must make living contact with the God whom our parents served, that this God be both the God of tradition and the God of personal experience to us. Then we say "God of Abraham," because this God is the God of those who are rooted to the right, those who serve God with deeds of lovingkindness. We say, "God of Isaac," because this God is also the God of those who serve God through prayer and sacrifice, rooted to the left, in service (*Avodah*). We say, "God of Jacob," because this God is also the God of those who serve God with Torah, being rooted in the middle. Abraham, Isaac, and Jacob were pure archetypes. Therefore, one cannot divorce oneself from any of these ways of serving. Only a Rebbe can establish the exact balance of Torah, service, and deeds of lovingkindness for each of the Rebbe's Hasidim.

Thus does Hasidism meet the problem of the usual incompatibility of religious intensity and tolerance. Without this approach, the intense adherence to one way would be heresy to the others. Hasidism teaches that there is integration (*hitkallut*) in the present order of the world (*tikkun*). The former order of chaos (*tohu*) carried the seeds of its own destruction, causing the "shattering of the vessels" when various objects collided with one another in their one-sidedness.

Out of the junk pile of chaos, God fashioned Man's animal soul. It can be of the "sheep," "ass," or "goat" variety. Hasidim cannot choose their own way unless they know the root of that other part of their being. Only a Rebbe can prescribe the way for them. No book can be written about such things. Reb Levi Yitzhak said long ago that the Rebbe of the generation is the "Tractate of the Love and Awe of God."

Hasidim would insist that neither Buber nor Heschel could replace the Rebbe. They could lead a prospective Hasid to one or another Rebbe, preaching one or another way. But without a Rebbe, the *becoming* of the Hasid would be frustrated. The "world" has no know-how; it cannot show the Hasid the way. When Hasidism first appeared, it found a Jew fettered by discipline, unable to become one with her or his inner destiny. The Ba'al Shem Tov and his disciples began to free the devout, in accord with the realities of the Divine Soul, Animal Soul, and Conscious Soul. Under their direction, an overdisciplined Hasid bloomed into spontaneity. But it is nonsense to say that Hasidism cast *all* control aside. One need only glance at the middle chapters of Reb Shneur Zalman of Liadi's *Tanya* or Reb Elimelech's *Tzettel Katan* to see that Hasidism taught the undisciplined how to gain control of themselves. The Maggid of Mezritch first taught his disciples "to discipline the horses so that they will know that they *are* horses" and then "to discipline the horses so that they will no longer *be* horses."

Techniques of prayer must be learned. Hasidism realized that it was not enough to say what one ought to do; it had to show one how to do it. Prayer, during the weekday, is a laboratory for the refinement of the animal and the rational soul. On the Sabbath, it is the laboratory for a soul's absorption in God. The ultimate, for the Hasid, is not "Heaven" or the "World to Come." The ultimate is to be absorbed in the Being of God. Under the Rebbe's guidance, Hasidim practice so that they might become virtuosos in their own field. In prayer, they not only pray to God but make *God* whole, for the sake of bringing about the union of the Holy One, blessed be that One, and the *Shekhinah*. Thus, as Reb Pinchas of Koretz said, "God *is* prayer."

Hasidism insisted on the need for *halakha,* since *halakha* served the most vital function of disciplining Man's will. In the mystical literature of the East, the solution to the problem of ridding oneself of the limiting self-will, which keeps God out, is sought in the realization that God alone exists, and nothing else has real existence. When the human identifies with the great Self of the Infinite, the human too is That. Hasidism holds that some humans can achieve the great realization this way. However, this way is barred to most of us. Some in the Western tradition have believed that it comes through mortification and consequent *apatheia,* for when there is no feeling of self, there is no will. Another way, counseled by Saint Augustine, is to "love God and do what you like." Hasidism says that this approach, too, is not given to many. Not everyone has mortified all desires by fasting, and not everyone is able to love God like a perfect *Tzaddik.* Most of us are somewhere between righteousness and wickedness, as the Chabad Hasidim say. Therefore, Moses implored God to give God's Self to Humankind in God's Will, construed in the leather of the *t'fillin* and the wool of the *tzitzit.* God acceded and clothes Himself in the *mitzvot,* which have now become the "limbs of the King." Individuals who shift to a *mitzvah-*centered life have no will of their own. Thus is the problem solved for those who are neither righteous nor wicked. Yet they must constantly attune themselves to be capable of fulfilling the Will and of understanding the Mind. The Hasid sees God's Will and Wisdom in Torah. First he surrenders his will to the Rebbe. He gives the Rebbe "power of attorney" over himself, vowing obedience to the Rebbe. The Rebbe soon transfers this obedience to God.

So there is an essential difference for the traditional Hasid between the teachings on Hasidism in Buber and Heschel and that of the living tradition. While Neo-Hasidism might be able to bring the Jew to the verge of accepting the yoke of God's kingdom, it cannot make the Jew capable of accepting the yoke of *mitzvot* and of continuing to function and develop. For spiritual direction, the Hasid must seek out the Rebbe. And each of the Rebbes has received a "double portion" from her or his predecessor, as Elisha did from Elijah. In the years since the assumption of the Ba'al Shem Tov, they are said to have acquired considerable experience in this area. So for the traditional Hasid, any talk of "decadence" or "decay" in the tradition is an egregious misrepresentation.

Hasidism and Jewish Renewal[12]

That is where I stood in 1960, when I wrote that critique of Neo-Hasidism. I was still a Lubavitcher Hasid and in the mood of apologetics and restoration. Eventually, I graduated that position and evolved a "renewal" perspective. You see, Hasidism used to be on the "growing edge" of the Jewish tradition. It was a radical movement attempting to vitalize its relationship with God. Conservatives want to be in the center where things are safe, but as with a tree, the center is dead matter. The livingness of the tree is on the outer edge. Hasidism used to be on this vital edge. But over time and in reaction to various historical circumstances, Hasidism has opted for the centrist position of safety and preservation.

Jewish Renewal differs from Restoration, which seeks to hold on to a dying or former paradigm. People in Jewish Renewal do not want to abandon sacred or cherished traditions or toss them out along with outworn cosmologies. We are now privy to information that floods us with wonder at the view of a wider and ever more complex cosmos, and we do not want to pawn our minds for the price of staying wedded to our tradition. Still, we look to fill our spiritual needs as experienced in the present with a maximum of tradition. To make this happen, we have to retrofit our spiritual technology to the demands of our era. We are sensitive to feminism, human potential, ecology, and whole-earth thinking.

Hasidism, though, is an eminently usable model for Jewish Renewal. Hasidism, with profound vitality, took a *sui generis* approach to Judaism without throwing anything out. For Jewish Renewal, the basic model of a "spiritual leader" is the Hasidic Rebbe. Yet it is traditional to think of a Rebbe as a *Tzaddik*—a saint. Knowing that we are not saints, in what way can we speak of the Rebbe as our leadership model? How do we dare even to apply the word *Tzaddik* to ourselves? Reb Shneur Zalman, the first Lubavitcher Rebbe, has priced *Tzaddik Gamur* ("the complete *Tzaddik*") out of our market. For the "complete *Tzaddik*" is one who doesn't have a shred of *yetzer ha'ra* (evil inclination, negative impulse) left. With great, great austerity, the complete *Tzaddik* killed the *yetzer ha'ra* in herself or himself. Who can even get close to this kind of a situation? And if that is what a *Tzaddik* is, if that is what a Rebbe is, then, who among us is a Rebbe?

But thank God this same Reb Shneur Zalman wrote a *sefer,* namely the *Tanya,* the first part of which he called *Sefer Shel HaBeynonim,* "The Book of the People In-Between." In the *Tanya,* he made a very important statement, that from the point of view of behavior, the *Beynoni* and the *Tzaddik* are on the same floor.

On the outer level, you cannot see a difference between a *Beynoni* and a *Tzaddik*. Whereas a *Tzaddik* is by nature totally good, a *Beynoni*, with great struggle and control, manages to control all thoughts, words, and deeds in such a way that she or he doesn't slip for one moment to become an instrument of the energy system of evil, in Hebrew, *k'lipah*. And when somebody asked Reb Shneur Zalman, "Well, what are you?" he would quote Rav: "I'm a *Beynoni*." The Talmud (*Rosh HaShanah* 16b) makes a similar point in the name of Rav, who also claims to be a *Beynoni*. The sages say to Rav, "If you are a *Beynoni, lo shavik mar chayya l'chol b'riyah*—you don't leave any space for any of us!"

In other words, if these saints see themselves as average, what does that make of us who are truly average? What is it we can really say of ourselves?

According to *Tanya*, we are at best *reshayim sh'aynam gemurim*; we are people who are not altogether wicked. That is the best thing that can be said for us. This means that even in behavior, we are very far from being in the halakhic black. So if that is the case, the question comes again: What right have we got to aspire to Rebbe-hood?

There is this wonderful story about a man who came to the Kotzker Rebbe and said to him, "Rebbe, my father came in my dream and told me I should become a Rebbe." The Kotzker laughed, and the man said, "What's the joke?" And the Kotzker answered, "If your father had come to three hundred other people and told them that you were to be their Rebbe, I would take it a little more seriously. That you have had a dream to be a Rebbe, I don't take too seriously." All of us can laugh out of that space, with that attitude. But here is what the teaching means: first the Divine flow, then the community, and then—only then—the focus point, the Rebbe. The Rebbe results from the Divine flowing into the world, working through a community that, in a sense, makes for itself a Rebbe. Without the community, there is no Rebbe. We must use Rebbe in this sense. It is not that we elevate ourselves to sainthood or raise ourselves above others. Rather, we are asked by the community to be their Rebbe because they see in us something they need.

Long ago, I wrote that *Hasid* is a relationship word, like *mother-father* or *son-daughter*. Just as you can't be a *son* without a *mother* or a *father*, you can't be a *Hasid* without a *Rebbe*. So if somebody says, "I'm a Hasid," I want to know "Who is your Rebbe?" Because *"ain melekh b'lo am*—there is no king without a people." It's impossible to have one without the other, without having the support of that.

Reb Moishe Kabriner once talked to a Hasid who said, "Reb Moishe, I know all about you—warts included—from way back. What do I have to believe about you so I could be a Hasid and you could be the Rebbe?" He said, "All you have to believe is that I'm a *kletzel hecher fun dir*, meaning that I'm—like the height of a tree stump—that I'm that much higher than you. That's all you need to believe." Because if you don't believe some of that, it won't flow "down" to you. The *Hashpa'ah*, the flow of Divine inspiration, won't come down.

You must not think that I'm advocating the continuance of hierarchy. Hierarchy is like a pyramid. It has a point on top and has all this mass of structure below. We are suffering from hierarchies and being choked by hierarchies. In a hierarchy, the one who is on top refuses to listen to the one who is on the bottom, despite the fact that there are many more on the bottom than on the top. What is the alternative? One alternative is to conclude that "everybody is equal"—but if everybody is equal, there is no flow; there is stagnation. Alan Watts used to call the *Tao* "the water-course way." Look how the water flows: *m'makom gavo'ah l'makom namuch*—it flows downward. Now, if you understand how this goes, there has to be a certain amount of raising up so that the wisdom can flow down. Inside of me, I feel what the *Gemara* says: "More than the calf wants to suck, the cow wants to give the milk." Especially at this time in my life, I feel it's so important to upload the files of my life's experience on other people, so the pressure here is great. On your side, the longing for the knowledge is great. Do you understand how we are in this wonderful relationship with each other? And it is not like that flat land of democracy.

So what is it? Not hierarchy, not democracy. I call it "organismic." I'd like you to hear that because I think that this is the foundation of the new Rebbe-work. The kidneys have to do the work of the kidneys, the lungs have to do the work of the lungs, the brain has to do the work of the brain, the spine has to do the work of the spine, and the heel has to do the work of the heel, and so on. This doesn't mean that my toe doesn't have access to my head. Step on my toe and you'll see! We are connected. We are organically connected.

To think about such issues, people always use models that make sense out of their life experience. So we are thinking of being organically connected, in other words, we think of the next paradigm in which Gaia brings us the organic model, the organismic model. Earth is alive; we are part of that; there are organs; cells make up organs; organs make up an organism. Organisms make up a social organism with other organisms all within the environment—that's how it goes. So the model is an organismic model, which is a lot better than either the hierarchical model or the flat one.

So we have people who are *reshayim sh'aynam gemurim*, "not altogether wicked," who have been called to do this Rebbe-work, who don't have all the tools that are necessary, but who, *b'chemlat HaShem*, "through the merciful grace of Providence," are picking up "breathing" and "postures" and "spiritual direction" from all kinds of places!

We get what we need, not necessarily through our tradition, but from other places, to make up for the pieces that we lost. And we also get ingredients, not only for the past, but those that are necessary for the future. These have to do with transformational psychology, with the brain-mind technology that's now coming down, which has to do with the expansion of consciousness so that we could get into larger and larger possibilities, which have to do with creating local area networks of people who work in dyads and triads and so on, so they can mesh their minds and work together. So I've come to understand that the Rebbe of the future is not going to be "the Rebbe" we knew in the past. For some time, the Rebbe will serve as a Rebbe, and when that's done, the person will have dinner and go see a movie and not necessarily be a Rebbe.

When we are playing—yes, playing—Hasid and Rebbe, something good happens. I like the idea of play, and I don't want you to think of it as "mere play." By "playing," we make sure we don't get stuck thinking that we always are that Rebbe. We understand that these are temporary roles that we assume for the benefit of that mutuality that we try to create.

I like to use the following example. I'm addressing an audience and I'm thinking, "What am I going to say next?" And the audience is wondering, "What is he going to say next?" During this time, the audience is feeding me a certain kind of energy. That's so important. The notion that I am speaking in the active form and that you are merely passive is wrong. You are very active. Your active listening creates in me the will to continue. If there were a conspiracy in which all of you decided to shut your minds against what I had to say, in two minutes my energy would be gone. I would be totally disconcerted. I wouldn't know what I'm doing. How can I teach if I don't have your attention? You're paying into the process by giving me your attention. I don't yet know what the group mind will want to reveal. And I've dedicated myself for at least the time we are going to be doing this together to be a *keli*, a vessel, for that to come through. If you would withdraw your energy, I would run away. I wouldn't have anything to do here. I'm here only because you help me with your energy. This is a very important point.

I want to make it clear that although we are not *Tzaddikim* and we are not Rebbes, we *may be* called to *function* as Rebbes. We recognize that this is not a permanent degree that we get for ourselves. Rather, this is an intermittent function that we allow ourselves, that we submit to, in order to be able to have access to regions that the normal consciousness doesn't have access to. If we want to live healthy as a people and as a religion, we can't do it unless we have some people who are the conduits of that energy. That is some small part of what Jewish Renewal has gleaned from Hasidism—models.

Renewal is not new. It has been going on from the beginning. Anything that is alive renews itself constantly. But there is also the teaching in Judaism that nothing has changed since Sinai. That is the architectural point of view. Many of the orthodox Hasidim insist that nothing has changed, and a lot of their energy has gone into rebuilding, to transplanting, the *shtetl* in a new environment since the Holocaust. But what is so interesting is that they didn't rebuild it; they improved on it, in one sense. Because if you have ever seen pictures from the *shtetl*, it is sort of funny to say, some of the *streimels* (fur hats) in the *shtetl* were pretty ratty. You look at the *streimels* today, and they are beautiful and nicely shaped. So they didn't have it as good in Warsaw as they have it now in Brooklyn.

My sense is that Jewish Renewal is basically an *avant-garde* of something that is going to happen later on anyway. When Reconstructionism first arrived on the scene, there were lots of people saying, "We don't want to hear it. We are against it. It is new; we don't want to have anything to do with it." But today, even in Orthodox settings, they are having bat mitzvahs, which Mordecai Kaplan first inaugurated in Reconstructionism for his own daughters. And it is similar with Jewish Renewal. You go to the Holy Wall in Jerusalem, and you will see people wearing the "rainbow *tallit*" I designed who have no idea where it came from. And if they had an idea, they might not wear it. Or they'll be singing Reb Shlomo Carlebach's melodies without knowing that this unconventional holy man wrote them.

Paradigm Shift[13]

In the teachings of the Hasidic masters given in this book, readers will encounter many ideas that will seem more than slightly out of step with today's thinking. More than that, some of the ideas will be offensive to modern sensibilities: the body is low, the earth is a kind of a prison in which we have to suffer and from which we must be liberated, Jews are superior, and women are somehow impure. And next to the teachings of joy that so characterize Hasidism, you might wonder, "What is going on here?" So it is time to talk a little about paradigm shift.

How you understand the universe and yourself when you are a child differs greatly from how you understand it when you have grown up. What you needed to understand in very simple terms when you were a child, you can handle the complexities of when you grow up. You can handle more paradox. You don't have to see things in black and white. I remember when I first looked at a computer terminal—it was dark and the letters were green or amber. Later on, the whole thing flipped when Apple showed that you could have a white background and black letters, and now they are in color. But my computer had a problem when it came to color. I wanted my screen to show over two hundred colors. But it just couldn't handle it. It could only handle sixteen. So your mind has to be ready to see complex things.

Think about how our conception of the universe has changed. We used to have the notion of polytheism, that there are many gods, because we couldn't imagine how the thunder god and the sun god could be the same god. So we separated them all out and put them into a hierarchy, because we couldn't quite see their unity, the complexity of one god containing all of these possibilities. Most of these gods were zoomorphic, meaning they looked like animals. Think of Ganesha, the elephant; Hanuman, the monkey; Sekhmet, the lioness; Anubis, the dog; and Nandi, the bull. And what did you feed those animal-gods? Human beings. Thus the big Minotaur needed to have a virgin every year to eat.[14]

After a while there was a switch. People were ready to say there is one God. And what did this God look like? Like us, anthropomorphic—in human form. God was seen as Michelangelo has it in his Sistine Chapel ceiling: an old man with a beard, touching the finger of the first human being. So what does this God like for sacrifices? A sheep in the morning, a sheep at night, as the Bible describes how the sacrifices had to be offered. And where is this anthropomorphic God? Far away: "My thoughts are not your thoughts"; we human beings were nothing in comparison. Sometimes this God would break in on us and come down. As the Bible has it, "And God descended on Mount Sinai." And it is very hard to meet God, because the very presence of God will kill you. "Watch out about the mountain," "Nobody sees My face and lives; you can see my back." And it may seem amusing now, but this was very real in the experience of the people of that time. God was seen as wholly other, completely different. And that "wholly other" notion of God was known as deism.[15] In other words, God is different and moves in and out in the universe. And if you wanted to go and find God, where would you go? You'd go to a holy place. A holy place was sort of impregnated with God-presence because God was in space.[16]

It was Abraham who took us from polytheism to deism. Remember, he meets this great being called Melchitzedek (*Malki Tzedek*), the king of Salem, and he does a ritual with bread and wine with him. And it is written that Melchitzedek "*vehu kohen l'El Elyon*," that Melchitzedek was a priest to God most high. At one point, we didn't quite understand what this meant. But now that we've found the Ugaritic tablets,[17] the tablets of the Canaanite religion, we begin to understand it a little bit better. *El* was the head of the Canaanite pantheon and was depicted as a bull, and *Ba'al*, his son, was depicted as a calf, and that is where the golden calf comes in. Abraham, in breaking the idols of his day, says none of these forms are God. Then he says, "We are made in the image of God"; therefore, God looks like a person. Later on, Maimonides[18] and others would interpret this and make it more spiritual, but if you read the biblical account of that time, it seems as if God spoke and appeared. Even to Moses, God says, "If you want to see Me, go hide yourself in the rock, and I will cover you, and you will see my back and not my face." And it happened just like that at that particular place and that particular time. So God was very much understood in deistic terms. Later on, with the prophet Isaiah, we move a little bit higher. And slowly the transition was made to theism.

Eventually, the Temple was destroyed, and Jews were no longer able to offer animal sacrifices. And by and large, ritual sacrifice is pretty rare nowadays, except in small pockets of the world, where they have chickens and Santeria.[19] We are for the most part done with animal sacrifices, with blood sacrifices. And what do we believe about God? Before, with deism, God inhabited space. There was a special mountain, a special place, in which God had chosen to make His name dwell. You made pilgrimages to that place. It was a holy mountain, a sacred place. And that was wonderful, but what happened when the Temple was destroyed and animal sacrifices were no longer being offered? People began to say, "God is not moving in the universe. God is so vast, so infinite, to say that God is moving doesn't make sense." In deism, God is smaller, as it were, and moves around in the cosmos. And now we come to theism, where God is spirit separate from the cosmos. You can't serve God in space because God is everywhere, and the Hebrew word that is being used for God sometimes is *HaMakom*, the Space, as if to say, "The whole cosmos is placed in that space, which is God." At this time in history, there was a translator of the Bible by the name of Onkelos.[20] And he no longer translated things literally. He took "And God came down" and translated it as "And God manifested." It was a way of saying that "we don't hold with this old belief anymore. It doesn't make sense." And if he would have translated it literally in those times, it wouldn't have been accessible, and the people would have rejected it. So by reinterpreting the meaning, in the new paradigm, God was Spirit. And the opposite of spirit is matter. God is not matter. God *made* matter. Matter is far away from God, because God is Spirit. Now, human beings are made up of a material body and a soul. And this was seen as the psychophysical parallelism, a world of matter parallel to a world of spirit. And God is a spirit in which matter is. There is a large universe of spirit and a smaller universe of matter. And how do we serve God when we no longer offer sacrifices? We speak words. "We pay for the bullocks with our lips," the saying goes. And from that you get the expression "lip service." But it isn't merely lip service. It had to be very accurate, just as when people were discovering magic and talking about magic. The formula has to be pronounced the right way. If you don't pronounce it the right way, you get into trouble. And where is God to be found if no longer in space spatially? You find God in time. That was a very important shift. All the many laws we used to have before, about bringing sacrifices and how to maintain the Temple, were now shifted into the Sabbath. You create a sanctuary not in space but in time.

Mircea Eliade,[21] a great scholar of comparative religion at the University of Chicago, spoke of this as *in illo tempore* time. There is regular time, and there is a time that is *in illo tempore,* "at that time" time. When you tell a story and you say, "Once upon a time," that introduction was the introduction that first was given in Latin when they would read from the Gospels. So the priests would read, *"In illo tempore,"* and then they would say, "Jesus went and did thus and such." It always began with *in illo tempore.* The calendar is made to go around with the shared experiences of people. If you live with a liturgical calendar, you live in *in illo tempore* time. Therefore, every Passover, you go out of Egypt. Every Shavuot, you receive the Torah. Every Christmas, Jesus is born. That is living in *in illo tempore* time. The birth of the Buddha gets celebrated that way also. The yearly celebrations that we have are ways in which we sanctify and mark time.

With the Temple gone, we no longer had that holy place to go to and find God. So where could we find God? In the ten days between Rosh HaShanah and Yom Kippur—in other words, not in space but in time. I once heard about some people who were preparing to celebrate Lent.[22] "Celebrate" is perhaps not the best expression when you are talking about the penitence that they are doing. A woman was describing how her family participated in an orthodox Christian ritual in which they stood in a circle and each family member was begging forgiveness from the other. And they did this at home. She and her husband first, and then with their children. And this became very real to her. She said, "I looked at my daughter and thought about how many times I didn't treat her right, I didn't treat her as a full human being because I was busy, I was this, I was that. I had all kinds of excuses, but it wasn't right." And so she asked for the daughter's forgiveness, and the daughter again asked for her mother's forgiveness. We do something like this at a wedding, prior to going to the canopy. We ask siblings and parents and children to forgive one another so that everyone can go in with a clean slate. And why was the Christian family asking forgiveness at that time? Because it was Lent. And Lent is the preparation for Easter. If you want to have God arise, have a resurrection, as it were, arise in you, you had better prepare for it. For Jews, this happens between Rosh HaShanah and Yom Kippur.

As Jews, it is hard for us to speak of God being incarnate in the flesh, but we do speak of God being incarnate in time. And Yom Kippur is the clearest God-time that we have. There are twenty-six hours of Yom Kippur (reflecting, as noted earlier, the fact that the Divine name, *YHVH*, adds up to twenty-six). In other words, you add an hour before and an hour afterward to make Yom Kippur enriched, as it were, with extra time. So you can see how God shows up in time.

There is a famous painting showing a man standing in the middle of a field. With one hand he is leaning on a spade, with the other he has taken off his hat, and there is a church steeple at one end of the picture. The painting is called "The Angels" because a bell is ringing at a time when the angels are singing in heaven, as it were. So the guy takes his hat off in the field where he is standing in an attitude of prayer, to join with the angels in the adoration of God, because the bell was ringing. Can you imagine living in a Muslim city, and you hear the muezzin's call,[23] "It is better to serve the Lord than to sleep! There is no God but Allah! *Allah hu akbar,* God is greater, mightier than anything else." We used to have the equivalent of that in the *shtetl,* a guy with a wooden hammer banging on the doors—"Time to wake up for the penitential prayers!"—before the High Holidays. What you see is that the timings of this sort, bells and so forth, call people to these things. And that is another way in which God is inherent in time.

Now the first Temple was destroyed around the year 600 B.C.E., in a time known among some people as the axial age, the age "when things turned." That was around the time when Socrates, Plato, Aristotle, Isaiah, Ezekiel, Jeremiah, Zarathustra, the Buddha, Mahavira, Lao-Tzu, and Confucius were active. It was like a blip on the radar of the Global Brain, as if the Global Brain was having an "aha" moment. The big "aha" eventually disappeared, but there were some people who codified the "aha" in each situation, and religions were formed as a result.

Now what happens between these paradigms, say, when polytheism is making the transition into monotheism, which is deistic and anthropomorphic? When this is happening, the old starts to break down, and usually, a battle ensues. Can you imagine people saying, "No, no, not this kind of invisible God who looks like a human being! God is a bull, a calf!" That is why they chose the golden calf. It was the comfortable "old-time religion" of that period, sort of a throwback. When you decide to let go of the old paradigm, there is always a struggle. People who say, "We have to do it just as our parents did," will insist and get very angry. It is a battle between two opposing points of view, different paradigms. Those who are holding onto the old are very tenacious and say, "How do you know that you are right? We have proven material here. What do you have to support something new?" But the old point of view cannot grow anymore. So it gets shattered. And during the process of dissolution, there is a sliver of time between these clearly defined paradigms when people go back to primary experience. But the question of the "old paradigmers" was right—"How do I know what is real and what is right if I can no longer trust the words that come to me from the past?" So the "in-betweeners" answered, "Let me experience it directly!" And the people who are looking for this direct, primary knowledge were often known as the gnostics. Their point was that unless you experience something yourself, you don't know what you are talking about, because words are inadequate to describe it.

So where are we now? I'd like to say we are in the shift to the place where everything is God, pantheism. The understanding that has come from mysticism and from people on the cusp of periods moving from past to present, people talking about primary experience, is that the body and the soul cannot be separated. It shouldn't be that they should be fighting one another, that you have to get rid of one in order to get the other. We want Wholeness, a holistic understanding, now. I believe that people are moving from theism to pantheism. There are some who don't like the word *pantheism,* the idea that God is everything. They prefer the word *panentheism,* which means that God is *in* everything. I, however, don't think that the distinction is real. What was the objection that people had to pantheism, God is everything? "Are you going to tell me that the excrement of a dog is also God?" And the answer to this would be—"Yes." What is wrong with that? It is only from the human perspective that we see a difference between that and *challah.* On the submolecular level, on the atomic level, they all look the same. And if you look from a galactic perspective, what difference is there between one and the other? So if "God is everything," why are you and I here? Because we are the appearance of God in this particular form. And God likes to appear in countless forms and experience countless lives.

If you would have mentioned this point of view when theism was dominant, you might have been killed. The theists would complain, "What you are saying is that there are no differences anymore? Does that mean that everything is right, everything is kosher? Where are the differences?" And those are good questions. We are not so far advanced yet that we can explain all these things, but deep down, the deepest level of the pattern is that God is everything. So it's not that God *created* the world but that God *became* the world.

The notion that people liked in theism and even in deism was that God said, "Let there *be . . .* " —*zap!*—and it was. And from this we got the notion that words are incredibly powerful. God created the world with words, and if we knew the right words, we could uncreate things, we could shift things. Many of the notions that came in Kabbalah and practical Kabbalah had to do with finding the formula so that you could change the pattern. Thus the word *abracadabra* (in Aramaic, *ibra k'dibra*), "created as it was spoken." Or take the expression "hocus pocus." It comes from the priest holding up the wafer and saying, "*Hoc est enim corpus meum*—This is my body." Through that act, "hocus pocus," the wafer is no longer bread. People got the sense that words are magical and can do lots of things. And we subscribe to this belief to this very day. At a wedding, when the groom gives the bride a ring and says, "*Harey at m'quddeshet*, . . ." they are married. I give you my word; I make a promise. It is binding; there is power in the word—or at least there used to be. I tell you, we have all lost the power of the word because we have gone journalistic.[24] So when I say, "I stand for this," "I give you my word," I am trying to make the word powerful again. And it is true that if your word is empty, your prayer life doesn't feel full. And if your word is full, your prayer gets filled. That is what mantras are about.[25]

What is the sacrifice now, if it isn't words? Now it is *time* and *energy*. The rich can't give any more than the poor where time and energy are concerned. That is the great sacrifice that we can offer. That is the one that we need to offer. So we offer energy in the service of God today.

Where may God be found, if not in space or time? In *person,* because it turns out that we are not doing so well with time today; time is not shared as much as it used to be. It has become secularized. Notice that we don't really celebrate noon when it is noon according to the sun. We do noon by clock time throughout each time zone. In other words, we have homogenized time. During my childhood in Vienna, I spent summers in a little village called Voeslau, which had its clock set five minutes later than Vienna's clock because noon came five minutes later. You see, people then really lived by the time; today, we have sort of made commodity out of it. Even time isn't working very well anymore. So what does that leave us with? We've got *person*—what happens on the inside and how much energy you devote to it. That is where we have God today. First we sought God in space, in *olam*. Then we started to look for God in time. And now we are looking for God more in person. Here is how it goes according to the traditional formula: "Seek ye the Lord where He may be found. Call upon Him, where He is near." We found God in space, in time, and now in person—and all simultaneously also.

Now in talking about paradigm shift, I am speaking of trying to understand a history of spirit, a history of mind. And that helps me explain these things. I can then take every writer of religious and spiritual material and acknowledge her or his great accomplishment of the time by going into that paradigm in which the individual appeared and taught. Then comes the question, "What good is such teaching today if it is obsolete?" The answer is that it is not obsolete. In ourselves, we have a primitive part that still acts as if polytheism were the truth. Do you understand? Look at the stock market; is it a "bull," or is it a "bear" today? We see those energies coming in, in that particular form. We act sometimes in the service of one or in the service of the other and not necessarily in the service of the *One,* All. When we touch a *Sefer Torah* and kiss it, what we are involved in is almost—I don't want to say idolatry, because we don't intend idolatry, but there is a tangible presence that we can hug, that we can kiss, that we can interact with. It is a very powerful thing, and that still lives in us. There also lives in us that dualism of spirit and matter. That is not finished in us yet. We have a sense that there is a difference between animal behavior—"Stop it! You're acting like an animal!"—and acting like a *mensch* and a spiritual being. We aspire to spirituality. Here again, we see that spirit living inside of us. But even all of this does not form a full reality map. So I put all these things into my reality map to understand it. And if I understand issues of *halakha* and renewal against this reality map, I can say, the good part of all these things we learned in the past is this. And when I ask myself, "What function, what process was going on?" I can find an answer.

Imagine for a moment that I am feeling guilty about something I shouldn't have done. If the Temple were standing, I would bring a sacrifice. Imagine it in terms of "Mary had a little lamb." Wherever Mary went, the lamb would go. So when Mary did something she shouldn't have done, she has to take her beloved lamb and say, "Dear God, I should have died for what I've done wrong, but I am offering you in my stead this animal that I've nurtured." Can you imagine what is going on inside Mary, seeing this animal slaughtered for what she has done and then having to eat part of it? Now, if I were to ask what is it that I need to do for my guilt today, I can learn something from the process of sacrifice then to get to the process that I have to go through today.

That is, in a way, reconstructing from the past. And that was an issue that Mordecai Kaplan and the Reconstructionists were talking about. I have to go and see what the function of a particular behavior was in the past and try to re-create that same function in the present. The reason I have spent time on this question is that it is always going to come up, and this is my thinking tool, my mind operating system (MOS). Each paradigm shift was considered heresy by the people who came before it. In other words, they will judge that what we are doing is wrong because we don't do what they have done in the past. That is why I say from time to time that many people in religion are driving by the rear view mirror. They are superimposing the past onto the present.

On Reading Hasidic Teachings

Now, the question that is relevant to the teachings of the Hasidic masters is this: How am I to understand sources that come from the past? The answer is, I cannot deal with the sources from the past unless I go back to the mind-set, to the reality map, to the paradigm of the past. If I try to judge the paradigm of the past with my understanding of the present, I am going to find myself in trouble. That is because I will judge everything as being lesser. "Look how funny they were to believe that" or "How stupid they were!" From that point of view, I wouldn't give credit to Plato, Aristotle, Moses, or Buddha. "He didn't know about quantum mechanics?" "Moses didn't know that $e = mc^2$?" If I go and judge it in this way, I cannot possibly estimate and esteem the true contribution of these people. So I must see them in terms of the world that they occupied and the worldview that they had.

Many books have talked about the lives and personal styles of the Hasidic masters, and there are many books of the Hasidic masters' teachings. But I believe that we still need to understand *how* to learn what they were saying, to look at things through their eyes and to apply their methods. For theirs was a unique approach to God and to life. It is not possible in any short presentation to transmit the whole of the wisdom they represented. What is more reasonable is to create a primer, a tool for working with the teachings. So what is presented here is not exactly "teaching" but rather the installing of software—software that will allow you to study the material to full effect.

Hasidic wisdom will take some genuine work and contemplation, but gathering knowledge is not a linear operation. For example, look at the process of reading a book. We don't often read it in one sitting. In between reading, we may eat or make a phone call and then get back to the book. It may take two or three weeks before you are finished with the book. But in your mind, the book has become one whole thing. Your mind integrates the experience of reading the book, even if in actuality it was fragmented. In a good whodunit, you're not going to know until the very last page who did it and why. But by the time you get there, the rest of the book begins to make sense. You know exactly how you got to that place with that particular answer at the end. Likewise, reading these teachings requires patience and an active engagement and questioning of the material. Keep the questions alive, for the answers are going to come. They may come from the environment, from your daily experience, or perhaps from your dreams.

What Francis Bacon[26] said in *Of Studies of Books* is also applicable to these teachings: "Some books are to be tasted, others to be swallowed, and some few to be chewed and digested: that is, some books are to be read only in parts, others to be read, but not curiously, and some few to be read wholly, and with diligence and attention." These teachings are of the latter type and require a different approach to reading. Some of the teachings will have to be unwrapped from their homiletical covers. Like a tightly rolled tortilla, before you get to the filling of it, you have to chew through some layers first. I realize that people might often like to get to the substance sooner, and they would like it to be unpacked for them, but you'll never be able to handle a Hasidic teaching if you don't learn to chew your way through this material. In some ways, we have been done a disservice by the encyclopedists who have given us nice, concise treatments of topics. They give the gist of the matter, and when you become accustomed to that, it is like getting perilously addictive "crack" in comparison to chewing a coca leaf. It is so distilled that you get 200-proof alcohol instead of a good wine. So it is important that you slog through it this way. You want to extract the essence from the bulk. The bulk may come from a cultural milieu very different from your own, but distilling it is an important element of your spiritual growth.

This is not a book *about* Hasidism. I don't want to talk about Hasidism as a static thing; Hasidism is an approach. It is an approach to Judaism. That is obvious from the way in which the texts deal with certain questions about the universe and about humanity. In learning to chew the Hasidic texts, we might glean something from this approach. So while you may encounter some difficulties, this book is really about helpful perspectives. Hasidism is very practical. So we are not exactly saying what Hasidism is in the sense of describing it but are rather introducing its approach.

So before you study this material, try meditating or singing a *niggun* as preparation. Then, when you have created the proper "space," read the selected teaching aloud. It doesn't work well to do it silently. These teachings were originally given orally, and when they are studied out of books, they are studied out loud. You may find it agreeable to study your teaching with a partner. Every once in a while, you may find that you have to put the book down and go over the material you have just read with the tendrils of your mind. Try to get a feel for doing this.

There is a form of meditation that might best be described as "rumination." Rumination means chewing your cud—tasting every word, reviewing every action, exploring every thought thoroughly. For example, somebody gives you a nasty look or says a nasty word to you. After you walk away, you ruminate on the situation. "What did he mean by that? Did I do something?" And notice when you ruminate, it isn't only a mental thing; it is usually accompanied by an emotional state, a feeling. Or if you get a compliment—"Ah, that felt so good!"—you ruminate on that. Yes, it is your reasoning mind that says, "Boy, did I wait a long time for that." Did you ever get the kind of compliment that you really felt you deserved but nobody in your family ever gave it to you? Then somebody comes and gives you that compliment, and you are almost moved to tears? Why are you moved to tears? It is like, "Oy, was I thirsty!" You felt that you so needed to get that acknowledgment, and that is like ruminating. You dwell on it, going over the thing, allowing it to arouse feelings. That is exactly what one does with these teachings.

How does one learn what one has not experienced? For those who have experienced faith or have experienced spiritual awakening, there is no need for explanation. But what about for those who haven't? There are some things that you can't really talk about if you haven't experienced them. And if someone tells you that it exists, you might say, "It's not true. It can't be true, because I haven't had such an experience." So how do you teach spiritual truths in the absence of primary experience? The answer is, you tell a parable. You give an analogue. As *A* relates to *B, that* relates to *this* spiritual teaching. And look how often this has been done in that way—the parable of the Good Samaritan.[27] You know, people think of the Samaritans as "goody-goodies." But when Jesus was telling the story, the Samaritans were seen as outcasts. There is a man on the road who is nearly dead from a beating given to him by robbers. First, a priest, a *kohen,* comes by and says, "I can't deal with you—you might die on me, and I'll become impure." Another Jew comes by and also says, "I can't deal with you." And finally, a Samaritan arrives, someone who in that society was "a down and outer," and he helps the man. Do you understand? Now, why is he telling this story? I don't know whether the story is fact or not, but the lesson in it is very clear. And the lesson is in the analogue. By telling the story in that way, you say, "I get it." Parables are like that. So in case you don't have primary experience, parables and the imagination can help. The Hasidic tradition is well known for its use of such parables.

Still, we come to things with our own perspectives and experiences, our individual filters. What are we to do about that? This is material from a different world, even for most Jews. And perhaps you are not even Jewish. You may come to this material from another religious tradition—Buddhism, say, or Christianity. And you might be wondering if it is possible to put aside what we believe in order to absorb this tradition in its own light. And while that is a noble intention, I say, welcome the filters. What is so bad about them? You bring something from your own experience to whatever you do. You will find the analogue to the teaching in your own tradition, in your own experience. Besides, removing your filters may not even be possible. For example, I haven't yet met anyone who has been able to put aside the filter of what it means to live in a mammal body. When I look at science fiction like *Star Trek*[28] and all the "exotic" characters they have, the Klingons and the Bajorans and so on, they still look like bipeds that are mammals. It must be very different to be a bird, but how can I relate to that? How would you put your mammalian perspective aside? I don't think that is possible. We can try to put these perspectives aside, but it ends up being an exercise in futility. The best thing that you can do is to have a certain kind of imaginal empathy. When you read about Reb Zushya or Reb Shneur Zalman and the encounters that they had and where they lived, exercise your imagination, and try to see them as if you were watching a movie. Out of that will come a closer connection. Still, it isn't possible to take everything that you bring to your imagination out of the picture. When I tell Zen stories, the Japanese Buddhists all end up looking like Hasidic rabbis. I just can't get rid of that completely. So don't strive too hard to get your preexisting mental images out of the way. Dig in and find the place in you that understands where these teachings were coming from, even when the thought is outdated or not so nice, and the experience will be one of profound depth.

A HIDDEN FIRE REVEALED

THE BA'AL SHEM TOV

(18 ELUL 1698–6 SIVAN 1760)

SARAH AND ELIEZER were pious Jews who lived in the small village of Okkup, in the western Ukraine. In their lives they had suffered great privations, but nevertheless, their hands were always open to any who might have a need. It was well known in the village that they received into their house with equal warmth both scholar and beggar; no one was turned away, no matter how disagreeable. So it was that Prophet Elijah arrived on their doorstep to test them. He knocked loudly at the door of the homely house on the Sabbath day, disguised as a foul and impious wanderer. Though this was a desecration of the Sabbath, and the guest proved irascible, the couple said nothing and took great pains to make him feel at home. Then Prophet Elijah announced, "Since you have not put a sinner to shame, you will have a child that will be a light unto Israel."

That great light, whom they named Israel, was born to them on 18 Elul 1698.[1] However, they were not destined to take joy in the child for long, and he was orphaned very early in his life. But before Eliezer died, he imparted to his son one vital directive: "When the Adversary comes before you, terrible to look upon, remember this—fear nothing other than God."

Upon the death of the boy's parents, members of the Jewish community took responsibility for the boy. But when they could no longer afford or were no longer willing to support the unusual youth, they got him a job as a *behelfer*, a school monitor. He also later found work as a synagogue beadle and as a ritual slaughterer (*shochet*).

Years later, the story is told of a *shochet* who came to Okkup to do his work. When he needed to wet the whetstone to sharpen his knife, he would spit on it and with his saliva hone the knife. An old Ukrainian who sat there, the one who plucked the feathers, shook his head in disapproval. The *shochet* asked him what was behind this, and he answered, "When I was young, I plucked the chickens that Yisrolick (the Ba'al Shem Tov) slaughtered, and when he needed to wet his whetstone, he wept on it, and with his tears he honed his knife."

But as beautifully as Israel performed these duties, he was not contained in them. He would go out for long walks in the woods and mountains, communing with God wherever God was to be found. Aryeh Kaplan has suggested that being deprived of human parents so early, the sensitive youth quite naturally and more fervently poured his heart out to his heavenly Father, seeking the succor of the Blessed One.[2] And nightly, while the town slept, he pored over the *Zohar*[3] and the works of the Holy Ari[4] by candlelight. For him, this was a personal dialogue between himself and the Creator, and thus it was concealed from the eyes of others. As far as his daytime acquaintances might know, he was merely a simple, if strangely judicious, young man.

Yet it was his judicious character that led many members of the community to come to him for the settling of disputes. And so it happened that while acting in this capacity, a visiting Rabbi, Efraim of Brody, recognized a spark of the youth's true character and offered him a marriage with his daughter, Channah. Young Israel readily agreed, but it was not to come off so easily. For before he reached home to tell his daughter of the match, Rabbi Efraim died on the road. When the contract was discovered among his belongings, only the name of the intended, Israel ben Eliezer, was mentioned. It gave no clue as to where such a person could be found or what merits the intended had to recommend him.

When Israel eventually arrived in Brody to claim his wife, the son of Rabbi Efraim, Rabbi Abraham Gershon of Kuty, a respected Talmudist and Kabbalist, was appalled at the prospect of his sister marrying this seemingly uncouth and uncultured man. He urged her to have the marriage annulled, but Channah would not hear of it. She trusted her father's judgment, saying, "Our blessed father made this contract, so we need not worry about it. It is certainly God's will."

The story is also told that the Ba'al Shem Tov insisted on having some words with her in another room visible to Reb Gershon, but out of earshot. There he spoke with her, and after a few minutes, she approached her brother and said that she agreed to the marriage. (Oh, how much I would have wanted to know what they said to each other!)

Her brother acquiesced and for a time even attempted to give Israel an education and make a proper Jew of him, with no success. He was a hopeless case, it seemed. To alleviate the tension, the young couple moved to a town near the foot of the great Carpathian Mountains, where they managed an inn. It was at this time that Israel met his teacher. At first the teacher came to the young man in visions, commanding Israel to seek him in the cave between the two mountains. Israel sought out the cave and found the man from his visions. For eighteen years he journeyed back and forth from the cave to the inn. Later it was revealed that this teacher was none other than Achiya the Shilonite, the teacher of Prophet Elijah. It is also thought that he had contact at this time with certain "hidden *Tzaddikim*," who some say were probably a circle of underground Kabbalists.[5]

On Lag B'Omer in 1734, the year that he turned thirty-six, Israel began to reveal himself. Two years later he was already known by the name *Ba'al Shem Tov*, "The Master of the Good Name," and had settled in Medzibozh. There had long been a tradition of wandering healers whom the local folk called variously *Ba'al Shem*, "Master of the Name." They were known as wonder workers, writing mystical incantations on amulets and prescribing herbs for healing. It is well known that Israel Ba'al Shem Tov was well versed in the use of these herbs, which knowledge he seems to have acquired in his time in the woods and mountains. However, he is distinguished from this group by the attachment of the word *Tov*, "Good," to *Shem*, "Name." Nevertheless, he seems to have made his reputation among the common folk in this tradition, first winning their trust, only to be their champion for the rest of his days.

Eventually, as his fame spread, he began to make many enemies among the learned elite. So it was that a prominent scholar, Rabbi Ya'akov Yosef of Sharograd, began to rail against him from the *bima* (pulpit). And soon thereafter, the Ba'al Shem Tov arrived in Sharograd, spinning complex and intoxicating tales in the marketplace. A crowd gathered and grew—and so enraptured were the townsfolk that no one even showed up at the synagogue for services. Worse still, no one even bothered to unlock the door, and Rabbi Ya'akov Yosef found himself locked out! Livid, he summoned the upstart Ba'al Shem to appear before him. It is hard to say what happened next, except that it did not go as Rabbi Ya'akov Yosef had intended. It is said that the Ba'al Shem Tov told him a story and then offered this advice: "If you want the horses to neigh, you must slacken the reins." Soon Reb Ya'akov Yosef began to show up in Medzibozh to listen to the master. Later, the great scholar would be known as Reb Ya'akov Yosef of Polonoye, the Ba'al Shem Tov's senior disciple and unofficial scribe. He was so favored by the Ba'al Shem Tov that the master once said of him, "All Ya'akov Yosef's works are pleasing to the Creator, Praised by His Name, and all his doings are in the name of God."

Eventually, the Ba'al Shem Tov gathered a great number of disciples, often like Reb Ya'akov Yosef, from the enemy camp. It seems that no one could meet the master without being overcome by his great love. Even his hostile brother-in-law, Reb Abraham Gershon of Kuty, became his disciple and came to live in Medzibozh, where he served as a tutor to his nephew. And it was to Reb Abraham Gershon that the Ba'al Shem Tov wrote his famous letter describing his mystical ascent of the soul to the palaces of the *Mashiach* on Rosh HaShanah in 1747. He reported of asking the *Mashiach* when Redemption would arrive and receiving the reply, "When all your teachings shall become known."

His tireless work went on for many years, and many people were graced to hear his unique teachings. Even as he lay dying in his bed, with his family and disciples surrounding him, he comforted them and continued to teach them: "I do not lament my fate. I know well that I shall go out through one door, only to enter again by another. 'Let not the foot of pride overtake me.'" With these words from Psalms 36:12, on the second day of Pentecost, in the year 1760, his soul departed from him and was gathered to his Mothers and Fathers. His body was buried in Medzibozh.

The primary authentic teachings of the Ba'al Shem Tov were, for the most part, preserved by his senior disciple Reb Ya'akov Yosef of Polonoye in his works *Toldot Ya'akov Yosef, Ben Porat Yosef, Tzafnat Paneah,* and *Ketonet Passim.* His teachings were also collected in other volumes, *Keter Shem Tov, Sefer Ba'al Shem Tov,* and *Tzava'at HaRivat (Testimony of Rabbi Israel Ba'al Shem Tov).* However, this last work, published in 1793, was not actually his "testimony" but rather a collection of sayings and fragments, which many experts consider to be authentic.

-------------------- ○ --------------------

Ecumenics of the Ba'al Shem Tov

> Straightforward are the ways of God,
> the righteous walk in those paths,
> and the wicked
> stumble in them.
>
> —Ba'al Shem Tov, *Tzava'at HaRivat*[6]

The *Tzava'at HaRivat* of the Ba'al Shem Tov is a book of prescriptions. All Hasidic masters made some prescriptions, usually a set of short notes, that they wrote for their disciples. They said, if you want to be one of my disciples, follow these prescriptions. That is to say, these are the things that are most necessary at this time and age to bring one to balance. So in the *Tzava'at HaRivat,* the Ba'al Shem Tov says, *Yesharim darkey*

HaShem, "Straightforward are the *ways* of God. . . ." *Ways* is in plural. Then he says, as the sentence continues, *Tzaddikim yelkhu bam uresha'im yikashlu bam,* "the righteous walk in those paths, and the wicked stumble in them." So why does he say *ways* and *paths,* in the plural? "Straightforward are the many ways," the "paths" of God. He is saying that sometimes you find one path blocked and there is another path open. Do not exalt any path above God. You may find one blocked for you, but it may not be blocked for another person. There are many paths that lead to God.

When you translate this into the discussion of religions and spiritual paths, it makes a great deal of sense. Sometimes paths are blocked for us and others are open. Once Reb Shlomo Carlebach, of blessed memory, quoting the Ishbitzer Rebbe, pointed out that for many Jews after the Holocaust, the path via Judaism was blocked. Many Jews could not get close to God until they first took a detour through Eastern religions, through other avenues, as it were. So the teaching of "many paths" is a very relevant teaching for us today.

Then, the sentence goes on, "the righteous walk by them and the wicked stumble in them." The point he is making here is that even the nicest teachings can be subverted by someone who has the wrong attitude or application of them. Imagine, if you will, someone in an argument about scripture vociferously screaming, "You should love your neighbor as yourself!" That is such an inappropriate application for that sentiment. The medium and the message have to fit together, and sometimes you find that the medium in which the message is delivered is not at all what it ought to be. So to speak of kindness in an unkind way just doesn't work. This, then, is how the wicked stumble in "the ways of God."

"The righteous walk by them." So people are capable of finding and following the ways that suit them, provided that they do not stand still. There is a great Yiddish book written by Menachem Boraisha called *Der Gayer (The Wayfarer;* literally, "the one who walks").[7] And as his dedicatory sentence, he uses *Sheva' yippol Tzaddik v'kam,* "Seven times will the Righteous fall and yet rise." Then he quotes from Reb Shneur Zalman of Liadi: "The *Tzaddik* is called one who walks, and in walking, one does not stand still, and the head bobs up and down, up and down, as you are walking, and you do not stand still." Even *halakha* means "the walking." So, to be open and fluid, "walking" is the way of the Hasid. When one is static and certain of life's limits, when one stands still, one is closed to the joy of endless possibilities, even on a spiritual path.

Franz Rosenzweig[8] taught that the whole problem that we have with becoming what we can become, doing what we need to do, may be the lack of a moment of generosity on our part, the failure to look at what is doable for us—in particular, to be open to what we feel an inner guidance toward. We all have had some experience with this. Remember those moments when you said to yourself, "I can't do that" or "What will people say?" We have to be generous with ourselves, with our inclinations, so that we are able to light on those "straightforward paths," "the ways of God."

The Unity of the *Mitzvot*

> *The Torah and* mitzvot *originate in God, who is the absolute Oneness. Love is connection to God, and therefore, when one correctly observes even a single* mitzvah *with love, then, through this* mitzvah, *he grasps part of the Oneness. All of this Oneness is then in his grasp, and it is as if he has kept all of the* mitzvot, *since all of them comprise a unity.*

—Ya'akov Yosef of Polonoye, *Toldot Ya'akov Yosef, "Yitro"*[9]

Maimonides writes that when a person keeps even one of the commandments (*mitzvot*), that person is then worthy of the World-to-Come (*Olam HaBa*).[10] The World-to-Come generally means that the person will not die with the body; the soul will continue to live in the Afterlife. One of the deep teachings in Hasidism is that you need to have a spiritual body if you are going to enjoy Heaven. Most people, if they do not keep the *mitzvot*, cannot enjoy the World-to-Come.

It is a very important value to do a *mitzvah*. A *mitzvah* means not only to do a good and kind act; it means to have embodied God in a particular act. You have taken God's Will and lived it. Very often, when people think of a *mitzvah*, they mean a kind deed—feeding the hungry, housing the homeless, "that's a *mitzvah*," they say. But a *mitzvah* is also keeping the Sabbath, putting on *tallit* and *t'fillin*, and eating *matzah* on Passover. And when these "connections" are made, the spiritual body becomes "filled out," as it were. The notion is that we come into this world with a physical body and have to build up a spiritual body, because without this, it would be like coming eyeless or earless to Heaven. You cannot see the beauty or hear the music of Heaven if you haven't got the organs.

The number 613 is significant in connection with *mitzvot*. That is the number of organs and limbs in the body; the sages speak of 248 limbs and 365 blood vessels or ducts. There is a formula in prayer that goes like this: *L'shem yichud kudsha b'rich hu u'sh'khintayh,* "I am about to do a *mitzvah*, a holy act; I am doing it for the sake of the unification of the Holy

One, blessed be He, and the Divine Presence," meaning that I want to tie the highest Godness with this here on earth. We want to make a connection. The prayer continues: "I am about to do one of those 613 commandments, and all the other commandments that are connected to it." What is that connection? Most of the time when people think of the world, the universe, it is from a mechanistic viewpoint: it is put together from individual pieces, as if reality was like an Erector set. A piece of this, and a piece of that, and you put it together. What is a human being, then? Human beings are sort of put together too, are we not? After all, we have a heart, lungs, and so forth. However, this point of view is forgetting the organicity of the human body. The heart is never fully a heart if it does not have the lungs to provide it with oxygen. The liver is not fully a liver without the heart. We are always doing all these things together—living is holistic. So when the teachers say that the *mitzvot* are 613, they mean to say that the *mitzvot* are an organism. And through them we are able to grow a spiritual organism.

According to teachings of Jewish mysticism, we reincarnate as many times as we need to in order to grow the full spiritual body so that we may enjoy Heaven in its fullness. Otherwise, we are deaf, dumb, and blind on the spiritual level. In this, it is similar to the notion of the hologram. If I eat *matzah* on Passover, that already includes *Shabbos* to a certain extent, that already includes being kind to people and remembering that you were slaves in Egypt. Each *mitzvah* has this organic connection, and by keeping even one properly, you already have a part in the World-to-Come.

On Reincarnation

From the time that the Ba'al Shem Tov was eighteen until he was thirty-six, he was taught secretly in a mountain cave by Achiya the Shilonite. But on that fateful thirty-sixth birthday, Achiya the Shilonite said to him, "It is time for you to leave me and to declare yourself in the world. I have taught you all that you need to know." The Ba'al Shem Tov responded that he had no desire to teach. Thereupon his master said, "Let me tell you a story.

"There was once a shoemaker in S'fat who was simple, knowing only how to *davven*. But once, during his bar mitzvah, he gave God, blessed be His Name, so much joy, He hasn't had as much since. So the Academy on High sent Prophet Elijah down to reward the shoemaker and to ask just what it was he did to give God so much joy.

"So one night, while he was performing the midnight prayer, he heard a knock at the door. Opening it revealed none other than Prophet Elijah, who said to him, 'If you will tell me what you did on the day of your bar mitzvah to make the Blessed One so happy,

I will come to you every day and reveal all the hidden teachings of Torah.' To that the pious shoemaker replied, 'If God did not tell you, I'm certainly not going to!' Elijah went back and reported this to the saints of the Academy. They were furious. 'Who does he think he is?' Then Elijah said to them, 'He didn't give us an answer, but he did give us a very important message. Our service to God, is for God, not for the all the saints of the Academy.' After this, the shoemaker was rewarded, and Elijah came every night to teach him personally until he became a very great soul for a very great purpose in the world.

"Now, Yisrolickel," Achiya the Shilonite said, "that shoemaker's soul is in you. The last time around, you were a secret saint. You have played that role, and this time around you have to be revealed. For the seeds that you sowed in that life now have to grow out and go beyond you. I have retaught you everything you knew before, and now you must teach it to others."[11]

This is what the tradition says about the Ba'al Shem Tov. It also says that this soul was also that of King David. So he believed in transmigration and did a lot of teaching on it. But the Ba'al Shem Tov was also able to recognize particular reincarnate souls, and he would help them with their particular needs. There is a wonderful story about him and fiddler who got pneumonia.

A fiddler is traveling with his klezmer band when he gets sick, and the band has to leave him with an innkeeper. The innkeeper feeds him and tries to take good care of him, but the fiddler is dying. And he knows he is going die, so he says to the innkeeper, "I'm sorry I can't pay you. I haven't got anything to pay you with. However, this fiddle of mine is worth something, so would you please sell it to settle my bill with you?" The fiddler dies, and the innkeeper leaves the fiddle hanging in his house on the wall and doesn't do anything about it.

The innkeeper is also a coachman, and so he has horses. One day, he finds a little horse on the road, and he doesn't know to whom it belongs, so he takes the horse and puts it in his barn and gives it some food to eat, but it is not his horse and it is pretty small, so he doesn't want to use the horse for pulling wagons and such. But one day, one of his horses gets sick and he has to use this little horse. The little horse turns out to be very powerful; it can easily pull the wagon and even heavy loads uphill. Soon the innkeeper has the little horse doing all his work for him.

The Ba'al Shem Tov comes to visit the innkeeper and says to him, "I'd like to see your horses, if you don't mind." So the innkeeper takes his guest into the stables and shows him the horses. And the Ba'al Shem Tov says, "Would you do me a favor? I'd like you to sell me this horse" and points to the little horse. The innkeeper replies, "It's not mine; I can't give it to you. Besides, it's the strongest horse that I have. This little horse is working better than any of the other horses I have; I can't see myself giving it to you." "All right," says the Ba'al Shem Tov, "what about this fiddle over here?" And the innkeeper says, "That fiddle used to belong to a musician who died here." The Ba'al Shem Tov asks, "Did he owe you something?" "Oh, yes, but you know, I never did anything about that. From whom could I go and collect that? I never tried to sell the fiddle." "Aha!" says the Ba'al Shem Tov. "Would you give me a statement to say that the debt of that musician is paid for?" And the innkeeper says, "Sure. I'd be glad to. I'm never going to collect it anyway. I'd rather give you that than the little horse." And he writes a note to say that the musician's debt is canceled. And the Ba'al Shem Tov stays in his house overnight, and the little horse dies that very night.

The next morning, the innkeeper says to the Ba'al Shem Tov, "What was that all about?" And the great man replies, "The musician owed you this money, and he couldn't find any peace in the Other World. So he came back as this little horse and was working for you in order to make up that debt. But once you canceled the debt, he didn't have to stay here anymore and could go on with his other life. He was released."

This is a remarkable story, and it tells us that this was not just a belief the Ba'al Shem Tov had but that he also acted on it. When I met Sogyal Rinpoche,[12] we had a wonderful conversation about the fact that all the Tibetan stories that he tells in his book about life and death, I could match story for story with parallel Hasidic tales about the Afterlife. This was one of those stories.

The first Tibetan that I ever met was Geshe Wangyal,[13] who was a professor at Columbia University and lived in New Jersey. One of the things that he asked me is, "Do you believe in reincarnation?" I said, "Yes." "Do you believe that human beings can also be reincarnated as animals?" And I said, "Yes." Most of the people who believe in reincarnation do not believe that, but in Judaism, at least in the Kabbalah, this belief does exist.

One of the ways in which mystical Judaism treats this is that sometimes you have to be reborn as an animal for a short time. The best job that you can do is to be reborn as a fish and to be eaten for *Shabbos*. That is the way the teaching goes. And there are marvelous tales about a Rebbe who eats up an entire goose one night because the person who was reincarnated in that goose needed the Rebbe to use the energy of the goose in prayer. And so he released him by eating him.

On the Simple Folk

Some people have asked me about the hierarchy on the spiritual path according to the Ba'al Shem Tov, and I think the only way to answer properly is with the following story, given in a letter by the sixth Lubavitcher Rebbe, Yosef Yitzhak Schneersohn.

Our Holy Master, the Ba'al Shem Tov, greatly loved simple, God-fearing folk and brought them very close to himself. His opinion concerning them was very well known, and it was also one of the major causes of the tremendous increase in the following that the Ba'al Shem Tov gathered in a short time. Many are the tales that speak of this.

Among his illustrious disciples, however, were some who could not accept this aspect of the master. It was very difficult for them to emulate the Ba'al Shem Tov's intimacy with the simple folk. Very often the Ba'al Shem Tov would send one of these disciples to learn a virtue like simplicity, trust in Divine Providence, uncomplicated faith, obedience, trust in one's master, or love for Yisrael from these people. Yet it was very difficult for the disciples to structure the virtues of the simple folk in their own being.

The custom of the Ba'al Shem Tov was that all the guests would join him at the first and last meals of Shabbat, and it was also his custom to take the second meal with his close disciples. To this meal, no one else was admitted. One summer Shabbat, something occurred that amazed and upset the holy fellowship of the Ba'al Shem Tov's disciples. Many guests had arrived for that Shabbat. The majority of the guests were simple folk who made their living from innkeeping, farming, handicrafts, tailoring, shoemaking, fruit and vegetable gardening, cattle and poultry raising, or trading at fairs and markets.

At the Friday night meal, the Ba'al Shem Tov beamed great love and friendship to the simple folk, giving the remains of his Kiddush wine to one, pouring some wine into his own special cup and serving another, that he might recite the Kiddush over it. To some he gave a piece of the Shabbat loaf, to others some of the fish or meat on his plate. These, as well as other intimacies, he showed them. And all this amazed the disciples, the members of the holy fellowship.

Now the time for the second meal approached. Those of the guests who knew that they were not invited to this special meal, which the Ba'al Shem Tov partook of with his intimate disciples, found nothing else to do except recite the holy words of the T'hillim. They entered the *beit midrash*, and without anyone arranging it in a formal way, they each began to recite the T'hillim. This must have occurred in the year 5513 or 5515, for among the disciples both the Maggid of Mezritch and the Maggid of Polnoye were already present.

Everything had its own order and system with the Ba'al Shem Tov. The disciples seated themselves in their usual order. During the meal, the Ba'al Shem Tov gave a Torah discourse and the disciples simply soaked in Divine Bliss. Usually they would sing many a tune at the table, and when the disciples saw how delighted the Ba'al Shem Tov was, they too became filled with a holy glee. Out of this deep inner joy, they reflected on their good portion and on their great privilege to be counted among the close disciples of the Ba'al Shem Tov.

There were some of the disciples who at that moment thought how all really was well and how much better it was at this moment than last night when all the unintelligent, simple people were present. Why did the Ba'al Shem Tov favor these simple people, who were unable to understand his lofty teachings? Why did he favor them with such great and wondrous intimacies, his wine in their cups, his own cup to one of them?

So preoccupied were they with their own thoughts that they did not notice that the holy visage of the Ba'al Shem Tov became clouded with great earnestness, and out of great absorption he began to speak: "Peace, peace to far and near. Our sages say that the perfectly righteous cannot reach and attain the level on which the penitent stand." He further explained that there were two ways of serving: the way of the *Tzaddikim,* of the righteous, and the way of the *ba'aley t'shuvah,* of the penitent. The simple folk, due to their humility and downcastness, walked the way of the *ba'aley t'shuvah.* They partake of deep remorse over the past, and they firmly resolve to live a good life in the future.

When the Ba'al Shem Tov concluded, his disciples meditated on their master's holy words while chanting the tune of a well-known *niggun.* Well did they realize that their holy mentor had read their secret thoughts and for this reason given them this very discourse. He had just explained the way of worship and service of the simple folk and shown why it is so exalted: because it partakes of and reaches the rung of the penitent, a rung that even the great saints are not able to attain.

Thus the Ba'al Shem Tov remained in Divine absorption during the singing, and when they concluded the melody, he opened his eyes and looked long and intently at each of his holy disciples, requesting them to place their hands on the shoulder of their neighbors so that their intertwined hands might form a circle. The Ba'al Shem Tov, who himself sat at the head of the table, was about to place his holy hands on the shoulders of the disciples nearest to him. In doing this, he would complete the circle.

He then commanded them to sing a tune and to keep their eyes closed and not to open their eyes until he told them to do so. At this point the Ba'al Shem Tov placed his hands on the shoulders of the disciples sitting next to him.

Suddenly, the disciples heard a delightful and longing sound, a melody of great yearning intermingled with suppliant weeping that would shock a person's soul. One was chanting and pouring out his soul, "O Master of the Universe! The Word of the Lord, it is a pure Word; it is silver sevenfold refined." Another was singing, "O dear Heavenly Father! Test me now and raise me up. Do refine my innards and my heart." And another was singing, "Father, Merciful One! Do favor me, O God; do favor me, for my soul does hide in Thee, and in the shadow of Thy wings will I hide until the storm will pass." And another was singing, "O Mercy, sweet Heavenly Father! Arise God, dispense with Thine enemies. Let those that hate Thee flee before Thee." And another was crying out, "Precious Father! Even a bird has found his home and a swallow a nest for himself, in which to put his fledglings, but Thine Altar, O Lord, my God and King . . ." And another was pouring forth his supplications, "Loving Father, compassionate Parent! Make me return to thee, O God of our salvation, and turn Thine anger from us."

The holy fellowship, hearing the sound of this singing, in which flowed the words of T'hillim, were deeply shaken. Though their eyes were closed, hot tears forced themselves through their eyelids, and their hearts were rent and shattered from the song of this supplication. Each and every one of the holy brotherhood fervently hoped that His Blessed Name would help him to be able to merit to worship on that level. The Ba'al Shem Tov raised his hands from the shoulders of the disciples who sat to his right and left, thus blocking their ears from hearing more of the song of lovely longing, the outpouring of the Psalms. Then the Ba'al Shem Tov commanded them to open their eyes, and they continued to sing the niggunim he prescribed.

The Maggid of Mezritch, in telling this incident to the Elder Rebbe, said; "At that moment, when I heard the song and supplication of the words of T'hillim, which was an outpouring of the soul, an immense longing of a delightful love, to which I hitherto had not attained, the slippers on my feet were wet from sweat and tears, and an inner turning originated from the depths of my heart. When the Ba'al Shem Tov concluded his singing and all of the holy fellowship was silent, the Ba'al Shem Tov remained in Divine absorption for a long time. And then he opened his eyes and said:

"The song you just heard was the song of the simple people, reciting the T'hillim out of the simplicity of the depth of their hearts and pure faith. And now, my beloved disciples, saints of the Most High, behold and see. Are we not merely the edge of truth? For the body is not the truth, and only the soul is truth. How much more so, the Holy One, blessed be He, Who is the true Truth, how much more does He recognize the sincerity of the simple people and their chanting of the Psalms!"

There is a statement in the Bible that says, "You are all standing before the Lord, your God, from the drawer of water and the hewer of wood until the chiefs of the tribes." Yes, the Ba'al Shem Tov had his great disciples, but he made certain that they knew just how close the simple folk could be to God, sometimes putting the disciples to shame. So I don't think that *hierarchy* is a word that you can apply to the Ba'al Shem Tov. There is a lot more organicity that goes with him. Before the Ba'al Shem Tov, there were many people talking about hierarchy: There are some people who are high and some people who are below (The Ba'al Shem Tov also discusses this in the story called "The Besht and the Mitnagged"). And what is the problem with that? The people on top do not listen to the people on the bottom. This was very much the case before the coming of the Ba'al Shem Tov. A circle, like the circle he created among his disciples, is a better figure to describe his thought. The people on top learn from the people below, and vice versa. This is the organically sound way.

The Merchant and His Wife

The Ba'al Shem Tov tells a parable about a merchant and his virtuous wife. They are on a ship tossed by the seas, and the merchant calls out to God to save them because of the merit of his wife's virtue. An idolater aboard hears this and scoffs, saying, "If I wanted, I could easily seduce your wife and procure her wedding ring as a sign of it." Well, after much effort, the braggart is unable to do it and finally resorts to bribing the maidservant to steal the ring. The merchant, seeing the ring, is devastated. And so he decides that he is going to test her himself. He puts her aboard a captainless ship, alone, and disguises himself as a sailor who will withhold food from her until she grants her favors to him. Finally, she is forced to give in. When she comes home from the mock voyage, she reproaches the merchant, saying, "I had such a terrible time and I had to give in because otherwise I wouldn't have had any food." The husband, seeing that she was indignant and did not attempt to conceal the situation, believed her virtue. And knowing that he was that very sailor, he knew she had not really sinned, because he was the one who had tempted her.

Eventually, he finds out that the idolater was faking the story with the ring, that he had had the maidservant steal it. So the Ba'al Shem Tov tells us that this is the meaning of exile for our people.[14]

The question is, who is the merchant and who is the wife? It is certainly clear that the wife is the Jewish people, in this case. She is always seen in this way as the "bride" of God, the virtuous wife of the merchant. The idolater represents the nations of the world that are sometimes causing us, by force, to convert and compromise.

This is how the Ba'al Shem Tov saw it. If it happens that we fall into temptation sometimes, the tempter turns out to be our Husband. In other words, behind the mask of the tempter is God. And when we are forced into a situation where we cannot "survive" except by compromise, then our loyalty is judged by the fact that we do not compromise without an internal struggle. The Ba'al Shem Tov was trying to say something good about our "story." He is trying to say to someone who has stumbled morally in her or his life that there is a way out. Do not think that the tempter who tempted you is anyone else but God. By reconciling with that, you can get out of having to accuse yourself.

The Blessing and the Curse

In Reb Ya'akov Yosef of Polonoye's book *Toldot Ya'akov Yosef*,[15] the Ba'al Shem Tov interprets the verse "And it shall be when all these things come upon you, the blessing and the curse, and you shall have regret in

your heart, and you shall return to the Lord your God." This is Deuteronomy 30:1–2. Here it is translated "And it shall be"; the King James version renders it as "It shall come to pass." The Hebrew for this is *V'Hayah*.
But when the text says *Vay'hi*, "It came to be," the Rabbis say *Vay'hi* is
always "*Oy! Vey!*"—something difficult happened that created the *Vay'hi*.
It was bad. But when it says *V'Hayah*, it is talking about the future, and
it is good. It is almost like saying the opposite of "the good old days." It
says, *Vay'hi Oy! Nebukh*, in the past, *Vay'hi*, it was bad. And *V'Hayah*,
"It shall come to pass," it will be good. "And it shall be when these things
come upon you, the blessing and the curse." So it is implied here that there
is a promise for a good future. Not everything can be translated. The difficulty with these texts is that there are connotations that do not come clear
for people unless they have studied this material before.

One can easily understand how "the curse," or suffering, could bring
one to repentance, but how could "the blessing" bring it about? Remember, it says, "It shall be when these things will happen to you, the blessing and the curse. . . ." If it was just "curse," everyone could understand.
It seems obvious how evil can cause a person to repent from the evil. But
how could the good cause a person to repent?

All right, let's take a little detour. I am the Ba'al Shem Tov, and I am
about to interpret Torah. What am I trying to do by an interpretation? I
am trying to modify reality. Remember, the Torah is given to us, almost
to the point, *Lo B'Shamayim*, "The Torah is no longer in Heaven; it has
been given to us." And because the Torah is given to us, we have a right to
study the Torah in our uniqueness. How we interpret something will make
a difference in reality. It is almost as if to say that this interpretation that
I am going to give determines how the world will come out. So the Ba'al
Shem Tov and later on Reb Levi Yitzhak of Berditchev and many other
Hasidic masters tried to create interpretations that would change reality
for the better. So the Ba'al Shem Tov, as he is about to interpret this, wants
to make it so that people would not necessarily have to be punished for
their transgressions but rather would be able to repent, to come close to
God because they experience a goodness, a grace; they experience a
"blessing." He wants to insinuate on the process of karma that some people can get better, can grow, can get higher and more holy because of
"blessing," and not just "curse." That is the instrumental thing that goes
into this interpretation. It is really important to understand that the interpretation is not merely information to elucidate; it is an attempt to shift
the template of reality in the way in which the master interprets it.

So the Ba'al Shem Tov explains it in the following manner: "It is written, 'A God of vengeance is the Lord, the God of vengeance shines forth'

(Psalm 94:1)." So in the way in which King David uses that psalm, he is saying, I do not have to "get even" myself; I can leave that up to God. In the long run, the person who deserves comeuppance will get comeuppance. It is as if to say, let me not be the one who is the instrument of that punishment. So the Ba'al Shem Tov gives us a parable. In the Gospels, it says that Jesus was not one of the teachers of the law, but he taught in parables.[16] What does it mean that he taught in parables? Why do parable teachers teach parables? Because there is a gestalt, a pattern, being created in a parable, and you can transfer that gestalt to something else. So right now, he is saying, I want you to understand something that is paradoxical. The paradox is, how could God give a "blessing" that causes you to repent? And he then relates this parable:

Once there was a peasant who rebelled against the king by desecrating the statue of the king. But the king, instead of punishing him, raised him out of his peasant status. He gave him higher and higher positions of responsibility until he was second only to the king himself. And as the king heaped reward after reward on the man, he became successively more aware of the king's justice. At the same time, he also became increasingly aware of his own injustice to this very king, and he suffered greatly inside for it. He had received good for evil. But this was all according to the king's plan. For the king knew that had he killed the peasant, the man's suffering would have been slight. But in blessing the peasant, the man was made to suffer terribly from guilt for a long time, realizing the virtue of the person whom he had rebelled against.

Now here is where some readers might get tripped up. Some might say, "Ah, so the king is doing the man good because he wants to 'tighten the screws.'" But that is not the situation here at all. The king is righteous, for, the psalm says, "A God of vengeance is the Lord." When the word *Lord* is translated here, it is actually *YHVH*. This is the four-lettered name of God, sometimes called the *tetragrammaton* (*tetra* is Greek for "four"). That name, *YHVH*, stands for the attribute of Mercy. So when you say "A God of vengeance is the Lord," in the Hebrew it comes out something like "The Kind One is a God of vengeance." So the original Hebrew of the sentence is already a paradox; it has a contradiction in it. How could the Gentle One be a God of vengeance?

The Ba'al Shem Tov says, I'll explain to you what the vengeance is. Now, as you follow that model, that peasant becomes more and more elevated. What does "elevated" stand for? His horizon gets bigger. Before the king does this, what were his horizons? The calf, the cow, the barn, and the outhouse. Now he is in the palace, and his horizon gets bigger and bigger each time he is elevated. His horizon gets larger and larger.

Now translate it not as a peasant but in terms of consciousness. The higher you rise in consciousness, the more you feel how wrong it was, what you have done. And what is the statue of the king? We are made in the image of God, so the statue of the king is you. Besmirching the statue of the king is like behaving in a way unfit for a *mensch*, one who is made in the image of God. That is not how the statue of the king should be dealt with. If a person were to respect the divinity of one's own being as the statue of the king, how much does it deserve to be adorned? Think about how much self-abusing addictions are desecrating the statue of the king. And the more consciousness we get to, the more regret we have about that.

If you short-circuit the process, you don't get fully conscious. In our day, we can look at it as a process, but then, the Ba'al Shem Tov had to deal with people who saw everything as God, "tit for tat." He is trying to get them to release the notion that God has to punish the sinner. He is trying to create a channel, as it were, another way of dealing with punishment. He says, could not grace also achieve this? Could not Divine compassion also achieve it? Does it have to be Divine vindictiveness? Is there not a better way to do it? Then, you might ask, why is any suffering necessary? If the peasant need not suffer physically, why torment him mentally?

Now we are touching on important matters. How does inner space get carved out? If I am totally living on the outside of myself, totally living in the world of action, if I never had to experience any suffering, I would not have any space for compassion either. In *The Chosen*,[17] Chaim Potok describes the situation of a brilliant young man who must learn compassion. He is an *illui,* a genius. However, precisely because he is so brilliant, he is contemptuous of people less brilliant. So his father did something that for him was not easy to do: he raised his son "in silence," without speaking to him in a personal way, only when studying. The rest of the time, the father speaks to the son through someone else. All the while, the son is frightened and longs for the personal connection with the father. He suffers, but the father suffers too. Yet ultimately the father explains, "When I saw who my son would grow up to be, lacking compassion, I knew what I had to do. Without having experienced any suffering, he wouldn't have been able to become the Righteous Man the world needs, because he would not have that space carved out on the inside." So the chisel with which God carves out space in our consciousness, in our compassion, as it were, is the chisel of suffering. Now, there is a difference between pain and suffering. This is also pointed out in Buddhism: pain is inevitable; suffering isn't. Suffering is something that comes out of attachment. Suffering is what we do with our pain and is unnecessary. In the parable of the peasant and the king, the king wants that suffering to achieve a certain end.

"And it shall be when all these things come upon you, the blessing and the curse, and you shall have regret in your heart." The Ba'al Shem Tov says, "When a person sins, he is in rebellion against God, the great King, the Essence of the Universe." Watch here, he is saying, we use the word *King* because we need an image, but beyond the image, he is trying to say, we are talking about the Source that begets worlds, that gives space to creation. Therefore, he says, "He is certainly worthy of punishment." Because remember, in the Ba'al Shem Tov's day, there were fantastically sadistic rulers like Peter the Great,[18] who personally executed people who rebelled against his cruel edicts. That was the notion of monarch that people had at that time. So when they were saying that God is a king, some of that image got transferred over. What the Ba'al Shem Tov is trying to do is get rid of some of that. He is intentionally subverting that notion by talking not about punishment but about the reconciling power of grace. So "God grants a blessing—and no suffering, or curse, could be more terrible than that." What would cause the man to suffer over that? The man needed to have a sense of the greatness of the king, in comparison with which he had done wrong. So the king uses a guilt that grows in proportion to the peasant's understanding of the quality of the king.

In Hasidism, this comes out especially in the writings of Reb Shneur Zalman of Liadi; what is it that we do to the king when we sin? Reb Shneur Zalman says, "Could you imagine taking the king's head and pushing it into the excrement of the outhouse?" Then he says, "In what way do we do that? Because at the very moment in which we sin, it is God invigorating us at that time." God is invigorating us, keeping us alive, and we take that energy, and in the very moment that I am sinning, it is, as it were, in God's face.

There is a twofold notion of sin. Catholicism speaks of two kinds of sin: venial sin and mortal sin. If a person says, " I want to spite God; that is why I am doing this," that's a mortal sin. "I could not help it; I was overcome by passion, by lust," is a venial sin. The venial sin may cause more damage than the mortal sin, but the mortal sin cuts the soul off from God. The venial sin only makes you a victim of the passion. In Judaism, this idea sometimes shows itself in another way, called *b'mezid* and *b'shoggeg*, or a *mummar l'chakh'is*, a *mummar l'ta'evon,* a person who is acting in a way that is rebellious against God out of wanting to anger God, and the other one is acting rebellious against God having been overcome by appetites. The Ba'al Shem Tov says that the more conscious a person becomes of having committed a sin out of appetite, out of not knowing better at the time, the more the person comes to realize that it was a graver thing than previously thought. Consciousness is making the person see that. This is the suffering that scours out the soul.

Now, in the end, the Ba'al Shem Tov says, "When the king sees that the peasant's suffering is greater than a punishment would have caused, the king forgives the peasant." Forgiveness means that the peasant does not have to continue grieving over his sin. One of the great teachings of Judaism comes with Yom Kippur, the Day of Atonement. It is when we go and say, "I've sinned; it's my fault, my great fault; I've done all these bad things in my life." But after Yom Kippur comes Sukkot, which is a celebration. So the notion is that I have to be able to celebrate after the atonement and really believe in it. One of the things that is considered to be a great wrong is if after I have done my penance and reconciled with God, I don't quite feel that God forgives me. That is like saying that I can sin bigger than God can forgive. Do you hear the *chutzpah* in that? My sin is so great that God is not able to forgive it! Basically, that is what Christians are saying about Good Friday. If you do penance and you find your refuge, as it were, in Jesus, then at that point payment has been made.

In Judaism, we do not think of repentance in terms of a person vicariously doing our repentance but in terms of a personal process of repentance, *t'shuvah*, "returning." The power of regret is to root out the habit of the compulsion to sin again. When I become habituated to something, it is almost like saying that without the "cold turkey" of regret and stopping it, I'll become compelled to repeat the thing over and over. I'll never get rid of it. So it is regret that sort of hollows it out of us; it is like the drill that the dentist uses to get rid of what is rotten. That has to continue until you get rid of the rottenness. But to believe that you always have to be in the presence of that regret isn't so good either. On the other hand, the higher we go, there is a teaching, "My sin is always before me." So, they say, did not King David get forgiveness? If God forgave him, why is his sin always before him? So they say, "Yes, God forgave him up to this level, but once he rose to another level, there was still something of the flaw to be fixed." So in our growth, we get to see that there is still more to be done about the flaws in our life.

THE TEACHERS OF THE AHA!

THE MAGGID OF MEZRITCH

(1710–19 KISLEV 1772)

AND

REB PINCHAS OF KORETZ

(1726–10 ELUL 1791)

REB DOV BAER was born in Lukatz, Volhynia, to Chavah and Abraham. His father was a poor teacher of Hebrew who was descended from renowned rabbis and could trace his lineage back to Yochanan HaSandler, a direct descendant of King David. When Dov Baer was about five years old, the family's home caught fire and burned to the ground. The boy, looking on and noticing his mother's grief, asked her, "Mother, why should you grieve so much over the loss of our house?" To which she replied, "I do not grieve for the house but over the loss of the family tree that was kept inside and that traced our lineage back to King David!" Then the boy announced triumphantly, "Don't worry, Mother; I shall start for you a new dynasty!"[1]

Very early on, Dov Baer showed himself to be a precocious child, and since his father was too poor to have him educated, a local rabbi took him on as his personal student. Later, the young man was sent to Lemberg (Lvov), where he quickly became one of the most distinguished disciples of Rabbi Ya'akov Yehoshua Falk, the famed author of the Talmudic commentary *Pnai Yehoshua* ("Face of Joshua"). Well on his way to becoming one of the outstanding scholars of his generation, Rabbi Dov Baer also studied Kabbalah and followed rigidly the ascetic practices of Rabbi Isaac Luria. However, these practices, undoubtedly combined with almost superhuman study habits, severely damaged his health. It is said that

Rabbi Dov Baer suffered from a weak constitution and lameness in his left foot.

Around this time, he married and began a career as a *maggid,* a preacher. He was not content to simply study for the good of all; he wanted to reach people. Very quickly, he became widely known and sought after in this function, preaching in Koretz, Dubno, and Rovno. But his weakened body made it difficult for him to maintain his preaching duties, and finally he sought relief for his ailing body. Following the advice of his mentor, Rabbi Ya'akov Yehoshua Falk, he sought healing from a popular folk healer called the Ba'al Shem Tov. In 1753 he took the long journey to Medzibozh. When he finally arrived and met with the Ba'al Shem Tov, he was immediately disappointed, finding himself disgusted by simple tales about coachmen and horses. Quickly, he readied himself for the return trip. Then the Ba'al Shem Tov sent for him once more. This time he questioned Rabbi Dov Baer on a deep Kabbalistic text, and of course, Rabbi Dov Baer answered correctly. But the Ba'al Shem Tov shook his head no and showed him that while he may have mastered the words, he had not yet mastered the sense. He had not understood the living reality. Thus Reb Dov Baer became a disciple of the Ba'al Shem Tov. Later he would say of his master, "He taught me the language of birds, the great secrets of the sages, and the mystical meanings of many things."[2] Eight years after their first meeting, the Ba'al Shem Tov died.

When the master lay dying, his disciples imploringly asked him, "How can you leave us?" The Ba'al Shem Tov replied, "There is a bear in the forest," an obvious reference to Reb Dov Baer. To some, this seemed a strange choice, considering that Reb Ya'akov Yosef was the senior disciple. But the Ba'al Shem Tov saw further. While Reb Dov Baer would provide the day-to-day leadership of the Hasidim, Reb Ya'akov Yosef would complete the scholarly works that would legitimize the movement throughout Europe. Later Reb Ya'akov Yosef himself endorsed the leadership of Reb Dov Baer, saying, "With the death of the Ba'al Shem Tov, the Divine Presence packed Her bags and moved from Medzibozh to Mezritch," the place to which the Reb Dov Baer moved his seat.[3]

From then onward, he became known as the Maggid of Mezritch and developed his own unique style of leadership. To Mezritch flocked the intellectual and spiritual giants of the age. They listened to the song that flowed from the Maggid's mouth and in turn poured it out to "thirsty" women and men throughout Eastern Europe. The Maggid trained an elite corps of generals to lead armies of Hasidim to Redemption. Most of his disciples went out and founded dynasties of their own, spreading Hasidism far and wide. In twelve short years, from the time of the Ba'al Shem Tov's passing to his own death in 1772, the Maggid had established a lasting foothold for the "way" of the Ba'al Shem Tov.

His counterpart in this chapter, Reb Pinchas of Koretz, was a younger contemporary also heavily influenced by the way of the Ba'al Shem Tov. Pinchas was born in Shklov to a learned Lithuanian rabbi, Abraham Abba. The son was a keen and devoted student of both Talmud and Kabbalah, applying himself with special fervor to the Zohar, which would become his lifelong companion and the wellspring of his teachings. He also rounded out his education with studies in mathematics and grammar.

It seems that Reb Pinchas was not inclined to accept a rabbinical post, or at least not just any post, and suffered great privations on account of it. To earn a living in the meantime, he took a job as a teacher of children near Polonoye, the home of Reb Ya'akov Yosef. After a while, he settled in Koretz, where he came under the influence of the Kabbalist Rabbi Yitzhak HaKohen. And although he would later move to Ostrog and Sheptovka, he remained to all Pinchas of Koretz.

On three different occasions, Reb Pinchas was privileged to meet the Ba'al Shem Tov. And although three meetings is not many quantitatively, they were enough to change his life. One must remember just how powerful a presence the Ba'al Shem Tov was. Sometimes it is said that Reb Pinchas was not a true disciple of the Ba'al Shem Tov but more of an associate. Whatever the case may be, the influence is clear enough. From the Ba'al Shem Tov, like so many others inclined to the Lurianic asceticism, he learned that the way of physical deprivation was not the only path to God.

At the passing of the master, Reb Pinchas was in favor of Reb Ya'akov Yosef's taking the reigns of the budding movement. Some of Reb Ya'akov Yosef's writings had delivered the message of the Ba'al Shem Tov, and Reb Pinchas called these "Torah from the Garden of Eden"[4] and classed them with the Zohar and the works of the Ari. Often he differed with the Maggid of Mezritch in his approach to teaching, putting his emphasis on practical ethics. However, despite their differences, it seems both were "chosen," as it were, by the master. For in addition to his deathbed approbation of Reb Dov Baer, "There is a bear in the forest," the Ba'al Shem Tov continued with "and Pinchas is a sage."[5] Reb Pinchas of Koretz died on the Russian frontier, making his way to Eretz Yisrael.

○

Maggid of Mezritch on *Tzimtzum*

For the effulgence of the Blessed and Holy One is far greater
than what the worlds can bear. But the Blessed One,
in many contractions and condensations, scales the
effulgence down so that we may be able to bear it.

—Dov Baer of Mezritch, *Maggid D'varav L'Ya'akov*

What does the word *Tzimtzum* (contraction) mean? If we talk about a new paradigm where God is everything and everywhere, if we talk of pantheism and panentheism, why does there have to be such a thing as *Tzimtzum*? Why must God step out of the way, as it were, to make room for the world? The *Tanya* of Reb Shneur Zalman of Liadi deals with this at great length. But let us look at it as it is talked about in the teachings of the Maggid of Mezritch.

The Maggid says that the teacher has to condense his teaching so that it will not overwhelm the fragile mind of the student, just as the father has to tell the story to the child in such a way that the child will be able to understand it. All of this is a way of saying that a certain scaling down is often necessary.

Now most people have a notion of God that is very small. I remember a little book by a man named Phillips called *Your God Is Too Small*,[6] and it had a little teddy bear on the cover. Very often when we talk about God, people do not get into what *Ain Sof* is really about—the "infiniting," the infinity going on in infinite dimensions. It is almost as if you were to make a googol to the googol power or an infinite sign to an infinite power. That is what we are talking about. Could you imagine the consciousness in a mind that is so constantly infinite and has to create space for our finite world? You can see, then, why there has to be an obscuring of that, a hiding of that infinite power-light-awareness, so that the little awareness that is in us can have a place to dwell. That is what is meant by *Tzimtzum*. It does not mean that God has literally removed Godness from this space; it only means that God has removed the Light.

Now, if you were to ask Reb Yitzhak Luria, "What is meant by Divine Light?" he would tell you *Hargashat shlemut haAtzmut*, the ability to become, feel, and realize the utter perfection of the absolute. If that utter perfection of the absolute were to begin to radiate right here, right now, can you imagine how we would be blown out? Thus a scaling down of sorts becomes necessary so that there should be room for our mind, our experience, to happen.

A Paradox: Praying for Oneself or Praying for the *Shekhinah*?

And to this our sages have said, "Thy fear be upon you,"
meaning that thy prayer be not fixed by rote. One should not
pray concerning one's own needs, but one must always pray
for the blessed Shekhinah, *that She be redeemed from Her exile.*
Thus all prayer must "be mercy and supplication," meaning
that one must always supplicate the Lord for the sake of the
Shekhinah, *who is called "Space," Makom, as it is well known.*
Thus the Zohar calls those who pray for themselves, and not
for the sake of the Shekhinah, *by the name of "dogs with harsh*
souls." For they are ever screaming, "Give me, give me."
And this is the intention of the sentence "One thing have I asked
from the Lord, only this [Heb. Otah, literally, "Her"] do I seek."
In other words, for the sake of the Shekhinah *do I seek this*
and so I pray before Thee—to correct the injury that has
been done through sin.

—Dov Baer of Mezritch, *Maggid D'varav L'Ya'akov*

He answered: What is God? The totality of souls. Whatever
exists in the whole can also be found in the part. So in any one
soul, all souls are contained. If I turn, in t'shuvah, I contain
in me the friend whom I wish to help, and he contains me in
him. My t'shuvah makes the him-in-me better and the me-in-him
better. This way it becomes so much easier for him-in-him
to become better.

—Pinchas of Koretz, *Midrash Pinchas*

The Maggid of Mezritch tells us that we should not pray for anything but the need of the *Shekhinah*, the Divine Presence. On the other hand, Reb Pinchas of Koretz, in his teachings, says that you should pray for anything that you need, even for the most simple things. So how are we to understand these two views?

Let me tell you a story of Reb Zushya. Reb Zushya of Onipol was the brother of Reb Elimelech of Lizhensk. Reb Elimelech was, you might say, the great ascetic of Hasidism, and Reb Zushya is the Saint Francis, liberating birds from cages and so on—a wonderful, warmhearted person. It is said that when the Maggid would utter the words "And God spoke," Reb Zushya would explode into ecstasy and have to be carried out.

So here is Reb Zushya. One day he arrives in a little town, looking like a beggar, and he sits in the *beit midrash,* the house of study. He is sitting there waiting for someone to offer him some food because he would not speak up. Finally, someone brings him some food—but he doesn't look at it or even touch it. Then he says, "Rebboina Shel Olam, dear God, Zushya is hungry! Zushya is hungry! Please give him something to eat!" Then he looks at the bowl, "You gave him something to eat!" And he makes a blessing.

With Reb Zushya, it is almost as if he did not want to deal with anybody else for his needs except God. So he is not talking about the *Shekhinah* right now. He is simply saying, "Zushya is hungry. Zushya needs some food." He is dealing with the basics of life with a very high level of intention. I think of the blessings associated with our daily routine, the blessing said after going to the bathroom, the blessings over the food. These things are so close to us and yet sometimes we hardly pay any attention to them at all. But imagine with what great intention you might say those blessings if you had prostate problems or if you had not eaten for a long time. Just think how you would thank God for every inch of the mundane then. So what does it mean to truly turn to God for all of our needs?

The question has been asked whether the prayers that we say in the synagogue or at home every morning and every evening are part of the rabbinic law or the scriptural law. Now if you ask which one of the two is of primary importance, you would say scriptural law "trumps" rabbinic law because it is written in the Torah. So is prayer a fulfillment of scriptural law or rabbinic law? Scriptural law demands that when you have a need, you ask God for that; rabbinic law is that you should pray three times a day. When you are fulfilling the rabbinic law of prayer, and in that prayer you ask for healing, help in making a living, inspiration or guidance—if you are merely reciting it because it is in the *siddur,* you are observing only the rabbinic law. But if you say, "O, *Ribbono Shel Olam,* I so need your inspiration! I so need your guidance; please help me understand!" you are transforming the rabbinic command into a scriptural command. You raise the level because of your own concern and personal investment in that need.

So why is it that the Maggid is saying that you shouldn't be praying for yourself but for the *Shekhinah* alone? I think of Reb Pinchas of Koretz, who asked rhetorically, "Who is God? And what is God?" and then answered, "God is the collection of all the souls." What a marvelous definition. Those familiar with Sufism[7] may know the words "Toward the One, the perfection of love, harmony, and beauty. The only Being, united with all the illuminated souls, who form the embodiment of the Master, the Spirit of Guidance."[8] There is no One more harmonious, more beautiful, and loving than that One that creates, sustains, and helps us all the time. When the Sufis refer to "the only Being," it is something different from the ordinary. We think we are a being, but we are not really a being; there is only one Being. Krishnamurti[9] also talks about this, that there is only one Being, and we are but one phase of that one Being, "united," or connected, "with all the illuminated souls." Who are they? They form "the embodiment of the Master, the Spirit of Guidance." In other words, whenever we receive some teaching, some learning, who is the Great Rebbe? "The Spirit of Guidance." Whatever we get through any guru, teacher, or Rebbe, it is only because the Spirit of Guidance is filtering through them. The Spirit of Guidance is the collective superconscious (not unconscious) of illuminated beings. Another way of saying it is that all the bodhisattvas[10] linked together in one local area network, as parallel processors, are producing that kind of intelligence and awareness.

So what is the *Shekhinah,* the Divine Presence, that the Maggid is talking about? It is often called *knesset Yisrael,* the gathering of Israel, in other words, all the souls together. When the Maggid is saying that you should pray not for yourself but for the *Shekhinah,* he means that there is an apparent separation to us between the clearly Divine and the Divine that is embedded in our experiential reality. And the Divine that is embedded, covered, in our experiential reality often feels cut off. It has a longing to be connected with the Divine that knows it is Divine. Reb Dov is saying that this deep longing is there in us, and what we should be praying for is not so much our own needs but the need of the Divine that is embedded in all of us. Often this is called the Divine immanence. What is immanent is what often does not feel the transcendence.

Some scholars have contended that because of this seeming shift from the everyday, the Maggid seems to have gone away from the way of the Ba'al Shem Tov. "He isn't so friendly to simple people as the Ba'al Shem Tov was," they say. Let me tell you, to the best of my knowledge, that is a libel. The Maggid's emphasis may differ from that of the Ba'al Shem Tov, but the Maggid was accessible to people. There are numerous stories of his interacting with simple folk also, and in fact he often sent his students to do some of that work so that they would live with the townsfolk and understand their needs. So do not be quick to see a strong dichotomy between them. Scholars, in their analysis, have a habit of doing that. They ask, What is it that differentiates the Maggid from the Ba'al Shem Tov?

Then they find a nuance and stick in the knife of dichotomy, creating an abyss from a tiny crack or crevice, a mere nuance. It is a conceptual illusion and a false division to me.

The Song of Songs Is Not Understandable

All scripture is holy and is the connecting link between
this world and the higher ones. Hence each portion can be
understood according to the world to which it is connected.
However, the Songs of Songs is not at all understandable.
It is sacrosanct and connects this world to the Ain Sof *infinities,*
which are beyond mind.

—Pinchas of Koretz, *Midrash Pinchas*

Many people did not want the Song of Songs to enter the official canon of the Bible—it was too raunchy for the taste of some. It describes the lover saying to the beloved, "How beautiful are your breasts," "How beautiful the belly is," "Your kisses are better than wine," "Your loving is so delicious, it is sweeter than the best taste to my palate." It is such a powerful book. So it happened that there was Rabbi Akiva, who himself was a person who knew what it means to be a loving partner with his wife. He pleaded with the rabbis to let this book into the biblical canon. He said, "All the Songs," meaning all the psalms, "are sacred, but the Song of Songs is the most sacrosanct of them all."

Reb Pinchas says that every book of the Bible connects you to another world. What does he mean by that? Look at Psalm 148. It is such a remarkable psalm: "Praise the Lord from the Heavens, from the earth, the whales, the sea monsters in the deep, fruit trees, and tall cedars, young men and maidens, fire and hail, snow and fog, mountains and hill . . ." This psalm connects you to this part of the world of which it speaks. There are some other worlds where "Sometimes I feel like a motherless child" or *Ei-leee, Eehhhh-leeee, lama azavtanee,* "My God, My God, Why hast thou forsaken me?" You can read different parts of scripture in this way. Some parts have to do with agriculture, and they connect you with that aspect of creation. Some connect you with what the angels are doing in Heaven, saying, "Holy, Holy, Holy is the Lord of Hosts." There are all kinds of scriptures that connect you to various kinds of things.

Every Friday, late afternoon, before you start the Sabbath prayer, you chant the Song of Songs. I remember when I was with my father, and I would hear him chant it tenderly and with longing the way he remembered his master doing it, "On my bed at night, I sought him whom my soul loves, I sought him and found him not." There was such fantastic longing in there. So all the songs were seen as if talking about God's "garments." Just as two lovers want to be with each other without garments, in direct contact, the Song of Songs is asking for that unimpeded contact. Reb Pinchas says, all the others connect you to worlds, but to the Infinite, they do not.

Now in the sense in which people who have experienced deep intimacy and love in sexuality, as it is discussed in *Tantra,* there are moments that feel "Eternal," where there is no *I* or *you.* It is beyond me or you; we are "One-ing" in a way that is bigger than both of us, and in that One-ing there is the Divine Presence. Most people in their lovemaking, and unfortunately in their prayer life, have the feeling that God has to be kept out of it. What a remarkable thing it is for people who can also have that prayerful connection in that deep union! Imagine the potential power in saying, "Now we are celebrating in our loving that there should not be any war ravaging the world." Can you understand that? To dedicate that wonderful energy, inviting the Presence of God into their being, in order to shift the karma of the world is a very powerful thing. It is sacralizing the sexual act, doing it in a sacred way. There is a lot of healing potential in this. Friday night is supposed to the most special time, in honor of *Shabbat,* to make love. However, this teaching is not emphasized by people that don't experience that; they won't talk about it. Reb Pinchas, apparently, has had experiences that made him say that this is the last word of his teaching.

This experience of One-ing also reminds us of *d'vekut. D'vekut* means "sticking to God." It is like being cozy with God, snuggling with God. That is what people are getting into when they are putting on the *t'fillin* and wrapping themselves in the *tallit.* They are experiencing closeness through those holy things. Perhaps you have seen Catholics kissing their rosaries or a priest kissing the stole before he puts it on. It is like saying, "I am now surrounding myself with and putting my aura in touch with God."[11]

THE ASCETIC SAINT

REB ELIMELECH OF LIZHENSK

(1717–21 ADAR 1787)

REB ELIMELECH WAS BORN to Meresh and Rabbi Eliezer Lipmann in Lapacha, near Tiktin. Though Meresh was unlettered, she was an extremely devout woman and may have influenced her sons, Elimelech and Zushya, as much as any of their great teachers. Reb Zushya once said of her, "My mother didn't pray from a prayer book, because she couldn't read. But she knew how to recite the blessings by heart and recited them with such intensity that where she had recited the blessings in the morning, the radiance of the Divine Presence rested in that place the whole day." His father, Rabbi Eliezer, was a generous and wealthy landowner who traced his roots back to the great biblical commentator Rashi. He tried with all his might to ease the suffering of his poverty-stricken neighbors and because of this was promised a great son by Prophet Elijah. Elimelech would later be called by some "the second Ba'al Shem Tov."

Both Elimelech and Zushya were educated in Tiktin, and it was there that they came into contact with a great scholar and Hasid, Reb Shmelke Horowitz. Though Elimelech did not enter the circle of the Maggid at that time, he learned from Reb Shmelke how to study with single-minded diligence and devotion. He also met there and benefited from Reb Shmelke's brother, Reb Pinchas of Frankfurt. But in these years, Reb Elimelech and Reb Zushya were in many ways students of one another, sharing in a spiritual partnership. To Reb Elimelech, Reb Zushya was a walking lesson in piety, and Reb Elimelech adored him. So it was that they set out together on the road of self-imposed exile, wandering from place to place to atone for misdeeds and to bring others to repentance.

For three years they did this, suffering through great poverty and sowing the seeds of many legends.

When this exile was finally ended, Reb Elimelech devoted himself completely to asceticism and his studies for fourteen years until finally, Reb Zushya persuaded him to visit the Maggid while he was at Dubno. Almost immediately, Reb Elimelech hailed the Maggid as his teacher. There, he also reacquainted himself with Reb Shmelke and met Reb Levi Yitzhak.

When the Maggid died, Reb Elimelech settled in Lizhensk, which under his leadership came to be thought of as the "Jerusalem of Hasidism." There Reb Elimelech maintained, as his master had, a court that was supported by *pidyonot,* contributions offered to the *Tzaddik.* However, it was said that not a coin remained under Reb Elimelech's roof overnight; he gave all of his money to the poor. Reb Elimelech taught his disciples how to be *Tzaddikim,* which they learned from his personal example. They learned by watching him pray, for he was renowned for his intensity in *davvenen.* He was also an advocate of practical Tzaddikism, which is to say, he was not simply a spiritual guide but also attended to the most mundane of his followers' needs. Not all *Tzaddikim* subscribed to this kind of leadership, but Reb Elimelech set a precedent that would be followed for long thereafter. Many great Rebbes of the generation paid tribute to him as their master, including the Seer of Lublin, the Maggid of Koznitz, Reb Mendel of Rymanov, and Reb Abraham Joshua Heschel of Apt. All of these, who had attended to the Maggid of Mezritch before his passing, acknowledged the leadership of Reb Elimelech. Reb Zushya interpreted the verse from Genesis 2:10, "A river issues from Eden to water the garden, and then divides into four branches," in this way: the Ba'al Shem Tov is Eden, the river is the Maggid of Mezritch, the garden is Reb Elimelech, and the "four branches" are his four great disciples.[1]

There is a story of Reb Elimelech from the terrible time of the Nazi domination in Eastern Europe. On one occasion, the Nazis thought to bulldoze the cemetery that kept the mausoleum of Reb Elimelech of Lizhensk. When they heard the pleas not to disturb the body of Reb Elimelech, they were amused and decided to have a look at this "great Jew." So they removed the lid that had laid there for more than 150 years, and there inside lay the body Reb Elimelech, seemingly untouched by the ravages of time. Filled with awe, the Nazis put the cover back in place and left the mausoleum intact.[2]

○

The Small *Tzettel* of Reb Elimelech of Lizhensk

1. When you are free at any time from Torah, especially when
   you sit by yourself in the room without doing anything,
   or when you lie down in your bed and you cannot sleep,
   you ought to meditate on the positive commandment of
"And I shall be sanctified in the midst of the children of Yisrael."
You must create in your soul the image, describing it to yourself
   in thought, of a great and fierce fire burning before you,
   its flames reaching the heart of Heaven, and you, for the sake
of sanctifying His blessed Name, break your nature and cast
yourself into that very fire. Since a good thought is reckoned
   as a deed by the Holy One, blessed be He, the result of this
meditation will be that not only are you not wasting your time,
but you are also fulfilling a positive commandment of the Torah.

—Elimelech of Lizhensk, *Tzettel Katan*

In 1942, in the days before they had copying machines, I bought myself
one of the big Lubavitcher prayer books, not the *Tehillat HaShem* but the
Torah Or—that's the real hefty one. I cut out from another book the
Tzettel Katan of Reb Elimelech and pasted it into my prayer book so I
could recite it, read it every day, and remember it, as Reb Elimelech says,
"This *Tzettel Katan* ought never to be removed from the book in which
you study." Usually included with the *Tzettel Katan* is also another short
piece called *The Way of Man*. Now as you read these, you realize that he
is giving his disciples a set of recipes—spiritual recipes. These were called
tzettel. *Tzettel Katan* means a "small note." So he wrote these out and
gave them to his disciples to read and work through every day.

He urges in the *Tzettel Katan* that when you have nothing else to do,
you should imagine that there is this huge fire and you, for the love of
God, are throwing yourself into that fire. That is how you want to serve
God. If you do that, with that intention, it is accounted to you as if you
had actually done it.

Once a big sinner came to Reb Elimelech of Lizhensk and said, "Master, short of
murder, I've done everything one shouldn't do. And I know that I will not be
accepted in Heaven, and if I die before I make amends for that, I'm going to be
roasted. So, Master, please help me! What can I do? I need a *tikkun*, a fixing for my

soul, because otherwise I'm going to be in Gehenna, I'm going to be in purgatory. I want to straighten this out." Reb Elimelech, hearing his confession,[3] says, "Well, one of the ways in which we had a person who wanted to atone for his sins execute it was to pour hot lead down his throat. And if you want, I'll do that for you." The man says, "Holy Master, will I be forgiven if that happens?" And he answers, "Yes." "All right," says the man, "let's do it tomorrow." "Ah, it can't happen so fast. You first really have to feel regret; you have to get it out of your system. It's not so fast that I'm going to pour the lead in." "How long will it take?" Reb Elimelech explains to the man everything he has to do to make amends for his life and says, "It's going to take a year." And the man follows him through all the things he prescribed. Finally, the day scheduled for the execution arrives. The lead is already liquid and boiling. Reb Elimelech sits the man down and puts a cloth over his eyes; the man once again recites his confession, asks God for forgiveness, and says the Sh'ma Yisrael. He is ready and opens his mouth to receive the lead. Reb Elimelech takes the ladle, dips it into a jar of honey, and pours the honey into the man's throat. The man sputters and swallows it down and then says, "What did you do that for? I expected to die!" And Reb Elimelech says, "By this time, you don't need to die anymore."

Reb Elimelech felt that the imaginal experience of that purgation was, if really felt, if really experienced, enough for atonement. It didn't need anything else. He sees this imaginal experience of offering one's life for the sanctification of God's Name, as a scouring, as it were, saying, "I defy my ego and its fears by imagining this."

I remember how I used to do a miniature of this meditation when I was riding from my home in Borough Park to the *yeshiva* on Eastern Parkway. I had to take the BMT subway to get there, and on the BMT there are those little places where the conductor sits at both ends of the train. I would go and sit in that little place because I didn't want to have to look at the ads that were on display in the car and get distracted. You know, a *yeshiva* boy having to look at Maidenform bra advertisements wasn't the best thing. So I sat in that little cubicle there, and I made up my mind that by the time we came Pacific Avenue, and the train would stop, I would die. So as we are approaching it, I'm getting ready, and it's coming in, and I'm hearing the brakes, and now, and now, and now . . . Ready! I'm gone. And I'll tell you something. At the time, I would get quite a charge out of that. It really worked for me. It was a way of saying, as a preparation, if I want to go into the world of the *Amidah,* the place where I can stand face to face with God, and offer my prayer, I want to be doing this from that place that is willing to say, "Death is OK." So you could see how Reb Elimelech would take this heavy medicine.

There was a great master named Reb Shmelke of Nikolsburg. In his day, if you were a prominent rabbi, you might be invited to become the rabbi of the city, which is a great deal more than being invited to the synagogue pulpit. Being invited to the seat of the rabbinate was like saying you're the chief rabbi of the place. It was a life contract that you were handed. And you were the chief magistrate also. Every legal question was brought to you. So you can imagine that the citizens wanted somebody who was truly an expert in the law; they didn't care so much about the sermons the person would give; they wanted someone to serve as chief justice of the Jewish community. So Reb Shmelke was invited to come to Nikolsburg in Bohemia to be the city's rabbi.

Shortly after his arrival in Nikolsburg, the townsfolk hold a big reception for him, but Reb Shmelke is in his study and isn't coming out. So his disciple, Reb Moshe Leib Sassover, goes up to the door of the study and listens to figure out what his master is doing. From inside, he hears Reb Shmelke muttering to himself, so he puts his eye to the keyhole and looks inside. There he sees Reb Shmelke going up and down the room saying, "Welcome, Reb Shmelke! How do you do, Reb Shmelke? Reb Shmelke, we are so glad to have you here in this town." He is going through all these introductions and compliments—the whole thing. Finally, he says, "Bah! Enough!" opens the door, and says, "All right. Let's go." And he goes to the reception.

Reb Moshe Leib says to him, "Rebbe, what were you doing in your study?" And he says, "The Rabbis have said, 'Let the honor of your friend be as beloved as your own.' In other words, don't insult anybody else. Treat others with the same respect that you want to have for yourself." But Reb Shmelke was reading it a little bit differently. He continued, "May the honor that you get from other people have the same taste as the honor that you give to yourself." Knowing that he was going to get all these nice things said about him, he went through the whole ordeal beforehand in preparation. He was just getting ready to handle the issue of pride.

However, later when Reb Shmelke would give sermons, he would give remarkable holy sermons, figuring that all these people were great and wonderful. But the people didn't relate to them. In the midst of his great and wonderful teachings, they were looking to have arguments with him, *pilpul,* and that's not what he was giving. Reb Elimelech realized that his friend Reb Shmelke is having trouble in Nikolsburg, and so he travels to Nikolsburg one day and asks the communal leaders, "May I preach in the synagogue, and could everybody be invited to come and hear the visiting preacher?" They agree, and the people fill the synagogue.

Reb Elimelech of Lizhensk starts out saying, "Once upon a time, there was this prince, and his father sent him to travel to Paris to study at the university there. With him, he sent a valet and a coachman. But after they started out to travel on the road, the valet decided to get rid of the prince, to kill him. He tells his plan to the coachman, saying, 'All the money that he has is going to be ours. From now on, you are going to be the valet and I'm going to be the prince. And this is how we are going to handle it.' Thereupon they kill the prince, but by the time they get to Berlin, the 'prince,' who was really the valet, has fallen ill. They call the best doctor they can find, the imperial doctor, to come and cure him. And the imperial doctor treats the masquerading prince with very refined medicines. But the medicines don't help him a bit. Now, the poor coachman, who is now the valet, sees that this isn't going to be any good. So he calls a horse doctor, who administers a good purge to the 'prince' that clears him out. And he gets better.

"So," Reb Elimelech says, "my dear friends, my holy brother, Reb Shmelke, he thinks that you are all princes, but I know that you are nothing but disguised valets. Well, I'm the horse doctor and I'm going to cure you guys." And he starts reading the people's foreheads and telling them the sins that they have done until he had chastised them all.

Reb Elimelech was a toughie, and he called a spade a spade. He got his young men to experience all these difficult things because he felt that that was going to bring them closer to the real light and to the greater love. *Amen.*

THE PASSIONATE DEFENDER

REB LEVI YITZHAK OF BERDITCHEV

(1740–5 TISHRI 1809)

WHEN REB LEVI YITZHAK was born, the Ba'al Shem Tov is said to have spoken these words: "A great soul is descending from Heaven, and he will speak up for the good of Israel." That great soul was born in Husakov, Galacia, to Soshe Sarah, a descendent of Rabbi Shmuel Eliezer Edels, and to Rabbi Meir, a well known Talmudist and Kabbalist, the sixteenth generation in his family to serve as a rabbi. Levi Yitzhak's talents were recognized very early, and he was sent to the *yeshiva* in Yaraslav and was soon to become known as the "Yaraslav prodigy."

When he was seventeen, he was married in Libertov, Poland, to the daughter of Rabbi Israel Peretz. Close to Libertov was Ritchvol, where dwelt Rabbi Shmelke Horowitz (of Nikolsburg), an important disciple of the Maggid. Meeting the saintly Reb Shmelke, he was quickly drawn into the mystic circle of the Maggid of Mezritch. Though he was a very young man, only in his twenties, it was not long before he gained a reputation as being one of the Maggid's major disciples. Upon Reb Shmelke's departure from Ritchvol, Reb Levi Yitzhak took his place as rabbi. But the growing opposition to Hasidim in Ritchvol, and throughout the region, soon overtook Reb Levi Yitzhak. On Hoshanah Rabbah, Reb Levi Yitzhak was forced to flee the city and his post with *lulav* and *etrog* in hand. Later he was driven from posts in Zhelikov (1765) and Pinsk (1771).

In 1785, he finally found a stable home as the Rabbi of Berditchev, where he stayed to the end of his days. In time, Reb Levi Yitzhak's gentleness and kindness overcame all opposition, and his influence was felt throughout the Hasidic world as a leader universally respected. He was so well regarded that he was often called on to be the arbiter of internal controversies that arose in the still budding Hasidic movement. Few individuals could be trusted by both sides. So it was he who was called on when controversies broke out between Reb Nachman of Bratzlav and the Shpole Zeide or between Reb Shneur Zalman of Liadi and Reb Abraham Kalisker. Reb Levi Yitzhak was a peacemaker, an advocate for all Israel.

Often he would travel to the surrounding communities to acquaint himself with the lives and needs of village Jews, to be sensitive to their problems. And like Abraham, he was known for debating with God for the people's sake. For no one knew better the difficult lives of village Jews and how hard they tried in spite of this to keep the commandments. Once, along with a group of others, Reb Levi Yitzhak watched as a wagon driver greased the wheels of his wagon while wearing his *tallit* and *t'fillin*. The others laughed and scolded the filthy man, but Reb Levi Yitzhak was amazed. "Look," he said to God, "how your servant praises and honors you, even while greasing his wagon wheels! Have mercy on such a people!" When Reb Levi Yitzhak died, Israel lost a great servant and advocate. Reb Nachman of Bratzlav said, "Whoever has eyes in his head will see that on the day that Reb Levi Yitzhak died, a great darkness descended upon the world."[1]

Songs of Adoration and Advocacy

> Where will I find You?
> and where will I not find You?
> If I go right,
> there is You.
> If I go left,
> there is You.
> Up, You; down, You; before me, You; behind me, You; in me, You,
> You, You, You, You.
> To the east is You.
> To the west is You.
> To the north is You.
> To the south is You.
> Where I go, where I stand, is You.
> Wherever I go, wherever I stay, I face You.

This was one of Reb Levi Yitzhak's songs, of which he wrote many. In one of them he says, "God, I'm calling you to court. Every nation has its emperor, its ruler. And what does that emperor do for his people? And what do his people do for him? They try and cheat each other as much as they can! But what about us—we are trying all the time to do Your will even though You don't have any soldiers and any sheriffs going after us. Still we are doing Your will. Isn't it a shame that You don't help us more? And so I am saying, the Russians say their tsar is a tsar, and the Germans say the Kaiser is a Kaiser, but I, Levi Yitzhak of Berditchev, say, 'You are greater than all these. Blessed and magnified be the Name of God. There must be an end to the sufferings of Your people, Israel.'" He goes from there into the prayer. What a wonderful way he had of saying, "You are so great my Lord, and we love you so much; so, I know you will help us out."

Teyku—Because Elijah Never Died!

Why, asked Reb Levi Yitzhak, do the Rabbis promise that all questions will be answered by Eliyahu the prophet when he comes to announce the Messiah and not by, say, Moshe himself, who then will be resurrected? And he answered his own question: "Moshe died, and we cannot hope to be helped in our current-day problems by Moshe, who completed his life, Peace be upon him. Since that time, the Torah has been placed in our hands, and if one's soul is from the side of grace, every thing is pure, permitted, and kosher, and if it is from the side of rigor, the opposite holds true. Yet each person according to his rung is a vehicle for the word of the living God. This is why the sages, realizing the need for grace in this world, set the *halakha* down according to the teachings of Hillel, for this is the world's need. Now, one who is alive and in this world knows well what the needs of the times are and the attributes we need to live by. One who isn't alive on this plane does not know the attributes we need to live by in this world. Since Eliyahu is existing and alive, never tasting the taste of death, and has remained all that time right here on this plane, he, and not any other, is suited to resolve our doubts.

—Levi Yitzhak of Berditchev, *K'dushat Levi*, 108b, Muncazs

Let's talk a little bit about *teyku*, which is Aramaic for "let it stand." Sometimes in the discussions of the Talmud, the Rabbis come to what some scholars regard as Talmudic "hairsplitting," delving into the subtlest differences between ideas. The Rabbis investigate things and want to find answers: What does it mean? With which or whose opinion should we concur? What is the case really about? What is the truth or reality? They ask a question as if to say, "Let us try and explore the thing so that we can understand where it is going." And at times they come to a place where there is no conclusion, and they cannot come to a decision, and so they say, "*Teyku*."

Now, some say that in addition to its meaning in Aramaic, it is also an acronym for *Tishby yitaretz kushiyot v'iba'yot* (*Tav Yud Kuf Vav*), meaning, "Prophet Elijah will come." Stating this acronym would mean, "I can't give you an answer now; we have to keep on searching." One of the ways in which you get real answers was called "a visit by Prophet Elijah." Prophet Elijah[2] is regarded as something like Hermes,[3] as it were, the messenger of God. If you have a conundrum and you seek a way out of it, Prophet Elijah will manifest, if you merit it, and will reveal to you the answer. So what the sages are saying is that you are going to have to wait until Elijah comes to sort this one out.

Many people have the notion that things are carved in stone, as the Ten Commandments were carved in stone. Whenever you think of something as carved in stone, it means it cannot be changed. So Reb Levi Yitzhak asks the question, "Why don't we ask Moses? After all, he is our immediate source of Torah, and shouldn't we get inspiration from him? Why do we have to go to Elijah?"

The teaching is that Moses is at one end of history and his life ended there. He "completed his life." And Elijah is at the other end of history, as it were. He was taken up into Heaven while still alive. It is said that there will come a day when Elijah will return: "Behold, I will send unto you my messenger, Elijah. And he will reconcile the hearts of the fathers unto the children, and the hearts of the children unto the parents." That is a very hard thing to do. And so on every occasion, like the Passover *Seder,* when we need intergenerational connection, or the circumcision, we invite Elijah to be present. Saturday night we sing *"Eliyahu HaNabi."* We need to make a connection between the Sabbath experience and the experience of the week. So we invite Prophet Elijah. He is the one who sees us through things and gives us the answers that we need.

In *The Autobiography of a Yogi* by Yogananda, there is a person called Babaji.[4] There is in Babaji an element that seems to show itself in every generation, a sense of some being that comes and goes. He doesn't quite belong to our world; he comes in when he is needed and then disappears. It is a similar situation with Elijah. Everybody else, we find out in the Torah, with a few exceptions,[5] is said to have died a natural death or was subject to dying. But Prophet Elijah, it says, took a fiery chariot to Heaven (2 Kings 2:11). You have some sense of that when you hear about the Ba'al Shem Tov taking the *Aliyat HaNeshamah,* the ascent. Well, Elijah is going up and down and is apparently dealing with a body that doesn't exactly come from this plane of existence, but one he can "thicken," as it were, to make it visible to us. He represents what is yet to come, but he also lived then; in other words, Prophet Elijah has a history.

When you look at the Bible, there are all kinds of prophets there. There are prophets like Isaiah, which are seen as literary prophets; they have produced for us the prophetic literature. Then there are some prophets like Elijah, who haven't produced any literature; there is no Book of Elijah like there is a Book of Isaiah. So what do we have of Elijah? We have him as a shamanic prophet. If necessary, he is able to do amazing things. If someone needs healing from leprosy, he heals the leprosy. If a baby has died, he brings it back to life. He can do all manner of strange things that other people cannot. In this he is very much a shaman.

Elisha,[6] his disciple, also performs this function from time to time when the king needs an oracle. When I was in Dharamsala with a Jewish group dialoguing with the Dalai Lama, we met the *lama* who serves as the oracle to the Dalai Lama. He is a very gentle and slight person, weighing not more than 120 pounds. And yet he wears a suit while performing this function that weighs over 250 pounds! When we talked to him, he told us (he speaks a pretty clear English) about what happens to him in the process. He gets so worn out that it takes him days to recuperate from the process in which he is being, as it were, possessed by that energy. So shamanic prophets, shamanic beings, who serve in that capacity, need an induction. They can't just "take off"; they need a catalyst.

Once, Elisha, the son of Shafat, was sought out when three kings, King Yehoshafat of Judah, King Jehoram of Israel, and the King of Edom, found themselves in dire straits and needed the counsel of the Lord. "What should we do?" they asked. "Isn't there a prophet around here?" So they went down to Elisha and said, "Give us a prophecy." And he said, "Get me a fiddler." So they called a fiddler, and when the fiddler fiddled a melody for him, he prophesied.[7]

The Bible says, "And it was, when the music was playing, the Spirit of God settled upon him," and took him where he had to go, and then he came out with the prophecy (2 Kings 3:15). We can see, then, that we have a different kind of prophet here with Elisha and Elijah. Remembering this, let's look at Reb Levi Yitzchak's teaching again. If Moses only sees until his dying day, he cannot see beyond his dying day. A Hasidic story will illustrate that:

A man comes to Reb Elimelech of Lizhensk and asks if he should go forward with a certain business deal. And the Rebbe says, "Yes. It's going to be good; God will help. You'll do very, very well." The man then goes to the Rebbe's disciple, the Lubliner, Reb Ya'akov Yitzhak, and asks him the same question. And Reb Ya'akov Yitzhak says, "You're going to get wiped out." So the man says to himself, "I asked the teacher, and he says I'm going to do well, and I asked the disciple, and he says I'm not going to make it. Which one should I listen to, the teacher or the disciple?" He decides to go with the teacher and makes the deal. It goes exceedingly well in the beginning, but he loses his shirt in the end. The man comes back to Reb Ya'akov Yitzhak of Lublin and asks him, "How come things turned out this way?" Reb Ya'akov Yitzhak says, "Because my master, my teacher, Elimelech, saw only until his dying day. And to his dying day, you were successful. But he didn't see any further. I can't see past my dying day either, but I saw further because your failure was within my lifetime."

So now Reb Levi Yitzhak says that every soul comes into the world with a kind of imprint from a particular branch of the Tree of Life. Some people come from the branch of grace (*Chesed*), and some people come from the branch of rigor (*Gevurah*). And sometimes when two souls like this meet, they feel as if they are banging their heads against a wall. If somebody comes from the side of rigor, and you are from the side of grace, it is difficult to get through to the other person; you want to say, "Why don't see it the way I do?" There seems to be such a basic *Weltanschauung*, a point of view inside, that says, "I can only see it this way." Thus we have individuals like Hillel and Shammai.[8] Hillel sees everything in the way of grace, in a gentle way, and Shammai sees things from the side of rigor. Both are necessary, and each, "according to his rung is a vehicle for the word of the living God." However, the sages, realizing the need for grace in this world, tipped the scales of the *halakha* in the direction of Hillel, to serve the needs of the world. Let me explain that a little.

Imagine that you are at the helm of the spaceship *Universe,* and you are asked to calibrate the karmic response of the *Universe.* You might think, if one could get a quick karmic response—for example, you do something wrong and you immediately get hit with the equivalent consequence—the *Universe* would run more smoothly. Maybe evil deeds will get the punishment they really deserve. But what would our life, our history, look like if that was the way of things? You would never be able to create anything. The backlash would be too harsh every time you made a mistake. So in the end, you decide to calibrate for a more forgiving *Universe.*

Think about this: if every time you drank a glass of chlorinated water from the faucet, your body responded the way it should respond to chlorinated water, without forgiveness, you would be in big trouble. In this sense, we have a very forgiving body, a very forgiving planet, and even a very forgiving society. If they were not forgiving, what would happen to karma? Say, if every time a mistake was made, the truly equivalent response was given, who could survive that response? Imagine if you never got a second chance. We might get slapped down so hard that we couldn't get up. It almost reinforces the wrong because we feel so down that we don't see the point in trying to get up. It leaves little room for hope and learning. If evil was always so strongly reinforced, time after time, by now we would be drowning in it. So there is a kind of forgiving element built into the universe. It isn't altogether forgiving, but it is a little bit forgiving. It gives us time; it gives us a chance to work things out. This is what is called *middat ha'rachamim,* the attribute of mercy.

It is said that when God created the world, in the beginning, He created the world in the attribute of justice, *ra'ah shayn ha'olam mitkayayem,* but seeing that the world would not be able to exist that way, *shittef bo middat ha'rachamim,* He added the attribute of mercy. So there is just a little bit more good in the universe than there is evil. This creates a kind of karma buffer. Every year on Yom Kippur, we see that there is a chance of more karma resolving. It is something like a compost heap for karma. There is a lot of garbage that gets piled there, but if it gets put in this place, there is a chance to somehow do the composting. That is built into the universe.

Right now, the world needs more Hillel than Shammai, because we haven't yet reached the kind of perfection that Shammai demands. God willing, we will reach that perfection and then be able to go with Shammai. But now it is the living grace and mercy of Hillel that is necessary. And it is only one who is alive in this present world who knows well the needs of the times and the attributes we need to live by. Those who are not alive on this plane do not know the attributes we need to live by in this world.

Very often people will refer you to the authority of this or that holy text, saying, "You guys have got it all wrong; that is not the way to do it." But you must ask from what time this text comes, from what paradigm? Yes, it may have been true in that time. But is it true in our time? The answer may be no. This is the hardest thing for religious traditions to have to deal with. For there are some people who come from the side of Shammai, of rigor, who say that the tradition is unbending; it never changes. They see it as hard and brittle. And then there are some people who see it as more adjusting or easy. "Since Elijah is existing and alive, never having tasted the taste of death, and has remained all the time in contact with this plane, he is suited, like no one else, to resolve our doubts." It is as if to say, he is the "livingness" and flexibility of the tradition. He knows our needs.

Joy Is the Mother of the Worlds

"A joyful mother of children" [Psalm 113:9]—read as
"Joy is the mother of children." God derives great joy from
the Tzaddikim, *and the anticipation of the joy, moved God to*
create the worlds, as it is in the writ, "The Lord rejoices in
His acts." Thus joy is the mother of the worlds.

Levi Yitzhak of Berditchev, *K'dushat Levi*, 102b, Muncazs

Aim habanim semaichah haleluyah, "Hallelujah, that the mother of children is happy." He is saying, "Happiness is the mother of children." Can you imagine, if you did not anticipate happiness, you wouldn't want to have the children? He is saying, "God derives great joy from the *Tzaddikim,* and the anticipation of the joy, moved God to create the worlds as it is written, 'The Lord rejoices in His act.' Thus joy is the mother of the worlds." It is a wonderful notion. Once, a Rolfer[9] told me, "Love, on the simplest physical plane, is gravity—two bodies in space attract one another." We speak of love most of the time in terms of feeling, but if you take the existential aspect of two bodies in space attracting one another, and if you see the exuberance of what life is, you get a sense of how joy is the source of creation. Reb Levi Yitzhak voices that, and Reb Nachman of Bratzlav also. He especially says, *Mitzvah g'dolah lih'yot b'simchah,* "It is a great *mitzvah,* a wonderful thing, to be enjoyed."

The Breath of Life

Believing that with every breath you receive new life can bring
you to hear what you heard at Mount Sinai. This is the meaning
of "You shall hear the sound-voice of YHVH, your God."
Without this [conscious breathing], you will only hear the words
of the Torah. However, if you will thus, at all times, merit
to focus on your being at Sinai, you will merit also to hear
the sound-voice of YHVH, your God.

Levi Yitzhak of Berditchev, *K'dushat Levi*, Muncazs

What a difference it would make if instead of reading scripture as dead scripture, we could actually hear that this is the central source of the universe saying, "Don't do that" or "Do that." If you really felt it enlightening you, or teaching you something, what a difference that would make. And how do you get there? By conscious breathing. People often ask if there such a thing as *pranayama*[10] in Judaism. And I say, there are very few sources, but they peek through from time to time. And this is one of them, peeking through.

Now, what is happening at Sinai is that you hear the "voice" like you never heard it before. What is it about religious truths that turn us off? It is as if we are saying, "Same old Cosmic Truths. So what else is new?" But what if you could hear it with "beginner's mind,"[11] like you are hearing it for the first time? *Chadesh yamenu k'kedem*, "Renew our days as when we first heard it." Think how invigorating and how involving it would become. How do you get to that place, to "beginner's mind," so that you can hear it that way? Reb Levi Yitzhak says, "Breathe right."

What Is God Preoccupied With?

> *What is God preoccupied with? The Original Thought in creating all the worlds was for the sake of the souls of Yisrael. And when the Creator focuses on the Original Thought, then He sustains only Yisrael and the worlds that do His will. But when, Heaven forbid, the Creator does not pay attention to the Original Thought, then even those who are not doing His will also are given sustenance.*

—Levi Yitzhak of Berditchev, *K'dushat Levi*, "Ki Tisa," Muncazs

Reb Levi Yitzhak is asking why is it that sometimes prayers don't get through. Does it mean that God isn't paying attention? You can imagine how difficult it must have been for people to maintain their faith in God during and after the Holocaust, considering the notions we Jews have had as to who God is and what God does. Reading the book of Deuteronomy, you get the feeling that if you do good and choose life, all good things are going to happen to you. And if you do wrong, all bad things are going to happen to you. And from Exodus, if Pharaoh didn't want to listen, he got the plagues. So you get a sense from the biblical accounts that everything is going be reckoned and that karma will be delivered swiftly and unerringly. But if that is so, we have a problem: why do some good people suffer and some bad people have it good? In fact, the *Tanya* of Reb Shneur Zalman of Liadi opens with that question.

In the past, people said, *Hester Panim*, "the Divine face is hidden." Sometimes the world is in such a situation that you say, "How great Thou art. Everything is beautiful. Everything is Divine. Everything is clear." And there are other times when it isn't so nice. And so people said that God was hiding His face. But this is not an answer, for a big question remains: Why? The stock answer to this has been, "In order to give us the freedom of choice." Without the understanding that God will reward or punish people, we would not be able to gain merit; everything that we would do would be very mechanical.

Why were we not programmed, then, to live that way? That is another question that can be raised. Again, because of the freedom of choice. I tell you, there are times when I am willing to say, "Dear God, you can keep the freedom of choice if you will make things a little bit better, make things a little more harmonious." But in the long run, with regard to what it takes for us to evolve, to become who we can be, the "hiding" makes sense. If we would have gotten everything we wanted and lived this very harmonious life, we wouldn't have evolved. Evolving is always something that comes through adversity. And those of us who have experienced that know that this is the way it is.

HEAVEN IS HERE!

REB MOSHE LEIB OF SASSOV

(1745–4 SHEVAT 1807)

REB MOSHE LEIB was born in Brody to Rabbi Jacob, a bitter opponent of the Hasidic movement. Moshe Leib, much to his father's chagrin, was, from an early age, attracted to Hasidism. Eventually, he left home without his father's permission to study for thirteen years under Reb Shmelke of Nikolsburg. When Moshe Leib's father found out what his son had done, he flew into a rage and rushed out to cut a rod from a tree. He put this in his room, intending to beat his son with it when the young man returned. And whenever it happened that he saw a better rod to beat his son with, he cut that one and threw the other away. This went on for a long time. And once, while cleaning the house, a servant mistakenly took the rod and put it in the attic. When this happened, Reb Moshe Leib asked the permission of his teacher to go home for a short visit. And when he entered the house, his father jumped up at once and began to search frantically through the house for the rod. While his father rushed about, Reb Moshe Leib calmly ascended the stairs to the attic, retrieved the rod, and laid it down at the feet of his father. The old man gazed into his son's earnest face and was overcome with love.

Reb Moshe Leib sought always to emulate Reb Shmelke's love of Israel, love of Jews. And when their studies were finished, the blessing of Reb Shmelke to Reb Moshe Leib was "May the love of Israel enter your heart." And it did. For Reb Moshe Leib of Sassov would come to embody that notion in its most profound sense. It was no empty epithet when it was said of him that he was the "father of widows and orphans." He would personally go to the homes of the bereaved and offer what comfort he could. There is even a story of his going disguised to chop wood for a needy young mother. He would spare no effort in helping the needy and raising funds for the redemption of captives, those unfortunate tenant farmers who had fallen behind in their rent payments and had been thrown into prisons by the Polish landowners. To redeem these captives, he would travel from town to town raising the funds and giving everything that he had. All the money he received, he distributed to the poor, asking no questions. When he was reproached for giving money to someone of ill repute, he replied, "Shall I be more picky than God, who gave it to me?"

It is said that Reb Moshe Leib Sassover was physically a giant of a man. But in spite of his size, he was known to be the most graceful of dancers. When his friend Reb Levi Yitzhak fell ill, Reb Moshe Leib laced up special shoes made of Moroccan leather and danced a holy dance, every spin and gesture of which was imbued with holy meaning. And through this "prayer," the Rabbi of Berditchev was healed.

When he died and had no more *mitzvot* to fulfill, he decided to do what he had done in life. He burst straight into hell and refused to leave until all its prisoners were released from their captivity. Some say that he had his way.

———————o———————

Arousing Love and Awe

> 8. *If the feeling of Love and Awe has become obliterated in you,*
> *you can arouse them through things of this world, until the*
> *desire will have caught on, and then you will bring it*
> *in to the service of the Holy.*
>
> Moshe Leib of Sassov, *Guide to Spiritual Process*

There is a basic notion that every soul has two "wings." These "wings of the soul" are Love and Awe. When the soul is free, fresh and open, and available for inspiration, it flies on these two wings. With one wing it is hard to fly; you must have two.

Rudolph Otto, in *The Idea of the Holy*,[1] talks about an experience he had in a synagogue in Algiers, I believe, on Yom Kippur. A German philosopher of religion, he was so struck by a sense of holiness in this place that he was unable to find any accurate way of expressing it. So he spent some years afterward trying to explore what gives us the feeling of holiness. He pointed out that there are two aspects to this. One is the *mysterium fascinans*, and the other is the *mysterium tremendum*. *Mysterium fascinans* is as if God is inviting us to check Her out. It is perhaps similar, if you are heterosexual, to what we experience in our teens about the people of the opposite sex, for instance. "Ah, so what is that all about? I want to see it more clearly. I want to be able to experience that." And that response, that fascination, is what you might call the wing of Love. It is the fascination that a moth has for a flame. "I'm willing to fly into that fire even if it burns me, even if it is going to extinguish me. I need to go into that place."

Then there is the *mysterium tremendum*. It is almost the flip side. You stay with the fascination for a long time, and you get closer and closer and closer, and all of a sudden you have the feeling, "If I take one more step, it is going to be fatal. God is going to dissolve me; I am going to fall into the abyss." It is terrifying, in a sense. One more step and I'm a goner. That Awe is the *mysterium tremendum*. And whatever is holy has these two wings.

In the story of Moses and the burning bush, the same holds true. The burning bush says, "Come on, come hither, come see what's going on." And Moses says, "Let me turn and see this. Let me go and check it out." He gets closer and closer, and suddenly, *"Take those shoes off! This is holy ground!"* So you see how these two elements work themselves out.

Now if I were to be in an "attuned" condition, I would have no trouble getting to Love and to Awe in relation to God. When the "doors of perception" are open, to go with William Blake,[2] I don't have any problem. Or if I am in the "beginner's mind," everything is fresh. But what happens when it is not that way? It is similar to when people complain of writer's block—maybe what I have is prayer's block. I don't know, perhaps you are a holy person and have never experienced that, but I want to tell you, I've experienced prayer's blocks, and *es geht nisht*. You might try and exert yourself, but still nothing happens. What do you do?

Moshe Leib of Sassov says, "Look, there are some things that scare you in the world, right? Go deeper than that fear, and you will discover that underneath that fear is that great Awe." Likewise, if you have something that attracts you, you can divest it of all those things that are temporary. What is it that attracts you? Is it the look, the taste? Looks change; tastes change; how much honey can you eat before you get tired of it? What is changeable isn't "it." So what is it that keeps on attracting me beyond anything that has "thingness" to it? If I get past that, I can get back to that Love. So instead of saying, "Don't bother with your fears," or "Don't bother with your loves," Reb Moshe Leib says, "Embrace them, get inside of them." It is the same advice that people like Ondrea and Stephen Levine[3] are giving. If you get phobic about your pain, it is going to hurt a great deal more. Go inside of it, and you'll discover something else, and you'll get past it. That is what Reb Moshe Leib Sassover is advising.

On Silent Prayer

You want to know about silent prayer? Here is how it is.
In all the requests and petitions in prayer, when a person feels
delight and joy that God has chosen him to serve Him and feels
that this God is so awesome, so infinite, so immense, may He
and His Name be blessed, such a joy arises that his heart cannot
contain it. He then feels forced to open up his throat and mouth
from whence a song wants to burst out from him. Then, if he has
any concern to bring to God, that God should have mercy
upon him, he need not even say it anymore, for he can do this
from simple humility in the midst of his heart.

There was once a conversation going on in *halakha* that dealt with the issue of required prayer. Since almost all of what we have in the prayer book, except for the scriptural passages, came from the Rabbis, it was held that the words that the Rabbis chose were the right words and the only right words. Therefore, they called it "the coin minted by the wise," and anything else was considered a "slug," improper for use. However, according to Maimonides (who sets out so much of our *halakha* for us), this is not how prayer started. Prayer started because it is written in the Bible that "if you have a need, you offer it to God." So that is a scriptural commandment, whereas all the other commandments as to what you are to say and how you are to say it come from the Rabbis. And in relation to the power and the value of prayer, or any commandment, a scriptural commandment takes precedence.

Reb Shalom Dov Baer of Lubavitch in his *Kuntres HaT'fillah* (Tract on Prayer) concerned himself with the question of how to raise prayer to the higher level. Many of us pray everyday by rote and follow the prescription of the Rabbis, so much so that there is even a controversy wondering if you actually fulfill your obligation of prayer without *kavanah*, without intention. And it remains so because we want to save prayer for those people who cannot bring themselves to the great intention by saying, "Even if you haven't fully intended, it is a good prayer." Of course, the reason is that you want to keep people involved in the act of prayer. Professor Abraham Joshua Heschel once told this wonderful tale, which is a *mashal*, an analogue:

A small town was without a watchmaker, so every once in a while, a watchmaker would come to town and fix the watches that were there. Whenever he came, people brought him all the watches they had. Some brought watches that weren't functioning well, but the owners wound them every day and let them work. These watches were very easy to repair. However, the watches of people who didn't wind them, those watches were very difficult to repair.

From this Professor Heschel drew the conclusion that if you say something by rote, it turns out really well, because the more easily you can actually get into it, the easier it is to repair.

So this deals with the issue of rote recitation, but as everyone who has improvised with music knows, if you have a certain riff that you know, you can improvise around that. So instead of feeling impotent and mute when a moment of difficulty comes in prayer, you have language symbols that you can use as a kind of grease for the wheels. For instance, "Let God answer you on the day of your troubles" (Psalm 20). And from that psalm impression, which has already run its track in your mind, you are able to say, "Oy! Rebboina Shel Olam, today I find myself in the day of tzores!" Thus a person has a repertoire that serves as an entry into the depths of prayer.

All of this has to do with verbal prayer, and there is a sense in which you have to say things, sometimes. Often when I davven quietly, if find myself moving more into mental prayer and not so much into feeling, because mental prayer doesn't often bring on feeling. "My soul goes out when I speak." Imagine, I might think to my wife, "I love you." It is not necessarily the same as what happens when I say it aloud, where heart gets involved and I begin to breathe into it. So speech is important.

There is, however, a situation where you might have something to say, and you can't say it out loud for a variety of reasons. Nevertheless, in the whisper with the eyes closed, a fervor takes you, and something important begins to happen, as with the prayer of Channah, the mother of Samuel. And someone like Eli the Priest, who was only used to people speaking their prayers aloud, upon seeing someone standing and praying silently with such fervor and expression, understandably thought that she was drunk. And I like the idea of that being perceived as drunkenness, because what would make him think that she was drunk if she were merely whispering gently? But the fervor, expression, gesturing, all that accompanied her prayer, made it seem as drunkenness to him.

So that sense of intoxication is exactly what made people who saw Hasidim pray in the beginning think that they were drunk. I need not go further than Rumi and Shams among the Sufis to talk about how wonderful that sense of intoxication with God is. Because during the kind of altered consciousness that intoxication brings about, there is a feeling that nothing else exists. Like in that love song, "I only have eyes for you," nothing else seems to exist at that time except the Beloved and what one has to say. So there is an element in that prayer that is not totally silent. And about this the Rabbis have said, "You have fulfilled your prayer, because the 'twisting' of your lips is also called a doing." In other words, it isn't just in the heart; it comes out in some other form of expression at the same time.

Reb Shalom Dov Baer of Lubavitch says, "You know, when you're standing there and are saying the words that the Rabbis have asked you to say, you put yourself into the situation. You get into *ada'ata d'naf-shey,* into situational feeling about the prayer, and then you are in the position that makes it a biblical prayer. You have raised up the rote situation into a real 'begging' for yourself." And in an essay that I wrote for rabbis on prayer, I spelled out that the Latin *precare,* "begging," is an important aspect of prayer, and in Hebrew we call it *bakashot,* "the begging."

Reb Moshe Leib Sassover asks, "You want to know about silent prayer?" This is kind of strange, because he was an ecstatic like Reb Levi Yitzhak of Berditchev. So why would he, all of a sudden, embrace silent prayer if all the time he was going on in great fervor? Here was a person who lived love in such expressive ways; if he was on his way to *shul* and heard a baby cry, he would show up late in *shul* because he went off to hold the baby.

On a mission to avert a terrible decree, Reb Moshe Leib and his master, Reb Shmelke of Nikolsburg, are crossing the Danube in a boat. Suddenly, it looks as if the boat would founder and they were both going to drown. And in the midst of this terrible situation, Reb Moshe Leib gets up and begins to dance. Reb Shmelke says, "What are you dancing for?" And Reb Moshe Leib says, "Soon I shall be Home with my Father!"

So you can see what kind of an ecstatic person he was. And all of sudden, here he is talking about silent prayer! What's going on? Well, the answer harks back to something called *bittul ha'yesh,* "the annihilation of self," the translation of which feels wrong to me. It's not that it is a poor translation of the Hebrew, but the words are a bad translation of the experience. It is more appropriately understood as "becoming transparent." When I become transparent and have a prayer, there is no "distance" between me and what I am praying for. I can imagine one of my children coming to me and pointing to a "boo-boo" and not saying anything, and it's not necessary to say anything because it is absolutely clear what is going on. And when you go to what Larry Dossey teaches about the empirical evidence of the power of prayer,[4] it is really clear that the less you give specific orders to God, the more likely it is that the prayer will work. Then it is not limited, nonlocalized, not locked into a particular time, and yet it has its power.

Now, following along with what Reb Moshe Leib is saying, "Such a joy arises that his heart cannot contain it," I want to say that sometimes it isn't joy that arises but pain that arises in the heart and cannot be contained. "Look and seek, O God, is there such a pain like my pain?" It is like showing it to God. Every editor says, "Don't tell them; show them. Don't describe; make it visible." So in the prayer, if I can hold out my joy, my guilt, my pain, my need for healing, whatever it is, without a word, and just stay in it, there is a fusion at that point where ego has become transparent and indistinguishable from what I am praying for.

When King David says, "And I am my prayer," we know what kind of prayer is taking place. "And I meet you, God, at a time of goodwill toward us." "O God, in Your great kindness, answer me in the Truth of Your salvation." Standing at that point and holding that up, I become the prayer, and it is at that moment that I break through to a time that is an acceptable time because I have transcended the locked-in moment. Then, in the psalm, you would expect that David would address God in the aspect of Mercy (YHVH), but instead he addresses the attribute of Judgment, which is strange. But because he does this, we can ask, "Why is the Judge Judging?" The answer: Because there is a Grace that needs to be maintained for the world, and if the Judge wouldn't Judge anymore, then the Grace would also disappear." So addressing the Judge, David is saying, "Behind Your Judgment there is that abundance of Grace, so I can expect that You will answer, not because I deserve it, but of the Truth of your salvation, because You are committed to salvation." Notice how much there is in our tradition that allows for that.

Now imagine that you were to be overheard engaging in "pillow talk" with your partner, and your words became public. You would be embarrassed, because that moment does not belong to anyone else. That is the kind of language you use only in great intimacy. It's almost like baby talk; it is a regression. Most people who don't have intimacy with God get into very formal language, the "vouchsafe" and "bestow" language, because they have heard their ministers and rabbis use it. But anybody who has had some intimacy with God, even to the point of being able to talk about one's sex life with God, there is some kind of inner . . . *disposition* is the right word for that, that allows me to talk about anything. And in fact, I can even transcend talking and just hold up my yearning and desire. So the likelihood is that I would have names for God that I wouldn't want anyone to hear, that I would have a language for God that I wouldn't want anyone to hear.

How do I demonstrate that there is a language without words? Well, we can do that with the *shofar.* With the blowing of that horn, there is the real sense of a cry. The Rabbis say that the *shevarim* and *teruah* sounds of the *shofar* are "whimpering" sounds. Psychologists used to talk about the "primal scream." They would say that unless you get to the place that evokes the "primal scream," you haven't gotten to the true source of the broken heart. In other words, ego will not let us reach our "primal scream," and so the *shofar* tries to get us to that place. Sometimes when Rosh HaShanah falls on *Shabbos,* and I don't want to blow the *shofar,* I ask people to scream, which gets beyond words, and in that scream we can share with people across generations, cultures, and languages.

There are some people who say, "When you see that nothing else helps, recite the Psalms." "He who wants to tell of the greatness of God, let him say God's total praise." Reb Pinchas of Koretz reads this as a Kabbalist and says, "If you find yourself facing *gevurah,* heavy decrees are on you, and you want to disperse them, say the entire *T'hillim,* all the Psalms." The 150 psalms are considered the strongest remedy of all. I remember the story of the woman living in Jerusalem as the German tanks of Rommel were approaching, who shouted, "Don't rely on miracles! Recite Psalms!" The sense was that this works. But Reb Pinchas of Koretz also said that "there are times when you can't even say that. At that point, just sit in the silence and hold whatever it is up to God silently, and this is an even better prayer."

DANCING FROM THE INFIRMARY

THE MAGGID OF KOZNITZ

(1733–14 TISHRI 1815)

REB ISRAEL, the Maggid of Koznitz, was born in Apt to Perl and Shabbatai, the bookbinder.[1] They were poor people and childless until very late in their lives when they received a blessing from the Ba'al Shem Tov. Their joy on one particular Shabbat filled him with such happiness that he foretold that they would have a son in their old age and that he should be named Israel, after himself. Though Perl and Shabbatai were desperately poor, they still saw to it that Israel received the finest education. His earliest Talmudic training was given by the Rabbi of Apt, and before long, his unusual diligence and precocity were recognized. Later he would go on to study in Ostrowiec and Horschov.

When his father died in 1761, he settled in Pzhysha, where he came under the influence of Rabbi Abraham of Pzhysha, a disciple of the Ba'al Shem Tov. Rabbi Abraham not only taught him Talmud but also Kabbalah and the art of *maggidut,* preaching, for which he would become famed. His brilliance in Talmud was such that even the great Mitnagged ("opponent" of Hasidism) and *yeshiva* founder, Chayyim of Volozhin, testified to his phenomenal mastery of Talmud and codes.

Eventually, he made his way to Mezritch. In preparation for his meeting with the Great Maggid, he tells us that he studied over eight hundred books of Kabbalah, but when he actually found himself in the presence of the Maggid, he knew, "I had not yet begun to study." However, Reb Dov Baer, the Maggid of Mezritch, said, "Blessed be the Holy Name! The

Note: This chapter was written by Zalman Schachter-Shalomi and Nataniel Miles-Yepez.

Almighty has sent a young man who can edit the manuscript of Rabbi Isaac Luria's prayer book. Now that you have arrived here, *Keter Yitnu* will be recited in Warsaw as well." That was to say, Hasidism would spread throughout Poland under his guidance, and many Jews would adopt the Lurianic liturgy and become Hasidim.

But when the Maggid of Mezritch died, Reb Israel took his devotion to Reb Elimelech of Lizhensk. His relationship to Reb Elimelech was different from the one that he had with the Maggid. With regard to Reb Elimelech, he would make a strikingly different comment than he had made about the Reb Dov Baer: "My knowledge of Kabbalah may be superior to that of my teacher, Elimelech, but I am not able to serve God in the way that he does, in the spirit of self-sacrifice, Love, and Awe." It is well known that before Reb Elimelech of Lizhensk died, he bestowed his four gifts on his four great disciples: to the Seer of Lublin he granted his "sight," to Reb Mendel of Rymanov he gave his "mind," his golden "speech" he bestowed on Reb Abraham Joshua Heschel of Apt, and his "heart" he gave to Reb Israel, the Maggid of Koznitz. And ever after, Reb Israel was known as a great master of *davvenen,* prayer.

After settling in Koznitz, the Maggid quickly acquired a reputation for being a great miracle worker, even as his namesake, the Ba'al Shem Tov, had been known. To supplement his meager income, he also took to preaching in the surrounding villages. The sheer amount of his activity was amazing, especially considering his extreme frailty. So weak was he that he could hardly rise from his bed and had to be covered with furs continually to be kept warm. And even when he came to prosper, never did he forget the grinding poverty of his parents. Thus he sought ever to rescue others from such poverty. He was a father to many orphans, many of which were raised in his own house. When a fire ravaged the Jewish quarter in 1778, he financed the rebuilding of the whole street, which was known after as the "Maggid's Street."

Aside from these activities, he was also known as a peerless master. He served as a counselor and guide not only to his own Hasidim but even to Polish nobles Adam Czartorsky, Joseph Poniatowski, and Prince Radziwill, not to mention great masters like Reb Simcha Bunem, the Holy Jew, and others. Even his friends, the Seer of Lublin and Abraham Joshua Heschel of Apt, visited the Maggid when their hearts were in need of renewal. Reb Israel died on the Feast of Tabernacles in 1815. When his soul departed, a great light of Polish Hasidism was extinguished.

○

Amalek and the Strength of God

The yetzer ha'ra *says to man, "Why do you exhaust yourself*
for nothing? You have committed so many sins they are
innumerable—it is impossible for you to repent for them all." . . .
The yetzer ha'ra, *the evil enticer, seducer, urge, drive, presses*
on and on this way, cooling one's connection to God,
and leading one away from His teachings.
Finally, one is thus led like an ox to the slaughter.
Therefore, God tells us, "Remember what Amalek did to you . . .
how he cooled you off on the way."

Israel of Koznitz, *Avodat Yisrael,* "Tetzaveh," 33b

Who is the "evil goad," the *yetzer ha'ra*? The Maggid of Koznitz says it is Amalek, the ancient nemesis of Israel. Amalek was that terrible force, the tribe that attacked the Jewish people on the way out of Egypt. Amalek came up from the rear, raiding and massacring the people at their weakest, before they had even gotten to Mount Sinai. Amalek exists on the inside, too, and attacks when you are at your weakest point, before you have reached your own "Sinai." And with what does it attack? Using *Gematria,*[2] the numerical value of the names of things, we see that Amalek has the same numerical value, 240, as the word *safek,* "question," "doubt." In other words, whenever you are about to commit yourself to something good and are getting "cold feet" on the good commitment, that is Amalek coming from behind, sowing doubts, and making it hard for you. Amalek also has the same numerical value as *mar,* "bitter," and *barzel,* "iron," 239 + 1 to point to the compelling power the *yetzer ha'ra* wields.

"The *yetzer ha'ra* says to man, 'Why are you exerting yourself for nothing?'" Notice that the *yetzer ha'ra* is asking a rhetorical question. It is not curious to know why you are exerting yourself in repentance, *it is telling you why*—"for nothing." Amalek is never a "question" in search of understanding. Its "question" is a cunningly designed tool for dismantling your good efforts. It says, "There is no point to the exertion. The depth of your sin for which you are repenting and your passion in it are so far greater than the depth of your lukewarm repentance."

Reb Levi Yitzhak of Berditchev, at the bedtime *Sh'ma,* would look back on his day and say that he was sorry for what he did not do right and that tomorrow he would do better. Then he chided himself, saying, "But Levi

Yitzhak, you said the same thing yesterday!" Then he would say,—"Yes, but today I mean it." The issue of this story, and the battle with himself, was the subject of a masterful sermon by the late Rabbi Milton Steinberg, who pointed out that after examining other options that are not really helpful, like that of lowering one's standards, taking a cynical—Amalekite—approach, seeking salvational help from a Savior, there remains only one way to deal with "our persistent failures," and that is the daily incremental movement of "Today I mean it."

Go back to times in your life when you have really struggled. Perhaps you have let someone down whom you really care about. Maybe it is God, or yourself, that you kept letting down. You can wrestle with those problems for years. You work with them and work with them and still they are dogging you. You repent and say, "This is the last time"—and it isn't. Again and again you make this affirmation, and again and again you slide back. Sometimes you have regret afterward, and sometimes you struggle just to have regret. You may even come to a point where you despair of the effort and are almost numb. You are "cooled off," becoming numb even to the sin. Then you feel hopeless, like "an ox being led to the slaughter." This is when even the sound of your own voice saying, "I'll change," or "I'm sorry," seems to mock you. Because, when you hear those words, which you have said so many times, on your lips yet again, you almost get a vision of all the "I'm sorries" piled to infinity. The size of that pile is ridiculous to the point of being overwhelming and frightening. Then, just on the heels of your completing this last "I'm sorry," a sibilant voice slips across your ears: "Liar! Your repentance is but a pile of empty promises, all broken. At least stop lying and be bold in the deed!"

This is the jumping-off point, as it were. Here is where the Maggid reminds us, "God tells us, 'Remember what Amalek did to you . . . how he cooled you off on the way.'" What is the lesson in this "remembering"?

If you learn how to be a scribe for writing a Torah, or for *mezuzot,* you learn how to write on parchment with a quill and a special ink. And you have to learn both how to write these letters and how to erase the letters. Now, the favorite word that they use for writing and erasing is the word *Amalek.* This is because of the remarkable statement that we have been hearing only in part: "Remember what Amalek has done to you on the way, when you went out of Egypt, how he met you and cooled you on the way when you were so tired. So it shall be when you enter into the land, you shall blot out the memory of Amalek, don't forget." Now, listen to that: ". . . Blot out the memory of Amalek, don't forget." Isn't that a *koan,* a paradox? "Make up your mind! Either erase the memory, or don't forget and keep it." The sense is that you will never have peace as long as Amalek is around. Amalek, *safek,* doubt, is insecurity of existence. Amalek is that something that can make our faith weaken as we are coming out. So we must erase the memory of Amalek, don't forget. That is to say, erase the chilling effect of the doubt, but don't forget that Amalek keeps lurking to pounce when you are unaware.

As I said before, Amalek is never a question in search of understanding. Hebrew has two words for question: *sh'elah* (a borrowing, seeking an answer) and *kashah,* an objection. Amalek raises objections to oppose the God it knows and wants to defy.

It is a destructive force, but it is redeemable. The way to redeem Amalek, the *yetzer ha'ra,* is to exchange its rhetorical question, *kashah,* for a true question, a *sh'elah,* one that seeks understanding. This elevation of the *yetzer ha'ra* is spoken of as "serving God with the *yetzer ha'ra.*" For even the *yetzer ha'ra* is the gift of God. Therefore, we do not shut it out or try to abolish it. Instead, the search for understanding is brought to the question, as it were, to redeem it. This, then, is how the memory of Amalek is blotted out without forgetting. Amalek's false question is exchanged for the true question. However, it is only the knowledge of what is exchanged that makes the exchange meaningful. So we must exchange and remember.

The Maggid of Koznitz was fond of quoting from Isaiah, and his favorite was Isaiah 40:31. The King James has it rendered very beautifully: "But they that wait upon the Lord shall renew their strength; they shall mount up with wings as eagles; they shall run, and not be weary; and they shall walk, and not faint." A slightly more literal translation might look like this: "But they who hope in *YHVH* shall change their strength. They will raise their organs as eagles. . . ." As we discussed earlier, the Divine Name is connected with the attribute of Mercy and thus it has the sense of "But they who hope in the God of Compassion shall change"—or "exchange," as the Maggid prefers it—"their strength." The reference to "mounting up" or "raising the organs," as the eagles do, has to do with a common belief at the time that when eagles molt, they are renewed, or reborn, to youth. They cast off the old body for a renewed body. However, it is interesting to note that the Latin from which the word *molt* is derived, *mutare,* actually means "to change." They "shall change their strength," changing one thing for another. A story will illustrate:

All of his life, Reb Israel, the Maggid of Koznitz, was very frail. His face was gaunt and his limbs so fragile, his circulation so poor, that he was wrapped always in furs for warmth and was carried from place to place atop a litter. But when the litter would reach the threshold of the house of prayer, he was transformed into another man. Once there, he would jump from the litter and move like a dancer, almost floating, through the room. And when he carried the *sefer Torah,* it seemed as if he leapt from person to person. And his *davvenen, Oy!* his *davvenen* was full of fervent ecstasy. But when the prayers were completed, the vitality invigorating him in prayer almost left his body entirely, and he was, all spent, once more placed on the litter to be taken home. Back atop the litter, his face was again wan, but it shone with the radiance of Divine love.

On another occasion, the Maggid was about to step into a carriage to attend a circumcision, and several people, seeing his fragile condition and knowing how he was usually taken to the *shul,* came forward to help him. Quickly, he pulled away and dismissed them. "Why should I need *your* strength? As it is written, 'But they who hope in the Lord will exchange their strength.' I shall exchange my strength for the strength of God, Who has more than enough for us all." And with that he got into the carriage with the vigor of a youth.

I personally met such a *Tzaddik;* he stayed in our home. I had fixed a nice room for him on the third floor, but he took lesser accommodations on the ground floor, as he had no strength to climb the stairs. But when I brought him to a public liturgy, he took charge of it, leading with a vigor that many of the younger congregants did not possess. He relied on invisible sources of support like Reb Meir'l Premishlaner, who said, "Whoever is attached to 'Above' will not falter and fall below."

That, in effect, is what we are doing when we serve God with the energy freed from the *yetzer ha'ra.* We are exchanging the tainted strength of the flesh for the pure strength of God; taking the doubt of Amalek back to its Source; gaining understanding, as it were. But why does he refuse to be helped? Is he saying that we don't need others on our spiritual path? No, he is simply making the point that though he seems to be weak in body, his true strength and sustenance is from the Lord. There are also tales where he gladly receives the help of others.

There was a time when the Maggid of Koznitz was very ill and nearing the point of death. He had exhausted his body almost to its limits. When his friend, the Holy Jew of Pzhysha, saw this in his mind, he immediately dispatched two disciples, who were talented musicians with beautiful voices, to Koznitz. The two disciples reached the town in time for Shabbat and greeted the Sabbath Queen with their music. When the holy sounds, moving through the house, finally reached the heart of the Maggid, his attendants immediately noticed that his face began to glow, his breathing grew deeper, and his fevered brow cooled. And when the music ended, his eyes opened as if he had just awakened, and he blessed the Holy Jew for sending him precisely the healing he needed.

The sense of this is that the Holy Jew of Pzhysha had attuned himself to the same Source as the Maggid and was therefore able to see the necessary remedy on the temporal plane. "But they that wait upon the Lord shall renew their strength; they shall mount up with wings as eagles; they shall run and not be weary, and they shall walk, and not faint." It doesn't say "he" or "she" or "one" who waits or is renewed; it says "they." What is the meaning of that plural? It means that we are not renewed as one, self-contained being. We are not renewed in separateness but in relation. Relation is filling the space between a subject and an object. It is the process bridging the two. Renewal is always a process of "togethering," of partnering with something else. For in truth, there is nothing in the physical world that is not of a dependent nature. The ego says we are separate and self-contained, and it is only by transcending this definition that we are able to tap the God-Source. Transcending, or becoming "transparent," as it were, to the ego allows us to be conscious of the Divine Organism. In this, one is no longer dependent on one's own strength but rather on the inexhaustible strength of God. When the ego withdraws into the primal organism, the "Waters of Love," the waters of renewal, are made available.

Think of the river, how it "runs and is not weary." So it is with us when we become transparent to the will of God, when we are attuned, so to speak, to the energy of God's creation, in harmony with the flow of God's Presence and Grace. This takes us to the issue of community. We are not alone, nor should we see ourselves as separate. "They" can also mean refuge in community, in partnering with others. Rising out of the deep morass of "coolness" is also achieved by community. The "river flow" of community, its effectiveness, is in the energy moving in the same direction. That energy will bear you up and on. What is the function of the community unit, or cell, in the organism as a whole? One liver cell has to connect and help another liver cell more than helping a stomach cell. Do you see what I saying? In this situation, where we are closer to one another, we have a more common destiny and a more common bond that we have to keep. Sometimes I have a feeling that if we took care of the local unit better, we would be able to be more compassionate to people far away from us.

Here is a Hasidic tale:

A man comes to the Maggid of Koznitz saying he wants to discuss a spiritual problem. The Maggid says, "Never mind the spiritual problem; what do you eat for breakfast?" And the man says, "Just a little bit of gruel." "And what do you have for lunch?" "A little thin soup." Now this man was a very rich person—Shlomo Carlebach, of blessed memory, would have called him "a millionaire." And he talks about how he hardly eats anything. So the Maggid of Koznitz says to him, "If you would like me to help you dealing with the matter of your soul and your spirit, I'll do this gladly. But first, you have a task to fulfill. Every day you must have a good goose for dinner, or a steak, and a really good wine." And he tells him that he should eat a luxurious breakfast and so on.

The disciples hear the Maggid talking to this man, and they can't believe their ears. A sinner is trying to atone for his sins, and the Maggid tells him to eat like that! So afterward they say to him, "Rebbe, what kind of a prescription is that?" And Maggid says, "If he eats a little bit of gruel in the morning, what do you think he gives to a poor person? If he eats well, he will give bread to the poor. But if he eats like the poor, he'll give them stones." The real healing, the true penance, for this person was to help others as the prophet Isaiah (58:6–8) declares: "This is the way I want to fast: break bread with the poor, the downtrodden beggar take into your home; when you notice one who has nothing to wear, give him clothes. . . ."

So this is taking care of the local unit in order to benefit the larger organism. But let's take it down even one more step, to the individual within the community unit. This story talks about living in community and how we must know who we are in that community if we are to be a support. We are not to be unkind to ourselves, or else how are we going to be kind to others? If we are not generous with ourselves, how will we have compassion for another? So this self-generosity is another way of exchanging our strength: if we do not treat ourselves kindly, seeking understanding of the rhetorical question, then how can we expect our spiritual needs to be fulfilled? That is what this tale is really talking about. On another occasion, a man came to the Maggid of Koznitz wearing sackcloth. And the Maggid said to him, "You think you have blotted out the *yetzer ha'ra* when in reality, it has just tricked you into that sack." Beating oneself up was not the way of the Maggid.

We must be acquainted with the ways of love if we are to give it. For the Maggid, this started at home. And it must start in the small things. I have a remarkable friend, Sam Keen, who wrote the book *The Passionate Life*,[3] which contains a chapter on "The Art of Loving" in which he says that when it comes to love, most people haven't learned *how* to love. First, learn to love a stone. When you have learned how to love that, love a plant. When you have learned how to love a plant, you can graduate to loving a pet. When you have learned to love a pet, maybe you can learn to love a human being. And he says, most of us are thrown into having to love a person, without any training in love. Learning how to love is a gradual thing. If you can learn how to relate to siblings or to the people you are with, you will see it will start to spread to others outside your little group. If you have it good, you will want other people to have it good too. That is how the Maggid presented it.

The Maggid was like that. He wasn't tough on sinners. He often taught that we shouldn't get depressed about our past sins, reminding us that Abraham regretted his past, his childhood, and the Lord said to him, "Dew is your childhood." You should consider it as pure dew. And this applies to the *yetzer ha'ra* too. For God made the *yetzer ha'ra* and the obscurations of the Light so that we might recognize the advantage of Light. So he says, "Don't take your humility so far that you consider yourself an evil person." In this way, he clears away that pure negativity about Amalek and shows us how loving, too, can get rid of Amalek.

A GUIDE FOR
THE EXCEPTIONAL
AVERAGE

SEVEN GENERATIONS
OF CHABAD REBBES

THERE HAVE BEEN SEVEN generations of Chabad Rebbes, each of whom had a lasting impact on the character of Chabad Hasidism. So we are going to walk through their lives sequentially while also touching on their specific contributions to Hasidic thinking.[1]

Reb Shneur Zalman of Liadi
(18 Elul 1745–24 Tevet 1813)

Reb Shneur Zalman was born in Liozna in Belorussia to Rivkah and Barukh, a descendant of the Rabbi Yehudah Loew, the Chief Rabbi of Prague. From an early age, Reb Schneur Zalman became famous for his remarkable intellect, having mastered the whole of the Talmud by the time he was twelve years old. By his midteens he had memorized most of the important texts of Judaism. At fifteen he moved to Vitebsk and married Sterna Segal, the daughter of a local businessman. After five years in Vitebsk, he came to a crossroads—to go on to Vilna and learn from the Ga'on[2] (the logical next step) or to go on to Mezritch and learn the way of prayer. He decided to go to Mezritch.

Reb Dov Baer, the Maggid of Mezritch, was the Ba'al Shem Tov's appointed successor. The Rebbe Reb Baer,[3] as he was called in Poland, was a genius in the creative process, and his greatest contribution was on the operation of the preconscious creativity of mind. Drawn to him, almost magnetically, were the most brilliant Torah scholars in the whole area. But they did not come to him for his skills in conceptual understanding, in the manipulation of concepts, but because in him the Torah was alive. When Reb Shneur Zalman had to make up his mind as to where he would do his advanced study, he decided on Mezritch because, he said, "in Vilna [the seat of Talmudic learning] one learns how to learn Torah; in Mezritch [he had heard] one learns from the Torah." Or as he said on another occasion, "Vilna represented study; Mezritch was prayer and the application of study."

The empirical secret of "know-how" was made available in Mezritch to Reb Shneur Zalman. And it was not accomplished by the denial of one's humanity. The teaching that won the young man from Liozna over to loyalty to the Maggid was what made the words "I have made earth, and man did I create upon it" experientially available to his students. In this it was pointed out that God seeks to reside with man in the observance of the 613 commandments, as the word *barathi*, "I have created," indicates by its numerical value, 613. The Maggid taught that "God has no need for the world for Himself, but knowing the desire of the righteous to lead the world to Him, He created the world for their sake." Never before did the generosity of the Divine Purpose in creation stand out in such bold relief.

The Maggid of Mezritch appointed his son, Reb Abraham, known as "the Angel," to initiate Reb Shneur Zalman into the way of Hasidism. He was truly a transcendental intellect, as evidenced by his opus *Chesed L'Avraham*. The Maggid, as it were, adopted Reb Shneur Zalman as his spiritual son so that the two "brothers" could share with one another the vastness of their knowledge and subtlety of their insight, the transcendental of wisdom wedded to practical understanding and knowledge. Reb Shneur Zalman's common sense often saved Reb Abraham's life and invested their relationship with humor and love. It was the perfect apprenticeship. However, when the prodigy returned to Vitebsk a Hasid, he was driven away by the Mitnaggedim. Eventually, though, he found a post as Maggid in his hometown of Liozna.

At that time, the *Shulhan Arukh,* the Code of Jewish Law, was in need of an updating. And though all the Maggid's disciples were giants in the Torah, Reb Shneur Zalman, at twenty-five the youngest of them all, was appointed by the Maggid to undertake this task. When it was completed, the new *Shulḥan Arukh* won great praise and demonstrated that the new movement was in no way undermining the observance of *mitzvot*. Reb Schneur Zalman was also instructed by the Maggid to turn his attention to Lithuania, the bastion of rationalism, the "brain basket" of Russian and Polish Jewry, which needed missionaries of the heart with superb mental equipment. He was the Hasid selected to speak to this community. He represented a blend of Lithuanian scholarship and Hasidic joy. However, the threat of the experiential to the conceptual, in a manner in which even a simple tradesman and artisan among the masses managed to live a life unified with God, immersed in His will and bathed in His Light always, could not help but create resistance among the Lithuanian scholarly elite, which as time passed became more and more aggressive in its opposition.

This opposition found its focal point in the great Torah genius, the Ga'on of Vilna, who was in many ways the unofficial head of European Jewry. However, during his lifetime, the "defense" against Hasidism did not involve violence or the foul play of informing against Hasidim to the government. So in 1775 Reb Shneur Zalman and his older colleague, Reb Menachem Mendel of Vitebsk, traveled to Vilna to see the Ga'on and to converse with him, being confident that their way represented not an innovation but a renewal of the flow from the inner wellsprings of Judaism and a return to its center—God. But the meeting was not to be. The Vilna Ga'on was persuaded by his mother not to meet with them. So great were the possibilities of this meeting that it was said by many afterward that had they met, a way to speed arrival of the Messiah would have been paved.

In 1772 the Maggid passed on. In all, Reb Shneur Zalman spent three years with his master, following him from Mezritch to Onipol. In 1777 Reb Menachem Mendel of Vitebsk, his mentor and fellow student of the Maggid, departed for the Holy Land, leaving Reb Shneur Zalman as the head of the Hasidic communities of Belorussia. Here he came into his own, refining and expanding his doctrines. In the field of experiential Jewish Living, in the empirical psychological know-how, his contributions are of great importance. Prior to the time of Reb Shneur Zalman, one could, with tremendous effort, achieve the rung of a *Tzaddik*. It had to be abrupt, but if one had the endowment, one could make it. If one did not have the endowment, it was not possible, except by way of mimicry, which suggests hypocrisy to those who have not yet achieved so high a rung.

So Reb Shneur Zalman asked, "Is man doomed to spend his entire lifetime as a poor sinner? A persistent failure?" His answer was a definite no. Thus he taught the way of the *Beynoni*, the man neither a complete *Tzaddik* nor, by the exercise of the power of his will and the control of his behavior, a wicked one. He allowed for an ethos that was conscious and deliberate, that would be graced with periodic liberation from the confines of the everyday self, having the skills and the insights of psychology. Reb Shneur Zalman equips the *Beynoni* to live a transcendental life.

In the world of thought, Reb Shneur Zalman is often identified with the opening word of his magnificent opus, the *Tanya,* or *The Book of the Beynoni.* It was in the *Tanya* that the way of Chabad—the utilization of the faculties of wisdom, understanding, and knowledge as they reside in the inner core of the soul—became the hallmark of Lubavitch Hasidism.[4] His was a rational and transrational method for the service of God. The fact that we concentrate here on his concept of the *Beynoni* doesn't diminish his other tremendous achievements in the fields of theology, philosophy, psychology, ethics, and Jewish canon law, which cover so much ground that justice could not be done to them in this limited context.

In 1798 Reb Shneur Zalman was arrested by the Russian government for sending money to the Holy Land, which was then part of the Turkish Empire. Thus this act was seen as aiding the Turks, enemies of the tsar. Reb Shneur Zalman submitted an appeal and was released on 19 Kislev. In 1800 he was again arrested and imprisoned for four months and ten days, being released in March 1801, when Alexander became tsar of Russia. Reb Shneur Zalman then took up residence in Liadi, on the estate of Prince Lubomirski, where he spent most of the next twelve years. When Napoleon's army approached Russia, Reb Shneur Zalman, not wanting to reside under the conqueror's dominion for even one day, took flight for inner Russia. Though it was commonly believed that Napoleon would emancipate the Jews, it was also believed that this type of emancipation would be destructive to traditional Judaism. Reb Shneur Zalman passed on during this period of exile in Piena, and the leadership of the Chabad movement came into the hands of his son, Reb Dov Baer.[5]

Reb Dov Baer of Lubavitch
(9 Kislev 1774–9 Kislev 1828)

Reb Dov Baer, his father's eldest son, was born shortly after the Maggid's death and was so named to honor the memory of Reb Shneur Zalman's great teacher. He had inherited the prodigious intellect of his father and seems to have been blessed with the transcendental qualities of Reb Abraham, "the Angel." For he was known to pray with burning intensity in utter stillness. When he was only fifteen, his father appointed him to guide the studies of the young married men of the court. In 1788 he married Sheine, the daughter of a pious teacher. When Reb Shneur Zalman died in the interior of Russia, Reb Dov Baer was there and remained until Passover. When he returned to Liadi, he found the city in ruins. So he decided to move the seat of Chabad Hasidism to Lubavitch, the "City of Brotherly Love." From that moment on, Lubavitch and Chabad were indissolubly linked. It would remain the Jerusalem of Chabad Hasidism until 1916.

If the Ba'al Shem Tov made available pure joy and will, the Maggid of Mezritch made accessible the creative processes of the preconscious, and Reb Shneur Zalman made applicable the treasures of wisdom, then the contribution of Reb Dov Baer of Lubavitch is that of broadening it all into conceptual understanding and contemplative know-how. His range of empathy with the minds of his Hasidim was profound. From a treatise in Yiddish on the ways of penitence to the most elusive and abstract mysteries of Jewish mysticism as they are elucidated in the *Imrey Binah*, Reb Dov Baer provided each category of Hasid with a text in which he would be able to verify, by his own experience, what Reb Shneur Zalman had set down in the *Tanya*. Of particular interest is his *Treatise on Ecstasy*.[6] Reb Dov Baer makes this elusive experience, which comes as a gift of grace and invades everyday consciousness, something that a Hasid might achieve and "steer." The many levels of ecstasy—those of function, of feeling, of pure intellect, of the will, and of delight—were all described in their process and in the way in which they could be achieved.

In 1823, continuing his father's support of Jews in the Holy Land, Reb Dov Baer established a colony in Hebron, the burial site of the Matriarchs and Patriarchs, which he supported financially. He longed to go there himself, for prayers recited in Hebron, he said, were particularly effective, as tradition held it to be the gateway to paradise. In the summer of 1825 Reb Dov Baer, for reasons of health, made his way to the hot springs at Karlsbad. On his return trip he met Rabbi Akiva Eiger, an opponent of Hasidism and one of the foremost Talmudists of the time. But this meeting would prove to be crucial in the easing of tensions. For Rabbi Akiva Eiger found himself impressed with Reb Dov Baer's scholarship, and Reb Dov Baer deeply affected by Rabbi Eiger's piety.

Just as his father had been imprisoned for his dauntless leadership of Hasidism, so was Reb Dov Baer. The subject of false accusations, Reb Dov Baer was imprisoned for two months in Vitebsk. Thanks to the intercession of certain dignitaries, however, he was released. His health no better from imprisonment, he made plans to settle in the Holy Land. Before going, he set out on a pilgrimage to his father's grave. He died on the way, one day before the anniversary of his release from prison and on his own fifty-fourth birthday. The leadership of the Chabad movement then passed to his nephew, Reb Menachem Mendel I of Lubavitch, who was also known as the *Tzemach Tzedek* after the title of his halakhic work, which corresponds to the numerical value of his own name.

Reb Menachem Mendel I of Lubavitch (29 Elul 1789–13 Nisan 1866)

Reb Menachem Mendel I was the grandson of Reb Shneur Zalman, the son of his daughter Devorah Leah and Rabbi Shalom Shakhna. In 1806 Reb Menachem Mendel married the daughter of Reb Dov Baer, Chayyah Mushka. He was treated as a son, and in 1827, at the death of Reb Dov Baer, took the reins of Chabad Hasidism.

Reb Menachem Mendel managed to break through the wall of prejudice that divided Hasidim from their opponents. So respected was he as a legal authority that even the opponents of Hasidism sent their legal questions to Reb Menachem Mendel for his responses, which were published under the title *Tzemach Tzedek*.

His tremendous knowledge of mathematics, astronomy, and classical philosophy placed him among the greatest minds of his generation. Reb Menachem Mendel was the great scholastic of Chabad Hasidism. Under him, the conceptual work that still remained to be done was accomplished. Rabbenu Saadiah Ga'on[7] and Maimonides were integrated with the Kabbalists Rabbi Yitzhak Luria and Rabbi Chayyim Vital.[8] However, Reb Menachem Mendel did not look for any easy compromise between these two ways of viewing reality, of meeting God, Torah, and Israel. The inner and the outer, the esoteric and the exoteric, are one, but the easy manipulation of concepts was not what Reb Menachem Mendel strove for. He strove to express the synthesis of true being between the inner and outer in order to winnow out true and secure knowledge. His *Derekh Emunah* reveals how successful he was. A soul committed to the unqualified observance of Divine commandments as stated in Torah will, for all its resignation to God's blessed Will, still seek to understand it, still seek to know the reasons behind His commanding. In this, Reb Menachem Mendel created a great synthesis of knowledge wherein the hidden and the manifest harmoniously paired to inform the soul and to conform it to the Divine intention of the commandments.

During his leadership, many complexities entered the Jewish scene. This was the time of the Enlightenment, and many Jews were abandoning their religious obligations for a place in the wider social sphere. And in Russia, a tyrannical tsar was inducting children into his imperial army with the hope of coercing them into acceptance of Christianity. These issues Reb

Menachem Mendel faced with fearless and active opposition. From his point of view, he was fighting for the very existence of the sacred and holy in Judaism. And yet, through all troubles, he was a model of serenity, a true man of knowledge.

On one of his travels to St. Petersburg to argue for free and untrammeled Jewish education, he was prepared to give his life, taking his burial shrouds along. He was there protesting the forced educational curriculum of the Russian government, which among other things required Jewish children to speak only Russian. What is wrong with learning Russian? Think of what the Native Americans went through when their children were taken away, forbidden to speak their own language, and forced to learn customs of their oppressors. Well, things of this sort were happening to Jews in Russia. So Reb Menachem Mendel came and said, "I will not permit this. I will not give my consent to that." It was a bold stand; some other rabbis were willing to collaborate with the government, but he was not.

At one point the minister said to him, "Could you tell me the reason why, when the ashes of the 'red heifer' are used to purify people who have touched a corpse, the one who burns the 'red heifer' and has the power to purify the people becomes impure?" Now this is a commandment that cannot be dealt with through logical reasoning. There is a paradox involved, and the minister had selected this question to stump the great rabbi. He said to Reb Menachem Mendel, "When you can give me the reason for this, I will allow you to have your way with your school. Otherwise, you will have to have the government school, because it stands for 'reason.'" Reb Menachem Mendel said, "I brought the reason with me. If you'll excuse me, I must return to my hotel. I'll be back in a few minutes." He went to his hotel, picked up a little bundle, brought it back in, and opened it up in front of the minister. In the bundle were the shrouds in which to dress a body to prepare it for burial. "What is the reason? What have you shown me here?" And Reb Menachem Mendel said to the minister, "When you can show me the reason for this, I will show you a reason for that." After employing this existential argument, he was placed under arrest for a while and then released.

Perhaps he would have liked nothing better than to be simply the literary executor of the writings of his late grandfather and father-in-law, as indeed he was, editing the *Torah Or* and *Likkutey Torah*. But his destiny made him the leader of countless Hasidim who swelled the ranks of Chabad. Indeed, he was so highly regarded in this role that even non-Chabad Hasidim looked to him for guidance. Reb Yitzhak Meir, the first Rebbe of Ger,[9] upon the demise of his master, Reb Mendel of Kotzk, said to some of his comrades, "Let us send someone to Lubavitch [to the *Tzemach Tzedek*] to see if there is place for us there." Only reluctantly did he agree to assume the leadership of Polish Hasidism. When Reb Menachem Mendel passed on, the Chabad dynasty was on sure footing and respected far and wide. He was succeeded by his son, Reb Shmuel.

Reb Shmuel of Lubavitch
(2 Iyyar 1834–13 Tishri 1882)

Reb Shmuel was the youngest of Reb Menachem Mendel's seven saintly sons. At twenty-one, he was already traveling and organizing support for the improvement of the lives of Jews under the tsarist regime. In 1866, when his father died, he inherited the main body of Chabad Hasidim, while others turned to some of his brothers, who also became Rebbes.

Hasidim feel that not only is the Rebbe a giant of the mind and spirit as a private individual but also that his mouth is an instrument of prophecy, that his counsels are as valid as those that came from the high priests' breastplate during the time of the Temple. An old and venerable Hasid, Reb Shmuel Munkes, who knew Reb Shneur Zalman of Liadi, came to hear Reb Shmuel give a discourse on Hasidism, after which he agreed that the line of Lubavitch Chabad had a true successor in Reb Shmuel of Lubavitch. But it was becoming more difficult to be a Lubavitch Rebbe. Not only did one have to find the activity most suitable for one's own being and one's own calling, but one also had to maintain and continue all the other activities of the past Chabad masters. With the will and joy of the Ba'al Shem Tov, the creativity of the Maggid, the wisdom of Reb Shneur Zalman, the understanding of Reb Dov Baer, and the knowledge of his father, Reb Menachem Mendel I, Reb Shmuel added the dimension of the imagination, where love and awe meet in beauty and in the highest aesthetic balance. Reb Shmuel was audacious in many ways. The form of his own teachings was more imaginative and suggestive than that of his father. Where his father was incisive, Reb Shmuel was the producer of insights. The student of his teachings moved from paragraph to paragraph with explosions of "Aha! Aha!" "Now I see it! Now I see it!" What was aural with his father became visual with Reb Shmuel. The meditative became contemplative in him. Many of the things in the *Tanya* needed restatement. It was almost eighty years later, in long discourses, that he would continue from week to week, Reb Shmuel restated the content of the *Tanya*, bringing his imaginative insights to bear on the material, to refresh his readers, to renew their motivation, to reinspire them, to rekindle their fervor, and to help them share his vision.

Reb Shmuel was not content with bringing a person only to the level of the *Beynoni*. At least for a short time, for at least a half-hour, he wanted each Hasid to experience the rich inner life, the ecstatic life, of a *Tzaddik*. Yet the intense vitality that made him seek out people who were far removed from the main springs of Judaism—in a hotel in Paris, on a train to the Riviera, traveling incognito everywhere he went. He did his work not merely on the basis of the reputation that his parents had built up or on the basis of his vast following but on the basis of his tremendous conviction, imagination, and charm. It was in his day that the personal counseling that the Rebbe gives to his Hasidim became a full science, the science of divestment and detachment from one to be able to invest oneself in another. Perhaps his father was easier to understand, but he was easier to feel with, and hence his impact was like that of the Ba'al Shem Tov: joyous and mysterious, wondrous and miraculous. One had to be completely attuned to him to understand the many levels on which he carried on a conversation.

In 1880 he was placed under house arrest. Shortly before his death in 1882, he asked three of his Hasidim among the exalted rabbis whether they did not think that it was time for him to move into more expansive quarters. They all shook their heads in agreement, not understanding that the "domicile" Reb Shmuel had in mind was that of Heaven. He was barely forty-eight years old when he, like the dove he described in one of his discourses, returned into the cleft of the rock from whence it had issued.

Reb Shalom Dov Baer of Lubavitch
(20 Heshvan 1860–2 Nisan 1920)

Reb Shalom Dov Bear of Lubavitch was the middle son of Reb Shmuel. In 1875 he married Sterna Sarah, the daughter of Rabbi Yosef Yitzhak Schneersohn of Avruch. At twenty he began to assist his father in his activities and two years later succeeded him. However, for several years he did not wish to assume the leadership. Rather than take on the crown of Lubavitch Chabad as Rebbe, he wished to cede it to his older brother and to walk secretly with his God. But his genius for the contemplative, the vast, the mind-filling, the intellectual and yet the functional delivered him to his true vocation. What would the head be without the two feet? The functions of victorious (*netzach*) insistence on eternity, balanced by the beauty and glory (*hod*) inherent in the service of the Lord, characterized his beliefs.

The world in his day had turned from the private and relaxed life of the village to the life of institutions. Lubavitch needed a *yeshiva*. It had to train Hasidim from the ground up. It had to train them in learning and in prayer against the onslaught of industry and the quickening pace of the era. It even had to train Hasidim to be impervious to torture and brainwashing. In 1897 he founded the Yeshiva Tomchei T'mimim.

Reb Shalom Dov Baer, called the "Maimonides of Hasidism," issued three manuals: *Kuntres HaT'fillah* (Treatise on Prayer),[10] *Kuntres Ha'Avodah* (Treatise on Work and Worship), and *Kuntres Etz Chayyim* (Treatise on Study). These became the working guides for students of Tomchei T'mimim, the Lubavitch Yeshiva. And Reb Sholom Dov Baer didn't just write about these things; he lived them. Nor did he forget the Jewish layman for whose mind and loyalties the struggles between the Haskalah "Enlightenment" movement, socialism, Zionism, and all the other isms alive in that day were fighting. He wrote the *Kuntres "Uma'yan"* (Treatise on the Text "And a Spring Wells Forth") at a time when he organized Torah-true Jewry in Russia under the banner of *Mahzikey Haddat* ("Those who hold fast to the law"). The most sublime doctrines of *Hasidut* found a simple and comprehensive statement in the *Kuntres "Uma'yan."*

His only son, Reb Yosef Yitzhak, who was appointed to executive leadership of the Yeshiva, was the living and accessible model to the students of Lubavitch. Having written the treatises on the functional aspect of the unitive experience, of contemplation, of the service to God, to changing man in the manner of tanning a coarse and callused hide into a supple and eager instrument of the spirit, of having trained people in the nondualism of the study of both the manifest and the hidden aspects of Torah, Reb Sholom Dov Baer provided the grist for the contemplative mills in exquisite philosophical work. During his day, the terms *o'ved,* "one who serves," and *maskil,* "one who lives the life of the intellect," came into their own in Lubavitch.

And yet he did not live in an abstract world. The Ba'al Shem Tov's call for *mammash,* "so-beingness," was still an active and real dimension of the Hasid's life, and so Reb Shalom Dov Baer would admonish the would-be conceptualizer, "If you want the ideas of God, these you will have. Heaven will give you everything of ideas, but Him, not at all. He is given to him who has given himself to Him and seeks only Him, untrammeled by concepts, labels and expectations." And this is how he trained his son during many a walk. He was both the stern father who would admonish his son while training him to truly pay attention to what the son's hands were doing (ripping off a leaf from the tree),[11] while at the same time he had been teaching him of the Divine design of the universe. Point by point he imparted to his son the knowledge of guidance and leadership, which Reb Yosef Yitzhak recorded in *A Treatise on Education and Guidance*. In the most up-to-date, sociological manner, the father charged the son to take note of different settings—urban and rural, different individual endowments—and to deny any relationship other than the one that is fully accepting of the other.

Reb Shalom Dov Baer was fully awake to the meaning of the present moment. Once a simple butcher asked Reb Shalom Dov Baer's son, Reb Yosef Yitzhak, a question about his father. "Tell me, your father, every time he teaches something, he says, 'Pesach is the greatest holiday!' and then he comes for Purim, 'Purim is the greatest holiday!' And when Shavuot rolls around, 'Oh, Shavuot is the greatest holiday!' I don't understand, how could they all be the greatest?" Reb Yosef Yitzhak says, "It depends—on Shavuot, Shavuot is the biggest holiday."[12]

A visitor to Lubavitch who had read some of the treatises on contemplative prayer and wondered if anyone was actually practicing so high a life was referred to such unassuming souls as Abraham David of Klimovitch and the young and the old Reb Hendel. The Rebbe's adjutant, Rabbi Gronem Esterman, and others, laid foundations in the souls of individuals that were hitherto unmatched. A new type appeared on the Jewish scene, the *tamim*, a wholesome student who studied at the Yeshiva Tomchei T'mimim.

When the Germans invaded Russia in the First World War, Reb Shalom Dov Baer fled into the inner country and lived at various places until he set his residence in Rostov on the Don. There he passed on from a typhoid infection in 1920. The reins of leadership under the Communist regime fell to his only son, Reb Yosef Yitzhak Schneersohn of Lubavitch.

Reb Yosef Yitzhak of Lubavitch
(12 Tammuz 1880–10 Shevat 1950)

Reb Yosef Yitzhak was the last Chabad Rebbe to be born in Lubavitch. When he was but fifteen years old, he was appointed to be his father's personal secretary. From then on, he was tireless in his activities to promote the spiritual and physical welfare of Jews everywhere. He participated in conferences, founded businesses and *yeshivot*, and distributed food to Jewish soldiers. In 1897 he married the Nechamah Dinah, the daughter of Abraham Schneersohn and granddaughter of Reb Menachem Mendel I.

Like Joseph the Tzaddik of the divine chariot, the foundation (*yesod*) of the flow of grace, the person who though bloodied remains unbowed. When Reb Yosef Yitzhak took the leadership of Chabad, he called on the loyalty of those whom he himself had trained in the Yeshiva Tomchei T'mimim to establish a network of schools of elementary and higher Jewish education in Soviet Russia, reaching as far as Georgia in the Caucasus Mountains and into Siberia and Kazakhstan. It was obvious that this activity was not too well liked by Jewish members of the Communist Party, the Yevsektsia. Their rabid anti-Judaism sought in the Hasidic leader their target for their lack of success in weaning Jewish people from holy loyalties acquired over millennia. If ever the question may have been raised whether Hasidism was a way only for fair weather but could not stand up under the storm and stress of constant emergency, danger, and even terror, here was the proving ground for Hasidism, where Hasidism came into its own.

In all, Reb Yosef Yitzhak was seven times in jail.[13] The first time was when he was a small child. And the last two times he was arrested by the Soviet government, for what they called "godly activity." The last time he was taken to the infamous Spolerka prison in Moscow, subjected to torture, and sentenced to death. However, Reb Yosef Yitzhak could not be broken. Not even when he was threatened with a gun held in the hand of an NKVD man, who said, "Many a man has changed his mind because of this 'persuader,'" to which Reb Yosef Yitzhak replied, "Only a person, who has many gods [passions] to serve, and only one world to serve them in, can be persuaded by your persuader. But I, who have only one God to serve and many worlds to serve Him in, cannot be persuaded by your persuader. I am not impressed." Still, they attempted to brainwash him but were unsuccessful. Later he said that what kept him together was that he was able to move into those worlds of Hasidic thinking that removed him completely from the grasp and the reach of the people who wanted to "burn him out."

When pleas for clemency came from around the world,[14] his death sentence was commuted to Siberian exile. At his departure, he triumphed over his guards by addressing Hasidic multitudes at the Moscow train station, pointing out to them that only the Jewish body was given into exile, not the Jewish soul, and that they must under no circumstances yield to that persuasion of the soul. When he was released on his birthday and later deported with an entire staff and library to Riga, Latvia, his activity on behalf of Russian Jewry did not cease. He began to pool his resources, visiting the Holy Land and the United States. He strengthened existing institutions there and returned to Warsaw to regroup the remnants of the Lubavitch Yeshiva, and the Torah service continued. On March 19, 1940, he arrived in New York, the new home of Chabad Hasidism.

During this stressful period of activity there continued a flow of hitherto unrivaled creativity in Hasidic thought, always with an eye toward practical application. The intellectual expansiveness of Reb Shalom Dov Baer's thought, the inventive and imaginative genius of Reb Shmuel, the scholastic scope of Reb Menachem Mendel I, the varied understanding of Reb Dov Baer, the seminal wisdom of Reb Shneur Zalman, the creative potential of the Maggid of Mezritch, and the release of pure joy of the Ba'al Shem Tov—all of these were present in this one individual and his teachings. It is no exaggeration to say that his writings surpassed the published works of his ancestors, in quantity, if nothing else. But there was much more.

Hasidism had to meet an ideologically complex world and respond with a statement of its own ideology. It had to meet the age of anxiety and transform that anxiety into creative drive. It had to meet psychoanalysis and show that not only are the conscious and unconscious, the body and the soul, the ego and the id, two separate continents but that the gulf between them could be spanned by light and intelligence so that the heart will learn to feel what the mind attains. Hasidism had to meet existentialism and meaninglessness. Perhaps in these areas more than any others has Hasidism made converts from the ranks of Jews whose Jewish background was almost nil.

When Reb Yosef Yitzhak passed away, he, great teacher that he was, left his spiritual testament in a homily—"I came to my garden, my sister, my bride . . ."—showing how the scope of Jewish history has always been one of investing God, the transcendent, into a way of life, a task that can be obscured only by the willful yielding to the spirit of folly, a task, however, that is not only possible of being fulfilled, but since God never tyrannically makes demands of His creatures, He not only gives the task but also the capability and means to fulfill it.

Reb Menachem Mendel II of Lubavitch (11 Nissan 1902–3 Tammuz 1994)

The seventh and last Lubavitcher Rebbe was born in Nikolayev, Russia, to Channah, the daughter of Rabbi Meir Shlomoh of Nikolayev, and Reb Levi Yitzhak Schneersohn, a grandson of Reb Menachem Mendel I of Lubavitch. Reb Levi Yitzhak was the Rabbi of Yekaterinoslav, a noted

Kabbalist, and also the student of Rabbi Chayyim Soloveitchik of Brest-Litovsk.[15] He was imprisoned by the Communists and exiled to Siberia. In 1928 Reb Menachem Mendel II married Chayyah Mushkha,[16] the second daughter of Reb Yosef Yitzhak of Lubavitch. He studied mathematics and physics in Berlin and engineering in Paris.[17] In 1941 he settled in Crown Heights, Brooklyn, becoming the chairman of the educational arm of Lubavitch. In 1950, upon the death of his father-in-law, he reluctantly assumed the leadership of the Chabad Hasidim.

Reb Yosef Yitzhak relied heavily in his educational endeavors on the talents, skills, and tireless work of his son-in-law and successor, Reb Menachem Mendel II of Lubavitch. The latter extensively studied Torah and was trained by his father-in-law, practicing all in which he was trained while at the same time becoming an expert in the exact sciences at the polytechnics of Berlin and Paris. Reb Menachem Mendel became the bridge between the teachings of his father-in-law and many a young modern Jew. *Yeshiva* students in all sorts of institutions bound themselves to him in loyalty, if only for having made it possible for them to remain unified human beings despite all the stresses that the two cultures exerted on them.

The scholastic brilliance of Rabbi Menachem Mendel I was his special endowment. The imaginative poetic fervor of Reb Shmuel he inherited asserted itself at many Hasidic gatherings. Two Israeli villages have become the laboratory of his spirit in the Holy Land. Moroccan Jewry was maintained by Lubavitch under his leadership. Kehot, a publishing house of immense scope and dimension, is an instrument of dissemination of Chabad knowledge. A network of educational institutions, from day schools and higher academies of Jewish learning, spanned the globe under his leadership. With all his majestic bearing, the more majestic for his unassuming humility, he was a model of one who bears the Divine yoke, fulfilling tasks often in spite of his personal convenience. His holy soul with the encyclopedic mind was a model of the Hasidic attainment of egolessness.

His correspondence was voluminous, as he answered all letters himself and saw by appointment anyone who sought to speak with him. Perhaps no other Jewish leader in his day had such a vast pastorate. A majestic source issuing the wellsprings of the Ba'al Shem Tov into the outer world, Rabbi Menachem Mendel II of Lubavitch was the embodiment of experiential empiricism of Torah and Hasidism in our day, the well-beloved seventh leader of Chabad since the inception of the way of wisdom, understanding, and knowledge as focused on the so-beingness of God, Torah, and Israel.

In 1994 he suffered a stroke, which eventually led to his death on June 12 (3 Tammuz). Many of the Chabad Hasidim believe that Reb Menachem Mendel II is the Messiah and have been promulgating the idea that he will be resurrected. The Rebbe died childless, and no serious candidates to succeed him have yet emerged. Indeed, the succession is a point of sensitivity and disagreement to this day.

BETWEEN PERFECTION
AND EVIL

*SEFER
LIKKUTEY AMARIM*
PART ONE
ENTITLED
SEFER SHEL BEYNONIM
("The Book of the People In-Between")

Collected from [sacred] books and from scribes of supernal holiness, whose souls are in Eden; based on the verse, "For it is exceedingly near to you in your mouth and in your heart to do," explaining clearly how it is exceedingly near, in a lengthy and a short way, with the help of the Holy One, may He be blessed.

—Shneur Zalman of Liadi, *Tanya*[1]

REB SHNEUR ZALMAN'S best-known work is called the *Tanya,* meaning, "It is taught," after the first word in the book. But if you look on the title page of the book, you'll see that there it is called *Likkutey Amarim,* "Collected Sayings." This was the original title. However, in order to distinguish it from the Maggid's work of the same name,[2] it was called the *Tanya.* But what did Reb Shneur Zalman mean by "collected sayings"? He means sayings that he has picked up. He doesn't want to give himself the pride of saying, "I have written a book." So instead he says, "I picked up some things here and there; most of this is stuff I've learned from my teachers." It is a statement of humility.

On that same title page, he also makes something of an opening statement. He is trying to say, "the path that I am about to teach you may look somewhat difficult for you, but it is actually a very direct path." This is what that cryptic statement "in a lengthy and a short way" refers to. And the sentence in quotation marks comes from Moses' saying, "Don't say that the Torah is across the sea, who will go across the sea and bring it to us, or that the Torah is in Heaven, who will go up and bring it to us down, but the word is very close to you, in your mouth and in your heart, that you might do it." In other words, it's doable. Reb Shneur Zalman wants his readers to know just this and is saying that he is about to tell them precisely *how* it is doable.

There is a wonderful story about the cookbook of the gypsy. Instead of saying, "To make an omelet, take six eggs," it says, "steal six eggs." Where do you get them from? You have to take them from somewhere. You steal them from the chicken who laid them, right? It is like when you hear someone say, "Thou shalt love the Lord thy God with all thy heart," and you want to say, "Yeah, how?" How can you legislate attitude and feeling? How could you command such a thing? And when it says, *K'doshim tih'yu ki kadosh ani Adonai Elohei'chem,* "Holy you shall be, for holy am I, the Lord your God," we say, *"Nu, nu,* I'd like to be holy! If I could, I surely would, stand on the rock where Moses stood! I'd do anything if I only knew how." The big question between moral preachment and actualization hinges on the skillful means. This is called *upaya* in Sanskrit. In Hebrew, you would call them *etzot,* which refers to those points of advice wherewith you can make a change and a difference.

The *Tzaddik,* the *Beynoni,* and the *Rasha*

> *It has been taught (*Niddah, *end ch. 3): An oath is given to him [before the birthing, warning him]: "Be a* Tzaddik *and be not a* Rasha; *and even if the whole world tells you that you are a* Tzaddik, *regard yourself as if you were a* Rasha."*
>
> Shneur Zalman of Liadi, *Likkutey Amarim— Tanya, Sefer Shel Beynonim,* ch. 1.

The first thing Reb Shneur Zalman does as he begins the book is give us a prescription. You hear him say, "We have learned that right before a soul comes down, they make her swear she will be righteous and not wicked." Just think about this for a moment. Don't think about it simply as an idea, because that will not make much of a difference. Imagine it is the moment before *you* are to become incarnate. You are still wandering around the *Bardo,*[3] as the Tibetans say, and there is somebody saying to you, "You are about to come to life, and we don't need people who are going to pollute this planet worse. So be righteous, and don't be a wicked one." You immediately say, "Yes, I promise. I promise." And *whoosh,* there you go!

This notion is to say that I made this promise, and this promise is in my guts, in my craw. And if I happen to deviate from it, I get a feeling as if something is not quite right; I'm not doing something right. So the whole issue of conscience gets explained by the oath that we have taken before coming down. Then, he says, "imagine you took the oath and said you are going to be righteous, and now the whole world tells you you are righteous, then, in your own eyes, you should feel like one who is wicked." Why is that? Because if you figure that you are all finished and all righteous, you are going to go off the right path. And besides, who knows better than you how wicked you really are? Then Reb Shneur Zalman goes on to say, "We find in the Talmud five particular types—a *Tzaddik* who prospers, a *Tzaddik* who suffers, a *Rasha* who prospers, a *Rasha* who suffers, and an a *Beynoni*."[4]

"You should be a *Tzaddik,* a righteous one, a just one, and not be a *Rasha,* a wicked one." What does that mean, and how does it change your place in the world? The book of Job raises the question, "God, why is it that good people are suffering and that bad people have it good?" and the Rabbis came up with an answer that goes like this. There are five categories of people: the *Tzaddik* who prospers, the *Tzaddik* who suffers, the *Rasha* who prospers, the *Rasha* who suffers, and the *Beynoni* (the intermediate one). According to the Rabbis, the righteous who have it good are extremely rare in the world. Everybody agrees that they are truly righteous and they live a good life and they really have it good. This is a *Tzaddik* who has it good. Then there is a *Tzaddik* who has it bad. He is such a wonderful *Tzaddik,* but he is always in such trouble. The perfect example of this was Reb Zushya of Onipol, the brother of Reb Elimelech.

Once some Hasidim came to the Maggid of Mezritch with a question. They could not understand the dictum that says, "You have to give thanks to God for what is good, and you have to give thanks to God for what is bad." They said to the Maggid, "This is such a strange statement. What does it mean?" And he said to them, "Go ask Reb Zushya." So they went to the little shack where Reb Zushya lived. Now, Reb Zushya was a poor man; he really had nothing but the clothes on his back. And, *Oy!* did he have troubles in his life; he was always the one who got whacked. So they asked Reb Zushya, "How could you be thanking God for what is bad?" He looked at them a little puzzled and said, "I don't know; I have never had anything bad happen to me."

That is a lot like the story about the king who suffered from melancholy. None of his doctors could cure him, and finally, along comes this healer who says, "I have a way to heal you." He says to the king, "If you would be healed of this melancholy, you must wear the shirt of a happy person." So the king asks the healer, "Are you a happy person?" And the healer says, "No." So the king goes to the vizier and says, "Are you a happy person? Could you give me your shirt?" And the vizier says, "I'll give you all the shirts you want, your majesty, but I'm not happy. How could I be happy? If I give you good advice, then it is your wisdom. If I give you bad advice, then I get into trouble. I can't be happy." So the king goes from one person to another, through the whole town, looking for a happy person to give him a shirt, and he can't find one. So now he starts walking down the road to another town, and he sees a poor farmer out there in the field who is singing very happily. And the king turns to him and says, "You seem to be a happy person." And the farmer says, "Yes, I am." Then the king says, "Can I have your shirt?" And the farmer replies, "I don't own one."

There are many variants of this story. In one, a man is being held in the jail of the local landowner who is trying to extort money from him. And every time the landowner comes and asks him for more money, he cries and says, "I haven't got! I haven't got! I haven't got!" So they keep him in the jail. One day the landowner is sort of tired of trying to squeeze money out of the man, so he sends one of his lackeys to do it: "Go torture him and get some money from him." Later the lackey comes back and says, "I think you ought to go and deal with him." "What do you mean?" The lackey explains, "I come in to torture him and he doesn't cry or anything; he's just laughing." And the landowner says, "Let the guy out. He doesn't have any money left."

You see, as long as he had something, he was protecting it by crying. So this is a *Tzaddik* who has it bad. Then there is a wicked one who has it good and a wicked one who has it bad. And finally, there is one in-between, a *Beynoni*—not very wicked and not very saintly. This, at least, is the way the Talmud talks about it.

Now, Reb Shneur Zalman makes a very important move from the way of the Talmud. He is not really as interested in behavior as much as he is interested in attitude and transformation. For the important part of this book is its transformational recipe. So he redefines these categories to fit this emphasis. And here is where Reb Shneur Zalman's farthest-reaching psychological contribution is made: in his concept of the *Beynoni*. Now, the word *Beynoni* is rather difficult to translate. Sometimes translators will render it as "average person," but this is a sociological fiction. Reb Shneur Zalman didn't intend any such meaning. For him, the *Beynoni* was an individual who fell somewhere between the *Tzaddik* (righteous one) and the *Rasha* (wicked one). So he begins his teaching by defining the *Tzaddik* and the *Rasha*.

For Reb Shneur Zalman, the term *Tzaddik* was a qualitative term, not a behavioral one. If it was merely behavioral, *Tzaddik* would simply have meant someone who behaves righteously more often than not but who might also desire things that are not according to God's will. Thus Reb

Shneur Zalman speaks of the "absolute *Tzaddik*" and the "conditional *Tzaddik*" and treats the *Rasha* in like manner.

An absolute *Tzaddik* in the qualitative sense is one who has completely mortified her or his own demons so that there is not even so much as an unconscious inclination to invest energy, or libido, toward evil. The absolute *Tzaddik* cannot even attempt such an inclination, since all fascination with evil has been completely eliminated. This person is totally devoid of evil. However, the *Tzaddik*'s disdain for evil is not at all fanatical; it is quiet and existential. This is the *Tzaddik* who is complete, the absolute *Tzaddik*.

The conditional *Tzaddik*, however, while not involved behaviorally in evil or inclined to invest libido toward it in any way, is nonetheless vulnerable to the potential for evil. There may be abhorrence for evil but it is not absolute, and the fascination for it still lingers at some unconscious level. This person has undergone a transformation, but there is still a little residue left, and so this is the *Tzaddik* who still harbors some evil. Yet in both categories of *Tzaddik*, the vital and decisive principle is the Divine Soul (*Nefesh HaElokit*), which shares a common ontology with God. Thus as a *Tzaddik*, one could not act against God, for it would be tantamount to acting against one's own nature.

By contrast, the absolute *Rasha* is totally under the governance of the lower bodily drives and emotional whims. Such an individual identifies with the Animal Soul (*Nefesh HaBehamit*), is one with its will, and—not being reason-directed—completely blocks out any awareness of the manifestation of the Divine Soul. This is somebody who truly doesn't give a damn about anything or anyone else—a truly malevolent person, devoid of good, totally bad. However, the absolute *Rasha* is really rather rare. More common is the conditional *Rasha*, driven by impulse, rationalizing but not quite rational, and conforming to pressures from both within and without—characteristics with which most of us can easily identify. This is a person who misbehaves from time to time. A person who commits even a single sin already belongs to this category. One still may have many good qualities because one is wrestling with the evil, trying very hard, but one doesn't always make it. We use reason as a tool for furthering the animal dimension of our nature yet delegate no control to reason over our emotions. We may, for example, be aroused to repentance (*t'shuvah*), Torah study, and the performance of *mitzvot*, but not on a primary level. At best, we may be involved in these peripherally, momentarily enveloped in the holiness they vibrate, but as we step back into our *Rasha* condition, all of this disappears like an illusion—though some traces of the experience remain at some level—and once again the Animal Soul is in control.

Finally, there is the *Beynoni*, the one whose character falls somewhere between *Tzaddik* and *Rasha*. The *Beynoni* has not sinned behaviorally, but neither has the *Beynoni* purged all evil. So on the level of behavior, and this is very important, the *Tzaddik* and the *Beynoni* are the same. The *Beynoni* doesn't do anything wrong, the *Tzaddik* doesn't do anything wrong, but the *Beynoni* still wants to do wrong. The *Beynoni* still has the urge to do wrong and has not overcome that urge. It has not been transformed as it has in the *Tzaddik*. So even though the *Beynoni*'s evil inclinations may fade during such ecstatic experiences as prayer and the celebration of sacred festivals, eventually they reemerge and become restored to their original strength.

Not too many people are of the category of *Beynoni*. To remain a *Beynoni*, one has to be able to keep repeating the decision that entails the recognition of the ontological definition of sin as idolatry. A *Beynoni* can therefore never act out in sin, for each sin would be akin to idolatry in that at the very moment that the sin is committed, all of one's energies draw from the evil energy system of *k'lipah*, the shells, rather than from the pure source of God. The *Beynoni*, recognizing this, makes a conscious and deliberate decision never to draw life energies from any source other than God, a decision that must thereafter be constantly nurtured and reinforced, often at great emotional expense. But while it is a seemingly impossible feat, it can be accomplished.

Now, with whom can I be most sympathetic? The *Tzaddik* or the *Beynoni*? We aren't talking about action here. We know the *ba'al t'shuvah* could in one moment become a *Tzaddik*, but that is a whole other matter. Here Reb Shneur Zalman is using categories so we should be able to understand how a person operates. "I don't want to be a *Rasha*, a wicked one. And I can't be a *Tzaddik* because I haven't yet transformed myself. So the person with whom I can most empathize in this whole business is the *Beynoni*." This is why he writes this book. He says, "I want to show you how to deal with that." So Reb Shneur Zalman writes this:

The *Beynoni*'s mode is the measure of every person. Let everyone aspire to it. For anyone can become a *Beynoni* at any time. The *Beynoni* does not abominate evil altogether, for this is a matter of the heart and not the same all of the time. But to forsake evil and do good in actual behavior, deed, word, and thought is something given to the human choice. For even when the heart covets and craves a physical passion—whether permitted or forbidden—one can prevail over it with one's willpower and say to the heart: "I do not desire to be a *Rasha* for even one moment, for under no condition do I wish to be severed and separated from God, as sins are wont to do. Rather, I desire to unite my *Nefesh, Ruach,* and *Neshamah* (animative, emotive, and intellectual manifestations of the Divine Soul) in the manner as they are invested in the three blessed garments of God: action, word, and thought. And I perform this by unifying God with Torah and the performance of *mitzvot* out of the love for God, which is implanted deep within my heart as well as in the heart of all of Yisrael who are called Lovers of Thy Name. Why, even the most lightheaded can offer his own soul for the sanctification of God's Name. Am I any less of a person? Indeed, how can I, too, become as lightheaded so that I may be able to do the same? Ah, but the truth is that a spirit of folly has entered such persons, making it seem to them that despite their sins they are still garbed in their Jewishness. They think that their souls are not distanced thereby from the God of Yisrael. They also forget that implanted deep within their hearts there is love for God. But as for me, I do not will to be such a fool as they, and deny the Truth.[5]

So if, as I said before, there aren't too many *Beynonim* out there, why does Reb Shneur Zalman say that the way of the *Beynoni* is the way for everybody? It is because when we talk about very few people fitting the category of *Beynoni*, we mean of actually being a *Beynoni*. If I had to put it into Alcoholics Anonymous terms, we are all recovering *Rasha*s; we're all *reshoim* in recovery. Even when we don't act out, it is still a one-day-at-a-time affair. And if you've ever had to deal with an addiction or a temptation, you know how true this is. So for as long as you manage, you are a *Beynoni*. And this is what Reb Shneur Zalman does for us: he gives us courage by that and tells us to hang in there for another day. Finally, someday all the troubles will be over. Potentially, everybody can be a *Beynoni*. But whether we have actually acquired the muscle to be able to say that over an entire lifetime we have never fallen prey to a sin in actuality, in thought, word, or deed, is a rare thing. So that is the point. We can aspire to that, but *are* we that?

Are There Really Such *Tzaddikim* Out There?

"I am only a Beynoni.*"*

—Shneur Zalman of Liadi

People sometimes ask me if I have ever known a *Tzaddik*. I believe, because they say it is so, that there must be at least thirty-six real *Tzaddikim* for the world to exist. But you know, I haven't yet met a *Tzaddik* that fits Reb Shneur Zalman's criteria, where I could say that this person doesn't have any more evil impulses. It's strange. I believe that I have met many people who have a strong *Tzaddik* "vibe," but I haven't yet met one that I felt was so much a *Tzaddik* that everything around and about the person was *Tzaddik*. If I were to say that in front of Lubavitch Hasidim, they wouldn't be so happy, because after all, I knew two of the Lubavitcher Rebbes, and how could I say I never saw a *Tzaddik!* But you know, *Barukh HaShem*, human beings have flaws. People are like Persian carpets: there is always a flaw. I saw some of the flaws, too; so what? But the archetypal *Tzaddik* I have never met. I have met a number of people who were accessible models of the *Tzaddik*, and I am happy with that.

I'll tell you a couple of stories about my Rebbe, Reb Yosef Yitzhak Schneersohn. He was a remarkable person. I first saw him after he had made the move to America. At the time, I was a Lubavitch Hasid and he was my Rebbe. When I knew him, his body was broken from the tortures he had be subjected to in Russia. He was paralyzed, had difficulty speaking, and could move around only in a wheelchair. But his presence was still vital and powerful.

In the *yeshiva,* it was a long, long day, and we had to be ready at seven thirty in the morning. That meant that often we had to get up around six or six-fifteen because we would go to dip in the *mikvah* to prepare for the day of spiritual activity. So we would come in at seven-thirty and sit and study *Hasidut,* especially the *Tanya,* for an hour or an hour and a half. And then we would meditate for a while and then begin our prayers. After that, it was time to rush to the refectory, have breakfast, and be ready at ten-thirty for the first lecture that we would get from the *rosh yeshiva,* on Talmud. We didn't get to lunch until two-fifteen, and there was a bunch of us who decided that we didn't want to go straight to lunch because we had been squeezing the bench a whole day up to that time, you know, and we wanted to move around a little bit. So instead of lining up for the food line, we would get there after the food line was gone and in the meantime we made a couple of points playing stickball or punchball from two-fifteen to two-thirty. But one of the teachers, who was teaching us Talmud, saw us and was upset by the fact that we, who were aspiring to be rabbis, could do such a thing, "play like little children with a ball." So this teacher comes down from where he is watching, takes the tennis ball, takes a knife out of his pocket, cuts it into little pieces, and tosses it down with disdain.

All right, that was that, and it was time to go for lunch, so we went for lunch. But one of our buddies didn't show up to eat with us. Back at the *yeshiva* we said to him, "Where were you for lunch?" and he said, "I just sent this letter to the Rebbe" and held out a carbon copy of a letter. He had run into his dormitory room and quickly typed a letter: "Dear Lubavitcher Rebbe, *Shlita,* I want to know what kind of a *yeshiva* you are running here. In the *Shulhan Arukh* it says you shouldn't be eating without warming up your stomach. A whole day we have been squeezing the bench and haven't been moving around. We are simply doing really what it says we should be doing. What right did this teacher have to come and take that ball from us and cut it into pieces? So tell me—if this was done at your say-so and with your consent, I don't want to be in this *yeshiva* anymore. Sincerely yours," and he signed it with his Hebrew name and his mother's name. We read it and said, "Oh, Yankel, what are you doing? You're going to have to pack your bags." But he was resolute. "I really mean it. I gave it to the Rebbe's secretary, and as soon as I gave it to him, he was on his way up to the Rebbe's office, and he took that letter along."

In those days, the schools would get milk in little six-ounce bottles. They were made of glass and had little cardboard tops. Over the next couple of days, there was no ball around, but we still didn't run to get our food. We still wanted to move around. So we made a game of seeing how many crates of empties we could push up and down. So there I was, counting, "Twenty-eight, twenty-nine," when everybody froze, looking up. I held the crates in the air to look up too. His secretary had wheeled the Rebbe out onto the porch in his wheelchair. He looked down at me and then turned his head very slowly as if to say, "All right, put it down." I put down the bottles, and he looked at us with a very benign smile, turned to his secretary, removed the lid from a box, and with both hands leaning over the railing tossed down a dozen tennis balls to us.

And the teacher who had destroyed our first tennis ball came running to catch one of the balls tossed by the Rebbe so that he could have a special memento, "A ball from the Rebbe!" So with all the Rebbe's important affairs, he was still concerned with the boys in the *yeshiva*.

He was also a miraculous person. The Rebbetzin, his wife, would go every once in a while to the refectory to taste the food that was made for the *yeshiva* boys. That was sort of her quality control. And so the cook was really inspired by that to make sure that the food was good. One day, she comes down and looks at the cook and says, "What's going on? Are you sick?" The cook replies, "I don't know. I haven't been feeling so well," whereupon the Rebbetzin explodes, saying, "From the whole world people come to my husband for prayer, and you, who are feeding our boys here in the *yeshiva,* if you're not feeling well, why don't you go and see him? Let's see what he can do for your healing." The Rebbetzin then grabs the cook and takes her up to the Rebbe's office. "This is the cook," she says to her husband. "She needs a *refuah,* a healing." The Rebbe looks at the cook, opens his desk, takes out a blank sheet of paper, writes a note, puts the note inside an envelope, seals the letter, and addresses it to a Viennese doctor who was living in Washington Heights at that time. He tells the cook, "Make an appointment and go see him." So she makes an appointment and goes to see him. She has the letter in her pocket, but she doesn't show it to the doctor. And the doctor looks her over and can't find anything wrong with her. At that point, she takes out the letter and hands it to him. He reads the letter and starts to examine her again. Then he orders that she be operated on the next week, and that operation saved her life.

He was truly remarkable, and those are the kinds of stories that go along with the teachings of the Rebbes. He was *human* and *extraordinary.*

Reb Yosef Yitzhak died in 1950, and his son-in-law, Reb Menachem Mendel Schneerson, succeeded him. And for a time I was his Hasid also. And he too was a remarkable Rebbe, all the more so for his ability to adapt to changing times.

I remember I once had a run-in with his "chief of staff," as it were, Reb Chaim Mottle Yisrael Hodakov.[6] He was quite a person. In Latvia, where every minority had its own educational institution, Hodakov was the minister of Jewish education. Hodakov was familiar with Dewey, Kilpatrick,[7] and everybody else who had written anything on education. I once came to see him and mentioned that I had figured out how the Rebbe in one of his writings, Reb Menachem Mendel, was answering some of the questions that came out of existentialism. I said, "In every generation, it is curious to see how the Rebbes always respond to what was going on in that generation." And he said, "No! It is always the same way. Each one is doing exactly what the other one had done before!" He was very rigid on this. He could not allow that there was movement, that there was a kind of dialogue going on, even if the dialogue was not explicit. Yet I had heard it explicitly. For example, it was Purim in the year 1951 and Reb Menachem Mendel gave a talk. I recall the words: "Scientists have found out that a small amount of quantity can release fantastic amounts of energy and quality. *Avraham Aveinu* was like nuclear energy. He was one human being only. But look what an explosion of spirituality that he brought about!" It was interesting that he used this language, but it is also not so far-fetched. He had studied engineering in France and for a while had even served the war effort by working in the Brooklyn Navy Yard to help design submarines. So it was not that he was not acquainted with modern science. But I always find that there are some who don't want to admit that the Rebbes interact with their environment, that they are adaptable.

Recall the story of the Ba'al Shem Tov and the mystic circle, when he placed his hands on his disciples and they were singing and the Maggid of Mezritch had the thought criticizing the Ba'al Shem Tov. And later on, the Maggid says that he only found his consolation when he saw in a supernal vision that Moses was teaching the little children that even the righteous are flawed because of the flesh.

There is an interesting story told of Reb Shneur Zalman. Once, when the Russian soldiers were coming for him, he slipped out the rear window of the house and began to run away, fearing that they might shoot him. Suddenly, he heard someone coming up behind him. He turned to see his Hasid, Reb Shmuel Munkes. He stopped, and Reb Shmuel said to him, "What are you doing running away? What's the matter with you?" And Reb Shneur Zalman said, "You don't want them to shoot me, do you?" Reb Shmuel replied, "If you are really the Rebbe, then nothing will happen to you. And if you are not, then maybe you deserve to be shot for impersonating a Rebbe." The Rebbe looked at him, turned back, and climbed back in the window.

Therefore, even a *Tzaddik* has a body, and in the body there arise all kinds of impulses and thoughts. So I don't know, if Reb Shneur Zalman could have written a book for the *Tzaddik,* maybe we would know the answer. But the question that I have is, if you really had to show a *Tzaddik* certificate, how many copies could he have sold? On the other hand, he writes a book for the *Beynoni* and everybody can aspire to be a *Beynoni* and that's what he puts in the book.

However, it is interesting that not everybody used that definition of *Tzaddik.* Because even Reb Shneur Zalman refers to those who say, "Well, if you have more good deeds than bad deeds, it adds up for a *Tzaddik.*" But that is a *Tzaddik* only by the statistics of behavior, not by the quality of really having been someone who is transformed into a *Tzaddik.* For Reb Nachman of Bratzlav, the true *Tzaddik* was not a Reb Shneur Zalman *Tzaddik.* Reb Nachman conceived more the person whose genius is inflamed with God and so is never the same two days in a row. For Reb Shneur Zalman there is the sense that a *Tzaddik* is mostly the same. Reb Nachman says, I've done everything that I could do in the body, and I don't want to hang around anymore—I don't want two days to be the same. He also says that each person has to find the spark within, the internal *Tzaddik,* because if you don't find the *Tzaddik* inside yourself, you won't find him on the outside either. Reb Nachman was talking about how the great *Tzaddik* on the outside was like the sun, but you have to have a moon inside of you.

I heard something very beautiful from Rabbi David Zeller.[8] He was talking about light, how the infinite light streams out. But you never see the light itself. You only see what interferes with the light and reflects the light. And this is still something that I'm working on to see fully. So it turns out that the best reflection of the light is the place where we are not quite transparent. In the New Testament, Paul writes, "Now we see through a glass darkly, but then we shall see as we are seen." This statement of Paul's is taken from an expression in Hebrew that was originally borrowed from the Latin. The Latin word *specularia* in Hebrew becomes *aspoklarya. Aspoklarya m'irah* in Hebrew is like window glass, totally transparent, and *aspoklaria sh'ayno m'irah* is like a mirror, which has that opaque reflecting character. So now we see as though in a mirror. It is as if you want to see the sun at a solar eclipse, the best way to do it is to see the reflection of the sun and not the sun itself. Otherwise, it will burn your eyes.

It has been said that a flaw is necessary for anyone who is a creature that is not God. That is the notion of an opal. It reflects the light and can be very beautiful, but it can also be like a cracked pebble. Which way is it? It is both. We all have a blind spot where we are finite and not infinite.

SOUL MATTERS

ALL RIGHT, we have gone over the categories; now let's go back and fill in some of the details we have glossed over.

The Animal Soul and the Body

Reb Shneur Zalman writes:

The explanation is to be found in the light of what Rabbi Chayyim Vital wrote in *Sha'ar HaKedushah* (and in *Etz Chayyim*, Portal 50, ch. 2) that in every Jew, whether a *Tzaddik* or a *Rasha,* are two souls, as it is written, "The *neshamot* (souls) which I have made," [alludes to] two souls. One soul derives from the *k'lipat* and the "Other Side" (*Sitra Achara*) and is clothed in the blood of a human being, giving vitality to the body, as it is written, "For the life of the body is in the blood." From it comes all the evil characteristics, deriving from the four evil elements, which are contained in it. These [characteristics] are anger and pride, which derive from the element of fire, whose nature is to rise upward; the desire for pleasures, from the element of water, for water causes to grow all kinds of enjoyment; frivolousness, ridicule, boasting, and idle talk from the element of air; and laziness and melancholy from the element of earth.[1]

Here he points out that we have an Animal Soul (*Nefesh HaBehamit*), an animal nature. How interesting it is that he speaks of the four elements, fire, water, air, and earth, and says that certain qualities derive from them. You can understand how laziness is an earth quality or anger is a fire quality, or how talking a lot is an air quality ("a lot of hot air"). And water is desire or longing. Let's say that I have an earth body and am sluggish, lazy. Or a fire body and I am racing and fervent. I have to deal with an Animal Soul through these elements. But is it all negative? Earth qualities make you lazy, the water qualities make you lustful, the fire qualities make you angry, the air qualities make you talk a lot, and Reb Shneur Zalman speaks only about the negative sides of those. Are there some positive sides? The answer is yes. These are sprinkled throughout the *Tanya*. When he speaks of the fire in prayer, the fire of fervor, the air of understanding, and the love for God that is like water, he calls it like water flowing, like water reflecting an image; so is the heart of one person to another person. So if we meditate on the kindness that God has done to us, how else can we respond but also with love? With earth it is a little bit harder to say what the good qualities are. But I think that they are the ones that ask us to be grounded.

Sometimes the Animal Soul is described in terms of actual animals. Chabadniks say, this guy is an ox. But don't get angry at an ox; you get a lot of harvests out of an ox. This guy is a lion, passionate and ferocious. This guy is a goat, stubborn. You don't get any wool, and if it is a he-goat, you can't even milk him. So they would talk about Animal Souls in that way. There is a wonderful person, Eligio Gallegos,[2] who teaches people about the totem animals in them. He says you can bring your totem animals to a powwow. If you have to make a difficult decision, you have to make sure that all the animals inside of you agree.

So we have an animal nature and a Divine nature. And you can understand that by separating them into these two things, you would get into a very tense relationship between the two. One wants to fly and go beyond, to transcend, and the other says, "I want my dinner!" This is the battle that the people have. What makes a *Tzaddik* is that a *Tzaddik* has so well tamed the Animal Soul that the Animal Soul is totally transparent to the Divine Soul and has no other will but that of the Divine Soul. But some confusion comes up around the relationship between the Animal Soul and the body, which is intensified by certain comments that Reb Shneur Zalman makes:

Just as the Divine Soul consists of ten holy *Sefirot* and is clothed in three holy garments, so does the soul that is derived from the Other Side, of the *K'lipat Nogah,* which is clothed in man's blood, consist of ten "crowns of impurity." . . . The abiding-place of the Animal Soul (*Nefesh HaBehamit*), deriving from the *K'lipat Nogah* in every Jew, is in the heart, in the left ventricle that is full of blood. It is written, "For the blood is the *Nefesh.*" Hence all lusting, boastfulness, anger, and like passions are in the heart, and from there they are disseminated throughout the whole of the body, rising also to the brain in the head, where one thinks and meditates on them and thus becomes skillful in them—just as the blood has its origin in the heart, from the heart it circulates into every limb, and also rising to the brain in the head.[3]

And later he says:

This ability and quality of connecting one's "knowledge" to God is present in every soul of the house of Yisrael by virtue of its nurturing from the soul of Rabbenu Moshe, peace be unto him. However, since the soul has garbed itself in the body, it needs a profound and powerful exertion, doubled and redoubled: First, one wearies the flesh, crushing the body into submission, so that it may not obscure the light of the soul. . . .[4]

There is a lot of confusion around the *Nefesh HaBehamit*, the natural part of the Animal Soul, and the habits of the body. And when Reb Shneur Zalman talks about this, it sometimes tends to sound like self-flagellation. However, it is not the body that he is against, because his master, the Maggid of Mezritch, made it very clear to him at one point when he was doing a lot of ascetic practices that "a small hole in the body makes a big hole in the soul. Just be careful to treat the body right." So it's not that they didn't want the body to be healthy. That is not at all what he was advocating. So let's get this straight. There is a difference between body and the *Nefesh HaBehamit*, the Animal Soul.

In Sufism, there is a teaching about the *Nafs*. The Arabic word *Nafs* is a translation of the Hebrew word *Nefesh*, and it stands for that selfish thing that seeks only its own pleasure. That is the saboteur of the desires of the soul. So Sufis advocate that one should wage the *jihad*, the holy war, against the *Nafs*. You see that kind of opposition. It is not the body; it is the series of habits and urges that represent the body, what Reb Shneur Zalman would call the Animal Soul. That is a big difference.

Let's say you are going to do tai chi, yoga, or chi-gung, or the doctor tells you to spend a half-hour a day in a "really brisk walk." That is my yoga these days. *Oy!* does my *Nefesh HaBehamit* not want to do it. "It's lousy weather outside." I come up with a thousand different reasons why I can't do it today. And then when I do it, I feel good, and my body feels good. So I see it is not the body. It is what disguises itself as the body's will; that is what Reb Shneur Zalman calls the Animal Soul. Or imagine that you have to take medicine, and you say, "I don't like this medicine. I hate this medicine. I have a gag reflex when I take it. But I have to take the medicine or I won't get well." Is it the body that doesn't want to take the medicine? The body is going to get healed with the medicine. What is that that makes you not want to do it? Let's take this in another direction, in which I think you'll be able to recognize yourself. What are the things that you know you shouldn't be doing to your body and you do them anyway? And why is that? Is it the body that wants you to do it, or is it a habit that you have given over to the body?

So Reb Shneur Zalman isn't pushing to break the body. What he is talking about is giving voice to the habits of the body and making them undeservingly strong. What he wants to break is the compulsion. He is saying that it affects the soul, that the two are inextricable. And the best way to deal with that is to say, "You want? Well, you can go on wanting." In Saul Bellow's *Henderson the Rain King*,[5] there is a scene in which part of him says, "I want, I want, I want," and then he says, "All right, what do you want? I'll give it to you." And it keeps on saying, "I want, I want." It isn't anything in particular, for he says, "I've given it food, women, everything, and it still keeps on saying, 'I want.'" I think Reb Shneur Zalman wants to break the compulsion of that. And when the body can become a good instrument for the soul, that is much better.

It is undeniable that the *Tanya* is lacking in positive language about the body, but that reflects the thinking of its time. Reb Nachman of Bratzlav tried to do a little to redress this situation, saying, "Everything your soul experiences you should also teach your body." But if we make this necessary distinction between the body and the Animal Soul, I think a lot of things straighten up around this issue.

The Divine Soul

The second soul of a Yisraelite is truly a part of God above, as it is written, "And He breathed into his nostrils the breath of life," and "Thou didst breath it [the soul] into me." And it is written in the Zohar, "He who exhales, exhales from within him," that is to say, from his inwardness and his innermost vitality that man emits through exhaling with force.[6]

Reb Shneur Zalman talks about the four qualities that make up the Animal Soul at the end of the first chapter and then goes on and says, "And now let me talk about the second soul, the Divine Soul." The Divine Soul is like a hologram of God, just as we speak of God as having the ten attributes of the ten *Sefirot,* the Divine Soul has these attributes too.

Now this particular section has some bearing on issues of meditation. So let's look closely at it with the original Hebrew, which is so much richer. Now, whenever you see the word *Yisrael,* this could be an inclusive rather than an exclusive word, provided you read it as "God-wrestler." So the Hebrew says, *V'nefesh hasheini b'Yisrael,* and often a translation will say, "of a Jew." So the translation limits it, rather than the Hebrew original. "It is truly a part of God above." What is so amazing is that when you go to the Hebrew wording, the English makes it sound really weak, because you can't quite say it the same way you can in Hebrew. *Chelek Elo'ah mima'al mamash. Mamash* has a sense of being able to touch it, palpably so. Reb Shneur Zalman is saying that the second soul, the Divine Soul, is truly a part of the living God, and so whenever we speak of a snippet of a hologram, it contains everything that is in the hologram. In the same way are we a part of God.

Now let's talk a little about the "as it is written" so that we understand it in context. How do I know that something is so? Today we say because we have empirical evidence. We have tested it and all of us have come to the conclusion that this is the way it is. In other words, we collude to say that we all agree that this is what we mean by this sign. Language falls under that kind of agreement. How do we know that a fact is a fact? My friend Reb Shloima often used to say, "everybody knows," speaking in hyperbole on how we agree about certain conventionalities. What does it mean that everybody knows? That it is generally agreed that this is so. At one point, everybody knew that the world was flat. So that was one way of establishing truth, we all agree. And it was at that time a self-evident truth. Nothing is self-evident, but when I want to say that we have a collusion to agree that this is so, this is our traffic control. We agree that this is so, and that is the collusion.

Now, if you believe that scripture is the word of God, the way that Reb Shneur Zalman sees it, it is *Chohmato u'retsono yitbarakh*, meaning "it is God's wisdom and will." The clearest test of anything at the time was "Where is it written?" And when you could say that something is written in scripture, that made it so; it was true. So whenever you are dealing with a society that lives by quoting from scripture, saying *Kemo sh'katuv*, "as it is written," or *Sh'ne'emar*, "as it was said," that provides immediate proof that this is so. The text is proof for what you are saying. And this is the way in which people dealt with these texts, as proof texts. It is similar to when people told time by the ringing of the bells of the town; it was very clear what time it was. So too with scripture. If you could prove something by scripture, Q.E.D., *quod est demonstrandum*, it has been demonstrated, this becomes clear.

We don't treat proof texts the same way nowadays. What does proof text mean for us? If I want to say that something is really so, we mean that it corresponds to a pattern that sits very deep in our reality map. So by referring to scripture, we want to say, this is a very strongly shared thing. First of all, I can't guarantee most of the time that scripture has been translated right. When I meet somebody who is a fundamentalist Christian, I often have problems with the way in which they quote from the King James version, as if this was the original way in which the text was given. It was not, and often the translation is faulty. Sometimes a big theological edifice is built on the mistranslations. I'll give you an example. In Isaiah, where the story is told that a child will be born unto us, it says "Behold, an *alma* will give birth." *Alma* has been translated in the Greek as *parthenos,* and therefore into English as *virgin,* a virgin will give birth, when the Hebrew word simply means a "young woman." So you have to check carefully what translations are saying. We use texts now not so much as a proof but as analogy. One of my friends says, "Treat the text no worse than an analyst would treat a dream."

"And God breathed into his nostrils the breath of life." You can imagine here somebody performing mouth-to-mouth resuscitation. There is blowing into. And what is happening at the other end? Taking the breath in—the in-breath. "And it says, He breathed into his nostrils the in-breath of life, *Nishmat chayyim.*" The out-breath is *Nefesh. Ruach* is breath. And the in-breath is *Neshamah.* So there is that first moment, and any of you who have ever been present at a birth and have watched the newly born take a first breath, it has such a powerful wow effect. Those are the moments that a Catholic would make the sign of the cross.[7] Because it is so awesome to watch a child take that first breath, and sometimes the cry comes.

So the point Reb Shneur Zalman wants to make is what happens in the out-breath of the one who gives the breath? From where do I breath? From my deepest place. If you watch breath, you get that sense—it goes so deep inside and comes out from so deep. So he is saying it comes from the very deepest place, not from the periphery of God, as it were. "He who exhales," says the Zohar, "exhales from within him"—that is to say, from his inwardness, from his innermost being.

For it is something of his internal and innermost vitality that a person emits through exhaling with force.

Speaking allegorically, the souls of Jews have arisen from the [Divine] thought, as it is written, "My firstborn son is Yisrael." You are children of the Lord, your God. That is to say, just as a child originates in his father's brain, to use an anthropomorphism, the soul of every Yisraelite is derived from the thought and wisdom of God, blessed be He. For He is wise—but not with a wisdom that is knowable. He and his wisdom are one.[8]

In a text called *Patach Eliyahu,*[9] Elijah opened the discourse saying, "Thou art wise, but not in known wisdom." In other words, we have a sense of what wisdom is about and who is the source of wisdom. So there was that sense of God's being the source of wisdom, but the wisdom that we know is only a reflection of a reflection of a reflection of the Divine wisdom. And what conclusion can we draw from the reflections? Just the quality of wisdom. The vastness of that wisdom we cannot get to. Now these anthropomorphic references to "father" and "child" that Reb

Shneur Zalman is using are based on something that the Talmud says: "Three partners are in a human being, there is a father, there is a mother, and there is God." Ram Dass[10] likes to say, "I am Jewish only on my parents' side." The meaning of this is that we have our parents' side and we have the Divine side from which we are begotten, as it were. If you think of what comes to us from the Divine aspect of our being, he says, we are of the very same substance, and the quote is, "What does the father give? Everything that is white. And what does the mother give? Everything that is red." Blood and muscles and everything that is red in a person. The red fluids are from the mother. Why do these people come to that conclusion? The monthly period and birthing makes that really clear to them. The white, that is what you see as semenlike. Now, people have found out that not only semen but serum and lymph are white, muscle and tissue and tendons are white. More than that, the spinal cord is white, and the brain is sort of whitish, too, and there is a fluid that the brain is bathed in. So the semen and brain fluid are seen to be as one and the same substance. And when you speak of the child, you are saying that what the father contributes is very much the same substance as brain fluid. In this analogy, the Divine Soul in each person is also of the very same substance, as it were, as what Reb Shneur Zalman calls the Divine brain.

The feminine will be the focus when he talks about the Divine Presence, the *Shekhinah*. But one can't make all one's points at once, and the point Reb Shneur Zalman wants to make right now is to say that each soul is "a chip off the old block." I say it in this light, humorous way, but there is a chant, "It is perfect, you are loved, all is clear, and I am holy." In which way can I say that "I am holy"? When I refer to the Divine Soul within me. I can say, with Hazrat Inayat Khan, "This is not my body; this is the temple of God." It is not just a body, not just flesh; something deep resides there. I remember having an old Hasid read this portion to me and saying, "Even at this time, we are still connected to God":

The way of this descent is analogous to that of a son who originates in the father's brain, and so even the nails of his feet come into existence by way of the drop of semen being in the mother-womb for nine months, evolving step by step, continually transforming until the very nails are formed from it. And yet through all this process, it is still bound and unified in a wonderfully essential oneness with the original essence, the father's brain, from which came the drop. Even now in the son, the nails are still nourished and live from the brain that is in the head.[11]

What kind of meditative tool did he give us here? The sense that we are never separated from God. He is saying that we are still connected at this moment. Can you be in touch with the Divine Soul? If you can be in touch with the Divine Soul, there has never been any separation. You are still one with God, just as the nails of the toes are still connected with the substance of the brain of the father.

Do you understand what he is saying? No, it is not where we are today with our science. But it is where people were in Reb Shneur Zalman's day, and he is using this as an analogy. So if you were to say that the analogy doesn't hold true by current medical understanding, that doesn't matter, and I'll tell you why. I have never yet found a pathologist who has cut a corpse apart and found for me the *sushumna nadi,* where the *kundalini* rises.[12] You see, we are not talking about the physical body at all; we are talking about something like an ethereal body, the "subtle body," as they call it in Hindu traditions. And what he is doing is using an analogy that we can connect with or at least his listeners could connect with. Today, we like to use more technical language. If I say "hologram," you can understand.

That is an important way of saying that nothing has changed. Today, when most people think of meditation, they think of having to empty one's mind or watching one's breath. However, in the case of the meditation of Chabad, which is the school Reb Shneur Zalman founded, meditation means planting in your awareness such a strong notion that it enters into your reality map; it creates affect and feeling. And most important, action directives come from that planting. So you can imagine somebody who feels suicidal paying attention to what Reb Shneur Zalman is saying here. It's not just that I *have* a Divine Soul but that I *am* a Divine Soul. Do you understand the difference? I have a body, but I *am* a Divine Soul.

Someone was sharing with me recently about a member in the family who was dying and was having a hard time dying. And we were talking about the thing that gives the hardest time is an identification that my "I am-ness" is nothing but my body. When my sister was dying from cancer, she also was having a really hard time. It was breast cancer that had spread all over, and she felt as if she would be forever locked into the crippled, no longer useful, painful body she was experiencing at that particular time. And when we talked about this some more and what it means to drive an old car to the junkyard and to get out before they crush it, she had such a sense of relief. She would no longer be a prisoner of that body. One of the teachings about the afterlife is to learn to say, "I am not my body. This body is worn out, but I have other organisms. I have a spiritual organism. I have a mental organism. I have an affective organism; only the physical organism is being discarded at this point. I am not dying just because I am giving up my body." The sooner you can make that distinction, the better. It is common in spiritual traditions to hear talk of death as "giving up the body"; sometimes it is talked about as "dropping the body," as if whatever was supporting it moved on. Hearing this, you get the sense of what it means to say, "What am I? I am a drop of the Divine ocean." It is another way of saying the same thing Reb Shneur Zalman is saying. What would be the ultimate thing that could happen? That the drop would flow back into the ocean and become one with the ocean. Am I diminished by that, or am I enriched by that? Jalaluddin Rumi[13] has this wonderful sentiment: "I was born a stone, and then I died as a stone. And I was resurrected as a plant, and I died as a plant. And I was resurrected as an animal, and I died as an animal. I was resurrected as a human being, and I died as a human being. I was resurrected as an angel, and I died as an angel. And then I was resurrected in God. O death, where is thy sting, if by thy means I have gained so much?" You could imagine that a caterpillar might be getting into all kinds of sadness, but somehow I have a feeling that caterpillars know that they are going to come out as butterflies. And do you remember the sign that Elisabeth Kübler-Ross used for Shanti-Niliah, her organization? It was a butterfly.

Now let's look at the very last part of chapter two of the *Tanya*:

As for what is written in the Zohar, the *Zohar Chadash*, to the effect that the fundamental factor is to behave in a sacred manner during sexual union, which is not the case with the children of the unlearned. It should be understood as meaning that since there is not a *Nefesh, Ruach, Neshamah*, which has not a garment of the *Nefesh* of the father and mother's essence, and all the *mitzvot* that it fulfills are shaped by that garment. Even the loving-kindness that flows to one from heaven is all given through that garment, and thus, through self-sanctification, one will cause the descending of the *Neshamah*, the sacred garment, of one's child. But however great a soul it may be, it will still need the father's sanctification.[14]

I'll tell you a story that will illustrate that a little bit:

Reb Shneur Zalman had a son named Dov Baer. And when Dov Baer was doing his prayers, you couldn't hear a sound from him. He was totally still when he was engaged in prayer. However, his secretary (sort of a butler) would come in while he was in the middle of prayer and take off his shirt and replace it with a fresh one, because the former was soaked with perspiration and tears. Both of these. In other words, there was no outward sign, but on the inside it was all cooking for him. One day, his father sends him on an errand to give a message to somebody in a small town. After he has completed his errand, he is standing there doing his prayers in the synagogue and he sees a man walking around and screeching his prayers, loud and noisy, all over the place. That was not Dov Baer's style at all. Later on he spoke to the man, saying, "What kind of a way is this to pray?" and then mockingly imitated him. And the man grabbed him roughly by the shirt and said, "Berel"—he called him by his first name, not showing him any respect—"what did your father have in mind when he made you and what did my father have in mind when he made me?" This so shocked Dov Baer that he immediately begged the man's forgiveness. When he came back to his father, he said, "Father, I haven't yet really begun to serve God. I've been given such a wonderful transparent garment, and other people have not had such a beautiful and transparent garment." And he was crying and he said, "Father, I have not put in as much effort as this person has put in." Later on, when the man came to visit Reb Shneur Zalman, the Rebbe asked that someone bring in some schnapps and some cookies, and he treated that man, and he said to him, "I want to thank you. You have made a Hasid out of my son. If you hadn't challenged him in such a way, he would have thought that anybody who doesn't measure up to his level is a low-life; he wouldn't have recognized how much work it takes to work through, to become more and more transparent."

The issue here is so clear, and this is what yoga and all these other things are about: to make the body and the Animal Soul, as it were, a more and more transparent and willing subject. To allow them to do what is required. So that is what Reb Shneur Zalman brings us to right now.

Nefesh, Ruach, Neshamah, Chayyah, and *Yechidah*

Let's look at the beginning of chapter three. I said before that *Neshamah* is in-breath and *Nefesh* is out-breath. You get that in the description of the first Sabbath, as it says in Genesis, "And on the seventh day God rested, and he exhaled." Imagine the sound of the exhalation as it passes the teeth and the shhh sound it makes. That is the same shhh one hears in *Nefesh*. To breathe out and to be in a place of rest. The out-breath places one in that sense of rest. With the in-breath you are breathing something in from the environment, and if you think of oxygen as that Divine thing that keeps you alive, then it is such a powerful act. Now, what do you breathe out? Carbon dioxide. So you get a sense of how this is. As I said before, in Arabic, the word for *Nefesh* is *Nafs*. If you are involved with Sufism, you will know that *Nafs* basically stands for the Animal Soul. And when they are talking about the *Ruh*, the spirit of God, *Ruh Allah*, they are saying this would be able to fly and do the adoring thing if the *Nafs* would let it. But the *Nafs* is sort of holding it back. So that is one way in which we talk about *Nefesh*.

If I were to come up with a description, I would say that *Nefesh* is the energy body, the astral body. *Ruach*, I would say, is a lot more the angelic body. *Neshamah* is closer to the Divine. So in *Ruach* you have the affect and the emotions; and the pure intellect that beholds the Divine with the clear mind, as it were, is the *Neshamah*. But there are souls still higher than the *Neshamah*, where the deep intuition resides, and these are called *Chayyah* and *Yechidah*. So there are five soul parts. Why five? Think about how many distinctions an artist might make with respect to the color blue. When you are so immersed in a thing, you begin to see many subtle distinctions not obvious to others. I think we have many words for soul in order to distinguish the levels, because they are not all the same. So it is a very particular kind of soul we are talking about when we say, "The soul that Thou hast breathed into me is pure."

In this system, we speak even of stones and plants as having *Nefesh,* animals having *Ruach,* and human beings having *Neshamah*. And the curious statement goes like this: "And God blew into his nostrils the breath of life, and the human being became a living being." *Vay'hee ha'Adam l'nefesh chayyah*. So, the *Targum*[15] translates it as *Ruach M'mallelah*, the human being became a speaking spirit. Thus they made the categories *domem tzomeach chay um'dabber*, inanimate, plant, animal, and speaker. A human being is seen as someone who can speak, who has language. And that is connected with *Neshamah*. I wouldn't say that there isn't a kind of rudimentary *Neshamah* available to animals. I wish I could understand the clicks of the dolphins, for instance. And people have learned to communicate with apes, so there is some kind of language there, and bees communicate using a kind of dance. So I don't know, from my perspective, I can't say more than that. But this is also connected with the elements. The element of earth is connected with the inanimate; the element of water is connected with plant; the element of air, breath, is connected then with fauna; and the element of fire is connected with human beings.

Concerning the *Nefesh* in stones, people often say to me, "Come on, how could that be?" But you know, some people believe that wearing a crystal will help them when they are not feeling well. What is active in that? It's a good *Nefesh* in that crystal that does something. And if my computer didn't have silicon chips inside, it wouldn't have memory. If that isn't *Nefesh*, I don't know what is. One can speak of the capacity to contain.

For animals, we speak about the capacity to contain *Ruach* also. And sometimes I think my cat has a *Ruach* that is hard for me to communicate with. She knows how to get to me, but I don't know how to get to her. But when I had a dog, I was really able to communicate with the dog's *Ruach;* that was a whole other thing. I think I had a connection. So when we talk about *Neshamah,* we are talking about human beings, and this also has to do with the brain. The reptilian brain is where *Nefesh* resides, the limbic brain is where *Ruach* resides, the cortex is where *Neshamah* resides, and the unformatted or yet to be formatted parts of the brain are perhaps where *Chayyah* and *Yechidah* reside.[16]

ATTRIBUTES AND GARMENTS
OF THE SOUL

Now, each of the three grades of distinction—*Nefesh, Ruach,* and *Neshamah*—consist of ten faculties, corresponding to the Celestial Ten *Sefirot* (Divine manifestations), from which they are descended, which are also subdivided into two, namely, the three "mothers" and the seven "multiples," that is: *Chokhmah* (wisdom), *Binah* (understanding), and *Da'at* (knowledge); and the "seven days of creation": *Chesed* (kindness), *Gevurah* (power), *Tiferet* (beauty), and so on.

It is a similar case with the human soul, which is also divided in two—*sekhel* (intellect) and *middot* (emotional attributes). The intellect includes *Chokhmah, Binah,* and *Da'at.*[1]

Here we see what this form of Hasidism is about: wisdom, understanding, and knowledge, the acronym of these three Hebrew words forming the word *Chabad.* What the Chabad Hasidim are doing is emphasizing a preferred style: just as Reb Levi Yitzhak is fire, feeling, and heart and Reb Elimelech is ascetic, Reb Shneur Zalman is the intellectual one. And sometimes this "intellectual" tag is applied critically. So let me say a little something about the marriage of intellect and devotion in Reb Shneur Zalman.

First, you must remember that we are reading the texts of people like Reb Shneur Zalman without their longing, without their melody, and without their prayer. And without these, they are going to seem dry, and that can't be helped. But remember when you are reading the *Tanya* that this same Reb Shneur Zalman, for all his wonderful intellectual capacity, was full of ecstasy when he was praying. The room where he prayed even had to be padded, because his ecstasy would take over and he could bump into things and he would begin to scream out in prayer, "I don't want your World-to-Come! I don't want your paradise! I only want You, You, You!" That doesn't come through in the text, but it's not because it isn't there. Books are filtered. The book was written in Hebrew and is being read in English. The book was written in nineteenth-century Russia under precarious circumstances, and where are we reading it now? And finally, we are no longer living in the context in which we used to study these things in the *yeshiva*. So the loss of immediacy can't be helped. The best we can do is try to conjure up an imagined context for the material.

Second, Reb Shneur Zalman uses a great many technical terms, but he does so in the context of Jewish culture in Belorussia and Lithuania. Many scholars there were like the "show me" Missourians. Their focus was study, study, study, and to get them to listen, you had to appeal to their sensibilities. So Reb Shneur Zalman said, "Let me show you a study that will open your heart." That is his way of sneaking it in. It had to be thoroughgoing for these "show me" people. You distract their minds by giving them complicated ideas they would recognize, endless quotes from the Talmud and the Zohar, until they say "uncle." Then they can look clearly and begin to feel the transformation it offers.

Third, let me say a word about the philosopher Baruch Spinoza.[2] Spinoza was not a very artistic person or an imaginative person, but he was a very intellectual one. And when he had to say something about how morals operate, he drew up a system of morals that was like Euclid's geometry. So you can see where his head was. He was all head. It is the kind of person you imagine with a big Adam's apple, a slight body, a big head, who looks at his body as merely that something with which to carry the head around. Everything is very intellectual for such a person. And yet he saw himself as someone who loves God. How could he talk about loving God? Well, his way of saying it was, *amor Dei intellectualis,* "I love God with my intellect." And you know, sometimes that happens for people. You have an insight into the nature of the universe, how it is made, how it is put together, and what its purpose is. And you say, "Oh, You did such a wonderful job!" You see, it spills over, as it were, from the mind into the heart.

For Reb Shneur Zalman, that idea is very important, because he says that you have to start with your *moach,* the *mochin* (*Chokhmah, Binah,* and *Da'at*), the "brains." What does he mean by that? Think of the brain. The right hemisphere has been compared to *Chokhmah,* wisdom. The left hemisphere has been compared to *Binah,* understanding. So the synthetic "aha!" of quality is in the right hemisphere. The analytical insight of coherence, trying to understand something thoroughly, is in the left hemisphere. And it is interesting that he said it this way before Langley Porter[3] and all the other people who did that brain hemisphere research. What is *Da'at*? *Da'at* is the cerebellum, the little brain in the back. And what happens in the cerebellum? That is the place where the switchboard is. We speak of it as the reticular formation system—what am I to pay attention to, and what am I to tune out? Millions of air molecules hit my eardrum, and I cannot hear them. Does it mean that I do not hear them? I hear them, but the sound gets filtered out through my cerebellum. When I focus on something and pay attention to it, and I don't notice other things, it is because the switchboard says, "The rest of it isn't important. This is a lot more important." Do you understand? *Da'at* is how we test reality. So we have *Chokhmah*, *Binah*, and *Da'at*. And these are called the brains.

Now *Chokhmah* (wisdom) is the source of penetration and comprehending, which is above *Binah* (understanding), the intellectual understanding and mentation—*Chokhmah* is above these and is their source. Notice the etymological composition of the word *Chokhmah*—*k'ch'm'h* ("the potentiality of what is"), that which is not yet registered and understood, or grasped with the intellect. . . .[4]

Let's look at how *Chokhmah* is spelled. *Mah* stands for "what." And if you turn *chokh* around, it is *koach*. *Koach* represents potential power, or strength. *Mah*, "what," also has some interesting linguistic peculiarities. Look at the relationship between *what* and *water*: *mah—mayim* in Hebrew, *qua—aqua* in Latin, *Was—Wasser* in German. Isn't it interesting that in all these languages you get a linguistic similarity between *what* and *water*? One day my wife was pouring some vinegar into a clear vase to clean it out because she couldn't get a brush into it. But because it was a vase and the contents looked clear, she told me it was vinegar. Well, what would have been my impression if she hadn't told me? It looked clear like water, and if I didn't take a whiff, I wouldn't have known what it was. It could have been muriatic acid. So it had to be smelled. It is basic for humanity to test water and to ask, "What?" Just keep that in mind. And what is it that I am asking when I ask, "What?" I am asking about the quality of something. *Qua*-lity, the "whatness" of something. It is interesting, when you have *quan*-tity, it is "how manyness." We don't have a good word for "howness." In English it would be *quiddity*, and I think some philosophers use it. In Hebrew, it would be *eikhut*. And if I want to discuss the "whatness" of a thing, I would call it *mahhut*. Now, it is easy to describe things as "square," "flat," "big," or "heavy." I could give all of what Aristotle calls the "accidents" of something. Those are the accidental parts, but what is the essence? Take that word, essence, from *esse*, "being," and we are back again to *qua*-lity. And who knows that in us, it is that part that is capable of concept formation, the conceptualizer. So that is not a left-brain situation but a right-brain situation. The left brain would analyze it into its components. This is what *Binah*, understanding, is doing. *Binah* is asking the question, "How is it put together?" *Boneh* is "to build." *Binah* is taking it apart so that you can understand how it was put together. Take the word *component* and now you *depone* what was *com*poned by the left brain. But it is the right brain, *Chokhmah,* that looks at something totally, holistically, and says, that is what it is, it is a "that." It is the total recognition of a thing. And so that is what Reb Shneur Zalman is talking about with respect to potentiality.

Here we are trying to understand how the mind functions. The right hemisphere represents *Chokhmah,* wisdom, and the left hemisphere represents *Binah,* understanding. Where the two of them meet in the cerebellum, at the little brain in the back, is *Da'at,* knowledge. Without this reticular formation system, without this switchboard, I would quickly be distracted from what I want to say or do. It tunes out irrelevant information. Now before there can be *Chokhmah, Binah,* and *Da'at,* you must have *kadmut ha'sekhel.* This comes before awareness; it is what in psychology is called a "psychological set." For example, you could be talking about the most innocent things, but if you had been talking dirty beforehand, the psychological set would predispose you to notice the raunchy stuff behind the new and innocent words. You would read something dirty into them. The psychological set sets you up, and that is called *kadmut ha'sekhel.* It has to do with a motivational circumstance, something that draws you to it. It is higher even than the conceptualizer and very often it has something to do with our love and the instinct for life. That is why that part of the soul is called *Chayyah* ("life").

Reb Shneur Zalman speaks of seven modes, which he explains later in the book, but I'll give you a preview of coming attractions. Attraction is a good word for the first one, it is called *Chesed,* grace. Again, like my Rolfer said, "Love on the most physical plane is two bodies in space attracting one another." You get that sense of attraction? It is also a sense of wanting to give, wanting to bestow. It is that sense of "I have an abundance that I want to give you. I feel so filled with goodies, I can't wait to share them." Then there is the other side, which says, "Is that the best way to deal with it?" You know, sometimes you have to have "tough love." "My kid stole, and if I bail him out this time and he doesn't go to jail, will he ever learn?" There is a time when you say, "This time I have to go the strict route," I have to go with rigor, *Gevurah.* So the right hand represents *Chesed,* grace, and the left hand represents *Gevurah,* strength, power, severity. What is between the right arm and the left arm? The heart. So that represents compassion, beauty, *Tiferet.* So Reb Shneur Zalman now has these three forming another section of a "body." The uppermost triad of *Chokhmah* (wisdom), *Binah* (understanding), and *Da'at* (knowledge) is like the head, and triad of *Chesed* (grace), *Gevurah* (severity), and *Tiferet* (compassion) are like the right arm, left arm, and heart at center.

Now here is the next triad, and this one is much harder to understand. It has to do with effectiveness and elegance. I can be very effective if I have a car that is built like a tank, you know. It is not going to break down and it is very strong, but it is also ugly. And then I have a Ferrari with beautiful lines, but it won't pull a trailer. *Netzach,* victory, is that powerful energy of function. And *Hod,* glory, is the beauty, the elegance that is there. Now, if *Chesed* is the right arm and *Gevurah* is the left arm and *Tiferet* is the heart, then the right leg is *Netzach,* the left leg is *Hod,* and the genitals are *Yesod,* foundation. And then comes *Malkhut,* kingdom, at the end. *Malkhut* representing, if you will, the feminine, or that which separates out; it is the seal of things. These are just a few short indications to guide you.

So these are the ten *Sefirot.* Where do we get the ten from? Reb Shneur Zalman is saying that this is the way it is in the universe, that this ten derives from God. The *Sefer Yetzirah*[5] often says, "ten and not nine, ten and not eleven," insisting that the number is ten. And this ten is made up of a three and a seven. These are the important numbers that will keep coming up.

One of the Hasidim once pointed this out, saying, "When the Kabbalah first appeared, it tried to bring to our understanding what God is like, and in order to explain it to us, it made God like a human being." Explaining that God's kindness is like the right arm and that God's severity is like the left arm, it uses the anthropomorphic understanding. "When Kabbalah came, it made of God a human; when Hasidism came, it made of the human a God."[6] It was a necessary development that first we should be able to ask, what can anyone say about God that makes sense? So the more we talked about God in personal terms, the more we could begin to relate. William James once asked a clergyman in New England, "What do you visualize when you stand in the presence of God?" And the minister replied, "I visualize an oblong blur."[7] I don't blame him for saying that, because he'd much rather say that than "I see a person" or "I see Michelangelo's God." So by saying an oblong blur, he is trying to do away with anthropomorphism. But I can't love an oblong blur. I can't confide in an oblong blur. I don't identify with that. So what we have done, we have each one of us tried to create a situation where we can speak of a personal God, a God who cares, to whom we can confide, share, and adore. And that is good, provided that we don't make an idol out of that. Because every once in a while, each of us has to break the mold of the God that we make for ourselves. So every Rosh HaShanah, every year at the High Holidays, I have to reconfigure my system as to who is God for me in the coming year. If I deal with the old God, I am going to be dealing with a childhood notion of God, and my relationship would be fixed at a very childish level. So I have to break the mold at least once a year to get rid of the old images that I have outgrown or made an idol of.

In the same way, there was a time in the Temple in Jerusalem when we offered animal sacrifices. And later it happened that the Temple was destroyed and we couldn't offer any more animal sacrifices, although they are commanded in the Torah. Now, some people say too bad, when we are able to build the Temple again, we will resume offering animal sacrifices. But they misunderstand something: it wasn't that the Temple was destroyed and therefore we could not offer animal sacrifices but that the form of offering animal sacrifices to God had already been outgrown. It was not a functional system anymore. So like a snake has to shed its skin, we have to shed the God images that we have.

What Reb Shneur Zalman is advocating is that as we assign to ourselves the notion of personality. For example, imagine that I have something wrong with me and the doctor says, "I am sorry to inform you that I may have to amputate your arm. But if I do it, you'll live." And some time later he says, "I have to amputate the other one." Then it's the leg. I would even go so far as giving up my eyes, you know, but if he says, "I don't have to do anything surgically to you except replace your memory, just give you a different identity, and then you can live a healthy life," the likelihood is, I would say it doesn't make any difference to me, I might as well die. Do you understand? Where does this come from? It comes from an understanding of what makes me a person is that I have my mind, my will, my feelings. Imagine what a terrible thing it was to give people prefrontal lobotomies. After that, the person was no longer a full human being and could not experience fullness of her or his own humanity. So what makes me a person is not my arms and legs; it is, following Reb Shneur Zalman, my *moach,* my *mochin,* and my *middot*—my mind, my feelings, and my will. Then the question is, how do I manifest these things?

Thought, Word, and Deed: The Garments of the Soul[8]

In addition, every Divine Soul (*Nefesh HaElokit*) has three garments—thought, word, and deed—which are expressed in the 613 *mitzvot* of the Torah. For when a person engages and fulfills all the laws that require physical deeds, and with his words he occupies himself in explaining all of the 613 *mitzvot* and their applications, and with the power of his thought he understands all that is understandable to him in the *pardes* of the Torah—then the whole of the 613 "organs" of his soul are clothed in the 613 *mitzvot* of the Torah.[9]

In chapter four of the *Tanya*, Reb Shneur Zalman starts talking about the soul, meaning the whole soul complex—Animal Soul, Divine Soul, and later on he brings in something that he calls the Rational Soul. The Rational Soul is a sort of intermediary between the Animal Soul and the Divine Soul. Because the Divine Soul is intuitive, the Animal Soul is reactive, instinctual, and emotional. The bridge is made by the Rational Soul. So the whole set of "soulness" is still not able to do its thing if it doesn't have the three garments. One of the garments is thought, the undershirt. Speech is the suit. And action is the coat. These are the three garments of the soul. Reb Shneur Zalman goes on to say, "I want to tell you, you can have dirty garments or you can have clean garments. You can have beautiful robes and you can have just lousy garb." How do you get beautiful robes? When you think those thoughts that God wants you to think, the commanded thoughts, then your innermost garment is a Divine garment, a splendid garment. But if you think thoughts that you shouldn't be thinking, either dirty ones or hateful ones or just foolish thoughts, what you are doing is taking a beautiful and holy soul and you are putting it into dirty garments.

Do you see how the notion of garments is understood? The *mitzvot* are the garments. What can I do for my mind? Reb Shneur Zalman comes with this remarkable understanding: "Every time I think, I put my mind into a Divine thought, something revealed by God, then my mind surrounds the idea." We say, "Do you grasp the idea?" My mind "grasps" an idea. But what idea am I grasping? I am grasping an idea of God, which then means, at the very moment when I'm grasping the idea, that the idea is also grasping my mind. To Reb Shneur Zalman, this is how we can have Heaven on earth. To put the mind into such a state that it is constantly in touch with the wisdom and the will of God—what more can I want? And to him this is a very clear mandate. Having the Torah and the commandments, I can wrap my soul in the garments of God. Think about the phrase "wrapping myself in garments." That is the original meaning of the word *invest*. So when I *invest* in something, it means I am putting it on as my garment, as it were. It becomes what I wear. Now you can see why it is so important that a person should have a repertoire of good thoughts.

Often when I talk to people who are doing spiritual eldering work [10] and getting older, I suggest that they should have a rosary of good memories. You come to the doctor's office, and you sit there waiting your turn, and what do you usually think about? All the complaints, your *kvetches*—this isn't right, this isn't good, poor me, I'm a victim. I like to use the tofu analogy. Tofu doesn't have any taste whatsoever. What makes tofu palatable and interesting is that you marinate it. Your mind is like tofu. It depends on what pickle juice you put your mind in. If the pickle juice is resentment and *kvetching,* this creates dis-ease, and you don't feel good. And if you marinate your mind in good things, you feel fine. Because, as Reb Shneur Zalman puts it, where the mind is, there is the rest of the person. Where the head is, there is the rest of the person. We have control. This is the thing that we don't "own" enough. We can learn the discipline of steering the mind. Most of us feel as if the mind is a toboggan we can't control. It is not true; we have freedom in the mind.

When people talk to me about the question of free will and predestination, they ask me which is true, freedom or predestination. I point out that there is no total predestination and there is no total freedom. For instance, I can't be a woman, and I can't be younger than I am right now. I am not free to change those things. But if someone were to point a gun at me and announce that I have but a minute to live, I have still have freedom in how to spend that minute. There is a beautiful story about a man who is hanging from a vine. Below is a tiger and above is a mouse gnawing on the vine. Pretty soon he is going to fall, but within reach is a luscious strawberry, and he spends that last moment enjoying this luscious strawberry. You have the freedom in your mind and the freedom to invest it in what you will.

Think about this in terms of programming. How nice it would be if, before you went to sleep at night, you could steer your mind toward what you would like to dream about or if, in the morning when you wake up, you could ask yourself, "With what do I want to fill my mind this morning?" Do you see why alarm clocks are so terrible? They wake us up in a burst of adrenaline; then we hit the coffee; then we have to make our way through traffic; and we are frazzled. No wonder, with such a diet upon awakening in the morning. Once in Bombay, I walked down from the hotel where I was staying to the harbor shortly after six in the morning. And the city's finest were promenading up and down and socializing, as apparently they did every morning. Thereafter, there were times when I just didn't want to sleep; I wanted to go down watch those people walk and talk to each other. What a civilized way of starting the day. Because they were already preparing, feeding the beautiful part of their soul by looking at the landscape, gazing on the ocean, seeing other people with whom they had friendly relations, and walking up and down. I witnessed the same thing in Rio de Janeiro. So the first thought upon arising is an important thing. The Buddhist teacher Chogyam Trungpa had a whole teaching about that first thought upon arising in the morning.

Let us now look more closely at the teaching of the garments, because the *how* of this is very important for transformation.[11]

The Hasidic teaching is that the soul, the *Neshamah*, differs from all material and spiritual creation in the fact that it is not a creature, a *nivra*. Angels, *mal'achim*, although they are spiritual, are creatures, *nivraim*. In other words, both matter and spirit have been created *yesh m'ayin*, *ex nihilo*, something out of a nothing. And suffice it to say, all of creation, this universe and the spiritual universes, are all creatures. However, the *Neshamah* is begotten of God, since it is of the very same substance as God, Blessed be He. In the same manner in which the child is part of the father, the *Neshamah* is *chelek Eloka mima'al mamash*, a veritable part of the supernal God. This is the decisive thing—it is not a severed, cut-off part of God but is rather part of God in the same sense as a brain cell is part of the brain. But even this is not completely accurate because the brain is made up of many brain cells and God is simple and not constructed from many *Neshamot*. And yet at the same time, each *Neshamah* is a part of God.

Our *chazal*[12] said that God fills the universe in the same manner as the *Neshamah* fills the body. On the other hand, the Elder Rebbe (Reb Shneur Zalman) warns us that while the *Neshamah* is affected by the accidents of the body, God is unaffected by the accidents of the world. Yet we can understand something about both God and the *Neshamah* if we see the Divine Presence indwelling in the spiritual universes and in this physical universe. So, too, does the *Neshamah* dwell in three modes of behavior: it must be "dressed," invested in any of the three garments, *l'vushim*, of the *Neshamah*. The three garments are *machshavah*, *dibbur*, and *ma'aseh*—thought, word, and deed.

First, let's look at the garment of deed, *ma'aseh*. It is obvious when we see a corpse, we realize and infer in a profound way that the dead body lacks something that is inherent in the living one. We do not see the *Neshamah*, but it is as if we saw it when we realize that a person acts in meaningful ways. Whenever a *Neshamah* is dressed in the garment, *l'vush*, of deed, *ma'aseh*, it acts like a subject acts on an object. The *Neshamah* via the garment of deed, or action, manages to manipulate the environment for its purposes. No *Neshamah* would wear *t'fillin* or eat *matzah* unless invested in the garment of deed and performing these *mitzvot* with the help of the body. The *Neshamah* could be thought of as an invisible being who becomes visible only by means of the garments she or he wears.

The garment of action is one that can be put on and taken off at will. In fact, each particular action and deed is a different garment. And there are functions that are holy in themselves. They are *mitzvot*, and they perform a very important function for the *Neshamah*.

The *Neshamah,* as it is dressed in the body, operates in the mode of *m'malle,* filling. It stands as if in the body and seeks to approach God, as if He stood outside of it in a *sovev,* surrounding, manner. Now, for all the holiness in the *m'malle* mode of the Divine indwelling, it is of a finite nature. It must be of a finite nature, for if it were of an infinite nature, it would not be able to dwell in any finite vessel. However, that which we, while living in the flesh, need to approach most and to make our very own is that which is beyond ourselves. God, as He is higher than creation and indwelling, is He Whom we wish to reach in *mitzvot.* Therefore, *mitzvot* come from the very high level of the Divine, from the level of *sovev,* the Divine radiation that is beyond and through the world as if it did not exist at all. Thus one may say that the indwelling God is the historical God, and the transcendent God is the eternal God Whom we wish to make our own in the *mitzvah* action. In God's grace, He confines the transcendent grace of His Being so that it can become a garment of light for the *Neshamah.* This is what happens when the soul invests itself in a *mitzvah.*

Since the *Neshamah* cannot reach these high levels unless it is "dressed" in a body and through the body in the garment of function, it has to come into this physical universe and live in a body of flesh. In order to achieve a higher level than its original level before it came down to invest itself in a body, it had to come down to this world of action. This, then, is the gracious purpose of God in the creation of the world, to enable a *Neshamah* to rise to the greatest heights after and through its descent.

Now, in the same way as the *Neshamah* acquires merit and the transcendental light by the action of the *mitzvah,* the opposite can occur when the *Neshamah,* by lack of vigilance, allows its intellect to become obscured and demented by the evil inclination, *yetzer ha'ra.* Then, like the deranged idiot who would dress himself in filthy rags, the *Neshamah* dresses itself in the function of evil. This is what we mean by an *aveyre.* The damage that this does, besides upsetting the cosmic structure and allowing the energy system of evil, *K'lipot,* to absorb the holy energies of the *Neshamah,* also stains the *Neshamah.* The stain that the *Neshamah* derives from an *aveyre* must be subsequently removed through repentance, *t'shuvah* (transgression), or *gehinnom* (purgatory).

There is also another group of garments, which are neither holy nor evil in themselves. They derive their energy from the system of *Nogah,* which, although a *K'lipot* system, is not altogether evil in itself. It is as if translucent, allowing light to pass through. The energy systems of the other *K'lipot* are completely opaque and do not permit any light of the *Neshamah* to pass through.

If one wished to use the following analogy, one could say that by doing *mitzvot*, the *Neshamah* manages to "stay in business." By doing *aveyres*, the *Neshamah* moves toward bankruptcy. But all the profit lies in the *Neshamah* dressing itself in the garments of *Nogah* for *mitzvot* purposes. Then, that portion of *Nogah* is added to *kedushah* on the credit side of the *Neshamah*. It would seem, therefore, that the *Neshamah* can only do good with holy garments and the neutral garments of *Nogah*. However, with garments of *K'lipot*, it seems that the *Neshamah* is unable to do anything profitable. But this is not so, because even the soiled garments, the filthy rags of *aveyrot*, contain, exiled within them, some Divine Life. Therefore, when a person exercises her or his will and does not allow her or his consciousness to be dimmed by the evil inclination and by free choice does not invest herself or himself in the filthy rags of the *K'lipot*, this deliberate act of resisting temptation frees the exiled Divine Life contained in the filthy rags. In abstention, this previously exiled holiness now accrues to the benefit of the *Neshamah*.

Now, if the *Neshamah* wishes to function vis-à-vis another *Neshamah* and is not interested merely in manipulating the environment, it dresses itself in the garment of word, *dibbur*. In this garment, the *Neshamah* relates to another *Neshamah* as subject to subject, as an *I* to a *Thou*. Speech and dialogue are also forms of behavior, only the garment of word is much more subtle than the garment of action. For by the garment of action we know merely *that* a *Neshamah* is active and alive; however, we seldom know *what* the *Neshamah* is like. We find that in the garment of *dibbur*, we can even get to know the emotional tone of the *Neshamah* that employs this "garment" in speech. Moreover, the garment of speech has the power of increasing the emotional amplitude. Thus if one speaks of a painful thing, one begins to weep after much speaking about it. For if one expresses one's *Ahavat Yisrael*, one's love, in speech, this love tends to increase in amplitude. Besides the emotional subtlety of speech, it can also convey thought in a limited manner. Speech serves as a medium of communication between two *Neshamot*. Whenever *dibbur*, speech, of *kedushah*, holiness, is the garment in which the soul dresses itself, all the modes that apply to the garment of action are also present in speech. Thus to study Torah and to express the learning in speech is a *mitzvah*, to study and to express the prayer in words is a *mitzvah*, and to speak of things that deal with *mitzvah* and that tend to being on the actualization of *mitzvah* is a *mitzvah* in itself. Many attitudinal aspects of *g'milus chasadim*, the bestowal of kindnesses, are greatly enhanced by loving and sympathetic speech.

However, since we have of late begun to treat speech in a light-headed way, there is far less commitment in speech than in action. And it is for this reason (and many others) that Hasidism speaks of *Assiyah l'eylah,* an action reaches far higher than words. Actions have far greater existential power than words. Yet words, before their devaluation in our time, carried tremendous power. The Holy One, blessed be He, created worlds with words. A person who holds words precious and uses them as if they were the most precious coin could also influence worlds with words.

In the same manner as more good is expressed through words, so does the *Neshamah* that dresses itself in filthy words suffer from greater contamination. This is due to the fact that the garment of speech is closer to the *Neshamah* than the garment of action. And yet all the words that one utters in one's daily life that are neither *mitzvot* nor *aveyrot* in themselves (provided they do not constitute *bittul Torah,* abandoning the Torah) can be sanctified and subsumed by holiness, provided one leads up to a holy idea in one's conversation. Thus the Rabbis have often counseled us that in everyday dealings with others, we should try to bring in a word of Torah, an idea of *yi'rat shamayim* (fear of Heaven). In this way, we are able to release and acquire all the merit of the Divine Life that was invested in all the words we spoke. So does the person who refrains from speaking lies, flattery, *nivvuleh* (foul language), and such by a deliberate act of will acquire all the holiness exiled in them.

Thought, *machshavah,* is the way in which the *Neshamah* expresses itself to itself. It is as if a part of the *Neshamah,* the "I" of the *Neshamah,* looked at the rest of itself, the "me," in order to understand itself. However, thought also comes in words, and words are also built out of letters. While the *otiyot* (letters of the alphabet) of thought share letter forms with speech, they are much more subtle and clinging to the *Neshamah.* The garment of thought relates to the *Neshamah* like an undershirt to the body, *guf,* or perhaps, to be more precise, like the skin to the body. It is almost impossible to divest oneself from one thought and invest oneself in another. The behavior of thought is not observable on the outside. However, it is the way in which the *Neshamah* observes itself and knows itself best. And while ordinary persons are unable to see into that garment of the soul, this garment is as visible to God as the garment of action is to other human beings. Man constantly lives in the illusion of the privacy of his *machshavah.* Exalted human beings, as well as the Hosts of Heaven, can make the *otiyot* on this page.

In most human beings who have not yet learned to master and subject the garments of thought to the power of the will, the arena of thought is a madhouse. A person who would in speech utter all the various thoughts streaming through his consciousness would be considered a psychotic. But most of us are in fact quite insane on the level of thought. Good and holy thoughts are jostled through the mind by pursuing evil ones—all against a field of neutral *Nogah* thoughts, which tend to make a great deal of noise.

Yet choice is granted to each person to divest herself or himself from one thought and invest in another thought. But the person who wishes to divest herself or himself from evil thoughts must have a great repertoire of good thoughts with which to displace the evil ones. Perhaps this is why our *chazal* said that an unlettered person cannot be a Hasid, because the most important arena of Hasidic enterprise is the garment of thought. Uncontrolled thought can lead to the worst *aveyrot* in action. A person who has a great many Hasidic teachings at hand is easily able to dispel thoughts of evil.

The more one is able to control the garment of thought by the will and the greater one's Hasidic thought repertoire is, the closer one can come to *hitbonenut*, which is the mainstay of prayer. Anyone who, after much work in the area of thought, is able to practice *hitbonenut* in great detail is later on able to come to an even higher level of thought, one in which the *otiyot* are extremely subtle and unobtrusive—namely, the level of *histaklut*, pure, still, and arrested contemplation of "the preciousness of the King."

Because thought is the closest garment of the *Neshamah*, almost like its skin, it can move all the other garments in the service of the *Neshamah*.

All the *mitzvot* that a person observes in thought, word, and deeds of holiness are indestructible. These garments survive bodily death. All of the celestial attainments of *Gan Eden* and *Olam HaBa* (the World-to-Come) come to the *Neshamah* through these garments which are a high, subtle, kind of Divine Light.

But there is another aspect to the garments. Not only does the *Neshamah* dress itself in these garments, but God also is dressed in these garments. Thus we are told that the person who takes hold of a *mitzvah* also takes hold of God. Thus, through these three holy garments, one is able to take hold of three levels of God. The garments are of the very same substance as His will. So even the greatest philosopher is unable to attain and reach and touch God because, as the Zohar says, no concept can contain Him in such a way that even the highest angels and *Neshamah*, which are to be found in *Gan Eden* and *Olam HaBa*, are unable to do. You and I are able to "dress" ourselves in God, are able to take hold of God, and are able to say each day, with all the love and fervor of the heart, and with all the faith of our *Neshamah*, "Blessed are Thou, Lord our God, King of the Universe, who clothes the naked."

THE VICTORY OF
THE RATIONAL SOUL

AT SOME POINT, you, like everyone else, need to make a decision about your nature.[1] This philosophical-theological homework needs to be done consciously. In the process, however, the image of self painted by others, roles that others have forced on you, often become unconsciously interwoven in your self-identity. Consequently, you might be innocently inclined to direct your energies toward the fulfillment of these introjected roles. Nevertheless, the overall image you maintain of yourself forms an essential identification. You may decide, for example, that you are essentially an animal, a part of the animal continuum (the lioness, too, loves her cubs, and so on). By dint of this identity option you are a reasoning animal, your rationale perhaps serving as a vehicle for the enhancement of your animal behavior. Once you have chosen this nature, however, you cannot expect to transcend the animal continuum, nor would you have any reason to do so.

On the other hand, you might also opt to imagine yourself as a Divine child of God, in which case you will perceive your body as an instrument for the Divine life. Before the advent of Hasidism, this was the only available alternative for the *Tzaddik*. And only by a heroic exertion of will and with the help of God were a select few able to reach this level. Others continued to fluctuate between the animal and the Divine. Still others (namely, the followers of Shabbetai Tzvi) identified the Divine Soul and the Animal Soul as one and the same, and confused them both in a single antinomian heave, hoping thereby to avoid the strain of the constant struggles between the two. But as was borne out by history, such an attempt at antinomian monism ends in a demonic fiasco.

Reb Shneur Zalman, however, proposed a fourth option: the human being, he taught, is Reason. Indeed, our primary soul, the arena of our life force, is the Rational Soul (*Nefesh HaSikhlit*), the final arbiter for most of us. The Rational Soul will align itself either with the Divine Soul (and only after much effort and with God's help) or with the Animal Soul (by choice or by default). By this system, the will is free, driven neither by animal nor Divine necessities, and is able to choose to perform the will of God or to transgress it and rebel. Though a person's will is totally free, it is nonetheless contained by reasoning and conceptualizing in order to maintain a beneficial relationship with other people and with the universe.

The difference, then, between the vehicle of the Rational Soul and that of the Divine Soul is that with the *Nefesh HaSikhlit* alone, one can only reach the God *idea*, but with the *Nefesh HaElokit*, one can reach God's Self.

Nevertheless, all of this would have solely philosophical significance were it not for another decisive dimension: The energies of mind, or reason (*mochin*), influence the affective modes, or emotions (*middot*). In fact, each *middah* is a consequence of a *sekhel*, an intelligence, a thought sequence or idea syndrome, consisting of *Chokhmah* (wisdom)—essential and qualitative truth; *Binah* (understanding)—truth in relation to other *sekhelim*; and *Da'at* (knowledge)—empirical truth.

If only *Chokhmah* were active in any given *sekhel*, the thought would be but a mere fleeting abstraction of an evanescent "what." If only *Binah* were operative, there would be a "how" without a "what." It is *Da'at* alone that provides the given, the "that." When I know *what* is, *how* it is, and *that* it is, I am involved in a meaningful situation in which I can act.

On the premise of these concepts, an innovative way of Divine service, *Avodah*, becomes possible, for we can then meditate on *how* God's Goodness operates via Divine Providence and *that* God, out of the pure goodness of the Divine Nature, acts benevolently toward us. When exercised at the proper depth of consciousness, this meditation will inevitably move us to experience a flow of gratitude toward God. This sense of appreciation issues forth from the Rational Soul; moreover, it forms a loving connection between the soul and God since the Divine Soul naturally loves its Divine root and source. The resulting experience is one in which Divine emotion blends with an *amor Dei intellectualis*.

Even by living a life directed by religion, the Animal Soul (*Nefesh HaBehamit*) is still constantly nurtured and reinforced. After all, kosher food, too, is pleasing to the Animal Soul. In like manner, each time the Animal Soul avoids any form of discomfort or exertion, its resistance becomes strengthened, and the "substance (matter) overcomes the form." Anxiety and frustration (*atzvut*), on the other hand, tends to dull the keenness of the perceptual judgment necessary for the Rational Soul to maintain a steady *Beynoni* mode. *Atzvut* evokes self-pity and, consequently, self-indulgence. Next, lethargy may set in (*accedia* is the scholastic term usually given to this malady). The Rational Soul is then no longer able to hold a firm grasp on a meditation, and the Divine Soul suffers *nefilat ha'mochin* (a falling of the mind) and *timtum ha'moach v'ha'lev* (a dulling of the mind and heart). This form of depression, begotten by the unmitigated anxiety, does not yield to homiletics or meditative exercises.

Here Reb Shneur Zalman suggests some remedial methods that might sound severe and drastic in comparison with the usually rosy portrayal of Hasidism by Neo-Hasidism.

Not given to any illusions, he even goes so far as to disqualify the Ba'al Shem Tov's method of raising up fallen drives, thoughts, and images, when it comes to salvaging the very delicate mode of *Beynoni*. His successor, too, Reb Dov Baer of Lubavitch, wrote three books on the subject, in which he prescribes a strenuous, painful program of intense penance, beginning with an exacting and austere discipline, for those seeking to reach the optimal heights of prayer.

Reb Shneur Zalman suggests that you convert your floating anxiety into objective bitterness and then integrate it into your sinful state. As a *Beynoni*, you need to turn all the potential energies of self-destruction toward the service of God. Instead of sulking proudly in your inability to soar toward Heaven, and rather than seething with paralyzing frustration and yielding to morose self-pity, you need to turn all these energies against your blocked *Nefesh HaBehamit*. Having done that, you must then sever your identification with your Animal Soul and free the rational soul from its enslavement to it.

Timing, however, is of great importance throughout this process, and all the necessary effort and exertion must not be expended prematurely. You must also weep over your lot of utter poverty and continuous inner struggle. You must become so broken in spirit that your only remaining reason for existing is God's creative and commanding Will. Nonetheless, this is your ultimate salvation, for after such uncontrollable weeping, one is renewed by God. Furthermore, the shell is shattered and a fresh joy will now be able to come through and fill you since it becomes thereby clear to you that God desires your service. Your sensitivity, too, is restored, and you can again render the decisions that impress the form upon the substance. Regression is of course possible. Reb Shneur Zalman counsels Hasidim to desensitize themselves against frustration and anxiety by deliberately inducing these moods now and then through *it'kaffia*, the suppression of the *Sitra Achra* (the "side of otherness"), which is achieved by depriving the Animal Soul of physical pleasure or by slowing it down to a less manic pace.

Then there is *it'hapkha,* the transformative process of bitter into sweet, evil into good, darkness into light, a process usually responsive only to the power of the *Tzaddik.* Nevertheless, the *Beynoni* works with *it'kaffia,* a process in which the *Nefesh HaBehamit* is deconditioned and virtually replaced by the assertion of a more humane, more Divine identity. In addition, there is a cosmic effect as well, as the *it'kaffia* process creates a rippling explosion of Divine Light and Life of higher orders in all of the universes.

Unlike the mind of the average person, terribly splintered in all directions, the mind of the absolute *Tzaddik* is Divinely unified, and the *Tzaddik*'s awareness is never split. In the same manner, the mind of the absolute *Rasha* would also be whole, a complete animal's tool. The *Beynoni,* however, is always caught in the split, always suffering from ambivalence, even when making a conscious decision. Judged constantly by both the good and evil inclinations, the *Beynoni* is at all times aware of the inner dissent between the two, even when rendering a good choice. When, as a *Beynoni,* you choose to love God, for example, you cannot experience that love fully; you can only will it as strongly as is within your power. You are at a further disadvantage as a *Beynoni* attempting to love fully because, being primarily self-directed, you are not much of a social creature to begin with.

In the final analysis, *Beynonim* always work with their will. There is, of course, much more to a person than will. Even if you will something, is it true? Is it honest? Is it authentic? Genuine? Saturated with too much experience, the *Beynoni* is not free from dissonant dissent and only a few moments after asserting the will to love God will experience the full emotional impact of a coarse temptation.

Does this mean, however, that the *Beynoni* is a hypocrite? No, says Reb Shneur Zalman, because reality is not determined by the Meaning put forth by humankind but by the Meaning that issues forth from Torah ("The Holy One, blessed be God, looked into the Torah and created the world"). *Beynonim,* then, tune in to objective transcendental reality, independent of their own inauthenticity. In a more profound way, the *Beynoni*'s nature is more fully authentic in that it is the very nature of the Divine Soul to offer *all* of oneself to God, and that includes the doubts, the ambivalence, and the contradictory experiences. Moreover, this ontological underpinning comprises the basis for meditations that can bring about profound emotive results. The question, of course, is, can any person do all this? And to that Reb Shneur Zalman responds with a resounding yes.

Yes. You need only arouse your natural love, which is so powerful that an Israelite cannot be persuaded or threatened to apostasy. Even the evil inclination, *yetzer ha'ra*, must constantly reckon with this omnipotent love for God and its resulting aggressive preservation of Jewish characteristic and identification, which constitutes the very power of Jewish survival. Thus regardless of how far from the path the modern Jew may have strayed, there is still the affirmation of "I am still a good Jew" or, in the words of the *Tanya:* "I am still standing in my Jewishness"—still a Jew in "good standing." For in the moment that they realize their self-deception and do *t'shuvah* (repentance), they could easily return to their basic nature, without having to create anything new in themselves.

But *Beynonim* must not allow themselves to be fooled, for in the realm of the *Beynonim*, every deviation from God's will is tantamount to a deviation from Judaism and thus a contradiction of the individual's very nature. The *Beynoni* must therefore take the existential stance to oppose even minor apostasies by equating them with the ultimate apostasy.

The way of the *Beynoni*, then, is costly. And it would therefore also seem that it is a mode only for a select few, as I said before, than for the average person. But the *Ba'al HaTanya* (Master of the *Tanya,* Reb Shneur Zalman) stresses the opposite. Now, let's move on and deal with a few of the hitches people have when they read the *Tanya*.

THE DUALITY
OF GOOD AND EVIL

The abiding-place of the Animal Soul (*Nefesh HaBehamit*), deriving from the *K'lipat Nogah* in every Jew, is in the heart, in the left ventricle that is full of blood. It is written, "For the blood is the *Nefesh*." Hence all lusting, boastfulness, anger, and like passions are in the heart, and from there they are disseminated throughout the whole of the body, rising also to the brain in the head, where one thinks and meditates on them and thus becomes skillful in them—just as the blood has its origin in the heart and from the heart circulates into every limb and also rises to the brain in the head.[1]

Often when people read in the *Tanya* about the evil that dwells on the left side of the heart, they get a little confused. After all, isn't our nature intrinsically good? Well, I tell you, I am very happy about the work of Matt Fox and for people who make the statement of "original blessing" rather than original curse.[2] On the other hand (there is always an "other hand"), why is it that some people with double Y chromosomes are hard to live with, act out in difficult ways, are hurting people? Why do kids show such selfishness and cruelty on the playground? Why, if we are originally good? A person who grew up never having experienced depravation may also end up not being a good person. Think again of the example from Chaim Potok's novel *The Chosen*. The father didn't talk much with his son because the son was so brilliant and so bright that he despised other people who were not on the same level. The father had to carve out a space for compassion in him so that the boy could learn to be kinder to other people. I'm not so sure that we could say that we come with original goodness. There is a lot that has to be transformed in us too. Go and look inside of yourself; I think that you won't find that your are so totally good. . . . Have you never felt envy? Have you never been angry? Have you never felt greed? So when people are talking about what happens on the inside, the issue isn't so much whether I'm good or evil but rather how I handle the impulses that arise in me. Let me illustrate this using the psychological concepts of source, drive, aim, direction, and object. The *source* is life, the libido. The *drive* is "Do something about it!" The *aim* is to discharge that drive, to finally be able to say, "I did what I needed to do." Over these three we don't have much control. As long as we are alive, the source is there, the drives are there, and the aim to discharge the drives is there. Over the direction and the object we have a lot of choice. In which *direction* do we want to discharge the drive, and on what *object* do we want to do that? There are kosher and nonkosher objects—a right way of doing it and a wrong way of doing it.

Now, what strikes us as evil, says Reb Shneur Zalman, stems from the left side of the heart. "Come on," you say, "if you were a surgeon and you opened up a heart, would you find a devil sitting in there?" Of course not. But it isn't much different from saying that at the base of the spine, there is a coiled serpent that rises up in *kundalini*. What is the point? That there is a certain kind of power like this, and it operates in that relationship to the heart. But to assume literally that evil sits in the left chamber of the heart is to misinterpret the metaphor.

What Is Evil?

Whatever is of the Other Side is abhorred by the absolute *Tzaddik* absolutely, by reason of his great love of God and of His Holiness, which is of surpassing affection, joy, and devotion, as is stated above. For they are opposed to one another. Thus it is written, "I hate them with an absolute hatred: I count them mine enemies. Search me, [my God], and know my heart. . . ." Thus, according to the abundant love of God, so is there comparable hatred toward the Other Side, and utter contempt for evil, for contempt is as much the opposite of real love as is hatred.[3]

What is evil to Reb Shneur Zalman? In his context, evil is anything that is not kosher. It means to him that the energy system of *K'lipot,* the shells, is what energizes that, and no matter what I do, I can't lift it. It is going to be stuck in my craw; I just can't do anything about that. But with the shells, what are we talking about here? Shells belong to walnuts, right? But just as the walnut has a shell that protects the nut on the inside and the shell is inedible, in the same way there is good that is often surrounded by something that is not so good and much harder. To explain this, the analogy of shells is used. However, I would like to call them by a different name. I like to speak of the *K'lipot* as energy systems. There is an energy system of good and an energy system of evil. Energy is the common factor. Even when I do something wrong, I am still energized. I have still got energy, but from where do I derive that energy? I cannot say that I derive the energy from, as it were, God's Goodwill, which is called the

Face of God. But I'm still getting Divine energy that helps me accomplish that wrong deed. In other words, I can go contrary to God's will and design by doing something that is wrong, that is evil, and at that very same time I am still being energized. So where does this energy come from? The teaching is that it comes from the Other Side of God, as if we are talking about the "backside." It is how people often pay their taxes. "I don't want to do it, but I have to, so here!" They give from the back, as it were, like a back-handed compliment. It is a similar notion with the *Sitra Achara*, the Other Side, and the *K'lipot* are the energy system of that Other Side.

So now, if something comes from the *K'lipah* of *Nogah*, which is not transparent but translucent, some light still comes through, and it is all the stuff that is kosher but not necessarily done for God's sake. This is covered in chapters five and ten of the *Tanya*. And in Reb Shneur Zalman's system, that is the way it goes. You find similar things in other systems. This thinking derives from the notion, "Why is it not kosher? It is not kosher because God considers this to be an abomination, something that instead of lifting you is going to drag you down, is going to imprison your soul." For instance, in the *sangha*,[4] a monk does not do things that are *treffa* for a monk to do. Or in Islam, one does not do what is *harram*, forbidden. In Christianity, such actions would be either a mortal or a venial sin. So you can see that the notion of what evil means is specific to each belief system. It is not abstract, the way a Greek philosopher would see it, that there is good and evil in the universe. Evil in many traditions is defined as whatever is against the express command of God. That is evil according to Reb Shneur Zalman's definition.

Hatred of Evil

But it is not completely extinguished in the case of the *Beynoni*; it is only so in a *Tzaddik*, about whom it is said, "My heart is void within me." The *Tzaddik* despises and hates evil with a complete hatred and contempt. . . .[5]

It often upsets a lot of people when they read that the *Tzaddik* is supposed to hate evil with this absolute evil. But I think we can deal with that by talking about aversion rather than hatred. The word *hatred* leaves a very bad taste in the mouth. Think of hate mail and hate crimes. It has sense of profound maliciousness. So if a person hates evil, isn't that person furthering the evil? If that were the case, it should upset us. Absolute aversion, by contrast, is a different story. It is not that I am going out of my way to find what is hated and attack it and kill it, as it were. However, it certainly doesn't turn me on, and when I get the vibes that it brings to try to turn me on, it turns me off instead. So that is basically what this "hatred" is about.

Stanley Kubrik's 1971 film *A Clockwork Orange* features a society that does aversion therapy on people. People are given the same stimuli that would ordinarily entice them into doing the wrong things and are then bombarded with induced pain; in that way, the body and mind learned not to want the wrong things. That type of training has a history. Many of the spiritual teachers of the past were advocating unhealthy forms of aversion therapy. So by saying to male heterosexuals that the woman you lust for is nothing but a sack of putrid waste, they created this aversion. It is different for a *Tzaddik* who is a complete *Tzaddik* according to Reb Shneur Zalman, because when King David says, "My heart is empty in me," he is referring to the left side of the heart, the left chamber of the heart, which at this point he says he has killed with fasting. Another way of saying it is that not only is there aversion against the evil but there is nothing in that person anymore that can be roused to that evil.

The Ba'al Shem Tov advocated the embracing of evil at its root. And I don't mean embracing the evil in a loving way but rather not spending energy fighting it, recognizing its source in God, and going to the Source. Reb Shneur Zalman contradicts this. In the *Tanya* he says, "Let him not be a fool to try and do what the Ba'al Shem Tov says. This was said only for the righteous, for *Tzaddikim*. If you are not a *Tzaddik* of the same level, then the likelihood is instead of your being able to lift it up, it will drag you down." That is Reb Shneur Zalman's advice for his customers, as it were. The Ba'al Shem Tov was offering something else, and so there were lots of people who said that his path was very dangerous. But this kind of distinction is somewhat artificial. It can depend on when you catch the teacher.

A man who adored horses comes to Reb Shneur Zalman. The man's whole life was horses. He was a trainer and rider. So he tells Reb Shneur Zalman about his passion for horses, and the Alter Rebbe says, "It is wonderful that you have this love, because the swifter the horse, the faster you can get where you are going. But if you don't know where you are going, with a swift horse you can go off the path." Boing! The comment went straight to the man's heart, and he turns away and starts to weep. And he says to Reb Shneur Zalman, "Is that how far I've ridden astray?" And the Rebbe says, "Yes. However, you have a swift horse, look how fast you can come back to the right path."

So it depends on when you catch them. But even if we use aversion, how could a *Tzaddik* get to that level? One of the Chabad Rebbes, Reb

Shmuel of Lubavitch, says, "A person should give himself the opportunity to live for fifteen minutes each day as a *Tzaddik*. That is as long we can do it." Now, notice that he doesn't say "to be a *Tzaddik*" but rather "to live as a *Tzaddik*, " which means, achieve a certain level of consciousness for a little while. Imagine that I'm now in this consciousness of the *Tzaddik* and someone comes up with something that is a temptation, an evil. In that consciousness, I have such an aversion for what is proposed, I am turned off by it; it doesn't have its usual power. So that is a good practice of reinforcement, even though it is not maintainable. For someone who is not in *Tzaddik* consciousness, however, this behavior would be disingenuous.

The Sanzer Rebbe calls a man over and says to him, "Tell me, if you found a wallet with two hundred rubles on the street, what would you do?" The man says to the Rebbe, "Oh, Rebbe, I would just try to find the owner and return it to him." And the Rebbe says, "You're a fool." So he stops another man and says, "What would you do if you found this wallet with two hundred rubles inside?" And the man says, "I'd pocket it." The Rebbe says, "You're wicked." He calls a third man: "What would you do if you found this wallet with two hundred rubles in it?" The man says, "Rebbe, I'd have a real battle with myself." "Ah," says the Rebbe, "you are right."

It's easy to say you would return the wallet intact. And that's the sort of answer you'd feel you had to give to the rabbi anyway. The second guy figures, "Why is he asking me such a silly question?" and admits, "Of course I'd pocket it," and the rabbi declares, "You're wicked." It is only when you recognize the battle that's going on inside of you, like the third man, that you come to the *Beynoni*'s aversion, which goes something like this: "In my life, I'm totally connected with the energy of God, and I so love God that to do something contrary to God's will is something I couldn't handle. If I did that, my consciousness would be cut off from God." It is an aversion driven by the resultant separation from the Beloved.

The Four Worlds and the Duality of Good and Evil

But we still have a problem. Isn't hating or being averse to evil engaging in dualism? Friday night, at the service, one of the psalms that we chant says, "Those who love God hate evil." In the past, people used to say, there is evil on one side and goodness on the other, and this polarity is unavoidable. The *Sefer Yetzirah* talks about the depth of good and the depth of evil. The notion is that this polarity exists throughout all existence. In Zoroastrianism and Parsianism,[6] it seems as if there are two gods, a god of goodness and a god of evil, battling with each other. And the god of goodness cannot win by himself but needs us to help. And if we do this, then goodness will prevail and bring the *Sishant,* the Messiah. And it is really clear that when you are dealing with the *Tanya,* it is very much involved in a kind of dualism. In other words, most of the time when Reb Shneur Zalman is talking about things that go on with good and evil, he is definitely a dualist. It is only when he goes up to the "higher regions," the higher worlds, that he becomes a monist.

Next, I'd like to look at evil through the Kabbalistic schema of the Four Worlds. But first I need to take a "time out" to say something about worlds in this context and the hermeneutics of words at different levels. Kafka's "Parables"[7] shows us that you can't always go by the simple meanings of words—you have to penetrate a bit deeper. For often it is the "echo," or the second level of meaning, that is intended. When I talk about "shadow" in psychology, for instance, am I talking about my physical shadow from light? Of course not. Obviously, you know that I am using that word to talk about something that has the same *Gestalt* as *shadow* has. Just as the physical phenomenon of a shadow works in relation to light, so does the shadow of psychology work in relation to inspiration on the inside; it is the dark places that are being made by the contrast with light. It is a similar situation with words like *worlds* and *shells.* When we talk about *worlds* in Kabbalah, what are we really talking about are worlds with particular characteristics, or *genres.* If I were to talk about the world of cinema, most people would know what I am talking about. If you go to Brooklyn and you speak of "the *yeshiva* world," everybody who is connected with that world will understand that you are referring to institutions devoted to the study of Talmud and rabbinics. The world of the physicist is going to speak one language, and the world of the biologist will speak another. This is what we mean by the word *world.*

So when we speak about the Four Worlds, we mean reality systems that are perpendicular to one another; they are dimensions of one another. If I say to you, "Between you and me (reader and author), we understand and appreciate one another and are not out to hurt one another," this fosters an openness, or a harmonious attitude, allowing for exchange. You might say that this openness is a "carrier wave" for exchange. Thus perpendicular to this physical world is a world of openness right now. So, too, the language that I use in order to communicate with you must be one we both understand and whose meanings we agree on. At the moment, it is English, and so it is clear that we are inhabiting a world in which English is the mode of exchange. So *world* here does not have any meaning so concrete as the planets and galaxies that may spring to mind but rather just realities that are intersecting.

Now let me show you something. Imagine that I have good on top and evil on the bottom. Between them are the degrees where they meet. Parallel to the good and evil is an ascending model of the Four Worlds, going up, from bottom to top, from *Assiyah* (deed or function) to *Yetzirah* (formation) to *B'riyah* (creation) to *Atzilut* (emanation). While we are in the lower worlds, more evil is present. And when we come to the upper worlds, there is less. And when we reach the high level, *Atzilut,* evil is gone; there is no more evil. So when someone speaks about the monistic One-ness, the person has already moved up to a much higher vibratory level.

Imagine if someone were to say that the 1992 atrocities in Yugoslavia[8] were not evil. We might say, "If that's not evil, then what is?" But where are we talking from? If we are talking from the lowest level, we have to contend with evil.

Now, Reb Shneur Zalman is talking about a *Beynoni.* The *Beynoni* happens to live between worlds and so is always dealing with half and half. I'll give you an example. Imagine that I decide to build a hospital, and I'm thinking about the hospital and the needs of the sick and how important it is to help them. In which world am I? Mostly up in the world of *B'riyah,* of thought. I'm planning how to build the hospital, how to equip the hospital, whom to hire. All these things are wonderful and easy, and the shadow side hasn't shown up yet. When does the shadow side show up? When the hospital has become real and people get sick because medicines are mixed up or they pick up strep in the hospital and we must deal with iatrogenic diseases. So when it comes down to the reality of things in *Assiyah,* things are not so good. In other words, down on that level of action, things are not necessarily good. The farther down you are on the level of practical things, the more shadow energy there is. The shadow cost of a highway doesn't show until it becomes reality and people start using it. The shadow cost of saccharine, which was developed to provide a sweetener for people with diabetes, didn't show until certain users of the product started getting cancer. Do you see what I am getting at? That kind of evil is different from malevolence.

Of course, there is also directed malevolence. There are some people, some beings, that really do have a malevolent streak about them. I remember a Jimmy Cagney movie, *Angels with Dirty Faces,* in which he is the friend of a priest but is himself a criminal. And all the kids in the neighborhood look up to him because he is a "big shot." However, just before his execution, the priest begs him to start screaming and carrying on so as to shatter the kids' illusion. And this kind of malevolence, at the last moment, is finally let go for the kids. I also feel there is malevolence in the way some people organize their lives. So when you speak of evil, you always have to check whether you are talking about evil as a cosmic force or as the shadow of the good. Are you talking about evil as something you have to overcome or as the "sparring partner" of the good? You know, if I didn't have problems in my life that appear to me as evil, I couldn't work on getting better. When you have a canary, you must give it gravel along with its food, because without some gravel in there, the canary couldn't digest its food. So people have looked at evil sometimes and said, "It is conducive; it is the sparring partner; it is the thing we need in order to grow and become better."

Satan, in Judaism, is not seen as a fallen angel. Rather, Satan is "His Majesty's loyal opposition." You need a devil's advocate. So the devil is the devil's advocate whom God sets up. And if you look at the book of Job, it tells you this story. It is Rosh HaShanah, the one time during the year that all the angels come and give reports, and Satan comes among them. With all the angels, God does a very quick job, "Thank you for the report," and sends them off. The one that God likes to banter with is Satan. God says to Satan, "*Nu*, what do you think of my Jobeleh? Isn't he a good guy? Isn't he righteous?" And Satan says, "No wonder he is righteous. Look, you give him everything he wants. He's got it easy. Take away some of those goodies and see if he isn't going to curse you for it." So God enters into a bet, as it were, with Satan, but never do you have a sense that God and Satan are enemies. All the angels are "yes men." The only one who can give God a run for His money, as it were, is Satan. It is almost like God needs to have Satan around to give Him a good conversation.

The Breaking of the Vessels and *Tikkun*

Even though the attribute of strength (*Gevurah*) seems to be the opposite of love (*Chesed*), since God punishes the world through it, its objective is still love. It is as Job's companions said to him, "Though your start was small, your end shall be greatly increased." The main purpose of the attribute of strength is to establish justice in the world so that God should be able to grant still more good.[9]

It is inevitable that you're going to experience labor. And then there will be a baby. When the Kabbalists talk about love, they mean *Chesed*. Strength is *Gevurah,* and then they get to beauty, *Tiferet.* And Reb Shneur Zalman is really talking about the three attributes of the *Sefirot.* So the big question is always, "Why would God have to utilize the harsh measures? Why is it that people have to die? Why can't we just be born and live forever?" These are always the kinds of questions that we are going to ask when we come to the hard places.

There are two kinds of evil, punishing evil and instrumental evil. If you do evil and you get zapped back, that is punishing evil—*malum poenum*, punitive evil. By contrast, instrumental evil is like the sparring partner to help you get better and better. But then there are some people who talk about what they call "surd evil," irrational evil that you can't justify. It is a sort of a nub of insoluble evil. And this is a hard one. It is difficult for me to talk about evil, but I can talk about malice. I have experienced malice, and I have experienced myself being malicious. And that is another thing. The question is, "Is the universe malicious?" I don't think I can go along with that. But we can't get rid of it either. It is there; it is in our craw. It keeps coming up like a grain of sand in an oyster that leads to the creation of a pearl. It is terrible and irritating, and you have to deal with it, wrestle with it.

Now you might ask, "Can you get rid of that evil by elevating the sparks of light embedded in the husks of darkness?" And that brings us to a thing that we haven't talked about, the Breaking of the Vessels. The lodging of the sparks in the *K'lipot*, in the shells. So strap yourself in for a little journey.

The mystical teachers grappled with the issue of where evil began. At which stage in creation, from the time of God's first saying, "Let there be something," did evil begin? From that great goodness and infinity, where did evil hook in? If you read the Bible, you come pretty quickly to Adam and Eve in the Garden of Eden. And we are told that if Eve hadn't eaten of the fruit and given it to Adam to eat, and if the serpent hadn't gotten her to do that, we wouldn't have evil in the world. It would be a wonderful world without any problems. But the Kabbalists are not quite happy with this, because in the garden with Eve and Adam was a tree of knowledge of good and evil—so there was already some evil around. Where did that come from? The Kabbalists push the envelope further back.

First the text says, "God created the sun and the moon." He created the two big givers of light—the greater one to shine by day and the lesser to shine by night. The strange thing is that the word *m'orot* ("luminary") is supposed to be written *mem-aleph-vav-resh-vav tav*. However, in the scripture, it is spelled *mem-aleph-resh-tav*. It is written defectively, which gives it a pun, *me'erot*, which means "curses." What happened? The moon came complaining and said, "God, it is impossible for two kings to wear one crown. And God said, "You are right. Make yourself smaller." Therefore, they say, "The first issue of evil came *mi'ut ha'yare'ach,* from the lesson of the moon." In other words, when the moon became smaller, waxing and waning, that is what brought about evil.

Every once in a while, I deal with a couple that is about to be married and I ask them to check with an astrologer to make certain that the moon is not "void of course" during the time that they have set for their wedding.[10] For when it is void of course, you shouldn't do any planning or make any decisions, because the likelihood is that things will not come out the way you are planning. In other words, it's not a good time. It is almost as if God is saying, "Oops." Nothing will go as planned when begun at that time. So following that line of thinking also, the moon was the origin of evil.

But then the Rabbis had to ask, "What caused the moon to complain in the first place? Something must have happened before that." The process keeps regressing, and you wonder if there is ever going to be a stopper for the regression, a point where you can't regress any further. Well, the Rabbis wanted to say, "You don't regress further than the *b'reshit,* the beginning. Don't ask what happened before. Beyond that moment, questioning is forbidden." And ever since that was said, Kabbalists have been especially curious to know what happened before. "What led up to that?" And this is what they came up with: In the beginning, when the will of God is becoming manifest and the Infinite fills all space, there is no place to create worlds. So what does God do? God removes some God-light from the place that is so filled with Divinity that there is no room for anything else. So that is the withdrawal, *Tzimtzum.* It doesn't mean that God isn't there anymore. It just means that the experience of God has been dimmed in that space. So now it is empty, void, nothingness. Buddhists also talk about emptiness.[11] And Kabbalists would say, "That is the space after God has withdrawn. No wonder that when the Buddha comes into that space, he can't find God there." God is hidden. That is an emptiness experience.

So now we have space to put worlds in, but how are the worlds going to come into being? Suddenly, a shaft of light comes through, from beyond that space that has been emptied. And this shaft of light flashes and is withdrawn. Now, let me explain. Inside the picture tube in a television, there is a raster that spits out light in pulses very quickly over the surface of the tube. It does such a very fast job, but the phosphor inside the tube is slow, so by the time the raster finishes one pulse, it seems like the next is there already. It is similar to fluorescent light, which seems constant but is really not. So a zap of light comes in and gets withdrawn, and what is left is almost like an afterimage. And that first afterimage is what becomes a vessel, a *keli*.

Then comes the next zap of light. And this zap is so strong that it shatters the vessel. But from what was that vessel made in the first place? It was made from light. So when the vessel shatters, it is like scintillas, like sparks. There are distant sparks flying all around that empty space. And this image is remarkable because astrophysicists tell us that they can still detect some radiation from the "big bang" that created the universe, and you can easily recognize the Kabbalists' model in the modern scientific model. Now in the Kabbalah, there are seven vessels that are created first and then shattered. So the light of the vessel was like laser light: it had one vibration and couldn't handle another. That is why the earlier vessel broke. So God decides that He can't "send down" the same kind of light again, so He makes vessels that are a little bit thicker. And the light comes now as spectral light, like the light that we receive from the sun, which has in itself all the seven colors. Its not so focused as laser light, so sharp. Therefore, it diffuses into all directions. So no longer is one particular *middah*, one particular mode of the Divine, in each vessel. Each one is already mingled with all the others. And the new vessels can handle the new light. So the second set of vessels are the fixed vessels. And the first ones are called *tohu*. And from them came the breaking of the vessels of *tohu*, the sparks of which lodged all over the place. And the higher the spark was in origin, the lower it lodged.

Now we come back to the question of surd evil. What happens with the sparks of holiness that are embedded in surd evil, that evil that we somehow can't dissolve anymore? You'll have to have a little patience. Reb Shneur Zalman in the *Tanya* talks about two ways of dealing with those sparks. One way he calls *it'kaffia*—you push it away from yourself, you bend it. If evil rears its head, if there is a spark that is embedded in evil that says, "I've got such a goody for you," and you feel attracted to it—"Just say no!" When you get to that space of saying no, you unmask that spark, and the spark is freed.[12]

The Zohar gives the following explanation. A king has a son, and he wants to make sure that his son is worthy of being a king. How can he be sure that the son will not be corrupted? So it says that the king has a friend, a courtesan, and he tells her, "I would like you to seduce my son." Now, she loves the king very much, and she will do what the king asks her, and she'll do the best job she can do, but secretly, in her heart, she hopes the son will spurn her advances and refuse to be corrupted. Because she also knows that this is what the king is hoping will happen. So the Zohar speaks of evil as the courtesan hired by the king to tempt the prince, to see if he will fall. When he does not fall, she can go back to being who she is, with all her beauty, and she doesn't have to play that part anymore. The spark has been freed.

Now, look at all the fairy tales—"Beauty and the Beast," the princess that has to be awakened, the frog that has to be turned into a prince. They all talk about the release that comes when there is a certain level of love. In this case, the best love that there can be is to say, "Dear spark, I don't want you to have to go into further incarnations, into worse and worse evil, to drag me down and to get yourself dragged down. I'm going to free you by saying no." And that is called *it'kaffia*.

The other way is called *it'hapkha*. *It'hapkha* is "to turn it around." If you have ever watched the sport of jai alai, you can get an inkling about this. It is a remarkable game. A baseball is nothing in comparison to the missile that gets thrown around in jai alai. You have this projectile coming at you from one side, and you have a banana-shaped receptacle with a handle that allows you to catch the ball and immediately launch it back in the other direction. If you catch it the right way, you can use the momentum from the projectile itself to send it right back. Otherwise, it could tear your arm off. The trick is to catch it right, not to get into its way, and to turn it around. So let's say a sexual temptation comes upon you. If such a temptation comes and you can say to it, "Aha, you've come to remind me that I should love God," that is sublimation. And they say that sublimation releases the spark. In this case, you don't say no, you say a kind of yes. It is almost as if you embrace that energy without doing the act. This is a little harder to do, not to get sucked in, as it were, into habits of the flesh. So Reb Shneur Zalman and others caution, *it'kaffia* is an easier road than *it'hapkha*. But those are the ways to redeem those sparks.

WOMAN AND
THE DIVINE FEMININE

A person must make a regular time in which to commune with his soul in order to cultivate the aversion to evil, for example, remembering the admonitions of our sages, "Woman is a vessel full of filth, . . ." and others. So, too, all charming things and delicacies are turned into a "vessel full of filth." Likewise, with regard to all pleasures of this world, the wise man knows ahead what will become of them, for in the end they will rot and become worms and dung.[1]

The assumption here is that we are talking to men. And it is true that this is a statement found in the Talmud. I can also find you statements of this sort in Saint Augustine,[2] too; they were all in the same boat at that time. If you read Sri Ramakrishna,[3] "Two things give people trouble—woman and gold." So you must realize that the matter comes up in every tradition. A male teacher says to his male students, how do I get you turned off from what you seek in a woman? I give you an image that says, "Look how dirty that stuff is." It is aversion therapy again. That's how some people did it in the Talmud, but the same Talmud also says, "Greater understanding has been put into a woman than into a man." "A woman of valor, she is the crown of her husband." "When your wife is short and you are tall, bend down and whisper to her." Treat her with honor. And if there is a question of buying a suit for oneself or a nice garment for one's wife, and one doesn't have money for both, the wife gets the first garment, says the Talmud.

Sometimes a man becomes aroused by desire for a particular person, but sometimes it also happens that a man becomes aroused in a generalized way that has the sense of "I want a woman." Do you know the difference? Gurdjieff[4] said once, "If you want a woman, have a woman. If you want a wife, choose carefully." One is about selfish pleasure, and the other one is about mutuality. For men in earlier times, aversive statements were used as a counterbalance to "I want a woman."

We could try to understand it by referring to the ritual impurity of the menstrual blood. But even that's not so good, because it seems to be saying that menstrual blood is dirty. And that's another problem that you have to deal with. Many women today object to the sense of contamination and impurity ascribed to menstrual blood—and rightly so. But we must all understand that what these texts are saying are intentional attempts at aversion. What is it that attracts you so strongly? And how do you counter that? I can't make the situation better or nicer; that is where the male writers of these texts were coming from at that time.

The Feminine in Judaism

It is this cause that is called the "world of manifestation," "matron," "nether matriarch," or "the *Shekhinah,*" from the phrase in scripture "that I may dwell among them."[5]

Someone who was taking some people on a vision quest wanted to know from me what to say to them about the feminine in Judaism. I was immediately reminded of something once pointed out by Theodore Reik. Go to any synagogue and witness the Torah service. Worshipers remove the Torah from the ark, and the Torah wears a great big crown, and they carry the Torah all around, and everybody touches and embraces her like a queen and kisses her, kisses the hem of her garment, as it were. Then they delicately undress her, place her gently on the table, roll her open, and read from her. Clearly, Torah is feminine. And *Shabbat,* the Queen, is certainly feminine. The *Shekhinah,* the Divine Presence, is certainly feminine. So the element of the feminine is embedded in Judaism, and the strange thing is that the very stuff that we threw out the door in the early days comes back in through the window.

In the pantheon of the Canaanites, the biblical idol worshipers, were Ba'al, and El, the bull god, and Asherah, the fertility goddess, and all that kind of "bad," "nasty" stuff. But when you look closely at them, the description was that El was the father God, a bull. Asherah was the mother goddess, the son was a calf, and the daughter was a heifer. So they were talking about the Divine family, the *familia shel ma'alah.* Isn't it strange how they use that phrase in Hebrew, so that the Divine family consisted of father, mother, son, and daughter? Many generations later, Rabbi Yitzhak Luria teaches us about the four aspects of the Divine *Partzufim,* the faces of the Divine, in the name of the Divine, *YHVH* (*Yud-Heh-Vav-Heh*). He speaks of *Yud* as the face of the father, *Heh* as the face of the mother, *Vav* as the face of the son, and *Heh* as the face of the daughter. So you can't get away from these relationships, because they are embedded in the deep structure of our reality system. The question is, "What is associated with it, and what kind of worship do you do?" The answer is what distinguishes true belief from idolatry. And when I point this out to people, I like to draw the four familial symbols from the *I-Ching*.[6] And what you see is Old Yang turns into Old Yin, Old Yin turns into Old Yang, Young Yang remains the same, and Young Yin remains the same. So instead of a hexagram, I put in a *tetragammaton*, the word written with the four letters *Yud-Heh-Vav-Heh*, which is God's name. So in the Chinese culture you also have these four possibilities for casting the hexagram. And when I do the *I-Ching*, I use a dreidel, which is a Hanukkah top with four sides, and that is how I build my hexagram, because each side stands for a different member of the Divine family.

Rabbi Yitzhak Luria also comes to the feminine from another perspective. All the time you hear people talking about God and soul as if God is masculine. But if you were to talk about God from the feminine perspective, you would say, "God birthed the world." Creation is a birthing process. Presaging feminism, Luria spoke about these spiritual processes, calling one the *ibbur*, meaning "pregnancy," and the second one *ledah*, meaning "birth." The third one he called *yenikah*, "nursing," nurturing, feeding from the breast. And so when we were in Egypt, our being in Egypt is considered to have been the pregnancy of our people. Our birthing was our going out of Egypt. You can visualize it as going out through the narrow birth canal. (Even the Hebrew name for Egypt, *Mitzraim*, means "narrowing.") God's nourishing his newborn people in the desert with water, with *mana*, with food, is much like the attention given to a newborn baby. That understanding is something that Luria brings to us. Those are some of the beginnings of feminism in the Kabbalah.

Luria talked about *ibbur* in another sense, and this is also described in the *Tanya*, where it says, "It may be possible, for a person who is under great stress, who needs the help of a saint who is no longer on earth, that an aspect of the spirit of that person will enter the person under stress and help that person overcome the difficulty."[7] And this is called *ibbur*. Think of it this way: Today, why are we interested in the teachings of the Ba'al Shem Tov at all? After all, I have mentioned paradigm shift, and he belongs to the past. Why bother with learning this now? The answer is that each holy being created, was, as it were, a software for enlightenment. When I think of the Ba'al Shem Tov, I see his teaching as a software for enlightenment. Now, I am not the Ba'al Shem Tov, but just as I have a word processor, I need a reality processor, a soul processor. So if I boot Ba'al Shem Tov, the booting of Ba'al Shem Tov is making the Ba'al Shem

Tov enter into pregnancy with me. So I can say that if I fill the RAM of consciousness with Ba'al Shem Tov, it is like being pregnant with him. We've all experienced this. If you ever got into a fad or a movement of some kind, especially in your youth, you will know what I am talking about. You were pregnant with the fad at that time. You were acting on that state of affairs. It had taken over your appearance, your personality, and it drove your parents crazy. And when a piece of music or something visual takes over my consciousness, I'm pregnant with that. So we have to be really careful what we want to be pregnant with. And a lot of what I think goes on in meditation when it works and becomes transformative for us is when we are pregnant with the right kind of thoughts. Someone once put it this way: "What is poetry? Virgin philosophy pregnant with meaning." So you have to understand it in the sense of having been impregnated, as if it has gone through every cell of you, through and through.

FEAR AND LOVE

This is called "Fear that is contained in love," the natural love of the Divine Soul that is found in all Jews, the inborn craving and will to be connected to its source in the light of the blessed *Ain Sof*. For by reason of this love and craving, it instinctively recoils in fear and [oppressive] dread from brushing even the very edge of the impurity of idolatry, Heaven forbid, which is to deny the faith in one God, even where such contact involves only pretense, namely, in word and deed, without any faith whatsoever in the heart.[1]

Here Reb Shneur Zalman is talking about the energy tap that can get us over all the humps. In other words, if you find yourself in difficulty in your inner life, there is a resource that is given to us, that is natural, built in to us, that can be tapped because of the natural love that we have for God. And what does he have to say about our natural love that is implanted in our heart? He says it helps in the performance of the *mitzvot*.

Now, how do we stimulate that natural love? Remember, Reb Shneur Zalman says, think these things and you will feel afterward. "You begin by telling it to yourself." And the form of meditation that he advocates is in other systems called discursive meditation. It is something like preaching a sermon to yourself. If we all do this, we can have our hearts filled with Love and Awe for God. He points out that we need two wings to fly. Love for God is the right wing, and Awe for God is the left wing. And we are only able to fly with both of these. Instead of the word *Awe*, translators often use the word *Fear*—the Love of God and the Fear of God—and you wonder, how can you fly with the Fear? But it is not really Fear but Awe.

Let me say a little something about different types of fear. When I was in the *yeshiva*, I asked my Chabad teacher and *mashpiyah* (teacher of *Hasidut*), Rabbi Yisrael Jacobson, of blessed memory, what was meant by *fear*, and he gave me this teaching. There are three Hebrew words for fear: *pachad, ai-mah,* and *yir'ah. Pachad* means something like *terror*: "I'm really scared." The word *pachad*, he told me, is related to the word

po-chad, "here it is sharp." If I come at you with a knife, it is very clear
what the danger is. You can see the danger, you can anticipate the hurt,
and that is a very objective fear. That is what we mean when we use the
word *pachad* for fear.

Ai-mah refers to a kind of paralyzing anxiety. It is related to *Aiyeh
mah*? "Where is it?" And *mah* alone is "What is it?" Imagine a voice
tremulously saying, "I don't know what it is, I don't know where it is, but
I got this uncanny feeling something is impending." In the Bible, this word
is used in reference to Abraham, when he is sitting and offering a kind of
sacrifice. He has split a bull and a sheep and has them arranged on both
sides of a central path. He is at one end of the path, in his *ohel,* his tent,
his tepee, and suddenly an eagle or vulture sweeps down and starts walking up the path to him between the two sides of the sacrifice, the *brit beyn
hab'tarim.* And it looks at him in a strange way, and the Bible says, *Ai-
mah chasheychah nafelet alav,* "A dark *ai-mah* falls upon him."

Every time I read that passage, I go back in my mind to being in the
tepee with Native Americans at a peyote ritual. In the tepee there is a fire
and a bird, the fire bird is moving closer, and closer, to the peyote button.
And it is an awesome thing because the only light comes from the fire that
is burning there. And you eat peyote, which is very bitter—*Oy!* I still get
a gag reflex when I think of that. But soon things begin to happen, and
everyone sings songs, and sometimes fears start rising up. It can be
unpleasant if the fire isn't very bright or if it gets too bright and it becomes
unbearably hot. So the fire chief has to do a real good job to control the
situation. You can imagine Abraham sitting in these circumstances when
the bird swoops in and this kind of fear seizes his heart.

You might liken this kind of fear to an impending *grand mal. Grand
mal* means "big evil." You know it's about to hit, and just before it hits,
there is a terrible sense of "here it comes," yet there's nothing you can do
to stop it. You feel the impendingness of it, but you don't know what
exactly it will be, what form it will take, or how long it will last—that is
the *ai-mah* kind of anxiety. The danger may not be clear, but you know
that something is terribly wrong. Nobody says that we need to have this
kind of fear of God. This fear has something malevolent about it.

The third kind of fear is *yirah,* and that is the one we always talk about
in relation to God—*yirat HaShem ta-horah,* "the *yirah* of God that is
pure." *Omedet la'ad,* "It stands forever." It gives you a connection; it is
the pillar of eternity. Interestingly, the three Hebrew letters that spell *yir'ah*
can be rearranged to stand for *ro'eh,* "to see," and *raoh,* "to see." It is
like the Latin *spectare,* "to behold," or *spicere,* "to see, inspect." Suppose
I'm alone in a room and I burp out loud. Then I realize that somebody is

standing over there at the door, and I have a terrible startle reflex—I am not alone; I am being seen. That is *re-spect*: I am aware that I am being seen. I act with respect, sort of looking backward at the situation where I am being seen. So *ro'eh* is "to see," and the fear of God is *yir'at HaShem*.

In the books, they talk about ten levels of fear,[2] the lowest of which is, anticipating Lawrence Kohlberg and his teaching about moral development, the fear of punishment, *yir'at ha'onesh*. That is, "I know that if I am going to do such and such a thing, God is going to zap me." That is the lowest level. The highest level is called *yir'at ha'romemut*, exalted awe. At times you get a sense of momentousness. It is a little like being in love and wanting very much to have your beloved love you back. I can't really explain it to you if you haven't felt it, but there is a sense of unrequited love. You love somebody very much and there is no return. How do you feel when you tell someone that you care for them and you haven't heard back from them yet? You have your heart in your throat, and you are wondering how they are going to respond. "Is this going to be OK? I hope they don't laugh." I come with all my devotion to that person. And so I would like that they should like me back. I almost have a trembling, and on the other hand, that great Love. Now, if you get fully into the feel of that, you might be able to understand how that would fly. And if ever you had a flying dream, how did you fly? So part of that dream is your knowing that if you don't keep on flying hard, you're going to drop out of the air. On the one hand, you are propelled by what attracts you, and you want to go higher, and on the other hand, you are afraid of being in that dangerous situation. I remember when I was on a mountain near Rio de Janeiro, strapped into a hang glider and running down a platform into the abyss, together with the pilot of that thing. You do a kind of imitation of Superman, and there is nothing between you and the ground. In a small airplane, at least you have a floor, something there to reassure you. In a hang glider, there is nothing to reassure you. And yet I felt great exhilaration. Do you see why Reb Shneur Zalman uses the image of flying? You need both wings to fly. And when you study Torah or do a *mitzvah* and you don't have both Love and Awe for God, it doesn't fly. In truth, most of the time when you attend services in synagogues or churches, it doesn't fly. But when you go and it flies, how wonderful it is. Inside of you, you have a sort of revelation, and you say, "*This* is what it is really all about."

However, sometimes you get into a position where the heart feels dull, and Reb Shneur Zalman talks a lot about this too, the dulling of the heart. *Timtum ha'mo'ach v'ha'lev*, the head is dull and the heart is dull. It all feels like too much work. What do I do then? Reb Shneur Zalman reveals a secret, and this is a wonderful secret that comes out in almost every tradition: You know what? You don't have to work at it! You're there already. All you have to do is get rid of the *illusion* that you're not there. Even if you don't feel it, so what? It is there; it is implanted in you. Just as your breath is implanted in you and your spirit is implanted in you, that willingness to do God's will and to seek to be close to God is implanted in you. All you need to do is recognize that. It is like saying, I have the software, but I have to load it and reboot the computer. If I don't pull it in, it's not going to work for me. This is the natural Love of God. And when we get tired of being cut off from that by the illusion, we'll see it. When you can't stand being cut off any longer, your heart will cry out, "I really want to connect with you, Lord!" That is natural and is implanted in us. That is why I like to say that we are *theotropic* beings. Just as a sunflower is heliotropic, turning to where the sun is, so we are theotropic, turning to where God is. The more conscious you become, the more you feel the attraction.

Is That Love in the Non-Jews?

For as regards Yisrael, this soul of the *K'lipah* is derived from *K'lipat Nogah,* which also contains good, as it has its source in the secret Tree of Knowledge of Good and Evil. The souls of the nations of the world, however, derive from the unclean *K'lipot,* which contain nothing good whatsoever, as is written in *Etz Chayyim,* Portal 49, chapter 3, that all the goodness done by the nations is done out of self-serving motives.[3]

Many people want to know if Reb Shneur Zalman felt that non-Jews had the same innate capacity. That is a difficult question to answer. For one thing, he didn't live here and now, feeling the security of this time. If only he could have seen and experienced what I experienced in Boulder, Colorado, when I was saying *Kaddish* for my father, maybe things would have been different. There with me were Allen Ginsburg and Jack Kornfield,[4] both Buddhists from Jewish families, concerned and helping me make a *minyan.* And when we came to the words in the *davvenen,* "They bow down to emptiness and void," I thought, in olden times in the *shtetl* they would say, "They bow down to a worthless nothing." But standing there with these Buddhists, I thought, "They bow down to emptiness, *shunyata,*" and "We bow down to the King of Kings." Do you see the parallel, side by side? It is a different story in this light.

It isn't quite true that Reb Shneur Zalman didn't recognize the potential in non-Jews. Once, a Russian officer came to interrogate him, and the officer said, "I want to ask you a question about the Bible. Why does God say to Adam, 'Where are you?' What kind of question is that? Doesn't God know where he is?" Reb Shneur Zalman replied, "The Bible commentator Rashi asked the same question and came up with the answer that God didn't just want to sneak up on him and go, 'Boo! I caught you!' So first he let him hear, 'Where are you?' That way God could enter into conversation with him." Then the officer said, "It must be deeper than that." "Ah," said Reb Shneur Zalman, "every time a person is anywhere, a voice comes and asks, 'Where are you in your life? Where are you *really?*'" Now he was teaching this man Torah, and the man wasn't Jewish. Yet Reb Shneur Zalman knew that if he spoke to the man in this way, there would be a deep response.

There is also a story about the tsar himself visiting Reb Shneur Zalman in jail, to see whether he was really a subversive. The guards dressed the tsar in the clothes of a convict who was about to be executed, and they figured that by leaving him in the same cell with Reb Shneur Zalman, while the tsar said nasty things about himself, they would hear Reb Shneur Zalman's unguarded responses. So they sort of pushed the tsar into the room, treating him like a prisoner, and Reb Shneur Zalman rises and greets him, "Your Majesty, allow me to say the blessing one says when one sees the sovereign of the country, *Borukh ata HaShem* . . ." And so he makes the *b'rokha* (blessing) for that occasion. Then, when the tsar asks, "How did you know?" Reb Shneur Zalman says, "The kind of awe that came upon me, when you entered into this room, could only have come because God gives this sense of awe for the sovereign of the country. I felt *Malkhut* (sovereignty)."

If Reb Shneur Zalman really felt that non-Jews were not worth his trouble, he wouldn't have gotten into this. Now here is the other side. If I want to talk to my kids and I want my kids to behave, I would say, "Is this fit for a rabbi's child to do?" You take the uniqueness of a situation, because you have a claim on that, and use it. Reb Shneur Zalman is doing that with regard to Jews. But I think there is a lot more, because take a look what it says in the first of the Ten Commandments: "I am the Lord thy God who redeemed you out of the land of Egypt in order to be your God." The question that the commentators raise about this is, "Why does it not say, 'I am the Lord your God who created Heaven and earth?'" After all, that is a bigger thing than leading some people out of Egypt. And here is the answer that they give, which is the same as that of Yehudah Halevi in the *Kuzari*:[5] "If He had said that, then the claim would have been, 'Why do you come to us when you can talk to everybody?'" The sense is that we have become committed to following God because we feel the grace that God has given to us specifically. This is a particular revelation and is something that we have the right to celebrate and enjoy.

But you know what? There is also surface tension. For we don't live in an environment where people are taking our kids away and forcibly inducting them into the army of the tsar, making them eat unkosher food, and coercing them through all available means to convert. So we don't have as much pain around these things. But you can imagine how much pain they must have felt. Many of us are aware of the Holocaust but lose sight of the antisemitism that has existed for two millennia. And I tell you, I'm not hankering that we find that consciousness back again. I am glad that we live these days in surroundings where, thank God, these things are not such terrible issues for us. We can go wherever we need to go and be accepted for who we are. It is all in preparation for a Messianic era, when we look at individuals for who they are, and "my house shall be a house of prayer for all people."

And at this point some people like to say, "Anybody can be a Jew if they want to; it is not ethnicity that counts." And that is true. A Jew is one who upholds the *mitzvot*. But that is not an answer. After all, shouldn't we respect the ways in which God has talked to other people, the different forms that God takes, the apparitions that come to people? And this idea is in the sources and must be brought out from them. If I were to say, *Himshilukha b'rov chezyonot hin'kha echad b'khol dimyonot,* you would say, "Aha." This is a prayer that is recited every *Shabbat* in the synagogue that says, "They have likened You in many visions, and throughout their visions You are One." That is the recognition that God comes in many flavors, as it were. Think of vanilla. If you want another flavor, first you make vanilla ice cream, and then you add the other flavor. I remember at one point when you wanted to buy a computer, you got sort of an average computer, which they called a "vanilla." If you wanted it to be dedicated to a particular purpose, then they would build that in. So I think there is vanilla religion and then there is the specific tradition. Here we are involved in a very specific tradition.

ANNIHILATION OF EXISTENCE
AND BROKENHEARTEDNESS

The level of Rabbenu Moshe, peace be unto him, surpasses them all, for about him it was said, "The *Shekhinah* speaks out of Moshe's throat." The Yisraelites experienced something of this at Mount Sinai, but they could not bear it, as the Rabbis say, "At each utterance [of the Divine] their souls took flight, . . ." which indicated the extinguishing of their existence. . . .[1]

What does it mean that through *bittul ha'yesh*, annihilation of existence, we can rise above ourselves? The language is the language of the past paradigm. In Mexico, there are people known as *flagellantes* because just before Easter, they beat themselves bloody and carry heavy crosses in imitation of Jesus.[2] And sometimes you find this antimaterial notion in Judaism. When we fast, it is sometimes taken to mean, "God will accept the 'sacrifice' of the blood and fat I lose during my fast, as if I were offering blood and fat on the altar." In other words, it is not from the sheep but from myself. It is like destroying something as if it were pleasing to God. That belongs to the past paradigm. Now we are talking about the destruction of the ego.

Imagine that your heart is made of stone; you do not feel anything; you are heartless. How do you get to feeling something? Well, you have to "break" your heart. "God is close to those whose heart is broken." The reference here is to pride and ego. Brokenheartedness is positive in the sense that when my heart is in one piece, I don't let anything out. I don't feel. What is it that makes me feel the Presence of God at one time and not at others? Often when I am really feeling shattered, my reaching out to God is very real, yet when things are going well, I don't feel much of anything. So in the past, the idea was to mortify your flesh, which is almost killing. The more you kill, the more the spirit is going to grow, to light up.

And so the Hasidic masters are using old language about the body to talk about the ego. If you do *bittul ha'yesh*, if you take your "selfness," your ego, and you annihilate it, you "bash" it, that is going to take you closer to the love of God. But today I don't even think it is a good strategy to bash the ego. I think the better strategy is to make the ego "transparent." We need an ego, but we don't want it to be "opaque." It needs to manage things for us, but we can make it transparent. And the whole notion of transparency is so that light should be able to shine through. This idea is a lot more consistent with where we are today. In the past, we dealt with the opacity by shattering the cause of the opacity, breaking it down. But you can achieve transparency without shattering. All you have to do is align yourself differently. However, this can be a scary proposition.

Most of the time when we meditate, we can steer. When we get into places that make us anxious, we can steer our meditation to less anxious places. One of the things about taking psychedelics was that you couldn't steer, and sometimes you would get caught on the "white water" of it all, and you got closer and closer to dissolution. So I don't want to say that the experience never has that element of fear, because you get the sense that one more step and it will be fatal—you will be totally dissolved. It must be a terrible experience for people out of their body to have to look in a mirror and not to see themselves reflected. They don't have the coordinates of the body to ground them, as it were. That is one of the reasons why we cover the mirrors in the house of a mourner. That way, the soul of the departed, which is thought to hang around for a few days, doesn't get freaked out looking in the mirror. *Roeh v'eyno nir'eh,* to have a center from which you see and not to be visible, must be very unsettling. That I am all subject and have no object to me can be a frightening thought.

However, you might think of it this way. Most of the time in our consciousness, we are at the center of our respective universes. We go around saying, "I want," "I need," and in this way we attract sustenance to ourselves. Right now, I am like the CPU and you, the readers, are like the peripherals. From that point of view, I'm the center. But if I am to bring sustenance to anyone else, I am going to have to do something different from my usual pattern. How would I attract sustenance to everybody and not just to myself? By becoming transparent, as it were. I am not asking for myself; I am identifying with all that there is, and I'm asking for that all. Often the word *nothingness* or *annihilation* carries with it a feeling that you have to destroy something in yourself. However, that is not the meaning it has in this process. It simply means that one needs to remove the resistance to the Light, to remove the resistance to God. It is the notion that I am a something when I am resisting and I cease to be a something when I am not resisting anymore. The obstruction is gone; I am at the level of nothingness. Then I surrender to the larger process. This is transmitting sustenance through attaching oneself to the level of *no-thing-ness*.

I am sometimes asked how the annihilation of existence relates to the end of time. Is there ever an end? Remarkably, in exoteric Christianity, exoteric Judaism, and exoteric Islam, there is always a story that has a beginning and an end, a point at which there is going to be a final judgment—"it's over." Once I meditated on that and got to it the following way. There is the last judgment, the final creature has been judged, and God is about to leave the Hall of Justice, as it were, and turns to the archangel Michael and says, "*Nu,* did I do a good job?" So there is still a later judgment—what Michael has to say. And Michael says, "Well, God, You did a pretty good job, but You know, uh, well, yeah, You did a good job." Later that day Michael comes home and talks to his wife and says, "You know, God asked me how I thought He did, and at first I wasn't so sure, but then I didn't want to start up with Him. Do you think I did right?" Well, Michael's wife says, "You know, . . ." So you see, it is hard to get to a regression stopper that says, "Beyond this nothing else will occur." This is not the first universe and it won't be the last universe. These things keep on going. Nevertheless, there is a remarkable teaching in the Zohar that says, "What is the ultimate thing that we want? What is the end after all incarnations? What can you hope for?" The Zohar says (in Aramaic), *L'ishta'ava b'guffa de malka.* In Hebrew it is *Le hisha'ev b'guff hamelech;* it means to be drawn in, ladled in, to the very body of the Sovereign. In other words, the drop has finally joined with the ocean, and all separation is gone. It also means that the outer form and all inner awareness of oneself are gone. It is like an actor saying, "I don't want to play this part anymore." Put in other words, it is like saying, "Here I am dying. I'm out of my body. I'm in the white light now. I have an opportunity to see my relatives, to watch the video of my life, to hear what they say at my funeral, and I can hang out for a while, but while I'm in the white light, I also have the opportunity to dissolve like a drop in the ocean, to be drawn in the very body of the Sovereign. Which one will I choose?" The Zohar offers the option of saying it isn't necessarily "over."

Depression

In actuality, however, there are two souls, waging war against one another in the person's mind, each desiring to rule over him and dominate his mind completely. Thus all Torah thoughts and Heaven fears come from the Divine Soul, while all other matters come from the Animal Soul, except that the Divine Soul is clothed in it. This is like a person praying devotedly while a *Rasha* prattles on to him in order to perplex him. Surely, in such a case, it would be best not to answer the *Rasha* with either good or evil but rather to pretend not to hear, in accordance with the verse, "Answer not a fool according to his folly, lest thou also be like unto him."

. . . There is still another aspect that the *Beynonim* must contend with, namely, that occasionally and even often they experience a dullness of the heart, which becomes like a stone, and the person is incapable, try as he might, to open to the "service of the heart," prayer. Also, at times he is incapable of waging war against the evil impulse, so as to sanctify himself in the things that are permitted, because of the weight that is on his heart.

. . . With regard to what is written, "In all sadness there would be profit," which means that some profit and benefit would be acquired from it. This phrase, to the contrary, indicates that sorrow by itself has no virtue, unless some profit is derived from it, that being the pure joy in the Lord that comes after genuine anguish over one's sins, at propitious times with a broken heart and a bitterness of soul. For through this, the spirit of impurity and the Other Side is smashed, as is the wall of iron that divides him from his Father in Heaven, as the Zohar comments on the verse, "A broken and contrite heart, O God, Thou wilt not despise"; and then will be accomplished in him the verses preceding this: "Make me hear joy and gladness. . . . Restore unto me the joy of Thy salvation, and uphold me with Thy generous spirit."[3]

I don't want this material to be confused with the material about the two souls waging war. So let's get that material straight, and then we'll move on. At one point Reb Shneur Zalman talks about the voice inside that is like the wicked sinner trying to attack you. This voice is like the cynic inside that catches you even when you say, "It's really not so bad." "Ha, ha, ha," it says, "you're just trying to talk yourself into it. You're whistling in the dark, you're really in a lousy place. You're a faker; you're a phony; you were never good for anything." It's an amalgam of all the introjected voices that we ever heard—those of siblings, parents, or other people who shamed us—and that amalgamated voice is still there, and we can hear it at that point. So what does Reb Shneur Zalman say? "Pretend to be deaf, without hearing; answer not a fool according to his folly." Tune it out sometimes. This is one way that Reb Shneur Zalman deals with things but is actually quite different and not to be confused with the way we will get into next.

Chapters twenty-five through thirty-one of the *Tanya* can be real life-savers because they deal with what to do when you get depressed. And you will see that Reb Shneur Zalman counsels, "Don't try to get out of it; go through it." So what happens when the mind is dull and the heart is dull? This is where the broken heart starts coming up. It is good to have a broken heart. And he notes that there are propitious times for sadness and the broken heart.

The propitious time is when you're feeling really bad. Imagine that you're going to check your biorhythms and you find that your mental, emotional, and physical rhythms are all below the line at the same time. *Oy*, is that a good time! In other words, you are already in a lousy place, so let every bit of that depression in. I hear Reb Shneur Zalman saying, "When you get into that abysmal depression, when you get to that place where everybody conspires to say it is not so bad and wants to cheer you up, it doesn't work!" So, he says, "overjoin" the depression; call yourself all the bad names—*atah, Rasha', ra', metu'av, um'shukatz*—you're bad, really *farshtoonken*. Heap it up even more, to the point where something cracks. What do you want to crack? Not yourself but your heart and mind. *Lev nisbhar venidkeh Elohim lo tivzeh*, "A broken and oppressed heart, God, You will not despise."

Today, when we say the word *brokenhearted*, we get a sense of tragedy. That is partly because we don't have good language for emotional states. Imagine a husband and wife. They are so furious with each other that they can't talk. And at that time all the communication that happens is as if they are talking back to back. They don't even show a real face to each other at that time. Then something happens where they explode and shout at one another. And after the shouting, one of them begins to cry. Then the other begins to cry, and a deep reconciliation comes. Do you know what I'm talking about? It is as if resolution couldn't happen as long as they were in a defensive mode with each other. As long as it was constantly, "I'm right and you're wrong," the heart and mind were closed. Why can't I see the other point of view until I cry? This is what we mean by the broken heart.

Another expression is "the circumcision of the heart." The Hebrew expression *orlat l'vav'khem*, "foreskin of the heart," is derived from a word meaning "that which stops it up." A heart that has been so insulated feels like leather, not like a heart that can feel. The point is that you can't make a deep connection until you have broken through that part. So here is where you have to think about experiences that you have had. Some people have had the opportunity of going to confession. In Catholicism, you are expected to make an act of contrition. What does that mean? To say, "I'm sorry, I did wrong." And most of the time, people come very cool to confession. They say, "Father, forgive me. I've done thus and such." And the priest says, "Say so many Our Fathers and so many Hail Marys and don't do it again. Make a strong resolve that you won't do it again." Then he says, *Ego te absolvo,* "I absolve you, and now you are clean. You can go and partake of the sacrament." But let's say that this is not a formality. And we come and say, "Father! Forgive me, for I have sinned! I really feel what I have done is wrong. Please, I would like God to like me again. I don't want to be on the outs with God." You can understand how a person would cry at this point. Then if the priest says, "Do you resolve not to do it again?" you'd say, "Oh, yes, I am ready to promise. Never again do I want to be so separated from God!" So that is how it is in Catholicism.

How do we see it over here in Judaism? Reb Shneur Zalman points out that most of the people who have written the liturgy for the goodnight prayer have not included a confession in it. In his own *siddur,* he has included a confession. He has also included Psalm 51. This is a song that David sang after Nathan the prophet came to him after he had been with Bat Sheba. David says, "Please keep on washing me from my sins"—scrub me, God, as it were. "Oh, God, don't take away Your Holy Spirit from me. I know I deserve to be cut off from You, I deserve not to be in Your grace, but please forgive me." And in the end he says, "I undertake to help other people to turn to You for good. Let me teach the sinners Your ways so that they might also return to You." I see what I have done wrong, and I would also like to help other people repair the wrongs that they have done. So in that form of the goodnight prayer, Reb Shneur Zalman says, "And say the whole Yom Kippur confession, if you feel like doing that at that time." He would like you to do it once a week for Thursday night. Why Thursday night? So that your heart will be awakened for *Shabbat.* Then you can enter the Sabbath without feeling burdened by the guilt of sin from the week gone by.

Each month, the day before the new moon is called *Yom Kippur Katan,* Little Yom Kippur. And there is a teaching to make that time work by saying, "I don't want to settle my debts only once a year; I'll get my bill at the end of the month. Let me straighten it out. It is not good for me to have to go around with that unpaid debt." Now from this place Reb Shneur Zalman comes and says, "Once you have seen how to deal with this burden, don't be afraid to make the depression go deeper." And when you hit bottom, your joy is going to come. It will well up again. You will feel reconciled. And in this reconciliation, you can make your next move.

Now, I know some of you may be hung up on making your depression go deeper. So let's look at the process a little more closely. First, you call yourself all the bad names; in other words, you join that nasty voice inside of you. Imagine I'm hooked like a fish. The more I pull, the stronger I'm hooked—like a Chinese finger puzzle. But if I'm pulled to one side and I go along with it, I might be able to disengage. It is as if that depression will not let me go if I pull in the other direction, because it needs to accomplish something. I like to call this "overjoining." I'll give you an example.

Once I came to a synagogue that was not an Orthodox synagogue upstairs; it was Conservative. But an Orthodox prayer service was held downstairs. So I went downstairs for *Minchah* before *Shabbat,* before I was to conduct a service upstairs. I was there in my whole Hasidic outfit, with the *streimel* and the *kapotte,* and a guy comes up to me and sneeringly says, "What are *you* doing *here?*"—meaning, what business have you got to be going upstairs in the Conservative synagogue, you who pretend to be a Hasidic rabbi? He bent in closer to me, and I said, "I do it for the money." He was so shocked that I should say it this way that he then said, "You must have other reasons too." Now, if I would have started to tell him all the other reasons why I was there, he would have said to himself, "Ah, he is doing it for money." I unhooked from his pull by overjoining him.

But then again, who knows what kind of a faker I am better than I? And who hasn't experienced that voice that says, "For all the things you have achieved in your life, you are just a fake. If they really knew how you faked them out. . . ." You who have been students may know about the paper you did so well on, where you took something from an old paper, you cheated a little bit with this, and you got a little something off the Web. You see, all the things we do for the practical part of our life can be interpreted from a cynical point of view that can smear us. We know that. So instead of fighting that and denying it, be able to say to that voice, "You don't know the half of it! I know even more than that, and you know what? I don't feel so good about it either." And then you get to that place.

Maybe you couldn't have done much better in those situations, but in psychotherapy, self-acceptance is what makes turnaround possible, and it can't come when there is denial. So what Reb Shneur Zalman is saying is, "Give up the denial. Join in the situation. Make it even stronger." Take the point of view of a perfect God looking at our cutting corners: accuse yourself and get unhooked. But this is to be done only at propitious times. You are not to seek this out. Engage it when it is happening. Reb Shneur Zalman is saying, "Even when you are already feeling that others things have gotten you down, that is a good time to do it." In every one of these cases, he empowers you. Isn't that interesting? Despite the fact that you are getting into depressed mode, he empowers you. He says, basically, we are always anxious, at least underneath. And the

Beynoni always experiences anxiety. He says, "All right, then, let the anxiety in, and you come out the other end."

In 1955 or 1956 I lost my job as a congregational rabbi. The administrators said they wanted "less English and someone more modern." I didn't fit, and I couldn't find a job. And I had a family to provide for. So I applied for a teaching position at the University of Manitoba. But the university would take me only if I shaved my beard! Well, I was a card-carrying Lubavitcher Hasid at the time, and Hasidim don't cut their beards. But I was desperate, and I talked them down to a little goatee. So the first time I went back to Lubavitch headquarters in Crown Heights after that, I kind of kept a low profile and stayed outside of the celebrations for a few weeks. Finally, my friend Reb Zalman Posner spotted me sneaking around from shadow to shadow and gestured to me to follow him. He led me over to a private corner and then laid into me, I mean, really lambasted me: "You cut your beard and sold out your Jewishness for a few dollars! . . ." And when he was done, he put his arm around me and said, "OK, now you can come in and enjoy yourself." To this day that still affects me and moves me to tears. You see, he took me through the shame. He took me into it and through it, which is exactly what I had to do.

However, there are times when this is not appropriate. I wouldn't suggest this to people who are severely depressed and possibly suicidal. With them the aim would be to shore them up and strengthen them. You would want to divert them with a lot of physical activity so that they begin to sweat and exert themselves. That can help overcome this kind of depression. But take a look, Reb Shneur Zalman is talking to a person who has committed to a religious life, who somehow, at least twice a day, says, "*Sh'ma Yisrael,* I believe in God, and I want to love that God." So he isn't exactly speaking to that abyss into which you would fall and from which, there is no coming up. It was Reb Nachman of Bratzlav who talked about that abyss. All Reb Shneur Zalman is saying is, break down the defenses periodically. It is like defragmenting your hard drive.[4] After a while, there is a lot of junk in there that will cause it to crash if you don't clean it up. The *t'shuvah* doesn't come without having that experiencing of regret.

Keep in mind, we are not talking about an absolute *Rasha*. In fact, he says, the imperfect *Rasha* is full of regret and is constantly saying, "Oh, I'm sorry." So he isn't talking about that kind of obstinate, totally malevolent person. The absolute *Rasha* has no access to regret where she or he is.

Another aspect of depression has to do with dealing with the bad things that happen to us. How do we deal with misfortune? Why did God let such a thing happen to me! The Rabbis wrote, "Just as one must recite a blessing for the good, one must also recite a blessing for misfortune." And about that I have a story:

Once there was a rich Hasid who had a caravan of merchandise being brought from the great fair at Leipzig back to Belorussia, where he lived. But catastrophe struck, and the entire caravan was destroyed. The man was wiped out financially; even worse, he lost not only his own money but also money he had borrowed to bring that merchandise in. So he was now in a very bad place. But had not yet been told of the calamity. So a group of his friends in Leipzig decide to go and inform him about the situation. They come to him and say, "Doesn't the Gemara say something about when bad things happen to a person?" And the Hasid replies, "Yes, it is written that just as for the good, you have to say a b'rokha for the bad that happens." So they say, "Let us tell you what happened to your stuff," and the Hasid faints dead away. So it's easier said than done.

In this is the notion of trying to pull yourself up by your own bootstraps. It is like saying, "How am I ever going to get out of this situation? If I am going to fight it, I'm going to have trouble. There is only one way to work it out: accept it for what it is." But how can I face the facts, sometimes terrible facts, and still believe that God is kind? So then come all the ways in which we play tricks on ourselves in our head. We start saying, "Well, I deserved worse" or "God gave me this one instead of that one." There is that element of always saying that God is just. "God in God's judgment is right." That right-making of God makes it so that we can at least count on God's help. No matter how bad the situation is, we can say, "Please be with me." There is a saying, "You promised Jacob to be with him in the fire and in the water." Note that it doesn't say that he won't get burned, and it doesn't say that he won't drown. It says that during his burning, God will be with him, and in his drowning, God will be there. That is a heavy statement, and it involves a heavy commitment. This is the point of gam zeh ya-vor and gamzu l'tovah, "this too is for the best."

Once Rabbi Akiva was riding a donkey and had with him a rooster and he was looking for a place where he could spend the night. Finally, he comes to an inn, but the owners don't want him there. So he has to camp out nearby with his rooster and his donkey. In the night the rooster dies and so does the donkey. And when each died he said, Gamzu l'tovah, "This is also for the good." So now he is alone at night camping out. The next morning he finds out that robbers came in and killed everybody in the inn. If the donkey had brayed, he would have been found and killed. And if the rooster had crowed, he would have been found and killed. So their dying saved him.

This is what the Rabbis tell about how you should meet misfortune. It isn't saying that pain doesn't exist. It says that as human beings, we do the best we can under the circumstances, and some of the "mind moves" we make are the things that help us out of trouble. Part of the Chabad way is to teach you mind moves to make it through difficult situations.

THE END OF THE JOURNEY

FROM THE MIDDLE to the end of the *Book of the Beynoni*, Reb Shneur Zalman talks about how to acquire Awe of God and how to acquire Love of God, and in the end, he asks about "sanctuary." Where is the sanctuary for God? In the past, we always taught that the sanctuary is the Temple. And now Reb Shneur Zalman wants to talk about the temple within, and that is the last chapter of the *Book of the Beynoni*. At one point he says, "I'll teach you a way in which you can have the Awe of God." So he points out that you have a little Moses inside, and you have a Moses awareness that will get you to the Awe of God. He says, "You want to be able to love God. Imagine a great king who takes a poor *shmegeg* who hangs out on a dunghill into his palace and there shows him great love. How will that person respond? Will he not respond with love? And then you start looking at all the good God has done for you. Is it not the same situation? And should you not respond with Love?" So these are the mind moves that you make to arouse feelings. That comes at the end of the first book of the *Tanya*.

Now let's look at how he leads up to this end. Perhaps some of this material seems technical and a little hard to follow. That is par for the course, but notice how he built the thing up. In chapters eighteen to twenty he was discussing the question "What does it mean to have natural Love and Awe for God?" What a remarkable thing. When people say in spiritual life, "It isn't that you have to achieve it, it is already there. All you have to do is remove the *avidya*,[1] ignorance. You are just not recognizing it." So we are dealing with nescience. But if you wake up to what you already know, you don't need any more; you have it all right there. That is one approach: everybody already has the yearning, that Love and Awe before God.

Once I participated in singing a wonderful Protestant hymn that goes, "Then sings my heart, my Savior God to Thee—how great Thou art, how great Thou art." That feeling is so natural for some people that you don't need to have very special things happening, and this is why people have peak experiences. Reb Shneur Zalman is not satisfied with that, and so he teaches a way of meditation called *hitbonenut*. In this meditation, you set things to your heart, you fasten your mind to something, and you see how God is indwelling in creation. He says, "You don't need to have faith to believe in the God who is the Creator of the Universe," that is almost given to be observed. What does it mean that you can "see" that? You can see it with your mind's eye. How do you see it with your mind's eye? You put it in front of your mind's eye. And a lot of this kind of meditation is just to put it there until it becomes a true reality for you.

Now, I've seen some people who do diagnostics. Perhaps you know someone or have members of the family who have gone to medical school. Medical schools don't give you much of a chance to be a human being; they pound medicine into you day in and day out. Do you know how hard it is to be an intern or a medical student? Before long, you don't look at your patients as human beings anymore; you look at them as symptoms. If you are a Rolfer, you might do the same. You have so internalized a way of looking at reality because you have held it in front of your mind's eye and taken it on. A particular map has been laid over your eyes, and it now seems natural for you that you see everything in terms of that map. Suddenly, you notice something that you didn't notice before you had the map. Just a small thing; somebody else wouldn't notice it at all. But because you notice that, your behavior is changed around it, and others who can't see it don't understand. They wouldn't understand what you are getting excited over because you have so strongly fastened it in your mind that it is integrated with your reality map.

So Reb Shneur Zalman is trying to teach people something about meditation and prayer. Every time I feel that feeling moving in my heart, I will pray. But what happens when I don't feel that feeling moving in my heart? Am I not going to pray? I have to *davven* anyway. So there are some times when we pray out and some times when we pray in. You open the prayer book, and it says, "The soul of every living being shall praise Thy name." So maybe this morning you don't feel like it; you are sort of dull in your head and dull in your heart and you don't feel like it. But then you stick with it and finally you get into it. You may have seen people working very hard in their *davvenen*. They have the prayer shawl pulled over their head as if to say, "I want to shut out everything else. I just want to concentrate on this one thing." "If my hands were to be like wings, I would fly. If my feet were to be like deer hooves, I would run to you." These things are part of the prayer book, and at the time that you don't feel like it, you are not praying out, you are praying in. So what Reb Shneur Zalman is showing us in the late chapters is how to create the natural Love and Awe that we have for God, how to fan it with the intellect so that the heart will get to feel that. That is a remarkable part of the *Tanya*.

The Sanctuary

May this be their solace, to be a comfort to them.[2]

You have a shrine room or perhaps a corner in your house where you keep your shrine—your "God corner." That is where you keep your candles, your incense, some pictures, and these kinds of things. Why do you put everything in this corner? Isn't God everywhere? Is there less of God in the bathroom than in your shrine room? I say yes. Well, it is not that God is less there, but my awareness of God may be less there. So I need to have signs that will draw me into that consciousness. Most of the time, what we do is create external means. And that is what sacred places are. Churches, synagogues, and temples are external means we have created in order to be able to say, "This is where God resides." So here comes Reb Shneur Zalman, saying, "In our heart, in our innermost being, is where God resides."

Now I'm going to step out of the *Tanya* for a moment. The physicist David Bohm[3] says that there are four explicate dimensions, the four dimensions that we know, and six implicate dimensions. The implicate dimensions are sort of rolled up; they are there, but we don't know them that way. In the explicate dimensions—length, width, height, and time—God is immanent. In the implicate dimensions, God is transcendent. If some of the implicate dimensions weren't here, the explicate dimensions couldn't exist. It is as if those six dimensions are sort of rolled up in those other dimensions that we cannot tap with our regular consciousness, and the reason we can't tap them is that they are implicate, not explicate; they are not "out there." Those dimensions are where the aspects of God that we can't get to with our mind, our senses, or with anything else, reside because they are so deeply hidden. That is the transcendent; that is where the Infinite is hiding.

Now what Reb Shneur Zalman is saying is, "I would like you to make a sanctuary for the implicate order." This is putting it into modern language, of course. How do you make that sanctuary for the implicate order? He says, "You make it by faith in the transcendent part." And this has something to do with an earlier statement, "You must never let the oil dry on your head."[4] Where does this oil come from? And the flame of the soul often remains hidden; what makes the flame of the soul burn? The answer is the practice—the practice of the rituals, the practice of the commandments—that is what gives the flame of the soul a chance to burn higher. That is the fuel, the oil.

I used to wonder, "What is it that makes a car go faster?" When I first got my driver's license, I couldn't understand how acceleration worked, and it was explained to me that when you step on the gas, more fuel goes into the cylinder, so it makes a bigger flame inside. If the flame gets bigger, then, boom, boom, it goes faster. So I finally got it. Now, if I would like to get the engine of my soul to go faster, I have to light it up; I have to put in more fuel. And what is the fuel that makes it run? That fuel seems to be the study of Torah, the fulfillment of the commandments—that is what makes that fuel increase. When there is an increase of that fuel, it burns brighter. And when the flame burns brighter, more space is created in the sanctuary. There is more manifestation in the sanctuary, and there seems to be an increasing transparency. So now, in the heart, *Malkhut* of *Malkhut* of *Assiyah* looks through and there shines *Malkhut* of *Malkhut* of *Yetzirah*, in which shines the *Malkhut* of *B'riyah*, in which shines the *Malkhut* of *Atzilut*. Do you see? There is sort of a gradual melting away of the opacity that exists until the flame burns at full throttle in the heart.

What would it be like to be a *bodhisattva*—to feel compassion for every creature in the world? Do you think it would be easy? It would feel like both ecstasy and agony. The agony is that with everybody who is suffering out there, you would participate in their suffering fully. Most of us want to run away when we hear that somebody else has got troubles; we make ourselves opaque to that. The saint, the *Tzaddik*, the *bodhisattva* stays with that and still has compassion. So there is heart space being created, and along with it a place where the sanctuary is made. I wish we all would be able to achieve what we build temples and sanctuaries for, in our own inner beings, in our own hearts. How wonderful that would be. And that is where Reb Shneur Zalman takes us at the end of the *Sefer Shel Beynonim*. So what we covered up to now was simply a road map for reading the first book of the *Tanya*. Keep the book around, and from time to time, just open up to any page for the inspiration it can give you. Likely it will be like an oracle; you will turn to the "right" page, and something good will come out for you.

THE WORD THAT CREATES

SHA'AR HA'YICHUD VE'HA'EMUNAH
AND THE REST OF THE TANYA

"Know this today and take it into your heart that *Hava'ye* is *Elokim* (God is the Mighty One) in the heavens above and on the earth below; there is none other." . . . It is written: "Eternally, O God, Your word stands firm in the heavens." The Ba'al Shem Tov, of blessed memory, explained this as "Your word," which You uttered, "Let there be a firmament in the midst of the waters . . . ," these very words and their letters are standing firmly and eternally within the firmament of heaven and are eternally clothed within all the heavens vitalizing them, as it is written, "The word of our God shall eternally stand firm" and "His words are eternally living and standing firm. . . ." For if the letters were to disappear even for an instant, God forbid, returning to their Source, then all the heavens would become nothingness and disappear completely, and it would be as if they had never existed, just as before the words "Let there be a firmament."[1]

The second book of the *Tanya*, called *Sha'ar HaYichud VeHaEmunah* (Gate of Unity and Belief), talks about cosmology. To Reb Shneur Zalman, the whole universe is created by the words of God, by the letters of the Torah, and he points out that you must not make the mistake of thinking that creation is like pottery. A potter takes clay and makes a pot. What is the creative part of the potter? Just to give it shape. The potter didn't make the clay. But when God creates the world, God makes the substance and also gives it the form. And how does it all come together? It comes together through the letters of the Torah. Everything that exists is a combination of the letters of the Torah, and that is what gives it life.

You know, if you took a snippet out of a book from a Hasidic master and were to hand it to me, the likelihood is that I would be able to identify the master who had written it. I once had a remarkable student at the University of Manitoba. If I told him a sentence from the Bible and then asked him to do it like Reb Shneur Zalman or Reb Nachman or Reb Elimelech, he would close his eyes and begin to say it in their style. Can you imagine having a really wonderful pianist playing "Twinkle, Twinkle, Little Star" in the style of Bach, Mozart, and then Brahms? Every Hasidic master has a deep signature. Reb Shneur Zalman's is in certain sentences that he uses over and over again. One such sentence is the one with which he opens the *Sha'ar HaYichud VeHaEmunah: V'yada'ta hayam vehashevota al l'vavekha,* "You should know it today and set it on your heart," *lei YHVH hu Elohim bashamayim mima'al v'al ha'aretz mitachat,* "that *YHVH* is *Elohim,* both in the heavens above and the earth below." *Ain od,* "Nothing else." There is no encore to that; this is just enough. It boils down to this: "How could there more than Infinity?"

If one were to take that sentence and spell out his mission, it would be to go around to the world and to tell people, "Know, today! Don't wait!" And you can know. What can you know? You can know that the Great Beyond and the One; all is identical, heaven above and earth below, *YHVH, Elohim,* nothing else exists. This is the Endless Being. And this is the mission Reb Shneur Zalman has set for himself, to go around and to make sure that as many people will get this message.

The Zohar also uses a phrase that Reb Shneur Zalman was fond of: "Why did God create the world? In order that creatures would know Him"—to be able to take finite beings and bring them to the appreciation and recognition of the Infinite. That is why the world was created. So there is a statement that we say on Rosh HaShanah, when we pray, "God, would you please renew Your contract with existence?" You know, if God didn't hold to the contract that He has with existence, existence would disappear. What keeps existence in being? Ah, God has spoken. But does God divide time into past, present, and future? No, because the name *YHVH* means "the One of ever-making being," "the One who brings into being." That is always. And if that "attention" were to stop, there would be nothing here. Can you understand? We don't see ourselves as ephemeral like that. Even if you kill me, there is still a moment of life leaving the body. So it is hard for us to conceive that one moment we are here and another we could be gone. And not by death; it goes deeper than that. The very substance of the universe wouldn't exist. It is energized constantly by Divine Speech. That is what Reb Shneur Zalman calls it, and that is what his whole book is about. He is trying give you a cosmology, a cosmogony of how the world comes into being.

When you read the Bible in English, in Genesis, it says, "And God said, 'Let there be . . .' and it was . . . ." "Let there be" is such a polite English translation, as a gentlemen might say, "Would you kindly allow this?"

The Hebrew is *Yehi or!* "Light, *be!*" It is so strong; it is in the imperative. "Be, O light! And there was light." It is like suddenly turning something on that didn't exist before; all of a sudden it is there. What makes it happen? The switch turning it on from nonbeing to being is Divine Speech. Turn it the other way around, God withdraws Divine Speech, and everything ceases to be. But God doesn't have a mouth like we have, so what do you mean by Divine Speech?

When Cecil B. De Mille was making the movie *The Ten Commandments,* there was a big question about whether God should speak in a tenor, baritone, or a bass voice. And you can understand, if you produce a movie with God in it, you have to have a voice in there. But could you imagine, if the technology existed, hearing it only inside your head?

There was a time in history, says Julian Jaynes,[2] when whenever we got something from our intuition, from the right hemisphere of the brain, we assumed that it was a voice that spoke to us. Nowadays, we can get stuff from the right hemisphere without having to go through that long walk to say there was a voice that spoke to me. Now, I don't know if you have had experiences of voices speaking to you with great clarity, saying, "Yes," "No," "Do this," or "Go there." But many people have had experiences like this, even if it is a onetime thing. So some people get this very clearly, and the best way in which the Torah can describe it is to say, "And the people saw the voices": *V'ha'am ro'im et hakolot,* "And all the people they saw the voices." That may seem a strange way of speaking, but those of us who have had these deep experiences will tell you, they are experienced in what is called synesthesia, as if the knowing jumps the senses. The sensory organs get so flooded that you don't know whether you are hearing or seeing. So, you can get a glimpse from that of what is intended by Divine Speech.

Then Reb Shneur Zalman asks, "How is it that these "ten sayings" that the Torah records (God created Heaven and earth; let there be light; let there be firmament; let there be dry land; let there be plant life; let there be sun, moon, and stars; let there be fishes and egg layers and birds; let there be mammals; let there be human beings; and also counting "In a beginning" as a "saying") cover all of creation? More than that exists in our world. So where do stones come from? It doesn't say, "Let there be stones." Where did stones come from? It says that there was water already, that the spirit of God was hovering over the water, but it doesn't say, "Let there be water." So this is a puzzle. If everything comes by Divine Speech, how does that work out? Reb Shneur Zalman offers this remarkable teaching: "The combinations keep on combining." What you have in creation is sort of a primary energy coming through, in his thinking, twenty-two letters in the Hebrew alphabet. And they combine in all kinds of combinations and permutations, and this is how reality is created, from the stone to whatever is happening right now, at this very moment. It all comes from those combinations of letters. Now for us this may not seem the best metaphor. So the question is, how do we understand what he means to say? You see that there is a wonderful pattern in which from simplicity emerges complexity. We are moving to ever-greater integration and complexity in our brain structure, and the way in which we are in the world, the way in which we relate to other creatures, and the way in which we begin to understand the necessity for the snail darter and the owl, they are all needed here because they make up this totality that we are. We are intimately interconnected. All of creation keeps on moving toward greater and greater complexity and integration. So that is sort of a modern counterpart to what Reb Shneur Zalman develops. Don't take his metaphors too literally. He was using metaphors that worked for his immediate audience.

There are twenty-two letters in the Hebrew alphabet, as we spell it out today, and much has been written on how the world was created from them. I've seen a lot of wonderful teachings on this; some of it I find inspiring, and at the same time, from the point of view of history, it makes no sense at all. The letters of the Hebrew alphabet and the shape in which we have them today came after the Babylonian exile. If you have seen the paleo-Hebrew alphabet, the alphabet that was earlier, it doesn't look the same as the current letters of the *aleph-bet*. And yet so much intention and so much teaching has been written about the mystery of the letters in the form in which we have them today. From a historical point of view, this is untenable. But from the point of view that reality wants to reveal itself to us in as many forms as it can, I want to buy in to that. Bhartahari was a Hindu philosopher who spoke about the letters of the Sanskrit alphabet in the same way. People in Islam say that the Arabic alphabet is what was used to create the universe and there was a man by the name of George Lamsa, a Christian teacher coming out of the Syrian tradition, where they still use Aramaic in their worship, who said that the universe was created from Aramaic letters.[3]

But let's look at this business of creation from the letters. In the imaginary world of *Star Trek* are what they call "replicators." You ask it for something, and it materializes it. So how do you make the replicator give you "Earl Grey tea, hot"? How does the replicator know how to do it? Now, I am not talking as if there exists a real replicator. But watch the way it lives in the myth. Someone can go and make a program, and that program is going to give you Earl Grey tea. Or you walk into the "holodeck," a room that creates interactive holograms, you set up a program, and all of a sudden a whole interactive reality gets created. So the replicator is Gene Roddenberry's way of explaining what the *Tanya* wants to explain. We are all saying that somehow there is a formula that holds everything together, and if there are differentiated forms, the best way to talk about those forms is to say, this is this kind of algorithm. It comes in this particular formula, and out of that formula, when that formula is input into what can produce something, a certain reality gets created around that. So however you explain that to yourself, it gets done in such a way that the infinite suddenly creates differentiation. Once again we use the word *language,* as in computer language. Creation language is almost like saying, "In the beginning, God *languaged* the universe, and this is how it came about."

Reb Shneur Zalman talks about the misunderstandings around the word *creation.* When people usually talk about creation, what they are really thinking is *formation.* The potter makes a pot out of clay. Then she goes to the market and the pot of clay still remains. She hasn't created the pot; she has only shaped it. Most of the time, what we human beings call creation is really shaping, giving form, but we don't create the substance ourselves. Yet when we speak of God as the Creator, God starts by bringing the very substance into existence. And in Reb Shneur Zalman's view, creation wasn't a onetime thing; it is a constant creating. If God were to break off for a moment, all would disappear. That is what is meant by the word *create,* the complete origination of the form, the substance, and everything else about a thing.

Now, if I could look at the formula for lead and just change a few numbers in there so that the formula would suddenly say gold, wouldn't that be wonderful? That is what the alchemists were chasing. They all had a sense that somehow, *abracadabra,* "as spoken, so it was created," that in this magic something came into being, because it was made with words. So you can make things happen with words, and if you knew the right combination, you could take it apart and put it back together differently. You can make something appear, and you can make something disappear.

What is the formula, you might ask, that Satya Sai Baba uses to make *Vibhuti?*[4] In other words, materialization carries a sense that somehow it is being done. Rabbi Yehudah Loew of Prague takes this clay and shapes into the form of a human being and writes one of the Divine Names on a piece of parchment, cuts open the soft clay, sticks the paper in, closes the clay up, and what was clay becomes a living body—the Golem.[5] This Frankenstein-like being then goes around and helps people in tough places. He is a little stupid, like a computer; if you don't direct it on when to stop, it'll keep on going. So you say, "Fetch water," as in "The Sorcerer's Apprentice,"[6] and he'll keep on fetching water endlessly until it is a disaster. You would have to say, "Fetch water until this is filled"; otherwise he would just keep on fetching water. There is the story of the Golem who was activated by this formula. In this understanding, the whole universe is put together using this formula, and you can create and change it.

The Talmud contains a number of statements that assure us that in doing this or that holy deed, we become partners with God in the creation of the world. How? It turns out that a certain amount of the formula, of will, is given over to us. Do you want this world to exist? OK, I'll make you a partner in willing this reality. And you might say that the human language, from the perspective that everything is *maya,* or emptiness, keeps our world together; our phenomenal world hangs on this language we are using together. We are all colluding to think in this way, to do things in this way. So you can understand why a person would say most language is not sacred language. It is language with which you shop, curse, and do everything else you do. But if you could speak the *lashon ha'kodesh,* the holy tongue, in the holy language, you could create and uncreate. Therefore, prayer is seen to be extremely powerful in the holy tongue and in these particular formulas that have to be recited. Some of the formulas are measured out with a precise number of words. And you must not add or omit a word, because that would change the power. So when *Kaddish* comes up on the days between Rosh HaShanah and Yom Kippur, you have to recite an additional *l'eyla,* saying it twice (*l'eyla v'l'eyla*), but you have to contract the two words together so that the word count remains the same. It is as if to say, don't mess with that, that is very powerful stuff. People feel the same way about mantras.

Then Reb Shneur Zalman comes up with this:

It is written: "For a sun and a shield is *Hava'ye Elokim.*" This verse is explained as follows: "Shield" is a covering for the sun, so that the creatures will be protected and able to bear it. As our Sages, of blessed memory, have said, "The *Olam HaBa,* the Holy One, blessed be He, will take the sun out of its sheath, and the *Rasha* will be punished by it. . . ." Now, just as the covering shields and conceals the sun, so does the name *Elokim* shield and conceal the name *Hava'ye,* blessed be He.[7]

It is written, "For a sun and a shield is the Love of God." A sun and a shield. Who is the sun? *YHVH* is the sun. Who is the shield? *Elohim.* That is how he says, *Ki shemesh umagen YHVH Elohim,* "The shield is in such relationship to the sun as the name *Elohim* is in relation to *YHVH.*" What might it mean that the relationship between *YHVH* and *Elohim* is the same kind of relationship as between the sun and a shield? The teaching goes, if God were to take the sun out from his shield, the sun would be able to shine fully and completely, and we would all be burned. Think of the shield as a good ozone layer. It is the shield for the sun. But what is behind these words? What is the relationship between raw God-ness, as it were, and the God-ness that reaches us, that is the same relationship as *YHVH* and *Elohim*? There is something tremendous behind the shield, and it creates a real sense of awe, or amazement. Professor Abraham Joshua Heschel liked to use the phrase "radical amazement" for this awe. I'll tell you a story about that:

Back when I was with the University of Manitoba, Professor Heschel was visiting a synagogue in Winnipeg and was scholar in residence for that weekend. And it was a remarkable weekend, but it was sort of sold out. Friday night, you couldn't come just to services because it was this weekend that he had come in, and most of my students couldn't manage to get in. So I did a retreat with the students at Hillel, and we studied the writings of Professor Heschel for that *Shabbaton,* and on Sunday he came for an hour to Hillel house. We had prepared for his coming and had come across the phrase "radical amazement." And one of my students asked him, "Professor Heschel, what's this 'radical amazement' that you write about?" Heschel made an angry face and said, "Look with what he is challenging me!" and started blowing his horn in an amazing way: "Here you are talking to me like this, I teach from coast to coast, and da da da da da," making a big thing of it. My poor student was wiped out. And then Professor Heschel turned to him and said, "Would you mind bringing me a glass of water?" And when the student returned with the glass of water, Professor Heschel held it up and began to rhapsodize beautifully about water. "Where would we be if it weren't here? We are water. We live with water. We live off of water. We are in water, a drop of water, a universe reflected in that." And this poor student was awestruck, and Professor Heschel looked at him and said, "That's radical amazement!"

The point is always to get to the moment where you get surprised by the Divine. That moment is called *Akheyn atah El mistater,* "So here you are hiding God." Or as Jacob says the morning after he had the vision of the angels going up and down, "Here I was in God's place, and I didn't know." It was an "Oh, wow!" moment.

So when Reb Shneur Zalman talks about the sun and the shield, he wants to tell us that nature, what we see with our eyes, is the shield. However, if it weren't for the sun behind the shield, we wouldn't have life. We wouldn't exist. It is the shield that makes the light accessible to us and gives us a chance to have our separate existence. So the world lives by that light that shines forth from *Ain Sof,* from the Infinite. It is like Huxley's consensus reality filter:[8] if we directly perceived the nature of what is, we couldn't handle it. There would not be anything left to apprehend. Hence there is a filter. And yet the filter is there not to obstruct but to allow the information we can handle to pass through to us. So how clean is the filter? A filter can get clogged, you know. In fact, this is what Yom Kippur is about. Like the sanctuary of the Holy Temple, the sanctuary was like a God-filter, to let God into our world—and to let the world up to God, because that is what we did; we offered sacrifices. And every Yom Kippur, the filter had to be cleaned out because it was clogged. That is one of the images that is being used. It had to be wiped, it had to be cleaned up. So follow me through another step, because this is going to get complicated.

If I say, "The Light that flows out from God is giving me life and invigorating me," what do I mean? Could there be an "out" from God? What do I mean, "out from God?" We are all inside of God. Think about this. All these miles away from the sun we receive sunlight. Do you think there is any sunlight an inch into the surface of the sun? Of course there is. Then what being does the sunlight inside the sun have? Reb Shneur Zalman says, "That is the being that all of reality has in God." Since it is happening inside of the Divine, what is going on in this seeming reality? How do we have a world?

Still, these are His Restraining Powers, to make hidden and concealed, through *Gevurah* and *Tzimtzum,* the life energy that flows into them, so that Heaven and earth and all their manifold variation should appear to be independently existing entities. However, this *Tzimtzum* and concealment is only in the lower worlds, for in relation to the Holy One, blessed be He, "Everything before Him is considered as actually nothing," just as the light of the sun within the sun is nullified. And *Gevurah* does not, Heaven forbid, conceal for Him, may He be blessed, for it is also not an independently existing entity—given that *Hava'ye* is *Elokim.*[9]

So he begins to teach us about *Tzimtzum*. He says that God has to remove that light so that there should be space for the world. And then he says, "There are some people who claim that God has removed Himself completely, because they understand the idea of *Tzimtzum* in a simple way. What did God do? God removed Himself and made a place for the empty space to be in. (Remember that "empty space," because we are going to meet it again when we discuss Reb Nachman and the "Torah of the Void.") So how does God create this empty space? As Reb Yitzhak Luria says, *Tzimtzem et ha'or litz'dadin,* "It sort of shoved the light over to both sides, and where the light was not, space was created for the world." So the question is, "Is God still there, or is God not there?" If you say that God is there as God was before, then there is no place for the world. But if you say God is not there anymore, there couldn't be a world either. He isn't there to invigorate it. Do you see the paradox? Reb Shneur Zalman says, "I cannot agree with those people who say that God has truly removed Himself from the space that the world is in. Those people are wrong; God is still there." And he quotes another one of those phrases that he is fond of quoting, *Leyt atar panui miney*, "No space is empty of Him." It is another way of saying *yachid u'm'yuchad*, "one, unique, unified."

This mystery, that God is here and isn't here, Reb Shneur Zalman begins to explain in the differences in the word *light*. In the Kabbalah, people are always talking about the Divine Light. What do they mean? Reb Yitzhak Luria says, "Divine Light is *Hargashat shlemut ha'Atzmut*, the possibility that we can feel the utter perfection of the Absolute." Light is that by which we apprehend the utter perfection of the Absolute. Now, if you really were to get the utter perfection of the Absolute, it would blow you out. So what we get is only a tiny bit of that Light.

Here I want to say something about the figure-ground relationship. An optical illusion reprinted in many psychology books can appear to be either be two people in profile or a goblet. Some people will even say it is two people holding a goblet between their noses. Or think of most of the signs we see. Usually, they are red and white or black and white. One color is the ground, which the other is contrasted against, making the figure. Now what do we mean by "ground"? Ground is what the eye makes "invisible" in order to be able to see the figure. If I wanted to read the ground of a sign, it wouldn't make any sense to me. But if I read the figure against the ground, it does make sense. So in this case, a ground color is serving what emptiness is serving. And the letters of the figure are what gets placed into emptiness. The mind is not interested in the ground; the ground is invisible to the mind. I once wrote a piece in my *Fragments of a Future Scroll*[10] called "Finnegan's Awakening," which dealt with the figure-ground reversal. It is one of those very deep meditations.

There was a Christian theologian by the name of Paul Tillich[11] who spoke of God as "the Ground of all being." In other words, everything that is, that has existence, that is there, is there because the ground makes it possible. So it is the ground that makes the figure visible. But once I look and want to see the ground, the ground becomes the figure; and if God were to be a figure, then that would be an idol. Remember the whole business of idolatry—don't make a figure of God. So how can I see the Ground? I exist in the Ground, but I can't see the Ground, because the moment I see it, I have a figure. When do I see air, for instance? If I put smoke through it, then I can see it; otherwise I don't see air. And yet we live and breathe in it. That is basically the sense of the emptiness that contains something.

Now the Gnostics spoke of something that is called the *Pleroma,* meaning "that which is the everything." At one and the same time this is both the utmost fullness and the utmost emptiness that there can be. So the words *full* and *empty* are like a Möbius strip, like *yin* and *yang,* melding into one another. It is very hard to say more than that. When you have a statement about God being *Ain Sof,* the Infinite, sometimes this is *Ayin HaElokhi,* the Divine Nothingness, and sometimes we speak about the Divine Somethingness of that. The Sufis speak of *fana,* related to the Hebrew *panui,* empty, gone. It is like *bodhi svaha* in Buddhism: everything that there is is *om, gate, gate, paragate parasamgate bodhi svaha,* "gone, gone, gone beyond, gone completely beyond." The Sufis also speak of *baqa,* "that which is present." And then they teach us that *fana* and *baqa* are one. The fullness and the emptiness are one. And there are some people who are into finding God in the *fana,* in the nothing, and there are some people who find God in the *baqa,* in the something. The positive theologian would say, "God is this, God is that." The negative theologian says, "*Neti, neti,* it is not this, not this."[12] And the radical theologian, says, "It's both"—there is a dynamic relationship with both.

Reb Shneur Zalman says there is *da'at elyon* and *da'at tachton,* supernal knowing and lower knowing—*Ki El de'ot YHVH,* "About God, one can say two things." One can say, "God is, and where God is, nothing else is." Or one can say, "God is the nothingness in which everything else is." And it is very hard to say both at the same time. Therefore, when we begin with the world of *Assiyah,* the lowest world, we would be saying, "Where this world is most palpable, God is least palpable." When we come up to *Atzilut,* there is nothing else but God. And all of these are true as long as you continue on the chain of being. You go from this level to other levels.

So this is Reb Shneur Zalman's introduction on how the universe comes into being. He completed twelve chapters, and that is where the *Sha'ar HaYichud VeHaEmunah* ends. I really wish that he would have continued and spelled it all out. There was a time when I really lived with this part of the *Tanya,* looking at everything from that perspective of the reduction of light. What does this obligate me to do? I see that there is light shining through, but I still can't see very well. I want more light, more light, more light. When Goethe[13] was about to die, his last words were, "More light." We want more light. Have you ever been to an ophthalmologist who dilated your pupils and then shone that white light into your eyes? It does not cause physical pain, but I can't stand it. It's not like it's going to burn out my retina or like looking at the sun, but I just can't stand the brightness. So this is our dilemma. We want more light, and when the light comes, we say, "Oh, not too much!" This is the understanding of Divine Light and the filters it has to go through and how it hides itself so it can do its amazing trick of energizing me to exist. If I were to see it happen, I would disappear. It is as if I can only be because it is hidden inside of me. We are back to the implicate order. It is there, but it can't show itself. If it would, I couldn't be. That is the meditation of the God who is hiding in everything and playing peekaboo with us. But it isn't that God is just hiding, God wants to be discovered in this hiding. The Ba'al Shem Tov described how his grandson came to him one day and said, "I've been playing hide-and-seek with my brother, and I was hiding, and he didn't come and seek me out." The whole game of hide-and-seek depends on your not being so well hidden that you can't be found. But you also can't be so obvious that you can be found without effort. That is what makes the game interesting.[14]

Igeret HaT'shuvah: Book Three of the Tanya

With this arousing of mercies following the contrition, evil and the Other Side are no longer nurtured from the life energy emanating from the lower *Heh,* as noted. (The latter *Heh* returns to its own place, uniting as before with the *Yud-Heh-Vav*. This will suffice for the understanding.)

As there is a "restoring" of the *Heh* above, so too will there be below in the Divine Soul within man; no longer do "your sins divide." It is said that "He cleanses" those who return to Him, to pour over and cleanse their souls of the defiled garments, the "externals" that the Talmud describes as "encrusted. . . ."[15]

In reading things like this, much of your spiritual yearning gets affirmed, and you are inspired by that, but it is also disconcerting. You begin to see the flaws that you have never noticed in yourself. You see the ego traps and all the things you've done wrong that you want to fix. How are you going to go about doing that? The third part of the *Tanya* is called *Igeret HaT'shuvah*, "Letter of Repentance," in which Reb Shneur Zalman spells out how to go about doing repentance.

We have a custom at weddings. Before you go to the wedding canopy, there is the veiling of the bride. At the veiling of the bride, I usually gather together all the blood relatives into a room, to ask them each to forgive each other, because its impossible to grow up in a family, with siblings and parents, without having some secret anger. And you don't want people to have to go into the next phase of life with all this karmic load. So that is why bringing in those people is so important. That way they can forgive each other and really bless each other. It is a very powerful thing. On one occasion, a young girl was present while we were doing this forgiveness, and she wanted to know how to do it. I tell you, it was a wonderful thing that she asked this question. She really wanted to know how to do it. It was as if nobody had ever showed her how to do forgiving. So I said to her, "Could you imagine that you have a beautiful shiny white dress on, and here comes this big clump of mud and dirties it? You would want to clean it off, wouldn't you?" "Oh, yes," she said. "Could you imagine then, instead of the mud being on the outside on your dress, the mud is on your heart?" "Uh huh." "And being angry with people and not forgiving them is like mud on your heart." "I sure want to get rid of that," she said. "OK, how are you going to go about doing that?" I suggested that she close her eyes, raise up her hands in her imagination, and draw down some golden light and let it flow over that mud on her heart until it was all washed away. In this way she really understood forgiving.

Do you understand how important it is, just as with this child, to respond decently when somebody says, "You ought to . . . ," and starts giving you advice and you want to say, "I've been trying to do it myself. You don't have to scold me—show me how to do it"?

This is the issue in all spiritual direction work. When you have achieved any kind of light and any kind of closeness to God, you begin to feel "*Oy!* do I have to clean up my act." Reb Shneur Zalman takes that whole notion and breaks it apart in the following way. He says, "If you take a look at the Divine Name, *YHVH, YH* is the connection that is so eternal, nothing can make it dirty. No dirt reaches that high level of our connection with the soul. But with the *VH*, the lower part, it happens all the time." It gets muddied and gets involved and so on. So that has to be cleaned up and brought back to the *YH*. The *YH* and *VH* should be together. Bringing back is *lehashiv*, "to make it come back." The word *t'shuvah*, he reads as "that which makes the *VH*, *tashev VH*, it brings back that part of the Divine that has become separated and dirty." That is the work that has to be done. So you say, "Wonderful, how do you do it?"

You see, he is not talking only about what happens in your feelings; he is also talking about the purification that has to happen. Even if you have done some things unintentionally, some things are tacky; they stick to you. How do you get rid of them? Most of the shamanic smudging with incense and sweats are trying to do this kind of cleaning. And it is not just cleaning up what you have done; it is taken for granted that if you have done something wrong, you will fix it up first, but having fixed it up on the outside, it still doesn't cover the damage that has been done on the inside. That needs to be repaired too. Fasting is how to handle the thing on that level. But then Reb Shneur Zalman starts saying that the heart also has to come back in repentance. And what keeps the heart from coming back? It doesn't feel forgiven.

The solution Reb Shneur Zalman offers for this is one he shares with Reb Levi Yitzhak of Berditchev. Reb Levi Yitzhak tells us that forgiveness is our right, and he tells this story. A child asks to have an apple, and his papa says no. So the child speaks a blessing: "*Barukh atah Adonai Elohenu melekh ha'olam boray pri ha'etz.*" Now the father is in a dilemma. Unless he gives the boy the apple, he causes the child to have a sin for having made a blessing in vain. So he has to give him the apple, and that is how the kid gets his apple. Says Reb Levi Yitzhak, "What right have we got to say that God forgives, 'Blessed art Thou who forgivest sin'?" He says it amounts to the same thing. We come to God and we say, "Whether you want to forgive or not, 'Blessed art Thou who forgivest sin.'" By making the blessing, we bring it about; we make it happen. It is almost mechanical. Reb Nachman of Bratzlav also points it out in his language. He says, "If you believe that you can spoil things, you must also believe that you can fix them." If I make an impact, I can do something positive. And in fact, that seems to be the job, to go and do the fixing. So there is that level of fixing, and there is also the level about trusting that forgiveness is a possibility. I think that is the hardest thing for people to believe, that karma is fixable. But then, we have Yom Kippur, and Christians have Good Friday, both of which say, "Yes, there is something that you can do about karma." So I want to tell you a story from the Zen Buddhist tradition:

In a Zen monastery was an old man who used to come every day to the dharma talk. And when it was over, he would bow and disappear. Noticing this, a novice asked one of the elder monks, "Who is this old man who turns up every day?" And the elder monk said, "When I was a young novice, I asked the same question about the same old man. And that elder monk, who was an old-timer like me, said that he had asked the same question also. This guy has been coming here forever, as far as we know." One day the old man doesn't show up, and the roshi says to the monks, "Today, prepare a grave where the roshis are buried and come with me." And they go and get together a bier on which to transport a corpse and get all the funeral stuff ready and begin to chant. The roshi (the abbot) takes them out into the field and there is a bush there, and he points underneath the bush, and there is a dead fox. They pick up the dead fox, do the chants, and bury it with all the honors of a roshi. But the monks are very puzzled. What is going on? After the funeral is over, they ask the roshi, "What was this all about?" And he replies, "Do you remember that old man who used to come here every day?" "Yes. What happened to him?" "Well, you see, only when he came here was he permitted to take human form. At all other times he was in the form of a fox. And that was sort of a punishment incarnation. Why was he punished? Because he was once a roshi at this monastery years and years and years ago, and people came and asked him the question, 'What happens when you are enlightened, does the karma stop, or does the karma continue?' And he taught that the karma stops. And because he taught that, he was punished by being reincarnated as a fox because he was teaching wrongly. But the last time he came to me, he asked me what happens to karma when one is enlightened, and I said, 'Enlightenment is enlightenment and karma is karma.' He thanked me and died right afterward. He was enlightened when I said that to him, and his karma stopped."

This is known as the *koan* (paradox) of the fox. Go figure it out. He had gotten this karma as a result of teaching that karma stops, and now he gets the teaching that karma does not stop, and when he really gets it that way, karma stops. It is not a rational thing. In a sense, that is what Yom Kippur is about. It is trying to get you to the place where you do all this, "I've sinned—I've done this and that," and at the same time you also have to believe that forgiveness is a possibility. And that feeling of being forgiven produces a deep sense of liberation. Much of Christianity is built around that—going to confession and making an act of contrition and doing penance and feeling that you have been absolved. The sense of having sinned no longer hangs on to you (unless you let it). I tell you, there were some people in the Jewish community who were not happy about the fact that someone wanted to come to the war criminal Adolf Eichmann just before he was executed[16] and reconcile him with Christ so that he should be forgiven. "Look what this person has done," they said. And yet at the same time, if you were Eichmann and genuinely contrite, could you imagine what it would have meant to you? "I don't mind dying, but I have to die in such a way, knowing there is no way for me to fix what I have done." And some people don't believe it can happen. The hubris, the *chutzpah*, of people is to think that they can sin so big that God can't forgive it. And that is what this whole third book of the *Tanya* is about. It is to explain what the means are for being able to create that *t'shuvah*, that reconciliation.

Igeret HaKodesh and Kuntres Aharon

Therefore, my beloved ones, my brothers: incline your hearts to these words I have expressed with great brevity (and please, God, personally I will speak to them at length). . . .[17]

The fourth and fifth sections of the *Tanya—Igeret HaKodesh,* "Sacred Letter," and *Kuntres Aharon,* "Latest Treatise"—deal with Reb Shneur Zalman's various letters. Some of the letters answer those written by his Hasidim, asking him for clarification on teaching, which he provides. Some are pastoral letters to his Hasidim. In one pastoral letter, he chides the men for talking in the synagogue. He says—and this has in fact come to be true—that it has now become a place for socializing, and the vertical connection has been cut. He would like to have people love each other and be warm and friendly; that is part of "love your neighbor as yourself," and he has at the beginning of the prayers that one should say, "I accept upon myself the positive commandment of loving my neighbor as myself." And with that you go into prayer. But to be able to spend the time in the sanctuary without talking and just make this prayer time, paying attention to the vertical connection and not to the lateral connection—can you imagine what it would be like to come into such a place? That is what it says in the Bible: "Into the house of God let us walk with sensitivity." Sensitivity means feeling it. If I don't walk with sensitivity, if I trample in, I'm not going to feel anything there. So that is one letter that he writes.

In another letter, he writes to his Hasidim, "Now that I have been jailed and released and a sort of victory has come for Hasidism, please don't go around lording it over the other people who were your enemies before." He tells them to act in a conciliatory way. In other letters, he writes to them about collecting money for the Hasidim who had gone and settled in the Holy Land because in those days there were no agricultural settlements and the people lived simply on the dole that they received. Why should people do that? Well, it isn't any different than it was in Lhasa, Tibet. The people who were in the countryside and were working, bringing in their offerings to the monks, and the monks were doing *puja* for them, were doing service for them. So to have people who sit and study Torah and pray for you in the Holy Land was considered a wonderful thing. To this very day, you can send a fax that someone will take to the Wall in Jerusalem and put the name of the person you prayed for in there. So if someone needed some special prayers, one would send a message off to the Holy Land to the people who were there. And for this they felt the people had a right to be supported. They were sort of the monks of that system. There is a place called Unity in Missouri where a perpetual prayer is maintained. There is always a crew praying.

That reminds me of a mission the Rebbe gave us in the early 1940s. The question was, "Do thoughts create bad karma? Do they put something out into the universe?" It was 1942 or 1943, and the previous Lubavitcher

Rebbe, Reb Yosef Yitzhak, urged us all to go through the streets reciting "holy words." He told us this was "*l'tahair et avir,* "to clean up the environment, the air is so polluted." In other words, if you put out some holy words, they will cause to precipitate and remove some of the garbage that is hanging in the air. That concept is really very important. Can you imagine having a meditational sanitation department? Well, we used to have that in every town. When I read about Teresa of Avila and the little convents that she had, what they were doing, I saw that they were in perpetual adoration, they were cleaning up the atmosphere for a whole diocese. And in every *shtetl* where you had people sitting in the *beit midrash* studying Torah, they were doing the same kind of a thing. Today we don't honor that enough. We don't see it as productive. And I have the feeling that after a while, we're going to learn how everything else on the level of action is energized by the people who are holding the field for us in prayer. And if you come to the Wall, even at two or three in the morning, you'll always find someone there holding the vigil, holding the consciousness. So that is why Reb Shneur Zalman had to write out letters to people, urging, "Please send in your donations to be sent to the Holy Land."

The Writing of the *Tanya*

Although many other Hasidic masters have released some fireworks of their own, Reb Shneur Zalman is special for sitting down and writing it all out. And some of his Hasidim said that this was the hardest part. In all of the *Tanya,* the word *Atzilut* is never fully written out. It was always written *Atzi',* with a little abbreviation mark. Why? If he had written out *Atzilut,* he would have been so caught up in the ecstasy that he wouldn't have been able to continue writing. It is extremely difficult to reach that high place and at the same time stay together. So the hardest thing for him was to write a book in such a consecutive order when each time he had these great explosions of insight along the way. So they say that when he held back, saying, "I don't want to go and fly off; I need to write this book and continue," this was the hardest part of his work. You can write about mundane things with greater ease, but if you write about that which takes you out, it is very hard to stay grounded enough to continue writing.

I remember when I was first learning the Sufi invocation "Toward the one, the perfection of love, harmony, and beauty, the only Being." By the time the others were past "harmony and beauty," I wasn't there anymore to finish the rest of it. It is such a wonderful statement. So for Reb Shneur Zalman to keep himself together to write this out was a great, great achievement.

RADICAL HASIDISM AND THE CHALLENGE OF CHANGING PARADIGMS

THE HASIDIM were by and large not much interested in politics; they didn't think that political action was the way to go. There was always the sense that you serve God, do what God tells you to do, and let God take care of politics. Well, that worked for a while, but then the tsarist regime decided to outlaw the private schools that the Jews had for themselves and force their children to go to government schools. What would have been so bad about that? Well, just ask Native Americans and Eskimos about how they feel about the forced education of their children, about being forbidden to speak their own language, about having their names changed and their culture uprooted. And so it was that Reb Menachem Mendel I of Lubavitch, among other people, stood up against the government as it became more and more recognized that political action was necessary. And by the turn of the twentieth century, there was already the possibility of having Jewish representatives elected to various government bodies.

And for those who no longer saw a future in Europe, there was Zionism.[1] How did the Hasidim look at this new movement to go and settle in Palestine? First of all, they were the kids already on the block before the Zionists showed up. Reb Shneur Zalman's friend and teacher Reb Menachem Mendel of Vitebsk had traveled to the Holy Land; some Hasidim had settled there, and many in Europe sent money to support those already in Palestine. Later on, there was a group called Hoveveh Zion (Lovers of Zion), largely religious Zionists who wanted to settle in Palestine. They arrived on the scene earlier than the Zionist organization, which wanted to create a secular state of Israel. So you can understand what kind of reaction Zionism provoked from many Hasidic masters. They said, "We did not leave Israel by our choice, and we are not going back by our choice. God sent us forth, and God has to bring us back. Any other solution is going to backfire in the long run." Sometimes you get to wondering if there isn't something true about that. So many Rebbes gathered together, and at first they were against Zionism. But then there was a split in the ranks. Some of the Hasidic masters supported Agudat Yisrael, the Orthodox party, and it turns out that Agudat Yisrael is now the core of the religious parties of Israel. And there were still others who said no to Agudat Yisrael and yes to the group called Machzikey Hadat, "those who hold on to religion." So basically, there were some people who decided that political action was appropriate for Orthodox Jews and others who said, "Yes, an Orthodox organization will help strengthen the religious needs and structure of communities that we want to help. But we are not going to help anything that has to do with politics, because that is corrupting to us." So there was this split. Then there were some other Hasidic masters who said, "How could anyone be against going back to the Holy Land? It is so important, it is a holy commandment!"

After the Second World War, when Jews first got out of the camps in Europe, all the important Hasidic books we had here in America were printed in Poland. And very often they were printed on poor-quality newsprint because the surviving Hasidim couldn't afford to pay for better-quality paper for them. And they were printed in the smallest typefaces so that a great deal could be printed in a small book. Sometimes the books were produced not from originals but from matrices (papier-mâché casts of pages of type), meaning that each successive print was weaker and more difficult to read. I have a Hasidic book that was printed in one of the camps where the people who had just been released were waiting to be resettled—that is how hungry they were for books.

Since 1940, the amount of Hebrew publishing here in the United States has been immense. When the Lubavitcher Rebbe came to America, it became more and more important to make writings available in English. In fact, modern Hasidim have flooded the world with Hebrew works. When Russia opened up, they printed the first translations of the prayer book into Russian so that they could take it into Russia. I remember, before the Iron Curtain came down, every time some friends traveled to Russia, they would take along religious implements. They would take *mezuzot, t'fillin,* and prayer books and then go to the synagogue and try and leave them inconspicuously. Now that the door has opened up, it seems miraculous. Like a tree that has been severely pruned, there is a lot of new growth. And this new growth is going with a lot of vigor. At this point, the new growth is mainly in structure, and it hasn't yet grown to great spirituality, except in a few extraordinary forms. One of them I found in a book that comes from Israel now, from the Slonimer Rebbe, Reb Shalom Noach Brazovsky, and the whole book is based on consciousness and faith and staying in touch with that consciousness. More and more there is growth toward a renewal of the meditative work.

In Warsaw prior to the industrial revolution, if you wanted to go and visit your Hasidic master, you would walk, like the Kotzker Hasidim would say, *Kan Kotzh furt men nisht, kan Kotzk gayt men, wile Kotzk iz doch bim'kom Hamikdosh,* "You don't travel to Kotzk, you don't share the pilgrimage with a horse, you walk there, because Kotzk is in the place of the Holy Temple." And on your way there, a lot of important inner work gets done while you are on the road, on the pilgrimage. And what goes on in your heart is a preparation every step of the way. But then the industrial revolution came and the whole economy of the *shtetl* shifted. This meant that people who wanted to make a living would be drawn to the large cities. For example, if everyone is going to Mexico City, people have a hard time making a living in Chiapas. But if they could go to Mexico City, they think they could make a better living and have a better life. So a lot of the people left the small towns. And because of the war between Russia, Austria-Hungary, and Germany, many of the Hasidic masters found refuge in larger cities. One settled in Berlin and several settled in Vienna, and they never went back to the little towns in Poland they were from. The Lubavitcher Rebbe, the Piasetzner Rebbe, and the Gerer Rebbe all settled in or near Warsaw. So the large cities became the Hasidic centers. Imagine what a switch this was. Before, when you went to the Rebbe, it was like traveling to the guru in his ashram. Now, instead of going to a small, secluded place, you went to a big city, where there was a whole other set-up and a lot of other distracting things going on. And instead of traveling as you did by foot and having to spend a lot of time in spiritual preparation, you took the train and got there overnight; you went to see the Rebbe with much less preparation.

And because the Hasidic way, at that time, had become more interested in preserving the mode and the ritual and the ways of ancestors than in innovating, the Hasidim were still holding on to their rural style in the urban setting. It didn't work, and many Hasidic masters despaired or made compromises with the city, but they did not restructure the Hasidic enterprise to fit the urban situation.

In the chapters that follow you will meet a selection of radical teachers of Hasidism who did seek to restructure the Hasidic enterprise and reignite the embers of the Hasidism of the Ba'al Shem Tov, in their own day. Some of them belonged to the traditional Hasidic milieu, like Reb Nachman of Bratzlav and Reb Arele Roth, and others, like Reb Hillel Zeitlin and Reb Shlomo Carlebach, lived outside of that world and hoped to bring its fire to a new world. In all of these masters, I would say, there is a recognition that the world is not what it was and that there must be Torah for the individuals of today. All of these men were trailblazers, and many of them had to endure the pain of birthing a new paradigm—the abuscs of those not yet ready—not to mention the pain of losing an entire world to that Atlantean chasm that was the Holocaust. But their legacy to us is all the more valuable for their courage and love.

DREAMER OF ARCHETYPES

REB NACHMAN OF BRATZLAV

(1772–18 TISHRI 1810)

ONE OF THE MOST UNIQUE personalities of Hasidism was undoubtedly Reb Nachman of Bratzlav.[1] He was the son of Feige, the granddaughter of the Ba'al Shem Tov, and Simcha, the son of Reb Nachman of Horodenka, the Ba'al Shem Tov's friend and disciple. Indeed, the future Rebbe of Bratzlav was born in Medzibozh in the very house of the Ba'al Shem Tov.

From an early age, Reb Nachman showed a marked bent toward the spiritual and even engaged in a severe asceticism. Once, after fasting for an extended period, his nose began to pour blood, yet still he persisted. His aim was nothing less than the complete subjugation of his bodily desires. On the other hand, he was very connected to the natural world. Like his great-grandfather, he spent countless hours in the woods and mountains speaking to God. In these years, he made a thorough study of the spiritual injunctions and teachings implicit in the Bible, Midrash, and Talmud, which would later serve as the basis for his first literary work, *Sefer HaMiddot.*

After his marriage and a troubled stay in the house of his father-in-law, he moved to the town of Medvedovka. This is a shadowy period in the young Rebbe's life. But in 1798 the shadows began to recede when he made a journey of incalculable significance for the rest of his life. It was then, with his disciple Reb Shimon, that he left to visit the Holy Land. Clearly, for him, this was a journey of tremendous mystical import. In Constantinople, just before his departure for Israel, he concealed himself in rags and drew abuses from fellow travelers as a means of "descent" before "ascending" into the land of sacred history. After taking only four steps on the holy soil, he declared his purpose accomplished. However, he would stay for some six months, visiting many holy sites and establishing a friendship with Reb Abraham Kalisker, a disciple of the Maggid of Mezritch.

His *aliyah* seems to have been the decisive event of his life, the source and secret of all his later teachings. For nearly all of the teachings we have of Reb Nachman date from after this period and serve almost as a coronation for his new emergence in the Hasidic sphere of influence.

In 1800 he moved his court to Zlatopol, which was near Shpola, where Reb Aryeh Leib, the Shpola Zeide, had his seat. Soon the Shpola Zeide began attacking the ways of Reb Nachman, and a great controversy ensued. It was likely an issue of territory, and in this encounter, it must be mentioned that Reb Nachman was defended by none other than the venerable Reb Levi Yitzhak of Berditchev, a known arbiter. A propos of this, Reb Nachman's later teachings often refer to feuds between *Tzaddikim*, which he relates to the concept of *Tzimtzum*, a Concealment of the Divine Radiance. In 1802 he moved to Bratzlav, whose name he would bear from thence forward.

In Bratzlav he met his most talented student and personal scribe, Reb Natan of Nemirov, who would assemble the master's teachings and edit them for publication. The study of these works, especially the *Likkutey MaHaRan,* became the foundation of Bratzlav Hasidic study. The Lubavitcher Hasidim are the only other Hasidim who study the works of their teachers in such a way. The first collection of the *Likkutey MaHaRan* was published in 1808, and the second was published posthumously in 1811.

In 1806 he began to tell his famous stories, which contain some of his most profound teachings. These Reb Natan faithfully recorded as he heard them directly from the lips of Reb Nachman. Today these tales are retold well beyond their limited Hasidic and Jewish spheres.

After the death of his infant son, Reb Nachman set out on a mysterious journey in the middle of the winter. In that time, his wife died and he contracted the tuberculosis from which he would suffer the rest of his days. Eventually, he removed his court to the city of Uman, which was the burial place of numerous Jewish martyrs. There he actively engaged many Jews who were part of the movement called the Haskalah, the Enlightenment. These were modern, free-thinking Jews who saw themselves as emerging into a larger world. His friendships with these men shocked and puzzled many of his Hasidim, but Reb Nachman clearly saw this activity as an extension of his holy purpose in the world. Reb Nachman died from his tuberculosis during Sukkot in the year 1810. To this day, his grave in Uman is the site of pilgrimage of Bratzlav Hasidim every Rosh HaShanah.

O

Reb Natan of Nemirov (1780–10 Tevet 1845)

Reb Natan Sternhartz was born in Nemirov, Podolia, to a wealthy non-Hasidic family in 1780. At age fourteen he married Esther Sheindel, the daughter of Rabbi David Tzvi, the Rabbi of Sharograd, a known opponent of the Hasidic movement. After his marriage, he lived for two years in the household of his father-in-law, pursuing his studies of the Talmud. But at sixteen he returned to Nemirov with his wife and became enamored of Hasidism. He began to visit a number of *Tzaddikim*, including such masters as Reb Zushya of Onipol, Reb Levi Yitzhak of Berditchev, and Reb Barukh of Medzibozh, the grandson of the Ba'al Shem Tov. But it was not until 1802, when he was twenty-two years old, that he met his Rebbe, Reb Nachman of Bratzlav.

It was not long before Reb Natan's considerable literary talents were noticed by Reb Nachman, who immediately employed the younger man as his secretary. From then until 1808, when Reb Nachman's condition worsened, Reb Natan took dictation of Reb Nachman's teachings and was even allowed to copy the master's original notes. After 1808, when Reb Nachman was no longer able to participate in such activity, Reb Natan recorded the important teachings of Reb Nachman from memory as they were given on various occasions. In this way, Reb Nachman's great works, *Likkutey MaHaRan, Sippurey Maasiyot,* and *Sefer HaMiddot,* came to be. Such was the value of Reb Natan's work that the master himself remarked, "If not for my Natan, no memory of my teachings would have survived."

However, Reb Natan's literary activity did not stop there. He also recorded even the most casual of Reb Nachman's remarks and a great deal of anecdotal material. He was also the author of numerous *novellae,* or extrapolations on the works of his master. In the end, Reb Natan was known as the most prolific author among the Hasidim.

After the death of Reb Nachman in 1810, it was Reb Natan that almost single-handedly forged the unique mold of Bratzlav Hasidism. So committed was he to the dissemination of Reb Nachman's teachings that he actually set up a printing press in his own house in order to bypass state censorship. Though he was sometimes the object of scorn and jealousy among the "old guard" Bratzlavers and was never permitted to enter their inner circle, Reb Natan was the living, teaching, growing edge of Bratzlav Hasidism for a new generation. Through his writings, recruiting, and revival of tradition, Reb Natan became the model of a disciple and temporal leader for future generations of Bratzlavers. Unlike other Hasidic communities, there would be no successor to Reb Nachman. To this day he remains the Rebbe of Bratzlav communities the world over. In many ways, Reb Nachman is the ideal master, while the role of accessible master is filled by a leader within the community who "embodies" the ideals of Reb Nachman. And this was a teaching that Reb Natan propagated. Many derogatively refer to them as the "dead Hasidim" for this belief. However, the designation is hardly true to the situation.

Unfortunately, Reb Natan, like his master, would also be the focus of several controversies. Aside from being alienated from the inner circle, more explicit attacks on him were made. One resulted from the fact that he had composed prayers based on the teachings of Reb Nachman. This was felt to be a blasphemous activity. Prayers were to be composed from Divine inspiration, which had ceased in the biblical period. Another persecution began around a misunderstanding. A group of Bratzlavers who did not recognize Reb Natan's leadership had offended the Hasidim of Reb Moshe of Savran, who, not realizing the difference, began in turn to attack Reb Natan and his group.

In 1822 Reb Natan visited the Holy Land, and in 1845, some thirty-five years after the death of his beloved master, he too went to his rest. His progeny, both literal and spiritual, would be some of the great torch bearers of living Bratzlav for generations to come.

Introduction to Bratzlav: What Reb Nachman Knew

Reb Nachman knew what modernity is all about.[2] It would be hard to find a better statement anywhere on the dilemma that confronts a would-be seeker in our modern (or even postmodern) age.

You've seen through the superficial glitter of the comforts and luxuries that our age has to offer. You've transcended the drive for "success" and status achievement that so plagues our society. Perhaps with the aid of one or another of the psychological self-help techniques that abound these days, you've made a serious turn inward and taken a good and thorough look at yourself.

You know now that the journey must take you further. There is a sense, one that you don't possess the words to articulate very comfortably, that your striving is somehow for the "religious" or the "spiritual." These are not words you, earlier in your life, thought you'd ever hear yourself using, but here they are. Now you have begun to turn, with ever so much hesitation, toward one or another of the spiritual traditions. Perhaps you turned first to the East, Judaism being so utterly discredited in your mind by your parents' synagogue and your bat or bar mitzvah. Or perhaps you did turn to Judaism, looking to the Orthodox or Hasidic communities to give you a way to God that you had never really been taught had any place in your tradition.

Somehow you haven't found there what you wanted. Now you begin to recognize what Reb Nachman saw nearly two hundred years ago: the old paths just don't work anymore. Our ancestors, so it seems to us at least, for countless generations knew who they were and where they were going. If they sought out spiritual knowledge, both the right books and the right guides were there. But the roads have changed; the maps no longer work as they used to.

All this is to say that modernity—the turning of the age that began about two hundred years ago and received its greatest thrust from the growth of science and technology and now seems ever more to be racing to some dreadful climax—that modernity has to be taken seriously. The revolution of the last couple of centuries has so transformed us that we are no longer the same people as our ancestors were; our experience of living is so changed that what appeared vital, exciting, and renewing to them is often just so much drudgery to us. How can the old means possibly compete? One aspect of religious teaching, accept it or not, was always an explanation of the natural order and how things got to be the way they are. We are light-years away from even our grandparents in our ability to take the old explanations without a grain of salt. Another function of religious life, to choose a totally different area, was that of entertainment, of bringing a bit of color into the generally drab lives lived by premodern people. But how could we expect the primitive form such entertainment took to even begin to compete in a world of our colorful, dazzling, and ever-advancing media? The same is true of such issues as rest and leisure, craftsmanship and pride of achievement, attitudes toward the human body and toward sexuality, and all the others.

Some seekers have reacted against all this, as you well know, and have decided to pick another time and place—a medieval Tibet, for example, or eighteenth-century Poland—in which to live. They have constructed small universes for themselves and have paid a dear price personally and intellectually but in some cases have reached remarkable spiritual attainments. To these people we can only offer our blessings—but it is not with envy that we see them. The life of the spirit must move forward; the God who created those earlier ages made this one and also the ones to come. It hardly seems likely that His will would be for us to live in one age while play-acting at being in another. The *shtetl* or the old-style monastery created in the middle of the global village is problematic in another way as well: the walls have to be built so high, in order for it to survive, that we fear little light will come in and that the darkness will provide a new breeding ground for claims of superiority, uniqueness, and the insignificance of the people outside. It is often with mixed emotions that I see students of mine move on from our eclectic new-age spirituality into an Orthodoxy, even when it is Jewish. More than once I have met them again on the way out, psychically battered by an attempt to do something that was just unnatural to them.

On the face of things, we live in the worst of all ages for the life of the spirit. Grand traditions that have survived for countless centuries seem to be collapsing, sometimes under their own weight; loyalty to the old ways, for Jews as for many others, once a hallmark of the community's continuance, is now hard to come by. Men and women over the past hundred or so years have increasingly come to identify themselves, their goals, and the meaning of their lives in secular terms. Even the onetime greatest mysteries—birth, death, origins of the cosmos, illness, and healing—have all been dealt with in confident, if not entirely satisfying, secular terms. The fact that daily living and the daily press confront us constantly with such questions as the ethics of abortion or the artificial prolongation of life, survival after organ transplants and the possibilities of building human communities on the moon, all tend to make it ever more difficult to find room for the mysterious handiwork of God anywhere in our lives. Faith itself, the inner turning at the very center of our religious selves, has come to feel awkward and out of step with the times. Again, Reb Nachman saw it coming: "There will still be a time before Messiah comes when more than one person will cry out over faith. Whatever righteous ones there are in those days will cry out over faith until they turn hoarse, just like I am doing now—and it won't help. . . . Surely in those days there will be no community like ours, a coming together of people who truly want to hear the word of God. Surely there will be a few such people in that generation, but they will be scattered. . . ."

We seem to have lived through what Reb Nachman and others imagined, in more ways than one, as the worst of all possible times for faith. Now the number of scattered seekers is growing, and the call for a true community is being heard again. Perhaps by the merit of those who followed the good Rebbe's advice never to despair, come what may, now the times seem to be changing once again. We who have refused to give in to the secular vision of the modern age, joined by countless new seekers who come to us as refugees from the very heart of the secular, now need to look at our age and see what has happened. The consciousness of the new emerging age allows us to look back at our modernity and see how much we missed the point of it and failed all along to really grasp its meaning.

The movement of the world and of our lives is one that ever takes us closer to, not further from, our Source. This one sentence sums up my faith claim as a religious guide and teacher. We may not always understand that movement, one that sometimes seems to lead us away from things "spiritual" as it has led us near to them—but we must learn to trust its flow, to know that there is guidance in our lives and that the Divine Will may be fulfilled in us in some of the very ways that we least expected. God retains the right, if you will, to surprise us. Human life as a whole and the life of every individual are both progressive revelations of that Source's presence, though not necessarily in any particular way or through any exclusive channel.

I can best articulate these notions of progressive revelation and the changes of the age through the language of an old metaphysic. As I use it, however, I beg the reader to understand that it is used as a suggestive and poetic, rather than a dogmatic, formulation of things. If the paper would only allow it, I'd really rather sing it than have it come to you flatly as prose. But let's give it a try.

"The world exists for six thousand years," say the Rabbis. "Two thousand are chaos, two thousand Torah, and two thousand the age of the Messiah." The Christian mystic Joachim of Fiore said the same in his way: his three ages were those of the Father, the Son, and the Holy Spirit. In both traditions there exist long histories of speculation (often just calculations of when The End is coming, but sometimes more profound as well) around these theories. At first glance such grand overviews seem awfully simplistic and hardly worthy of regard. I believe, however, that they may be of some help to us here.

Let us clock the ages a little bit differently than they did in the Middle Ages and begin with most ancient human memory rather than the beginning of the world (about which, after all, we have some rather different ideas). The first age is that of "chaos." God is distant, far beyond the world. He speaks rarely, and then only on the great mountaintops, to people in the midst of transcendent experiences, lifted up beyond this world. It is what our pagan selves learned most at Sinai: God is not the idols or illusions that we carry with us everywhere we go, making them think what we think and permit what we desire. God is in fact other, above the world, speaking to us in the voice of command, frightening us enough that we shrink away from Him. That was an age in which it was best to be a follower; the great religious teachers (in all parts of the world) went up to God, but most of us felt happier and safer waiting for them at the base of the mountain and following their teachings when they came down. We preferred to be Israelites rather than Moseses, to be Christians rather than Christs, and so forth. We took the rare human who had been with God as the leader to be followed rather than as the model to be copied. Now and then the leaders themselves saw through the inadequacy of this response (as when Moses says to Joshua, "Would that all the people of God were prophets!"), but social reinforcement and natural human awe of this distant and overwhelming God worked the other way.

The God of the Age of the Father ("God the Father"? Or dare we call Him "God the Chaos"?) had to be served in distant and awe-provoking ways. Sacrifices, blood—first of humans, later of animals—were required to come before such a God. Every meeting with Him was thus a meeting that contained death within it, as though frightening us by the constant grim reminder of our mortality was essential to the religious act. In this most dramatic way, such service required an act or deed, and without such a deed it would be deemed unworthy.

The second age, that in which the great religions took the institutional form in which we have received them, is called the Age of Torah. This is the time when received teachings, the wisdom of the ancients, came to the fore. No longer did magnificent lone individuals and their ascents to God dominate the scene; now it was the community living the holy life on earth, inspired by the teachings of the ancients, that was most important. To be sure, there still were great climbers and seekers in every tradition; Shankara and Chaitanya, Akiva and Luria, Augustine and Teresa all belonged to this time.[3] But their revelations and those of many like them were of a different order. Mystical rather than prophetic, the revelation sent seekers back toward their own tradition, opening for them a deeper reading of the word as they had received it but not calling for the founding of a wholly new order.

In worship, this is the age of the Word; Torah is the Word of God. For the Christian, Jesus is the word enfleshed, hence "the Age of the Son." The sacrificial deed is replaced by the prayerful word. Deeds remain, of course; Judaism is the best testimony to that. But the deed is required because it is the word of God, the commandment, not because the deed itself has power. On the contrary: one who says, in this second age, that the deed's power is separate from or higher than that of the word would probably be accused of heresy if not of magic. Standards change.

If we look at these two ages closely, we may say that there is movement between them toward a greater constancy in the life with God. No longer does the spirit belong only to those who climb the mountain; it resides in the people (or the church) and its Torah here below. The distant God of

Sinai has come closer through His Torah. "It is not in Heaven," the Rabbis remind us. Torah is here on earth; as we study it, live it, speak it, we come as close to God as most humans are meant to be—such is the teaching of the second age. No wonder that a good many of its mystics and visionaries wrote their works anonymously or attributed them to ancients.

Among the last great religious movements in that second religious age—and not only for Judaism—was Hasidism. Coming on the very eve of modernity, it represents the second age of religion trying to transcend itself; it steps forward and peers beyond the blinders of its age but then moves back again out of understandable fear or hesitation. Its original claim, that *kavanah* (inwardness) is what true religion is all about, was still too revolutionary for its day. Its move toward transcending specific ritual by turning every human act into a vessel for God's presence also showed it to be well beyond its time. Of course, it had to retreat from these positions; *halakha* had to be defended; outward conformity had to be proclaimed as good both for the peace of the community and for the sanity of the individual in that still very convention-ridden world. Outer culture—ghetto or *shtetl* for us Jews—reinforced the inner life of spirit, and even the surrounding world, hostile as it may have been to Jews, shared the general religious assumptions about life. For us, however, all this has disappeared. Born into rootless modernity, already two or three generations from any real life within the tradition, all paths seem pretty much the same. A resident of the global village, you feel yourself as capable of adopting a Tibetan Buddhist or Vedantist identity, for purposes of seeking, as you do, to return to a lost Hasidic past.

As you try other traditions on for size, none of them quite fits. True, statues, incense, and pictures of the guru are rather alien to you, but then so are *t'fillin* and prayers in Hebrew. More significant than this, the reality maps offered you by the traditions don't really seem to fit either. As you begin your attempt to go through Jewish teachings, someone tells you that there are 613 commandments and that these correspond to 613 mysterious limbs of your spiritual body. Your spiritual body, however you try, just doesn't feel it that way. When you start looking at the teachings of the Kabbalists with all their diagrams of the upper worlds, sometimes you feel just as alien as if you had stumbled into something out of the arcane world of Mahayana Buddhism.[4] And this certainly isn't what you feel within you; it was simplicity and wholeness you were seeking in the spiritual path, not complex diagrams of how to get to the destruction of religion the more conservative it became. But the age of the Ba'al Shem Tov was far from what some later followers would make it out to have been, and the original impetus that moved it should not be lost on us.

Reb Moishele, the Bratzlaver of Kopiczinitz

There is a wonderful Bratzlaver melody that I learned from Reb Shlomo Carlebach, which he told me he learned from Reb Moishele, with whom he used to hang out in Vienna. Reb Moishele was the son of the Kopiczinitzer Rebbe[5] and in line to become Rebbe himself, but instead he became a Bratzlaver Hasid. You have to understand what an amazing thing this was, for the son of such a distinguished Hasidic dynasty to become one of the "dead Hasidim." In some ways it wasn't fitting for the descendant of a Hasidic house to abandon the way of his fathers to embrace the way of Reb Nachman. For Reb Nachman didn't always have a "respectable" reputation; there were many people who were not sure about him.

Kopiczinitz was an established house from both sides. The Kopiczinitzer line came from the Apter and the Ruzhyner. And Ruzhyn was sort of the citadel of Hasidism. There was a time when every Rebbe traveled to Sadagora to meet the Reb Yisroel, the Ruzhyner, and to get his stamp of approval, as it were. When a young man would come to Ruzhyn to see the Rebbe, he would come into the court and see the Ruzhyner looking at him from afar, and he felt he was in the court of the king. And in a way he was. The Ruzhyner drove in a carriage with six horses, which at that time meant Polish nobility. In his house, even the spoons were gold, and his table was built in such a way that around it was an amphitheater. He had his carpenters build bleachers so that his Hasidim wouldn't have to jostle one another. And there he would sit at his table surrounded by all his Hasidim in tears, and the place would be very quiet, and he would speak with a very fine voice, maybe a total of fifteen or twenty words at that whole meal. *Oy!* did that stay with the people.

Reb Yisroel of Ruzhyn was the son of Reb Shalom Shakhnah, who was the son of Reb Abraham *HaMalach*, the Angel, who was the son of the Maggid of Mezritch, the successor to the Ba'al Shem Tov. Reb Abraham, the Maggid's son, did not live very long, but he was a very special person. He and Reb Shneur Zalman were great friends and studied together. The Maggid said to Reb Shneur Zalman, "You will teach him the manifest part of the Torah, and he will teach you the hidden part of the Torah." So the Maggid had great confidence in his son. Reb Abraham also wrote a book. And if everything in *Hasidut* is gold, the Angel's book is platinum. There is a real *Eidelkeit*, a gossamer quality, to what he writes. He doesn't write much, but what he teaches is highly original. What he says about the *Sefirot* puts a whole new twist on the concept.

His son Shalom Shakhnah was raised in the house of Reb Nachum Chernobyler, whose granddaughter he married. But Reb Nachum didn't know how to deal with him because Reb Nachum was still from the time of those old-fashioned Rebbes for whom "poverty is the greatest joy that we can have because then everything is dependent on God." And here he has Reb Shalom Shakhnah, who is nobility to the Hasidim. So their ways don't quite go together. Like his father, Reb Shalom Shakhnah doesn't live very long, and his son, Reb Yisroel the Ruzhyner, is orphaned. When Yisroel of Ruzhyn is still a child, he comes to the great wedding that took place in Ostilla. And while he was there, his little prayer sash fell off. The elder chief of Rebbes at that time was Reb Abraham Joshua Heschel of Apt. And when the prayer sash fell to the ground, the Apter Rav bent down and picked it up and put it around little Yisroel. All the people who saw this asked in wonder, "Rebbe, in what way does this child deserve that you should do that?" And he winked back at them, "I'm only doing *g'lilah* with the Torah." Before the Torah is put back in the ark, one man holds the Torah while another rolls it together and puts the sash on it. So "I'm just doing *g'lilah* on a Torah" was an acknowledgment of who the Ruzhyner would grow up to be.

The Ruzhyner had six children who became the great Rebbes of Galacia. And the Ruzhyner's granddaughter would marry a great-grandson of the Apter Rav who would become the first Kopiczinitzer Rebbe. So Kopiczinitz is Hasidic royalty from both sides. Professor Abraham Joshua Heschel was of that line and could have led this dynasty. People would say of him that had he been a Rebbe in Poland, he'd have stolen the Hasidim from all the other Rebbes.[6] So you can imagine how great was his talent. And Reb Moishele was Professor Heschel's cousin who became a Bratzlaver Hasid. He left that "royal" house for Bratzlav, where the Hasidim were mostly poor. You know, if you want to be sort of an Episcopalian Hasid, you go to the Ruzhyner's children, you don't go to the Franciscan Bratzlavers, those poor folks. Why did he do it? As you read on, may you also get to feel the radical ("from the roots") attraction that characterizes the way of Reb Nachman.

Do Not Despair!

If Reb Shneur Zalman was a man for the head, Reb Nachman was the one who told us how to live through the ups and downs. Reb Nachman Bratzlaver says, *Gevalt, Yidden, zeit aich nisht me'ya'esh! Gevalt, Yidden, zeit aich nisht me'ya'esh! Gevalt!* "For Heaven's sake, Jews, do not despair; do not despair!"

In fact, he wants to go so far as to say, "There is no such thing as *ye'ush* at all. There is no such thing as despair." For, if you think about it, "How far can you fall? Can you ever fall out of God?" Then he continues on the flip side, "How far can you rise? Can you ever rise above God? Underneath, there are always the Everlasting Arms, no matter how low you fall. Even in *gehinnom* (purgatory) you can come to know God. And there are some souls in *Gan Eden* (the Garden of Eden) who haven't yet met God." So he is saying that there is nothing to keep us from God. There is no *place* of despair. And even the obstacles in our lives are a blessing. "It is the wise man who does not get hung up by the obstacles." He says, "God loves Man very much, because God is *hofetz chesed,* desiring to give us grace, but God is also an *ohev mishpat,* a lover of justice." So when somebody undeserving wants to come close to God, people say, "That *paskudnyak!* What right does that sinner have to come close to God?" So out of duty, God has to put some obstacles in the person's way, but since God still loves the person, what does God do? God condenses and hides in the obstacles.

So Reb Nachman says, "A person who is wise knows what has happened, but a person who is a fool does not realize it." And, that is already written in the Torah, *va'yar' ha'am,* "and the people saw the obstacles," *va'yanu'u, va'yamdu me'rachok,* "and they stood from afar." *V'Moshe,* "and Moses," who was wise, *Nigash el ha'arafel,* "went into the dark obstacle," *asher sham ha'Elohim,* "the very place where God had hidden Himself." Thus Reb Nachman says, "You must not despair. Look at the obstacle itself. Fix it in your mind. Love the obstacle, and all of a sudden you will be able to see God, who hides in the obstacle itself."

> *Whether you have been granted a high rung or a lesser one,*
> *you must not be content to remain there but always aspire*
> *upward. Believe and know! It is necessary and possible for you*
> *to go on and on. In this progress, if you should fall into a lower*
> *rung—even into the "bottomless pit"—you must not despair.*
> *No matter what happens to you, wherever you may be and*
> *to the best of your ability, seek His Blessed Name. For it is here*
> *that one can also cleave to Him.*

—Nachman of Bratzlav, *Meshivat Nefesh*

Now here in the *Meshivat Nefesh* we have Reb Nachman's disciple Reb Natan of Nemirov's reconstruction of his master's words. And in this he kept on pushing the notion that there is no such thing as despair. Now, some people feel that this kind of talk is simple-minded—a good-humor man meets Norman Vincent Peale.[7] They feel like they are being fed positive thinking gimmicks. It makes me think of Bishop Fulton Sheen,[8] who said, "Be a mirror to reflect everybody, and then be a glass through whom the light can shine." It is wonderful stuff but a little gimmicky. So I can understand why people feel this in Reb Nachman. It is sort of a "feel-good" message, and you figure that the person saying it drives a fancy car and lives a very comfy life and tells other people, "Don't despair!" But this is not the case with Reb Nachman.

I remember an occasion when a celebrated theologian had said something wonderful and very aesthetic about Jesus, and Howard Thurman walked up to him afterward, and said, "Did you ever preach in the ghetto? Did you ever preach this to the poor?" You understand, he had to make the theologian see that what he was saying sounded very beautiful and was good theology, but when you speak to the poor, you really have to come at it differently. And while on the surface it might seem smooth rhetoric, underneath we are dealing with powerful *etzot*, counsels. For Reb Nachman knew the dark places. So his is not a naive, "Damn the torpedoes, full steam ahead!" attitude. He knows that often we are at the mercy of an environment that pushes us into situations that cause us to topple down the mountain.

Nature

Reb Nachman, like the Ba'al Shem Tov, had a profound connection with nature. He said, "One must *davven* sometimes in nature. One must forget the social universe and enter into the natural universe in order to be able to rediscover prayer." When he was a boy, he would sometimes ride out on a horse into Medvedevka. He would ride and ride until he was deep into the open universe; then he would get off the horse and go and stand near a tree. He would look up in wonder at how the tree was reaching upward, how every leaf was reaching out to God—how the tree was praying. And he would be caught up in the ecstasy of that moment, and sometimes the horse would return home without the rider, and his family would wonder what in the world had happened to him. Or he would go out on a boat in order to get into the flow of the river. He wanted to see how all of life is a flowing river. Often he forgot to take the oars along and would end up floating for hours on the river. He felt a powerful connection to the natural world.

So this became part of his counsel, for he says, "You must from time to time get into nature." And he stresses this in his Torah: "Why is it that we bring greens, foliage, into the *shul* on Shavuot? In order to remember that the Torah was not given in a building." Do you see how wonderful this is? You get involved in a sunset, a sunrise, in nature, and there is something new that begins to happen. To many people this sounded dangerously "pagan." Many saw that deep and natural experience that begins to happen in our soul as a little too close to the hot core of the sensual. But perhaps we need the "pagan" situation in order to transcend it; and if we do not meet the pagan situation, we may never be able to find the *Ribono Shel Olam,* the God of the World, very much involved in the world, the God who hides in the obstacles.

Unlike others, Reb Nachman taught that "there is no such thing as vile passion." Natural impulses were to be harnessed into a team. He said, "People say to God they have to follow their passion," by which they mean something like a wild horse. He says, "What is passion?" He says, *Essen darf men?* You have to eat? *Shloffen darf men?* You have to sleep? It is a *mitzvah* to have children. So, where is the wild passion? Notice how we are driven to life that is not truly our own because we are hung up on the romantic view that we are not fully human unless we are clutched by an uncontrollable passion, a great aesthetic situation in which we have no control whatsoever. In art this might be the lack of the control of the medium in which one expresses one's being. Very often artists may not be capable of putting a line where they want to put it because they haven't learned the *craft* and so they cannot master the *art.* The craftsmen can truly be artists because they have something to express, but we clamor for expression and self-expression before we have built a self that is worthy to express something. So in Reb Nachman, nature is not to be crushed but to be put into the service of the King, the Sovereign One.

In contrast to the natural world, Reb Nachman says that there is another kind of world, an unnatural one that we ought to shun, because that world is a liar. It is a social world, the source of illusions. Reb Nachman says, "When someone goes around with a closed fist and says, 'What have I got here?' What have I got here?' Everybody says, 'Ah, what I want she has!' and then the one with the closed fist says, 'If you want it, come with me. I'll give it to you later. Come on, come on.' And the whole world would follow the one with the closed fist, and in the end she opens it and there is nothing in it." It almost sounds like a story by Kafka, doesn't it? "We are following an illusion. We are putting our desires into the empty hands of the world."

In this unnatural world, people follow after illusions, after money. Reb Nachman says, "Money. *Di velt mach't gelt. Fun der zeit vos di velt shteit mach't men gelt. Vu iz di gelt ahin gegangen?* We have been making money ever since the world began; what happened to all the money?

Money is not a reality." He tried to shock us into seeing that it is not an end but an instrumentality. It is not what is real.

Hitbodedut—Personal Prayer

Reb Nachman would tell his Hasidim, "If you really want to pray, you have to at certain times put the *siddur* (prayer book) away. And you have to speak to God as one person speaks to another." He also counseled that they should speak in Yiddish, the vernacular of the people, as opposed to the sacred tongue. He says, if he didn't feel bad about the fact that there are so many centuries already in the *siddur,* he would say that the *siddur* should be translated into Yiddish and people should pray from it in Yiddish. Why is that? Because in the language we are most comfortable in, we are best able to express the language of our hearts. So if you are to pray to God in a real way, you sometimes need to pray in the language natural to you. So Reb Nachman counsels that after *davvenen* or before *davvenen* one should *davven* without the *siddur, Un zich a durch reden mit dem Ribono Shel Olam,* "to have a conversation with the Creator of the World." To his dying day, this was the mainstay of his practice. Bratzlavers suggest that you take an hour out every day for this practice. But I think to talk about taking an hour out and making it a discipline is already the structuralizing of Reb Natan. You know, Reb Nachman would close the door and start saying, "*Oy! Ribono Shel Olam,*" and talk things over. I don't think he was saying, "Now is my hour to talk to God."

The suggestion that we pray in the vernacular is something that sometimes strikes us as not particularly Jewish—only Protestants do that, right? The Catholics pray in Latin and the Jews pray in Hebrew and only the Protestants have enough sense to just come out and say, "God! I need this and I need that—please give it to me." And by the way, praying in the vernacular is a true way of fulfilling the obligation of prayer because to fulfill *t'fillah d'oraitah,* the biblical obligation of praying as it is spelled out in the Torah, is to be *sho'el tz'rakhav,* to ask for what one needs.

When his disciples were standing around Reb Nachman shortly before he died, he asked his grandson, who was still a small child, "Will you pray for me, please?" And his grandson said to him, "*Zeide,* what will you give me?" Reb Nachman said, "What do you want me to give you?" And the boy answered, "*Zeide,* you have a gold watch. If you will give me the gold watch, I will pray for you." The disciples started to laugh, saying, "*Oy! bist shoin a Rebbe.* He is already willing to take like a Rebbe, before he starts praying." Then Reb Nachman said, "But he is right. Only a person who is really involved in something can pray." And Reb Nachman gave him the watch. Then everybody was waiting to see how the child was going to pray. He opened his mouth and said, "*Ribono Shel Olam,* You are a Good Doctor. And you can heal. Please heal *Zeide. Amen.*" And everybody laughed again, and Reb Nachman said, "Why do you laugh? This is it precisely. You asked me often to pray for you, and what do you think I did? I did that same thing. I said, '*Ribono Shel Olam,* You can do this, and so please do it.'" You see, there is a certain kind of literal simplicity about it. We always think that we must find a fancy mode in which to do things, but that isn't true. It is a real way in which to do something, to do it simply and with intention. That is how things really get done. So, says Reb Nachman, the most desirable virtue is to be a *prostak*—a simpleton.

Praying the Torah

> One Hasid asked Reb Nachman to prescribe for him how
> he is to conduct himself in becoming closer to God, and
> Reb Nachman recommended that he study Torah. The Hasid,
> however, complained that he did not know how to study Torah,
> and Reb Nachman replied, "Through prayer one can come
> to accomplish any good thing, in Torah, Service, all holy things,
> in all kinds of service and to benefits in every universe there is."

> —Nachman of Bratzlav, *Hishtapkut HaNefesh*

Reb Nachman said that everything you study, every time you learn Torah, what you learn should be translated into a prayer. "*Me darf machen fun Torah a t'fillah,* all your learning you must make a prayer of aspiration to God, to help you make the thing come true." Let's say you learn from the Torah that you should rest on the Sabbath. You might say, "Oh, *Ribboina Shel Olam,* let me merit to have at least one hour in my life where I would experience what *Shabbos* means, to live *Shabbos* like you want me to live *Shabbos,* to go to that place where the commandment, the prescription, the teaching, is taken so seriously. I don't think I'll be able to do it unless You help me. I've got no chance whatsoever without You." You might implore God: "Please make it real for me."

Reb Nachman tells Reb Natan that this is the way to learn Torah. And he does it in a statement that is almost like a throwaway, once, kind of offhand. And Reb Natan then sits down and works through the whole book of the *Likkutey MaHaRan* and takes every teaching of Reb Nachman and reworks them as prayers. Sometimes when I want to understand something that I can't quite grasp in the *Likkutey MaHaRan,* I go to Reb

Natan's book of prayers to gain insight into the analogous teaching. I'll
give you an example from the teaching "Torah of the Void," first as it is
in the *Likkutey MaHaRan* and then as it is in Reb Natan's prayers:

TORAH OF THE VOID

God,
for Mercy's sake,
created the world
to reveal Mercy.
If there were no world,
on whom would Mercy take pity?

So—to show His Mercy
He created the worlds
from *Atzilut*'s peak
to this Earth's center.

But as He wished to create,
there was not a where.
All was infinitely He,
Be He Blessed!

The light He condensed
sideways
thus was space made
an empty void.

In space—days and measures
came into being.
So the world was created.

This void was needed
for the world's sake,
so that it may be
put into place.

Don't strain to understand
the void!
It is a mystery—not to be realized
until the future
is the now.

Now
speaking of the void

we must say two things
—opposites—
"is-ness" and "is-not-ness."

Void means absence of God
for the world space's sake.
But in truth's deepest truth
God is still there.
Without His giving life
Nothing is "is-ing."

Thus we speak of the void.
There is no way to realize
the void before the future
is come to be now.

There are
two kinds of
unbelief:

One kind
originates
the "outering" sciences.
The questions raised by them
are to be answered.
"Know what to answer
the unbeliever":
Outer knowing is rooted in
the order of holiness.

Once there was light,
much and powerful,
holy light,
and it was in vessels
—too much light,
too much power—
and the vessels burst!

When the vessels burst
the fragments
of Holiness
took form
becoming the "outered" sciences.

So,
even of Holiness
there is offal:
Just as there is sweat
and hair and excrement,
so Holiness too
has its offal.

Holy Wisdom, too, has offal.
"Outered" wisdom
is the offal of the holy.
And when this offal is used
to twist the world,
you have sorcery.

Once, also, source-ery
was rooted
in a high wisdom.

He who can
should strive to avoid
the trap
of the "outered" sciences.
But whoever falls
into the trap
is not lost forever.

Seeking God
one can find Him there,
in the shards of Holiness
which give life to the sciences—
even in the very symbols
in which the sciences
express themselves.
For as long as there
are reason and rhyme—
and words—
there is Holiness
in the form of sparks.
As long as there is life
in the word, God is there.

As long as there are sparks
unbelief allows for re-ply
and for the return.
"Know how to re-ply to the Epicure."

But there is another kind
of unbelief.
Rooted in un-wisdom,
though profound it seems
and unrealizable
—its profundity is nonsense.

Such non-sense is thought wise.
One who is not learned
will be stumped.
Caught in a web by false reason,
How can he unmask it?
If he has no knowledge
he think the dissembler wise.

And the philosophers
have all kinds of questions
—objections to true knowledge—
not rooted in wisdom
but in un-wisdom.
They turn answers into questions.
Rabbi Akiva says,
"All is foreseen
and freedom is given."
This is an answer,
a paradox—
but a fool of the void
turns it into a question again—
"If all is foreseen,
how can man be free?"
The paradox twisted into
a question
is the folly of the void.

Because human sense and reason
know not how to settle the issues,
the questions seem profound.

In truth there is no settling
these Issues at all.
They come not from sparks
of holy somethings,
but from the void,
and it is void even of God.
So there is no way to find Him
there—
no way to re-ply—to repent.

If one could find Him there
there would be no void
but Infinitely He.
Therefore there Is no way
to answer this unbelief:
"He who comes there cannot return."

How can Yisrael face the void
and live in it with Him?
Such thought is void of words.

Yisrael believes
and leaps, passes over,
all the sciences,
even the lore of the void
because even in simple faith
they believe
that He fills
and surrounds the world.
And the void?

It is nothing but
the no-thing, which takes up
no space at all.
All it does is separate
between the Divine that fills
and the Divine that surrounds
the world.

Without the void
all would have been One.
But then

there would not have been
any creature—any world.
So the void is a kind of
Divine Wisdom of not being
so there can be division
between one kind of being
and another.

This wisdom of not being,
the wisdom of the void—
cannot be realized!
It is not a something,
but it makes all somethings possible.
Each something is infused with
God
and surrounded by God:
There is in between
a void that is not.

This cannot be known
by knowing
but it can be "faithed"
by "faithing" past and through it.

This is why Yisrael is called
Ivrim—Hebrew, "through-passers."
And He is known as
the God of the Hebrews.

> —Nachman of Bratzlav, *Likkutey MaHaRan* 1:64

Now here it is in Reb Natan's prayers:

> Oy! *You who do great things beyond our understanding,
> miracles without number, Lord of all. Beyond, beyond of
> anything that we can attain, and there is no beyonder than You.
> You fill all the worlds. You surround all the worlds. You are
> beyond all the worlds. You are underneath all the worlds.
> You are in between all the worlds. There is no space empty
> of You. You created Your world in the beginning out of so much
> goodwill, out of so much compassion and mercy, which You
> needed to reveal in the world so that the world should get to
> feel your compassion. And out of Your love and out of Your
> goodness, You wish to reveal Your goodness and Your mercy*

in the world. So you took Your whole divinity and condensed it,
and You turned the entirety of Your great light aside, Your
infinitely great light aside, pushing it away to the sides, and there
You made this empty space. And in the midst of it You created
all of creation. From the beginning to the end, and all this You
did in order that You should be known in this speck of dust,
in this little world so that we should know You all the time.
Therefore, I come to meet You, to entreat You, my King, my
God, let my prayer go out to You. Be kind, have mercy on me,
take pity on me and all of Yisrael, Your people. Guard me, save
me from all kinds of heresy and denials. Let them not come into
my heart; let them not rise into my consciousness. I do not wish
to come to philosophies, to raise questions and get lost in all
the conundrums of the philosophers; I don't want to get lost
in the outer wisdoms. . . .

—Natan of Nemirov, *Likkutey T'fillot*

Do you hear that? Everything that was in that teaching Reb Natan has now turned into a prayer. He is offering it up as if it were a prayer. That is so wonderful. So nothing Reb Nachman says to Reb Natan gets lost. Sometimes he gives him a bit of advice that another person would treat as nothing. There may have been ten other people around who heard him say this about prayer, and they thought it was something clever. But they didn't heed it, didn't do it. A teacher gets such great *nachas* (pleasure) when she or he gives a hint and somebody follows that hint and later on comes back and says, "I tried that and it really worked for me."

Chiddush and Finding God in the Dark

There were times when Reb Nachman said, "I'm a *chiddush*—nothing like me has ever happened before. What I know is so special, there isn't anybody who has ever understood it the way I understand it." All the other masters would say it came down from Sinai, and Moses knew it really tops, and every time it comes down it gets diluted—"Nowadays, who are we in comparison with them?" That is the usual run of the second law of thermodynamics as applied to revelation. It is running down, it's running down. And Reb Nachman comes up and says, "There couldn't have been anybody like me before. The reason is, I had a great-grandfather who was the Ba'al Shem Tov—figure that one out." The Ba'al Shem Tov's daughter was Udel, and Udel had a daughter by the name of Feige. And Reb Nachman was the son of Feige and her husband Simcha. And

Simcha himself was the grandson of a man named Reb Nachman of Horodenka, who was one of the Ba'al Shem Tov's buddies, even during the silent times. So Reb Nachman saw himself as sort of a thoroughbred from both sides. But then after all the seeming self-adulation, he decides that all that counts for nothing and says, "I'm a nobody. I'm a nothing. I have to start afresh. I have to start anew." What is going on with that? How can he say both?

That is why when Art Green wrote a book on Reb Nachman, he titled it *Tormented Master*.[9] It is a wonderful paradox. If he is a master, he shouldn't be tormented, right? But here you see that he is indeed a master and he is indeed tormented, and you have to deal with it. There are some relevant questions we should ask. How old is he? He didn't live past the age of thirty-eight (I feel odd when people say you've got to wait until you are forty to study Kabbalah; if Reb Nachman had waited, oh, what we would have missed!). And what did he die from? Tuberculosis. Think of other writers (Kafka, Rilke) who died of tuberculosis and what effect it had on their expression. Who was his teacher? You realize that Reb Shneur Zalman of Liadi could always have a chat with the Maggid, to connect and refresh. Reb Nachman didn't have that. He was a crazy kid running into the forest, getting married very young, drifting for hours, getting lost. Even the Ba'al Shem Tov had Achiya the Shilonite to teach him. Yet there is no tale of Reb Nachman being taught by such a mysterious teacher. He had to start from scratch.

So when Reb Nachman studied the *Gemara*, he learned it like nobody else before. Because when you know how everybody else thinks and your thought is not like everybody else's, in a world where Talmud suffuses the conversation, where all these people studied in a particular way and you haven't studied in that way, your uniqueness tends to be obvious. Reb Nachman comes at things from another angle, and he sees them differently. His approach is original. But can he be sure that he has understood everything right? How does he know? This may explain why nobody speaks about doubt in as friendly a manner as Reb Nachman does. You see, it is all happening in his own mind, under his own authority. That is why it is so important that he didn't have a Rebbe. It is so much easier to say, "Oh, I got it from this great authority, so I don't have to worry about the process. All I have to do is trust that the great holy master got it from God." But he is saying, "Never mind that I didn't get it from the mouth of the holy master who got it from God. I'm the holy master who got it from God. And I see how fickle that process is. I don't know when I'm imagining and when it is revelation."

So this uniqueness and feeling of alternating extremes comes out in his teachings. And there it is dealt with also:

Thus to merit repentance and returning, become expert in these two ways of halakha: *"surging forward," desiring and working always to be on a yet higher rung toward God; and "drawing backward," holding fast to His Blessed Name, no matter if you fall or what station in life may be granted you. When you have become skilled in this, you will realize that His Right Hand is always extended to receive penitents, who in contrition for their sins have amended their lives.*

—Nachman of Bratzlav, *Meshivat Nefesh*

It became a part of Bratzlav teaching—to deal with the highs and lows. And it is important to understand that they don't happen at the same time; they alternate. These are the vicissitudes of life, and we can serve the Holy Sovereign in the highs as well as the lows. Reb Moshe Leib Sassover says that a person should have two pockets. "In one pocket, one has nothing but dust and ashes. And in the other, one has, 'For me the world was created.'" So sometimes you go into one pocket or the other, but God is always present.

If you start looking for a model of who could give you insight into Reb Nachman, it is very difficult, because he is so complex. But I believe there is a connection between Reb Nachman and Saint John of the Cross,[10] especially when he talks about the Void. There are not too many people in Judaism or in Christianity who are what are called *apophatic theologians,* saying that God is more in the darkness than in the light. Most people want to talk about the great light and the great bliss. Very few are willing to talk about that fatal abyss that is God, to speak that language.

And you have got to understand how new this whole way of doing things is, finding God in the dark. It is written, "The people saw and they moved back and they stood from afar. And Moses, he entered into the cloud"—into the dark where God was. And Reb Nachman wrote: "When the people saw they couldn't find God in the light, they moved and stood from afar. But Moses, who knew, went right into the deep and cloudy darkness," knowing that there he would find God. You see what he does just by emphasizing certain words differently? That well-known biblical passage suddenly takes on fantastic depth. So he didn't have to go much into process; he was just breaking ground, opening doors. Reb Natan works with this and invites people to watch that process in themselves.

So when Reb Natan describes something, he goes into a lot of detail: How did you first fall? How did you find your way out? He is more descriptive of the process. Reb Nachman does less of that, and you therefore accept his teachings on that basis; he projects a confident vibe, often with a tear drop in his voice. The confident vibe has a sense of *ha'levai* ("would that it be thus") to it.

So with Reb Nachman there comes a profound understanding of both the depths and the heights. He knows what it is to be in the dark place and not to be overcome by it, and so he projects great confidence. He has a real appreciation of himself. He asks, "What's the first thing that you remember? Can you remember when the taste got into the apple? Can you remember when the light was still burning? What's the first memory?" And then he says, "Well, I'm the youngest, but I'm really the oldest, because I remember even the Nothing." That is wonderful. And he says how fearsome it is to fall into the abyss, how even Moses has trouble with the silence in the abyss. He talks like somebody who has experienced that. About being in the dark, he sometimes talked about how difficult it is to find a good point, but there is no way of getting back until you have found at least one good thing about yourself. And he says, "If you can't be *mechayyah* (invigorated) yourself, if you can't invigorate yourself over anything else, then at least be *mechayyah* that God has chosen you to serve God as a Jew." That you can invigorate yourself with. It's not even a point that depends on you.

The Writings of Bratzlav

Reb Nachman, himself, wrote very little. What he did write is pretty obscure and difficult to read. This is not because he wasn't any good at it but because his writing was for him. It was more a taking of notes on his amazing mental processes. He really was fascinated by what was happening in his head. So what he wrote was mostly notes. But Reb Nachman's *magnum opus, Likkutey MaHaRan,* is clearly more than mental notes. This book was written in a wonderful way. Reb Nachman would call in Reb Natan, or he would give a teaching, and the next day Reb Natan would ask the Rebbe to review and make corrections to the teaching Reb Natan had taken down, saying, "This is what I was able to put down from what you said yesterday." He was very much Reb Nachman's amanuensis. And Reb Natan was a good writer. One of the issues that I have with Buber is that he accuses Reb Natan of having spoiled Reb Nachman's tales.[11] I would swear on a stack of Bratzlav books that he didn't distort the tales. On the contrary, he listened attentively and he put it down in writing and he was very, very careful about it. And he wrote things down in two forms—in Yiddish, as Reb Nachman first said them, and in Hebrew. The Hebrew was his polished version. That was his way of sketching things out. But this sketching was done in great detail. Sometimes he would repeat something because he heard the Rebbe repeat it. So the primary book of Bratzlav literature, the *Likkutey MaHaRan,* was written in this remarkable way with Reb Natan.

This work was published in Reb Nachman's lifetime and had his seal of approval, as it were. And the teachings that continued after its publication were gathered into a second volume of the *Likkutey MaHaRan* that was published by Reb Natan posthumously. It is called *Likkutey Tinyana,* "Second Collection." Concerning these works, Reb Nachman left his disciples with amazing instructions. One instruction was that they should study it and work through the material very carefully themselves, to go through cycles of reading it. This is rare in Hasidism. Another instruction was that if they are so moved, they should write *novellae* on it.

Now, the *novella* is a very interesting thing in Judaism. A lot of the literature in *halakha,* regular Talmudic material, goes as follows: "Such and such is written in the Talmud, and if you study that, certain questions arise. These questions have been discussed by this school and by that school, and such and such arguments have arisen, and there are these possibilities of reading the texts and there are other possibilities of reading the text. Now, if I read it in one way, one question arises. If I read it in another way, another set of questions arise. So how are we going to deal with that?" You see, it is a very tight intellectual process. So when somebody reads such a report of Talmudic thinking and studies it carefully, weighs it in her or his mind, one way of reading it, another way of reading it, and then zap, something happens, something hits, eureka! there is a way of harmonizing both ways of reading it. If you drag in such and such a concept from another place, the whole puzzle fits together; it harmonizes that material in a flash of insight. Such a flash is called a *chiddush.* And when somebody asks you, "Where did you read that? Where did you get that from?" "I just got it! It occurred to me. It was a brand-new thought, as if I had penetrated to a new level of Torah." So that is a *chiddush.* Think of a *novella* as a new *chiddush,* an inspired flash, a new take on the material.

So sometimes you come across books that are called *Chiddushey Torah, novellae,* new takes on Torah. Most disciples of Hasidic masters didn't dare to write *chiddushim* on their Rebbes' writings; that might imply that the works weren't complete in themselves. To these disciples, the words came down holy. But Reb Nachman encouraged his disciples to write *chiddushim.* He was saying, "This is a process. If you get involved in that process, insights will occur to you too, and those insights are part of the same teaching. You keep on working the wake and making it wider. So you should write and keep writing." Taking this advice, Reb Natan began writing his own stuff. Reb Natan wasn't as "flash" and "aha!" as Reb Nachman, but he was very good in weaving the systematic and theological issues together. And this was a very important value for a Hasid. It was very important for each disciple to show that in the seemingly simple statements of the master. "Oh, what deep stuff! Do you think he is talking only about horses, the Ba'al Shem Tov? Of course not!" And so in the same way, you would take any story the Rebbe would tell or any simple teaching the Rebbe would make, and you would turn it over to one of the disciples who was really sharp. That disciple would work with that and come back later, saying, "*Oy! Oy!* Do you think you can just take my master on one level? The depth, the depth, the depth!" He would show how an apparently simple saying of Reb Nachman threw light on everything. This was the way of Bratzlav Hasidim to keep on enlarging the thrust of the teachings of Reb Nachman.

Dreams

One should not underestimate the value of Reb Nachman's aesthetic moves—he was so comfortable in the world of imagination. Maimonides and many others in normative Judaism were not happy in the world of the imagination, but Reb Nachman was quite comfortable there. And nobody recounts dreams with such detail, despite the fact that the dreams are not very flattering. You might be tempted to edit the material in your dreams, so that you can say, "Oh, I have such exalted dreams!" Well, Reb Nachman reports dreams in which he forgets everything and people revile him. You see almost a Kafkaesque quality in him. He doesn't know what he did wrong, but everybody is whispering behind his back. You don't find too many people who will talk about themselves in this way.

In the winter of his thirty-eighth year, shortly before his death, the Bratzlaver said: In my dream, I sit in my house, and no one enters. The thing so amazed me, I went into the other two rooms, and there was no one there. So I went outside, and I saw that people were standing in circles and whispering about me. This one is mocking me, and this one winks knowingly in my direction, and this one laughs, and this one shows *chutzpah* against me, and so forth. Even among those who were my Hasidim, there were some who were against me. Some of them looked at me with scorn and whispered against me.

I called one of my men and asked him, "What is this?" He answered me, "How could you have done such a thing? How could you have done such an awful sin?" I did not know at all what they were talking about or why they were making fun of me, so I looked for that man, that he should go and gather a group of my people. When he came back, I considered what to do. I decided to travel to a different country. I came there, and even there, there were people standing in circles and whispering about me. Even they had gotten to know the thing. So I went and sat down in a forest. Five of my Hasidim came with me. They sat with me, we sat there, and as we needed something to eat, we sent one of the men to buy it. So I asked him, did they already stop making all that noise against me? He said that the tumult was as great as it was before.

An old man came and said to me that he wanted to speak to me. I went with him, and he said, "How could you do such a thing? Are you not ashamed before your ancestors, your grandfather, Reb Nachman, and your grandfather, the Ba'al Shem Tov? Why aren't you ashamed before the Torah of Moshe and the holy forefathers, Avraham, Yitzhak, and Ya'akov? What do you think, you will continue to stay here? You can't stay here always, and finally, you will not have any more money, and you are a weak man—what will you do? Do you think that you can go to another country? Consider either that they will know who you are or they will have heard of your deed. If they don't know who you are, you will not be able to earn your keep." So I said, "Well, if it is so, then what am I to do? Will I have a part in the World-to-Come?" He said, "Do you think that they will still give you a part in the World-to-Come? Even hell is not sufficient for you to hide there, for you have caused a great desecration of the Name." I said to him, "Go away. Here I thought that you would console me and speak to my heart, and you bring me such pain! Go away."

The old man went away. I feared that since I have been there for a long time, I might forget what I had learned, so I looked for the man whom I sent to buy the victuals that he would try and get a book for me. He went and could not bring me a book. It was impossible for him to get any book without telling that it was I who needed the book. I then had great pain, for not only was I in exile, but I did not even have a book and certainly would forget all my studies.

The old man came with a book. I asked him, "What have you got in your hand?" and he said, "A book." And I said to him, "Could you please lend me the book?" He gave it to me, and I took it, and I did not know even how to hold the book. I opened it, and I couldn't understand the meaning of the words, for it was to me like a strange language, in a foreign script. This caused me great pain. I was afraid for my own people; if they were to realize that I cannot even read a book, they too will leave me. So the old man called me to come so that he could speak to me. Again, he began to upbraid me for having committed such a grave sin without being ashamed, and even in hell there would be no place to hide. And I said to him, "If one of the souls from the Higher World were to tell me such a thing, I would believe him." He said to me,

"I am from there," and he proved to me that he was from there, and I remembered the story of the Ba'al Shem Tov, who had also thought at one point that he had lost his part in the World-to-Come, and he had said, "I love Him Whose name is blessed, even without reward in the World-to-Come." And I cast my head back with great bitterness, and as I cast my head back, there gathered about me all the great people, and the old man said to me that I should be ashamed before them, before my grandfather and all the forefathers. And they said to me, "The fruit of the earth is for beauty and for pride." They said to me, "We are very proud of you." And they brought to me all my people and children. All of them consoled me greatly. With such great bitterness had I cast my head back that even he who had transgressed the entire Torah would have been forgiven for it. And the rest of the good, I don't tell you, though it truly was good.

Stories

Reb Nachman told stories to his Hasidim that are just wonderful. You have to imagine how primed the situation was for these stories. First of all, you would have warmed up with a little schnapps and a few *niggunim,* melodies. And then the lights would be dimmed and he would begin to tell the stories. I imagine that he told them in a little singsong. One of them, "The Seven Beggars," is truly amazing.[12] This is just a small part of the story.

You see, there is a hill, and on that hill is a stone. From that stone there wells a spring. Now everything has a heart—the world as a whole has a heart, and the heart of the world is a complete form, with a face and hands and feet. And even the nail on the toe of the heart of the world is more heart than any other heart. And the hill with the spring, this hill is at one end of the world, and the heart is at the other end of the world. And the heart and the spring are opposite each other. And the heart longs and yearns always to reach the spring. And the longing and the yearning of the heart is wild. And the heart is also always crying out because it wants to reach the spring. And the spring, too, craves the heart. Now, the heart has two afflictions: one because the sun pursues it and scorches it, because it cannot bear the heart's longing for the spring; and the other because of the sheer exhaustion from its yearning and longing. But when the heart must rest a little to regain its breath, a bird comes flying there and spreads its wings and hides it from the sun. Then the heart rests a little. Yet even then, it looks across to the spring and yearns for the spring. So why doesn't the heart go to the spring? Because it stands facing the hill, and it sees the top of the hill where the spring is, but as soon as it tries to move toward the hill, it no longer sees the top, and then it can no longer see the spring, and it might—God forbid!—die of longing. And if the heart died—God forbid!—of longing, the whole world would be annihilated, because the heart is the heart of the life of every living thing—and how could a world exist without a heart?

And therefore the heart cannot move. And the spring . . . the spring has no time. For it has no day, and no time in the world at all, for it is above the time of the world. And the time of the spring is only when the heart gives it a day as a gift. And when the day is about to end, they begin to bid each other farewell. The heart and the spring tell each other parables and sing songs to each other with great love and with great longing.

And the true man of grace, he has charge over it all. And as the day draws to its end, the true man of grace and good deeds comes and gives the heart a day. And the heart gives the day to the spring. And the spring, again, has a day. And when the day comes, it also comes with parables and songs in which are all the wisdoms. And there are differences between days because there are Sundays and Mondays and so on, and New Moons and festivals. And each day comes with its own songs, according to the day.

The story is not so much prose as poetry. But that is the way Reb Nachman was teaching people. Read it again, and then you must wonder about and ponder the thing, and then you will see what beautiful depth there is in the *prostak*, a simple Jew who tells other people Jewish things.

The Parable of the Master of the Field

There is a Field
where grow Trees and Plants
of beauty indescribable,
ineffable preciousness,
fulfilled is the eye,
that glimpsed it once.

"Trees," "Plants,"
holy souls are they
growing, becoming.

Naked, erring souls
befogged, outside
the Field of bliss,
longing, yearning
to be mended,
to be rooted again
in their own place
in the Field of bliss.

Great souls,
others cluster about them,
also err outside,
having gone out
unable to return.

Wait they must
for the field's Master.
Only he can mend, replant.

Some can be mended
only by another's death,
another deed.

Yet must he beware
for he may have to
yield his life to gain.

Even then he may not prevail
except he be the greatest
among *Tzaddikim.*

—Nachman of Bratzlav, *Likkutey MaHaRan* 1:65

Who is Reb Nachman talking about? Obviously, he is the master of the field. And obviously the trees and plants of the garden are his Hasidim, who are the official followers. Then there are some people he wants to fix, who are not inside. He would like to be their gardener too. Now, if you had to name names, who would those people be? There were some *maskilim,* "enlightened" or "modern" Jews, in Uman, where Reb Nachman was living at that time. And in those days, these men could not be counted as part of a *minyan* because they were considered fallen men. One of them was a pharmacist, and another was Reb Nachman's landlord, and from time to time, the story goes, the Rebbe would sit and play chess with these guys. Can you imagine what his Hasidim must have thought? I can imagine Reb Natan coming in on this scene and being mortified. Why is the great Reb Nachman hanging out with these guys? So there is something real behind the metaphor. And Reb Nachman was willing to break out of the insular community to reach those Jews.

Reb Nachman's Wake of Comfort

I fall more in love with Reb Nachman whenever I teach about him and see the effect that he has on people, even today. It is the way in which he catches the imagination. I could teach you some teachings of Rebbes that would leave you cold; there is no way they could get you to the place of the "dance" or to the "flame." But Reb Nachman is always warm. And disciples in his day were turned on by his vibrancy. The thrust was for them horizontal. And what keeps coming out is that he creates a wake in which we are comfortable, emotionally and spiritually. He doesn't say much to leave you uncomfortable. Even in the "heavy" places, he has gone ahead of us and offers a reassuring voice. He has been there and has come through. So it feels really comfortable to be in his wake and to see the light spreading from there.

Reb Gedaliah Aharon Kenig (1921–23 Tammuz 1980)

Reb Gedaliah was born in Katamon, Jerusalem, to Eliezer Mordecai Koenig.[13] He was the foremost disciple of his master, Reb Abraham Sternhartz (1862–1955), the great grandson of Reb Natan of Nemirov. When he met his teacher, Reb Gedaliah was already well versed in Torah but engaged with his master as if he were a mere beginner. All in all they completed eighteen cycles of studying the entire *Likkutey MaHaRan* together, and in that time, Reb Avraham passed on to Reb Gedaliah the oral tradition of Bratzlav.

Reb Gedaliah was well known for his boundless patience and kindness, not to mention his willingness to teach each and every person who came before him, including many women. He was the author of *Chayyey Nefesh*, numerous unpublished works, and commentaries on the *Likkutey MaHaRan* and *Tikkuney Zohar.*

It was his life work, as he saw it, to rebuild and reestablish the community of S'fat, the city once home to the mystical community of Rabbi Yitzhak Luria. This was to fulfill the last request of his beloved master, Reb Avraham, who specified the very tract of land and said, "If Bratzlaver Hasidim will bring Rebbe Nachman's mission to S'fat, it will benefit the entire world." Eventually the land was acquired, and a community slowly began to take shape.

In 1979 Reb Gedaliah made a trip to the United States to arouse interest in the S'fat community and succeeded in opening many doors for Bratzlav. The following year, before a trip to England, he entrusted the mission of rebuilding S'fat to three of his sons and passed on the leadership of the community. While in England, Reb Gedaliah died suddenly from tuberculosis. He was buried on the Mount of Olives in Jerusalem. His son, Reb Elazar Kenig, is now the spiritual leader of the S'fat community, which continues to grow and prosper.

Reb Gedaliah was deeply rooted in Reb Nachman's "Torah of the Void," which deals with the sciences and traditions outside of Judaism.

REB GEDALIAH KENIG AND THE BRATZLAV IDEAL

Each science
has its own song:
Each science
issues from a melody.
Even the void's Unwisdom
has a melody of its own.

"What was wrong with the heretic?"
"—When he rose,
Greek songbooks fell from him.
All day he hummed the song
of the Greek."
The song and the heresy—
each depend on the other—
the wisdom and its tune,
the science and its scale.

For heresies fall
in book-loads
from one who sings the tune
of heresy.

Each wisdom draws from its own
melody.
Even the higher ones,
they draw from melodies higher
Up, way up,
to the point
of the first emanation,
beyond which
there is only
nothing
but the Infinite Light
surrounding the void
which contains the
something.
With the wisdoms
arising from some melodies.

Certainly in the beyond
of the void
there, too, is wisdom,

but it is infinite
and only the Infinite One
attains to it.
And His wisdom cannot be reached
at all:
There is nothing there
save faith—
to faith Him, Be He Blessed!—
that His Light endlessly embraces
the all,
surrounds all worlds.

And faith—
she, too, is a song,
a tune unique
to faith.

Even those who worship stars
and constellations
mistakenly
have for each star,
for each zodiac sign,
a special tune—
which they sing
and by which they celebrate
in their prayer houses.
Conversely,
in Holiness's true worship
each faith
has a special tune and song.

And the song which is
uniquely singing of the
faith most high,
the faith transcending all
wisdoms and deeds
in the world—
That faith in the Self
of the Endless Light,
bathing all worlds,
it too has song and tune,
beyond any other

belonging to wisdoms and creeds.
Yet they all derive a note,
a phrase, a pattern or inspiration
from that most high tune
which passes all understanding.

And when
the future to come
will be now
and all nations will have clear lips
turned upon them,
all calling with the Name
HVYH
and all faithing Him,
then will be upheld
"Sing from the heartsprings of faith"
the tune most sublime.

Now only a Moshe-*Tzaddik*
merits to know this tune
which is the song of silence
Be still.
Thus rose the *thought*
beyond words or expression.

And this is why
"Then will Moshe sing,"
for that song
has not yet been sung,
for it is a dead-raising
song of silence.

And through the *Tzaddik*'s *niggun*,
when in him tongue-tied Moshe
sings,

all lost souls
rise from the abyss,
and find their way from void.
All tunes are reabsorbed in
the song of silence,
all heresy integrated and dissolved.

Tune and word
in the *thought song*.

And this is why God says
to Moshe,
Come to Pharaoh,
the obstacle to freedom,
the void-maker,
for I have made heavy and hard
his heart,
for in the void
only the hard questions
and contradictions remain—
So.
Moshe has come there
where no one may come,
for it is a God-void
which God voided
"so that I might set forth
My wonders
in its midst."
The wondrous creation
which needs a void
to be put into
"In order that you may tell
in the "ear-ing"
of son and grandson."

For in the creation,
in the something
you can tell and talk,
for there is multiplicity—
names and forms,
letters and phrases,
notes and songs,
all for Mercy's sake.

For all Mercy was condensed
so that the world could contain it.

    —Nachman of Bratzlav, *Likkutey MaHaRan* 1:64

What is it that makes true devotees exceptional? That they emulate in life—and in death—the master they love. When we look at Saint Francis of Assisi, coming down from the mountain with his *stigmata*,[14] we can see how he so embodied his love for Jesus that he took on the five wounds of the master. Reb Gedaliah Kenig was a Bratzlav Hasid, and he died from tuberculosis, from bleeding in his lungs and choking on that blood. And this was precisely the way in which Reb Nachman of Bratzlav had died. So one can get a sense of what that emulation meant to him. It went to the extent of becoming somaticized. And this is the power of Bratzlav, for Reb Nachman had died some 170 years earlier. Reb Gedaliah's living master was a direct descendant of Reb Natan, Reb Abraham Sternhartz. So there is the accessible master and the ideal master in Bratzlav.

With Reb Gedaliah, I had such a sense of close spiritual friendship. We would have wonderful talks; the patience that he had, the way in which he would hear me out, was truly wonderful. Once we got into a discussion about God "communicating" with other nations. And in his image, it was like India got it all from Abraham. Aren't the Brahmins from Abraham? There is a funny story around this that I didn't want to tell him at that time.

When I had first gone to India, I was in a place in Bombay where there was a synagogue of the *Beney Yisrael*, the Jews who had been in India since King Solomon's time. So that congregation was known as *Magen Hasidim*, the shield of the pious, of the Hasidim. And this was kind of strange because usually in Hebrew it is *Magen Avraham*, the shield of Abraham. So I asked a man there, "Why are you are called *Magen Hasidim*?" "Because," he replied, "*Brahm* is God, and *A-Brahm* is "Not-God," as if one were professing atheism. *A* attached to a word signifies "not" in Sanskrit. So to call this *shul* the "shield of Not-God," of the atheists, as it were, would give the wrong impression to people. And it was a wonderful *shul*. The *siddur* was printed in Hebrew characters on one side and Devanagari[15] on the other side. So I said, "Read to me the translation of the *Sh'ma*." I wanted to see how they translate *Adonai*. It comes out, "Hear O Israel, *Rameshvar* is our God, *Rameshvar* is One." *Ram* is for *Rama*, which means "pleasing" or "delight," and is a name for God in general in Hindu traditions. *Eshvar* is for *Ishvara*, which is the word for "Lord." *Ishvara* is also a "chosen deity," so it becomes "*Rameshvar*, the High Chosen Deity, is our God, the High Chosen Deity is One." It was wonderful to see that.

But Reb Gedaliah, in his reasoning, figured that the Hindus had gotten it all from Abraham because Rashi's commentary says that Abraham sent his children to the lands of the East, empowering them with some magic names that didn't come from the highest places of purity. So Reb Gedaliah said, "That's how they got whatever truth there is there." Then I said, "You can say this very well about India, but what are you going to say about China?" and I started to tell him about Lao Tzu and showing him the similarities. And he let it all in and then came back with, "Well, this must be a residue from when God went around with the Torah from nation to nation and talked to them." But in saying that, he had already made a shift. It came directly from God and not via us, and that was a remarkable shift. But he was a remarkable person.

But again, he was following the remarkable model of Reb Nachman. For Reb Nachman was saying, "Even from the fairy tales of the *Goyim* there screams forth the glory of God." You don't hear anybody else saying things like that. And he also says in the "Torah of the Void," that "every wisdom has a song, has a melody. And the songs that they sing in their houses of worship also contain in their melody the great wisdom." I imagine how fascinated he must have been hearing some singing, maybe some chorale music coming out of a church, not wanting to hear it and so wanting to hear it. So following this model, Reb Gedaliah also pushed the edge. He was the one person in *Meah Shearim* (the most stringently observant neighborhood of Jerusalem) who taught women; none of the other rabbis would bother with that. And they got on his case because he created an expectation that other women pressured their men to follow, to do as Reb Gedaliah does. And of course they said, "Who are we? We can't be like Reb Gedaliah."

I once saw him coming out of his house, going to *shul*. It was so wonderful. Even now I see the picture in my mind's eye. He was already wrapped in the *tallit* and *t'fillin*. He didn't wait to get to *shul* to put them on. He put them on at home, and on his way he went already clearly focused every step of the way on going to *shul*—getting closer and closer to the place where he would talk with God.

One day, he told me about a man whom the community was about to go after and give a hard time. A meeting is held in *Meah Shearim,* and people stand up and are really beginning to say nasty things about this man, who somehow didn't live up to their expectations. So Reb Gedaliah takes the book of the teachings of Reb Nachman, the *Likkutey MaHa-Ran,* ascends the *bima,* and says, "I want to read for you a *shtikele* teaching of Reb Nachman." And it begins like this: "Be very careful with what you say, because after a person has lived his life in this world, *venifra'im mimenu mida'to u'sh'lo mida'to,* one has to pay for the guilt with your mind on it or with your mind not on it." Furthermore, it says, quoting Reb Nachman, "Don't judge anyone too harshly. When a person comes to the other world, they ask this question, 'What do you think if somebody has done such and such a sin?' And when you are talking to the authorities up in Heaven, you get to be very pious. 'For such and such a sin, terrible, terrible, five years of shooting, six years of hanging. It is a terrible, terrible sin.' *Lifney mi atah atid liten din ve'cheshbon,* before whom will you have to give a law and an account? The strange question is, why do you have to tell them in Heaven what the law is?" Reb Nachman says, "Because they ask you what is the law, and you give the harshest interpretation. Then they say, 'OK, let's make you a *heshbon* (an accounting): now let's see how many times you transgressed.' Why do you have to pay for it in such a way? It was *mida'to,* by your consent, by your consciousness. But *sh'hlo mida'to,* you didn't know that they were talking about you; you still think they are talking about somebody else." So Reb Gedaliah turns to the people and says, "You know, all that piety and that condemning that you are about to do, just remember that someday they'll hold it against you too." And he descends from the *bima.*

What a compassionate person he was. He taught me some *niggunim,* and he was the one who helped me when I needed to find out when you count *Da'at* and when you count *Keter* in the ten *Sefirot.* He said, "It depends which world it is in." And so I said to him, "In which world do you count *Da'at* and in which world do you count *Keter*?" He said, "You can figure this one out yourself." And when I told him "that in *Atzilut* and *Yetzirah* you count *Keter,* and in *B'riyah* and *Assiyah* you count *Da'at,*" he said, "You are right." It was just so wonderful that he gave me the space for my own "aha" and didn't rob me of my initiative. *Z'chuto tagayn aleinu,* may his merit protect us.

WHO WALKS ON THE EDGE
OF THE SWORD

REB MENACHEM MENDEL OF KOTZK

(1787–22 SHEVAT 1859)

THE UNCOMPROMISING Menachem Mendel Halpern (later Morgenstern) was born in the winter of 1787 in Bilgoray, near Lublin.[1] Leibish Halpern, his father, was a poor glazier. It is said that even as a child, Reb Menachem Mendel was secretive, stubborn, reserved, and brilliant. But he knew no peace and was unrelenting in his search for truth. He left Bilgoray to study rabbinics under the tutelage of Rabbi Yosef Hochgelerenter in the *yeshiva* of Zamosc.

At twenty he married Glukel, the daughter of Eliezer Nei of Tamashov, who bore him a son, David, who would later succeed him. However, Glukel died after the birth of their son, and he married Chayyah Halfin, the sister-in-law of Reb Yitzhak Meir Alter, later the Rebbe of Ger. During the period of his first marriage, it is said that Reb Ya'akov Yitzhak, the Seer of Lublin, sent for the brilliant young man to be brought to him. And under the influence of the Seer, Reb Menachem Mendel became a Hasid. But later he broke away to follow the elite discipline of Reb Ya'akov Yitzhak, the "Holy Jew" of Pzhysha. And with the death of the "Holy Jew" seven years later, he followed Reb Simcha Bunem who further refined the process of purification for Pzhysha Hasidim. Truth and perfection was the "art" of the Pzhysha school.

When Reb Simcha Bunem also died, a small group of devoted young men followed Reb Menachem Mendel to Tomashov. Hasidim used to say of this time in Tomashov, "A fire is burning Tomashov." The atmosphere of Tomashov was austere, but one did not go hungry. Here one was fed a fist full of teaching at a time.

During the Polish revolt of 1830–1831, Reb Menachem Mendel was a supporter of the cause. But when the revolt was quelled by the Russians, he was forced to flee for a time and changed his name from Halpern to Morgenstern. Later he safely returned to Poland and settled in the small town of Kotzk, whose very name would become synonymous with the search for Truth.

In 1840, the year he predicted that the Messianic era would begin, Reb Menachem Mendel shut himself up in his study and secluded himself there until his death in 1859. The nature of what happened to cause this is the subject of much speculation. Some say it was a mental breakdown of some sort, that Reb Menachem Mendel sought only to lead a very small and elite group of Hasidim to great heights but instead gathered a large following whose "maintenance" he found extremely taxing on his energy. Others believed that when the gates of Heaven did not open in 1840 because of their own sins, the Rebbe symbolically shut the door on the world.

It was also at this time that his devoted friend and student Reb Mordecai Yosef withdrew from Kotzk, taking a large number of the Hasidim with him. This is one of the tragic rifts in the history of Hasidism. However, students like Reb Hanokh of Alexander and Reb Yitzhak Meir Alter remained loyal to the Kotzker through his self-imposed exile. Indeed, Reb Yitzhak Meir really served as de facto leader of the community. And after the death of Reb Menachem Mendel, most of the Kotzker Hasidim transferred their allegiance to him and became Ger Hasidim. Reb Menachem Mendel of Kotzk destroyed all of his writings, but his influence reverberates to this very day.

Holding Fast to the Truth

People often make a connection between Søren Kierkegaard[2] and the Kotzker. Kierkegaard was saying that you cannot be a comfortable Christian, and the Kotzker says, "I haven't come to bring you comfort; I've come to needle you." What is a human being for? one might ask. And the usual answer would be "To serve God." But Reb Menachem Mendel said, "No! The purpose of Man is to drag God into our lives. To bring Heaven down to us." So he was a tough character and often compared to Kierkegaard, who was also uncompromising. Kierkegaard, too, had the same restlessness that demands almost annihilation in God, the strong fervor in his search for truth, the high crisis point that characterized the

Kotzker. Professor Heschel wrote a remarkable book about the two con-
temporaries, the Kotzker and Kierkegaard, called *A Passion for Truth*.

Reb Menachem Mendel was really concerned with a visceral experience of the Truth. He says, "Never mind what you have in your head!
Never mind what you have in your heart! What about your *pupick*?"—
that is, your belly-button or, by extension, your gut. That was the kind of
language that Reb Menachem Mendel the Kotzker used. In fact, that line
comes from a story about the Kotzker and a Lubavitcher Hasid:

A Chabad Hasid comes to the town of Kotzk, and Reb Menachem Mendel asks him,
"Tell me, what does your Rebbe teach you about *kavanot,* about the intentions that
you have in the *Sh'ma Yisrael?*" The Chabad Hasid excitedly begins telling Reb Menachem Mendel Kotzker about the Chabad system and describing many heady intellectual things. And Reb Menachem Mendel listens to him patiently and finally says,
"*Yeh, yeh ober dos hostu in kop! Un vos hert zich in pupick?*—What you have in your head is
not worth much. What is going on in your navel, in your gut?"

The point is really that very often it is not a question of the mind, of
the heart, or of the imagination—it is a question of the guts. And sometimes you have to get things done with your guts, by marshaling those
visceral forces in order to get to your strength. Reb Menachem Mendel
said, "The only person I like in the whole Bible is Pharaoh, the king of
Egypt." Why? He says, "Look, God threatens him with blood, with one
plague after another; *er halt zich bei zeins*—he sticks to his guns, he
doesn't give in."

How would one come to join such a group of Hasidim? I'll tell you. If the young man
had made up his mind that he was going to follow the way of Reb Menachem Mendel
and he came to Kotzk, he was to be put to a test, and of course nobody told him how
the test was to be conducted. On the morning of his second day in Kotzk, all the *chevra*
(companions) of the Kotzker Hasidim would get up very, very early and do their *davvenen* without waking the would-be Hasid. When the young man arose at seven, thinking he was up early, the rest of them were back in their beds, pretending they were
sleeping. They did not make much of a fuss of *davvenen* anyhow, in Kotzk, because Reb
Menachem Mendel told them, "*Mokdo,* the burning of the fire on the altar, is written
with a small *mem* because the flame does not want to be so big, but *tamim t'ihi'yoh im
HaShem Elohecha* is not written with a small *tav.* Perfect be with the Lord, your God,
this is written in very plain writing." So he did not want to see the big flame of fervor.
He wanted to see more of *dem emet*—the truth. It is written, "Open unto Me like the
point of a needle, and I will open unto you like the gates of a palace." So the Kotzker
said, "Yes, just like the point of a needle, *nor es darf zein a durch un a durch,* it should go
through and through."

When the Hasidim got out of bed, they said to the young newcomer, "Sit down and let's have something to eat before we *davven*." So they got some wine and some cake. And the young man didn't know what to do. He had never eaten before *davvening* in his whole life. Very upset, he said to them, "It says in the *Shulhan Arukh* that you must not do this." They all just shrugged and said, "Look who wants to be a Hasid. He wants to be a Hasid, and doesn't eat before *davvenen!*" And they really started to needle him about this. It was a tremendous pressure for the young man to put up with. Finally, they said, "Either you eat with us, or we throw you out!" The young man did not know what to do. Finally, somebody suggests a solution, "Come, we will go over to the venerable old Hasid with the long beard and ask him. And whatever he says goes." The disconcerted young man agreed, saying, "All right, I will go and ask this old man, and whatever he says, I will do." And the old man said, "Of course, everybody says to eat, *zei nisht kein narr,* don't be a fool, sit down and eat." So the young man sat down and the Hasidim gave him the wine and cake, and he began to make a *b'rokha,* but before he can say God's name, they grab him and throw him on the table. And he screamed, "*Gevalt, vos vilt ir fun mir?* What is it that you want from me?" And they shouted back, "Ha! You take the word of a human being just because the old goat has a long beard? You are going to *farkoif dein Gott,* sell your God short!" So that is how it was in Kotzk!

The point is that one has to be resolute, not intimidated, even by God. Nothing should divert you from the road on which you are traveling. People would come to Reb Menachem Mendel the Kotzker and not being a man of many words, he would ask them, "*Ver?*" And by this he meant, "*Ver bist tu?* Who are you?" And he would say, "*Vaned?*" He wouldn't even bother to say, "*Fun vaned?* Where are you from?" And finally, "What do you want?" One man to whom these questions were addressed on his first visit to the Kotzker felt as if Rabbi Akavya ben M'hallalel, the *Mishnah* sage, was standing there saying to him, "Where are you from? Where are you going to? And before Whom will you give an account of your life?" So you can see how these questions of the Kotzker penetrated a person with a sense of "*me tor zich nisht naren,* you must not deceive yourself!" This is how Reb Menachem Mendel put it: "*Lo tonu ish et 'amito,* You should not fool one another." Related to this is one of the Kotzker's most famous sayings, which became the ground for Martin Buber's *I and Thou:* "If I am I because you are you, and you are you because I am I, then I am not I and you are not you. But if I am I because I am I, and you are you because you are you, then I am I and you are you, and we can talk." In other words, "I'm not playing up to you, and you are not playing up to me. We have a core of authenticity." So what is a Hasid? A Hasid is one who does more that the law requires. The law requires that you should not fool another person, but the Kotzker says, you must not even fool yourself.

Parable of the Goat and the Snuffbox

On one occasion, the Kotzker complained that his Hasidim troubled him with trivial things, and he told the following story.

Once upon a time, there was a goat, and the goat had huge horns. And with his horns the goat supported Heaven. And this goat would eat the grass at a cemetery, a special cemetery in which there were Jews that were killed by Chmielnicki, and the soil was drenched with blood, and so a very special, succulent grass grew there, and it is the grass that the goat ate, and so his horns grew longer and longer and were able to lift up Heaven too. At this time, there was also a Jew who came out to the cemetery because he was looking for an old horn, because his *tabak pishkeleh,* his snuffbox, had gotten lost, and so he was weeping there in the cemetery. And the goat said, "Why do you weep, my dear Jew?" And he said, "Because I don't have a snuffbox." So the goat said, "Stop weeping. I will bend down and you shall cut off a piece of my horn and then you can fashion a snuffbox." And so the goat bent down, and the Jew cut off a piece of the prodigious horn, and he made a snuffbox from it. Afterward, he went to the *shul* and gave everyone a *shmek tabak.* And as the people were sniffing the snuff, they said, "Oh, what a wonderful fragrance it has!" And he said, "No wonder. I have it from a remarkable goat, and the end of the horn I made it from was in Heaven. So no wonder!" And soon the news spread, and everyone came running to the cemetery and began to weep before the goat, "Please give me a piece of horn." And the goat had such great *rachmones,* such great pity on these people that the goat bent down and allowed each one of them to cut from the horn. But in the meantime, who would be supporting Heaven?

Reb Menachem Mendel meant to show his Hasidim that their trivial requests were preventing him from upholding Heaven.

On Writing and the Kotzker

There was an attitude among some Rebbes that everything they had written during their lifetime should be burned when they died. The Kotzker made sure on his deathbed that Reb Yitzhak Meir of Ger, his friend and disciple, would burn everything that he had written. Why did the Rebbes feel this way? Possibly because they didn't want to leave the writings behind as karma that would keep them "earth-bound." If people hang on to what their teacher has said, that ties the teacher down to earth. And sometimes teachers feel, "I did my duty this time around, I played my role;

don't tie me to a gravestone." The Kotzker was especially fond of saying, "I'm not a *kvures Yid,* a Jew who hangs out at gravesides." That has to do with this side of life, and Reb Menachem Mendel had finished and wanted to take all of that stuff with him. However, it didn't work.[3] People still remember and recount the teachings and the stories, just as I am doing right now. There is always something that gets left behind, and so Reb Menachem Mendel is still troubling us with his uncompromising vision.

DEPLOYED BY GOD

REB MORDECAI YOSEF OF ISHBITZ

(1800–7 TEVET 1854)

REB MORDECAI YOSEF LEINER was born in 1800 in Tomashov to Rabbi Jacob. His father was of a distinguished ancestry, tracing his line all the way back to Rabbi Meir of Padua, who was said to be a descendent of King David. His mother, too, is said to be of a proud lineage. His was a wealthy family, and after his father's death he was fortunately able to continue his studies. When he was still very young, he was already thought to be a prodigy and was befriended by Reb Menachem Mendel (later of Kotzk). It was he who in 1819 took him to meet Reb Simcha Bunem of Pzhysha. The young man soon sold his possessions and moved to Pzhysha to be near Reb Simcha Bunem, with whom he remained until the latter's death in 1827. Reb Simcha Bunem liked the luminous, though frail, young man and is supposed to have said to him, "At present I am taller than you, but you are still young and will grow."[1]

After the death of Reb Simcha Bunem, he joined a number of others who became the Hasidim of his friend Reb Menachem Mendel of Tomashov. But even while a disciple, he was receiving petitions from Hasidim to become a Rebbe. Ishbitz tradition says that at the time, Reb Mordecai Yosef rejected the position of Rebbe, saying, "The time has not come yet for me to be a Rebbe, and I will be with you in one group until the year 5600 [1840]."[2] In Tomashov and later Kotzk, under Reb Menachem Mendel, he held a position of honor. Along with Reb Yitzhak Meir Alter, he was among the foremost of Kotzk Hasidim. Indeed, when the numbers of Hasidim swelled too large, Reb Menachem Mendel appointed Reb Mordecai Yosef to guide the younger Hasidim.

In 1839, after thirteen years of discipleship (Ishbitz Hasidim considered these his "hidden" years), came a decisive break with Reb Menachem Mendel in what is often described as the "Friday night incident."

The previous year, Reb Menachem Mendel collapsed and was ill for nine months. During that time, Reb Mordecai Yosef began to accept petitions and donations from the Hasidim who were coming to count on him more and more in the absence of their master. In the fall of 1839, Reb Mordecai Yosef came for the High Holidays to Kotzk. On the eve of Simchat Torah, he asked those who were close to him to bring Torah scrolls to his inn instead of to the Rebbe's *beit midrash* where they would usually pray. At the time, they did not understand the reason for this request, but they complied anyway. As the services of the Kotzker Hasidim were being led in the *beit midrash* that evening, Reb Menachem Mendel reportedly ran from his room into the house of study and grabbed the Torah scroll from the person who was holding it. Then, looking at the man, as though surprised, he returned it, saying that he thought it was Mordecai Yosef. Hearing about this later, those in Reb Mordecai Yosef's room understood that he had foreseen this action and had sought to avoid it. After this incident, the lines were drawn. This was the year before Reb Menachem Mendel entered his mysterious isolation and things were definitely beginning to change in Kotzk. After this "break," Reb Mordecai Yosef left Kotzk for Vengrov and then Tomashov and finally settled in Ishbitz, where he spent the next thirteen years. Obviously, the break was over more than just jealousy; a fundamental difference in attitudes had been growing for years. There would be tension between the two communities for years after, especially considering the many families and friends that were divided. However, the emergence of Reb Mordecai Yosef from the Kotzk shadow was of great and lasting significance. Reb Mordecai Yosef's teachings are among the most profound and original (and controversial) in all of Hasidic history. His great work, *Mei HaShiloach,* was published posthumously by his grandson, Reb Gershon Henokh of Radzyn.[3]

○

All Is in the Hands of Heaven

> *If all the accidental properties have been removed, and there is still something that finds favor, it is a sign that there is some good in it. And to this purpose the Torah speaks about the* yetzer ha'ra, *the inclination of evil, for in no other place does the Torah speak so clearly about the* yetzer ha'ra. *For it can happen that the* yetzer *of a person should so greatly overwhelm him that he cannot move; that his choice is completely taken from him*

and he cannot move, and then it is clear that it comes from God.
This we find in the Torah with Yehudah and Tamar.

—Mordecai Yosef of Ishbitz, *Mei HaShiloach*

Morris Faierstein has written an excellent study of the teachings of the Ishbitzer called *All Is in the Hands of Heaven*. In the Talmud it says, "All is in the hands of Heaven, except for the fear of Heaven." What this means in the language of the Talmud is that God's providence is total and controls everything except human choice. In other words, God is not going to force you to be religious; that is human choice. "All is in the hands of Heaven but the fear of Heaven." Then Reb Mordecai Yosef of Ishbitz comes along and says, "All is in the hands of Heaven, including the fear of Heaven." Now, you can imagine how a statement of this sort would be rejected by orthodox ideologues. It undermines the whole of human responsibility.

What experience would prompt a man like the Ishbitzer to say what he is saying? Even the fear of Heaven is in the hands of Heaven? Perhaps it is an experience of grace that floods him so much that he says, "I had nothing to do with it. It certainly wasn't from my ego." What else might prompt someone to say that? Since there is no space where God is not, and if you feel the totality of that situation, it melts away the business of choice. But if the Ishbitzer remained with that, it wouldn't be so simple. Because as he puts it, "Why is it that we have such a sense of responsibility? Why is it that we are given commandments? Why are we not treated like marionettes? If all is in the hands of Heaven, including the fear of Heaven, why is that we have an experience of the freedom of choice and responsibility?" His answer is, "That too is grace." That we feel as if we are participating in something special, that we can feel that our actions create a great contribution, is the gift of God. It is to give us the satisfaction of a meaningful life that somehow feels like we are doing something. *Sh'yih'yo nikra'im 'al sh'mo*, "Actions should be credited to the person's name." Why is it that God gave us the sense that we are doing something, that we have a choice? On the one hand, we know that we are being deployed by God, and on the other hand, we get satisfaction from a job well done.

So here is where the Ishbitzer comes in such a way that upsets and troubles many orthodox thinkers. There is an amazing story in the Bible about how Judah, the son of Jacob, the founder of the Davidic line and dynasty, goes to shear the sheep, and on the way he meets a *hierodule*, a sacred prostitute, on the highway. And she is veiled because it wasn't a personal affair with them. She represents the goddess, and before the shearing of the sheep, the sheep belong, as it were, to the goddess. And one of the ways to serve the goddess was to have intercourse with one of her priestesses. This is an understanding that comes from a modern reading of Canaanite religion. And one of the things that is a really abhorrent to Judaism is that the gift that you give to a prostitute must not be used as a sacrifice. You may not bring *etnan zonah*, the hire of such a sacred prostitute, and offer that as a sacrifice on the altar, again, in direct contradistinction to Canaanite religion.

From the point of view of the Rabbis, it does not read like this. They say simply that she is a prostitute who serves idols. So Judah comes to her, and because he doesn't have a sheep to give to her, he is forced to leave his seal and his tassels with her, his insignia of his being the ruler of the tribe. And the next day he sends someone down with a sheep to give her, but they can't find her, nor can they find his belongings. Indeed, no one has even heard of such a person. This is because she was no mere prostitute but was actually his daughter-in-law in disguise. She had deliberately done this because he had not dealt justly with her in the past. And three months later it is discovered that she is pregnant. When this is reported to Judah, the head of that tribe, it is assumed that she must have whored because her husband is dead. Therefore, he says, "Take her out and burn her." And they are about to execute her when she takes out the signs of office that he left with her before, and she says, "The one to whom these belong fathered this child." She doesn't say, "Judah fathered the child." She gives him, at this point, the option to deny that these are his, from which the Rabbis draw this amazing conclusion: "It is better to cast oneself on a pyre to be burned alive than to shame another person in public." Judah, on the other hand, goes out and says, "She is more righteous than I."

A little bit later in the Bible we come to the story of Zimri and Kozbi. Kozbi is a Midianite princess who leads a group of young Midianite women to the camp of the Israelites in the desert to offer to have intercourse with them. Zimri chooses that princess, and he is having sex with her when Pinchas, in great zeal, takes a javelin and kills the two of them in the middle of the act.

Now, this is all a long introduction to the Ishbitzer's statement that "Judah couldn't help himself." He says, "There are ten degrees in compulsion. The lowest level is when somebody gets all dressed up and goes out on the town and makes it obvious that she or he plans on "doing it" tonight. It is deliberate and very, very clear that this person is going to sin through fornication. The opposite is a situation where a person is doing everything that she or he can to avoid a situation but absolutely cannot avoid it. And so the Ishbitzer says, "When this happens, it isn't that 'the devil made me do it.' It may have served God that this act should happen. The Zohar says that by right, this woman, Kozbi, the Midianite princess, was really his intended mate and that Pinchas had succumbed to excessive zeal in killing them. He shouldn't have done it, but it accomplished an end that was in accordance with the law." Can you imagine teaching such a thing, that Judah couldn't help it because it was the Divine plan that the whole kingdom of David should come through disrepute? Remember, David and Bat Sheba in their adultery have a child who dies, and then they have Solomon. So all this barely acceptable behavior, even unacceptable behavior, is radically reinterpreted in Reb Mordecai Yosef's writings. You can imagine that a book that teaches such things would be absolutely anathema to normative-orthodox interpreters. If the Vilna Ga'on would have read this book, his people, all the Mitnaggedim, the opponents of Hasidism, would have said, "Shabbetai Tzvi! Heresy! What a terrible thing to say! What happens to the freedom of choice?"

When Reb Mordecai Yosef's grandson, Reb Gershon Henokh, published his grandfather's book, called *Mei HaShiloach*, "Silent Waters of the Siloam," he didn't seek anyone else's approval for printing the book, which in those days was unheard of. At that time, every book would need a *haskahmah*, an endorsement. Today, we have blurbs in the back of the book, but in those days, books were carefully read, and if somebody found something that was objectionable, he would declare that this book was not to be printed because it contained heresy. If nothing objectionable was found, the authority gave his approval, which was printed in the book. Reb Gershon Henokh didn't bother and just hired a printer. He traveled from Poland to Austria and had the book printed in Vienna. He had a whole bunch of copies made, and the Hasidim of the Ishbitzer in each town might have only one copy of the book, which they studied zealously. Reb Shlomo Carlebach once told me a funny story related to this.

They had one copy of *Mei HaShiloach* in a little town in the Ishbitzer *shtiebel,* the conventicle where they met, and every *Shabbos* the copy would disappear. And later, when someone went to the outhouse, the copy would always be found there. Well, you can imagine how angry they got: "How dare anyone take the sacred teachings of our master and hide them in the outhouse!" So they decided that they were going to check out who was doing this. One Friday night, they made it look like they all had gone home, but actually they were hiding out and watching. And in came a Sanzer Hasid, who picked up the book and made his way to the outhouse. The hiding men jumped out and grabbed him and flung him on the table and were about to whack him when he said, "How dare you whack me! The power overcame me! I couldn't help it! It must have been God's will!" So, being Ishbitzer Hasidim, they had to let him go.

So you can understand how that played out. Reb Shneur Zalman's view was an architectural view, like Maimonides', that "the Torah was given at Sinai and has been sort of pegged and standing in this way, and there is no dynamic to it." For the Ishbitzer, the statement was, *Z'khor y'mot 'olam biynu sh'not dor vador,* "Remember the days of eternity, and understand the years of generations." Now he is playing on a pun here that runs as follows, "There are certain teachings that are eternal, unvarying, and there are other teachings that change (*sh'not*) from generation to generation. You have to honor both." And then he says in one place, "In Deuteronomy, Moses' teaching is 'You must always do this; you must never do that.' In the book of Ecclesiastes, the teaching goes, 'For every thing there is a season, and sometimes you do and sometimes you don't, and it depends what time it is whether you do or you don't.' Well, by whom do you go?" So the Ishbitzer makes the move that is the traditional move, *Elu v'elu divrey Elokim chayyim,* "The words of these and the words of those are the words of the living God." But how can both be right? So until the Messiah comes, we take fewer risks going with Moses, because we aren't yet really clear on what is our own urging, coming from our own dark side, or are we following the sacred promptings of this moment? We can't be sure, so we go with Moses. But when the Messiah comes, it will be so clear, in every act, because it will be natural for us to respond to the truth of the situation. This is because we will be transparent to the will of God at that time. "For every thing there is a season," and you will know exactly whether it is a time to do or a time not to do. You can understand how radical this teaching was to people in the generation before.

For Jewish Renewal, the Ishbitzer's teachings have become very important as they represent an understanding more palatable to our modern consciousness. They have come down to us especially through the voice of Reb Shlomo Carlebach, who would often teach, "The Heilige ('holy') Ishbitzer said . . ." He would quote the Ishbitzer often because somehow the Ishbitzer's teaching spoke to our hearts. And it was Shlomo who first introduced me to the Ishbitzer's *Mei HaShiloach.*

Reb Mordecai Yosef's son, Reb Ya'akov, took the teachings of his father and expanded on them. And to this day we still don't have all the volumes of the teachings that he gave. But in this second generation of Ishbitz, the teachings of Reb Mordecai Yosef became more and more detailed. Just as Reb Shneur Zalman's son, Reb Dov Baer, took his father's teachings and elaborated and deepened them, so did Reb Ya'akov of Radzyn.

Reb Gershon Henokh of Radzyn (1839–4 Tevet 1890)

Reb Gershon Henokh of Radzyn was born in Ishbitz, the son of Reb Ya'akov Leiner. He was raised by his paternal grandfather, Reb Mordecai Yosef of Ishbitz. He married Hadassah, the daughter of Rabbi Yosef of Hurbiszov. By the time he was thirteen, he was already demonstrating his remarkable intellectual prowess, especially as a Talmudist. However, his was a creative intellect of the highest order and would not be limited even to such a broad subject as Talmud. Reb Gershon Henokh was also an accomplished musician and proficient in various arts and crafts. He gained so deep a knowledge of medicine that his prescriptions (in Latin) were much sought after and honored in many a Warsaw pharmacy. His linguistic facility was such that he was able to converse in a half dozen languages with people throughout Europe from widely different social spheres and all the while in traditional Hasidic garb. He traveled widely and conducted various researches in the empirical manner of a scientist.

When he was twenty-two years old, he became the Rabbi of Radzyn. It was around this time that he prepared and published his grandfather's seminal work, *Mei HaShiloach*. Breaking with tradition, he published the work without official sanction and with a non-Jewish publisher. On 15 Av 1878, he succeeded his father Ya'akov as Rebbe.

When he was thirty-three, he began work on his *Sidrei Tohorot*, which would assure his reputation as a Talmudist. This piece of pseudo-*Gemara* with commentary received accolades from many prominent rabbinic authorities when it was printed in 1873 but also became the subject of much controversy for the audacity of its author in producing it.

In 1887 he published a work on the lost tradition of the *tekhelet*, the blue thread that used to be a part of the *tzitzis*, the ritual fringes. After that, he embarked on a journey with his attendant to the Mediterranean to search for the *chilazon*, the creature from which the blue dye was taken. He visited the aquarium in Naples four times and even went to the Vatican to inspect the garments that reportedly had belonged to the high priest. Eventually, he discovered the *Sepia officinalis* that met the criteria of the lost *chilazon*, and on the eve of Shavuot 1888, he published another book on the *tekhelet* detailing his discovery and answering all objections. Reb Gershon Henokh also devised a method of separating and dissolving the dye so that nothing would have to be added.

On the first day of Hannukah 1889, Reb Gershon Henokh and twelve thousand of his Hasidim began to wear the blue thread, thus reestablishing the *mitzvah* of *tzitzit* to its original condition. This "innovation," too, was the subject of controversy among many rabbinical authorities. And unfortunately, the *mitzvah* did not "take" in the larger Jewish community. Today, only Radzyner and Bratzlav Hasidim[4] observe the wearing of the blue thread.

At circumcisions, Reb Gershon Henokh served both as *sandek,* holding the child, and *mohel,* performing the circumcision. He drank a fifth cup of wine on Passover and preferred the *etrogim* (citrons) of Corfu to those from the Holy Land. Even among the many and varied geniuses of Hasidism, Reb Gershon Henokh, though not widely known, stands out as a figure of unique brilliance and daring.

Reb Gershon Henokh of Radzyn and Renewal

> *. . . The priest is the one through whom everything that has gone awry is mended, completed, and corrected.*

—Mordecai Yosef of Ishbitz, *Mei HaShiloach*

Reb Ya'akov had a son, Reb Gershon Henokh of Radzyn, and he was the one who brought the teachings of the Ishbitzer into print without any stamp of approval, as no one would have given it on such radical teachings. So even in this we can see that he had the most remarkable *chutzpah*. But his *chutzpah* didn't end there. First of all, he packed a gun. Nobody would mess around with him, because he was really serious about it. He had foreseen what would be happening in the future, and it was his character to be ready for such things. He was not one to stand by meekly. He died before the Nazis came to power, but he had foreseen the way of things to come. And because of this, in his heart, he was very much connected to the attitude of the right-wing movement in Zionism called Betar. These were people who would later evolve into the Haganah and still later the even more right-wing Irgun and Stern Group.[5] What you had with them was the sense that we can't be led like sheep to the slaughter. We have to stand up for our rights, and now that the world has recognized that everybody has the right to citizenship, we should have the same right.

He continued the teachings of his grandfather, the Ishbitzer, and on his own studied Latin and medicine. In Warsaw the apothecaries and druggists all accepted his prescriptions. Could you imagine Hasidim coming to see him for a blessing for healing and him saying, "I'll give you the blessing for healing, and be sure to take this so and so many times," and giving out a prescription? He was not the only Rebbe to give prescriptions, but he was one of the few who actually took it upon himself to study medicine.

In the Talmud is a whole section that doesn't have any *Gemara*, commentary, and only has *Mishnah*, the oral Torah. There are six orders of *Mishnah*. One deals with agricultural law (*Zeraim*); another with the calendar (*Mo'ed*); another the laws of women and marriage (*Nashim*); the fourth deals with torts, that is, civil law involving damages (*Nezikin*); the fifth deals with sacrifices offered in the temple (*Kod'shin*); and the sixth deals with what is pure and impure (*Taharot*). You are physically impure if you touch a corpse, if you contract a venereal disease, if you are menstruating. The only book of that last order, *Taharot*, that has *Gemara* is the one that deals with the laws governing menstruation. All the other categories of *Taharot* don't have any *Gemara* because with the destruction of the Temple, it didn't seem that there was anything to discuss. These laws of purity and impurity applied mainly to the time when the Temple still stood. So Reb Gershon Henokh went through the entire Talmud with his encyclopedic mind and wrote a piece of Talmud called *Sidre Taharot*, pulling portions of information from all over the Talmud and creating, as it were, one more volume of Talmud. You have to understand what kind of a *chutzpah* this took. Nobody else dared to do that. It is not that he was innovative in the sense that he wrote things that didn't exist before, but he pulled together materials that existed elsewhere to address a void. So he gave interpretation to that part of the *Mishnah* that didn't have any interpretation before he came along.

Once, when he was jailed on some trumped-up charge, certainly not a crime (the Polish government didn't like Jews of independent spirit), he did something else amazing. From his cell, he asked for paper and pen. He recalled to his memory an entire book, which he then wrote a commentary on. What wonderful *chutzpah* this man had!

But perhaps his most profound act of *chutzpah* had to do with the *tekhelet*, the blue thread. A rule is based on the following reading of the Torah: "And the Lord spoke to Moses saying, Speak unto the children of Israel. Let them make tassels on the corners of their garments. And let them put a blue thread on those tassels." So where is this blue thread? Most of the time when you go to a synagogue, you won't find anyone with a blue thread on their tassels. Why? Because way back, when many people were exiled from the Holy Land, access to the Mediterranean and to those cuttlefish, the *chilazon*, from which the blue dye came, wasn't accessible. So the tradition of the blue thread died out. And if you can't have the blue thread, what can you do? So they divided the commandment of tassels and blue thread into two commandments and said, "I'll have the tassels, even if I can't have the blue thread." Since that time, everybody has gone on to have no blue thread and only the white tassels. Even Reb Yitzhak Luria, facing the situation of having to recite the passage about the blue thread, wrote in one of his commentaries, "In our day the blue thread is gone and not necessary," which sort of says, "You can relax about that." But it was not so for Reb Gershon Henokh.

Reb Gershon Henokh said, "Why can't we have blue thread? So we lost the know-how of it. Well, what we lost we can find again!" And so with his knowledge of Latin, he went down to the Mediterranean and figured out just what you have to change in Latin to make it Italian. You change some of the endings and do a little work with the syntax and you have a kind of basic Italian. So he went down to the Adriatic port of Trieste and started to walk down the coast looking for the *chilazon* that gives that blue dye. And there he saw some fishermen's wives hanging out garments that had that blue color. He started to ask them in this Latin-Italian what he wanted to know about the creature from which they got this blue dye. They explained to him where they got it, and he determined by using the legal descriptions that this was the ancient *chilazon*.

So next he had some *tzitzit* and wool sent to him, and he dyed some threads right there in Italy so that he could observe the *mitzvah* right away. Not only that, but I heard that he brought some of those cuttlefish back to Poland with him, setting up special saltwater tanks to raise them in. Then he did another remarkable thing. He wrote out all the objections that people might have against the "new" blue thread and answered the objections one by one. These he printed up in books, *Sh'funey T'muney Chol,* which is the biblical material about the *chilazon*. These he sent out with four sample threads to three or four hundred great rabbis in Poland and Lithuania so that they could tie them into their *tallitot,* endorsing the blue thread. But almost nobody endorsed the blue thread. Several rabbis tied the blue thread on their *tzitzit,* but the *tallit* that had the blue thread they made a blessing on in private and didn't take out in public. Reb Gershon Henokh, disappointed in the rabbis, said, "I answered all the questions that they could put to me in my books about the blue thread, except the one that could not be answered. Why, if this is the true blue thread, did not their own grandfathers discover it?" With the exception of the Bratzlav Hasidim, only the Radzyn Hasidim took on the restored *mitzvah* of the blue thread in that time. But today you'll find people in Jewish Renewal also attaching the blue thread from the Radzyn Hasidim.

I am especially fond of Reb Gershon Henokh because in him we have a Hasidic Rebbe who was interested in renewing something that had gotten lost. There was a sense of renewal there. "I don't want to leave it just because somewhere it got lost." You know, if you check out what has gotten lost in every religious tradition, sometimes it is quite damaging, like losing brain cells. If you look at Catholicism today, compared to where it was before World War I, there were novenas, vespers, and all kinds of services. All Catholics have left today is the Mass. It is as if to say, "They only shoot with the big guns today, and all the little devotional things that they used to have they don't have anymore." Many Jews are in the same situation: instead of having three daily services, they get together only once a week for the Sabbath. So loss happens. The tool chest gets smaller and smaller. And so Reb Gershon Henokh was interested in increasing it again and working against that diminishment.

A LATTER-DAY SAINT

REB ARELE ROTH

(1894–6 NISAN 1947)

REB ARELE ROTH WAS BORN in Ungvar, the son of Rabbi Shmuel Jacob. When he was nine years old, he was sent to study at the *yeshiva* of Rabbi Joseph Rothenberg of Krasnoye. Later he moved on to *yeshivot* in Galicia and spent four years studying under Rabbi Yeshayahu Zilberstein and Rabbi Moses Forhand in Hungary.

During World War I he lived in Hungary and spent time among some of the great Rebbes who found refuge in Budapest—Reb Issachar Dov Rokeach of Belz, Reb Israel Hager of Vishnitz, and Reb Zvi Elimelekh Spiro of Blazowa, who urged Reb Arele to become a Rebbe.

Reb Arele Roth married Simcha, the daughter of Rabbi Yitzhak Katz of Budapest, when he was twenty-two. Later he lived in Satmar for a time and attracted a small group of followers. In 1925 he departed for the Holy Land and established himself as a Rebbe in Jerusalem. When he returned to Satmar for medical reasons in 1929, his new status gained him many enemies, and he was forced leave for Beregszaz, where he established a well-respected *yeshiva* of his own.

After ten years, he again returned to the Holy Land, establishing a close-knit group of Hasidim known for the intensity of their *davvenen*. During these years he wrote many radical books on Jewish observance. He died in 1947 in Jerusalem and was buried on the Mount of Olives. After his death, his Hasidim divided between his son and his son-in-law.

○

The Rebbe with a Last Name

Reb Arele Roth was an anomaly to me. I never heard of a Rebbe with a last name before Reb Arele Roth. It was always the Belzer Rebbe, the Bobover Rebbe, or the Lubavitcher Rebbe. It was like saying the Santa Fe

Rebbe, the Boulder Rebbe. A Rebbe was always connected with some town. All of a sudden I am faced with a Rebbe with a last name, not connected to a particular town.

In 1959 I went to Israel, and at that time I was teaching at the University of Manitoba and I hadn't yet gotten my doctorate. And I was interested in pursuing doctoral studies under Professor Gershom Scholem, who was the great professor of Kabbalah at the Hebrew University. So I made an appointment with him, and it was a wonderful meeting. During it I said to him, "I'm interested in spiritual direction literature, and most of the things that I have read were from classical Hasidism and Chabad. Who is writing this material for people today?" And he said, "Reb Arele Roth." "Who is Reb Arele Roth? A Rebbe with a last name!" And he told me he lived in *Meah Shearim*. "Do you think I could find him?" I asked—I was ready to run to him—but Professor Scholem said, "No. He is gone already, but his son and his son-in-law are each running a section of the congregation." "How can I find them?" I asked. And he said to me, "Well, go down *Meah Shearim* street, and where you hear people shouting the loudest in their prayer, that's where they are."

By this time I was really curious, so I went and bought some of the books by Reb Arele Roth, and yes, I found them in *Meah Shearim*. And boy did they *davven!* They *davvened* up a storm. Their body movement was exuberant, almost violent; they were really exerting themselves and swaying hard with every word and shouting very loud. Whenever I would come and *davven* with them, I would be taken by their pace but not by the screaming. And I would go into a more meditative state because they were not rushing through the *davvenen*. In the average Orthodox synagogue, the best *davvener* is the one who finishes first. I once heard a famous violinist play Mendelssohn's concerto, and I wanted to scream, "Slow it down, man." He was so eager to show how fast he could play those difficult notes that he wasn't respecting the pace that the music wanted to be played at. But here were people who *davvened* very well.

Consciousness Commandments

May your Holy Faith
never be removed from me
nor may my joy and trust in You
be removed from me,
my seed and children's children,

all those who are to proceed from me
with Your help,
not from those who are related to me,
and from all Yisrael,
Your Holy people.

And may no moment of our life
from now on
for ever more
be empty of You.
Amen.

—Arele Roth, *Ani Ma'amin*

I never got to talk with Reb Arele's son-in-law, who was the head of one branch of Roth Hasidim, but I did talk with his son. I also picked up the books, and I was getting more and more excited about what I was reading. For years I had been pursuing a question that went something like this: There are 613 commandments in the Torah. How many of these commandments are not physical but are consciousness commandments (in Hebrew, *mitzvot hat'luyot b'lev,* commandments that are connected with the heart)? Because I felt that they were the core of consciousness.

There was a book called *Chovat HaL'vavot* (Duties of the Heart) that was written in the twelfth century by Bachya ibn Pakuda, a great mystic and philosopher who was very close to the Sufis. He wrote this book in Judeo-Arabic (Arabic written with Hebrew characters). And in it he pays special attention to the commandments that are connected with the heart, to the Oneness of God, Awe before God, Love to God, and understanding. For as much as the human mind can reach toward God, it should, and it should understand who and what God is all about. So it was very important to write these things. And here was Reb Arele Roth, who had done this very thing for modern readers. He had written a book, *Shomer Emunim,* and some remarkable letters to his disciples.

Reb Arele Roth wrote about the thirty-two ways of fulfilling the commandments. Now, how would you designate thirty-two in Hebrew letters? *Lamed bet.* And since in Hebrew numbers are represented by letters, *lamed bet* can also be read as a word: *lev,* "heart." So Reb Arele Roth came up with thirty-two ways—short aphoristic indications of where to put your consciousness. And running through them in this form does something to you. He also wrote a book that is as close as you can come to sexual tantra, but it was mostly on the no-noes rather than the yeses.

But you can't write a book on the yeses without it being considered pornographic. Sacred sexuality doesn't express itself so well when you write about it in that form. So he wrote about what one should guard against in *Taharath HaKodesh*. And then he wrote a book about eating, *Shulhan HaTahor,* "The Pure Table." It concerned not the etiquette around eating but how to eat so that you should be truly offering a sacrifice before God. Reb Arele Roth took the basic things that people do and spiritualized them. At one point he says, "Look at your plate when you have been served, and that piece of food that you most want to go for, set it aside, and decide that this is the one that you are not going to eat." Simply to exercise control. Elsewhere, he says, "If you are in the middle of eating, and then you say, 'Enough,' it is better than a fast day." Catch yourself in the middle, when your appetite is on a roll, and then stop and say, "That's all I need. I don't want any more."

In Reb Arele's letters and talks to his disciples before prayer he says, "If you want to pray with me, you must not think of appointments after *davvenen*—you must be prepared to expire in your prayer." In my imagination, I visited with Reb Arele Roth during the *davvenen*. The Hasidim would start the prayer, and when they would reach to the last place where one may interrupt with speaking, Reb Arele would turn around from his prayer desk, and all the Hasidim would rush up to him. And like a football coach, he would give them a pep talk about the *davvenen* so that they would explode in fervor in *davvenen* afterward. So one day, he looks around and sees a Hasid who is a little distracted and says to him, "Come here. You have some business to do after the prayer is over?" And the Hasid says, "Yes." "You are a little anxious about it?" Again, "Yes." Then Reb Arele Roth says, "Do me a favor: *davven* elsewhere. I don't want you to *davven* here today." The Hasid says, "Rebbe, why not?" "Because I only want people who are willing to die in the middle of the *davvenen.*" In other words, "If you are not willing to die in the middle of the *davvenen,* to expire, to give yourself over to God in the middle of *davvenen,* what do I need you here for? You are just a brake, not a motor; out with you!" And he followed his own advice. While singing the *Hallel* with all of his effort on the 6th of Nissan 1947, while taking *matzot*, Reb Arele passed on, singing, "The dead praise You not, those that go down to *She'ol*—We shall praise You, henceforth . . . and forever,—*halleluyah!*"

So Reb Arele Roth was a Rebbe for putting your money where your mouth is. And this shows in his poignant letters to his disciples. Very often when he was in the middle of writing Hebrew, he switched to Yiddish. During the time of the great conflagration in Europe, he would write, "*Kinderlech, vos iz den az men shtarbt?* So what if you die? If it so pleases the Master of the Universe, Who has strong medicines, to take one of His sheep and to offer it up in a way He wants to offer it up, who is to tell Him what to do?" It wasn't that he was telling people to walk into the furnace. He was telling them that they must not let go of the basis of their own faith just because they were moving out of the "fair weather" and into a very stormy time for Jews. How many of us are only "fair weather" Jews? So there is some of that Kotzk resiliency in him. I want you to understand who he was. He was special in modern Hasidism. He was not a dynastic heir, somebody whose father set him up; he was a self-made man, in a sense. He visited many masters, studied from them, and found one who really fed him royal jelly, and he became a remarkable Rebbe.

On Voiding Strange Thoughts

Any strange thought
that will tempt me to materialize any supernal light
or to think against the actions
and ways that are hidden and undisclosed
I regret it and void it as of now.

—Arele Roth, *Ani Ma'amin*

What does Reb Arele Roth mean when he says, "I regret and void any strange thought that will tempt me to materialize any Supernal Light"? So much of Judaism is halakhic. And because it is based on law, the following happens. Imagine Passover is coming, and I have cleaned my whole house, and there is no more *chometz* in there. But can I be absolutely sure that there is no more leaven in there? Have I been able to go with a microscope and see whether there was a minuscule crumb of bread under the radiator? I've done all my cleaning, but there may still be something I missed. So what do I do? The law says that I must not be the owner of any non-Passover items on Passover. How do I get rid of the things I couldn't possibly find? The answer is, I simply make a legal declaration, pronouncing myself not the owner of it any more. Then I say, "This material, this *chometz*, is *bottul*; I declare it to be *hefker*—it is now ownerless. I don't have any more connection to those items." And thereby I am able to say that those items are no longer holding me back.

Now let's say I have some thoughts that are not kosher thoughts. Remember in the story of the circle of the Ba'al Shem Tov, how the Maggid of Mezritch had thoughts that he was ashamed of. You can't necessarily control what thoughts will arise in you. The only control you can have is whether you harbor the thoughts and welcome them or whether you send them immediately away. Like when one confesses to evil thoughts, and the priest asks, "Did you entertain them?" There is an element of control there. But you can also make a legal declaration. Remember, *halakha* works in relationship to God and to spiritual things in this system. Therefore, I can say, "Dear God, I now make the following declaration: any thought, word, or action that is not according to Your will, I hereby declare null and void. I don't want to have anything to do with them. I know they come up and I know I get tempted. I know all of that, but I don't want to own them anymore." It is almost like saying, "Can I get rid of the karma?"

Now, what do we do about our tendency to anthropomorphize God? The answer is, one says, "Dear God, I can't help being a human being, having my sensation, my imagery, and everything operating on the basis of images." When I think about *Tiferet,* I might think "the heart of God." And when I get into prayer and am relating to it, these images become very strong, and they come alive to me. I feel a closeness to them.

I'll give you an example. In Psalm 73, it says, "In some ways, I'm nothing better than a beast, an animal." I don't have supernal consciousness. Sometimes I act like a beast to you. In which way? As Isaiah says, "I know where I can find my food, and I go there." I know where I can get my God-fix. And I'm doing it just like an animal going for its food. "Nevertheless, I'm always with you." In other words, "How could I not be with you? You are creating and sustaining me. The Psalm continues, "You have taken hold of my right hand." Which is to say, "I rely on You to lead me, to guide me. So if you take hold of my right hand, then in my imagination it is Your hand that is taking hold of me." So what have I done? I have taken a Supernal Light and have put a material image around it. As long as I do this because I have to make my heart connection with God, it is not so bad. But later, when I begin to reify that image and believe that indeed God has a physical hand, I get into trouble. So what can I do? "I hereby declare null and void the tendency to reify my images. I understand my tendency to want to materialize that, to want to give it shape. And because I understand my tendency, I hereby say, whatever I can do, dear God, I don't want it to be reckoned. I don't want it to create karma." So by declaring it null and void, it doesn't create karma. That is what Reb Arele Roth has in mind, and he makes a number of mental acts there in this long *Ani Ma'amin* where here says, "And here intend to fulfill this commandment" and "here intend to fulfill this commandment." Because he is talking not about physical commandments but commandments of consciousness. So when I'm thinking for a moment, "God is One . . . One . . . One . . . ," I am fulfilling the commandment of *Yichud HaShem.*

So this spiritual-halakhic connection is strange to us today. But it exists in other religions also. In Catholicism, you make an act of contrition, and you make an act of faith. And it is the same kind of situation with the Sufi *Zikr*, an act of consciousness, *Zikr Ullah*, and the *Wazifas* in Sufism. They all have their way of making an act of something. And therefore to make it as real as is possible.

But still you might say that this is an avoidance of responsibility. Let me tell you, in the early 1950s, many people were reading Jean-Paul Sartre and Albert Camus. And one of the things that came out of Sartre was that for every act you do, you take an infinite amount of responsibility. You are not only taking responsibility for what you are doing but also for the echoes of the echoes of the echoes of that act, the karma of the karma of the karma. You take total responsibility. In comparison with that, a person who is an Orthodox Jew has a beautiful "moral holiday," as William James would call it. It doesn't always have to be bound up by the results of the results of the results. "God tells me to do it, and I do, and let the chips fall where they may because I'm just a finite human being, and if I were to take on responsibility that is infinite, I couldn't handle it." Now, what is interesting is that I don't know of people who have taken that thing, to say that "the sin that I committed yesterday I declare null and void." It does not work that way in this system. What does work is, "I declare beforehand, as with the Kol Nidre, this is a new year starting up. I know I'm going to make some vows, I know I'm going to have this weakness, and I want to declare right here in front of the whole congregation, I am going to make vows—please don't take me seriously." Let them not take effect. It is humble to say, to acknowledge, that I get exuberant about some things and that I get weak about some things. So I want to create for myself external ways of holding on to something, but they aren't quite real. That is one side of it.

The other side has to do with a recognition of what the halakhic world is like. In the halakhic world, halakhic statements work. That is true for Catholics also. Look at the sacrament of reconciliation, which they used to call penance: "I declare before God almighty, and his son Jesus, and before Mary, and all the saints in Heaven, and all the angels, that I want to do God's will, and if I slip, I am heartily sorry for offending." So they too had a whole formula for dealing with this. This formulaic thing is basically medieval in the way it operates. So there are some prayers that almost are like contracts written to God to say, "This is what I intend to do. I affirm this and I know I might slip, but still I will affirm it."

There is a wonderful sermon given by Milton Steinberg that touches on this issue. It was called "Our Persistent Failures." And when I was in Los

Angeles for Yom Kippur in 1997, I told the congregation I was addressing, "Instead of me ad-libbing, coming up with a sermon of my own, I'd like this year to do something like a Mozart of a sermon, to give you a classic." And I gave that sermon of the persistent failures. This is just a portion of that.

At night, when he would go to sleep, Reb Levi Yitzhak would say, "Dear God, I'm sorry for the ways I deviated from your will today. I promise, tomorrow, I'll do better." Then God said, "But Levi Yitzhak, you said the same thing yesterday." And he quickly replied, "But today I mean it." So then Rabbi Steinberg starts saying, "Isn't that a silly story? In some ways it's a silly story. Doesn't that make it trivial?" And then he goes on to say, "Well, what are the options that are there?" So he figures out the options and says, "Well, maybe you should set your goals a little bit lower; then you won't have any failures." But he quickly dismisses that option. Then he goes into a nihilistic option and dismisses that too. Then he looks seriously at the option of Christianity, that I'm going to get bailed out of my failures by the Christ. And he dismisses that also. Finally, he comes back full circle and says, "I haven't got anything else to offer, 'but today I mean it.'" And then he adds, "When you look at that, it is possible that the angry person will at one point be a little bit less angry and the miser will be a little bit less miserly because he says, 'Today I mean it.' And in this incremental way, there may be hope." So that is the point of the sermon. And he is saying that our whole life is working with these persistent failures. But giving up on working with them isn't a viable option either. Therefore, one of the tools for Orthodox people was this declaring, making a declaration about "persistent failures."

LOVING THE LAND
AND ITS PEOPLE IS LOVING GOD

REB ABRAHAM ISAAC KOOK

(1865–3 ELUL 1935)

REB ABRAHAM ISAAC KOOK was born in Grieva, Latvia, to Rabbi Shlomo
Zalman HaKohen, who associated himself with the Mitnagged tradition,
and to Pearl Zlata, daughter of a Chabad Hasid, Rabbi Raphael, a disciple of the *Tzemach Tzedek*. His middle name, Isaac, came from his great-
grandfather, a follower of the founder of Hasidism, Israel Ba'al Shem Tov.
It is said that his mother sewed a button from the coat of a Hasidic Rebbe
onto her child's jacket so that he would walk in the way of the *Tzaddikim*.
Until his bar mitzvah, he was educated in his parents' home. But for the
next eight years he studied in various places, becoming known as the
Ga'on of Grieva and Ponevezh. Finally, for a year and a half, he studied
in the famed Volozhin *yeshiva*, with none other than Rabbi Naftali Zvi
Yehudah Berlin as the *rosh yeshiva* and role model for the young genius.
He received his *s'micha* (ordination) there and went on to take posts in
Zaumel (1888) and Bausk (1895).

All his life, he seems to have been troubled by the issues that divided
Jews, Hasidim versus Mitnaggedim, secular versus religious. He was truly
a seeker of unity and a builder of bridges. Though he was not raised in
the Hasidic tradition and as far as we know received no direct teachings
from any Hasidic master, he was thoroughly conversant with Hasidic literature, especially the thought of Reb Shneur Zalman of Liadi and Reb
Nachman of Bratzlav, and was in contact with various Hasidic masters in
later years. He also studied Kabbalah with various masters, most notably
Rabbi Shlomo Elyashev, known as LeShem. It was through his unique
blend of *halakha*, Hasidism, and Kabbalah that he forged bonds of unity
between widely divergent worlds.

In 1904 he immigrated to the Holy Land with his wife, child, and younger brother, taking a post as the Rabbi of Jaffa. And there he truly came into his own. Here we begin to see signs of his tremendous acceptance and respect for wide-ranging perspectives. He identified with the Zionist movement and was friendly with nonreligious pioneers, which did not endear him to the rabbinic establishment. At the same time, he also urged the *Halutzim*—the people engaged in setting up *kibbutzim* in Palestine—to observe the *mitzvot*. He engaged in a controversy with Eliezer Ben-Yehudah, the man largely responsible for reviving the Hebrew language. Ben-Yehudah endorsed Herzl's idea of a Jewish state in Uganda rather than in Palestine. To Rav Kook, this was incomprehensible. The very essence of the Jewish people was tied to the Holy Land. For him, the dream of a renewal of the Jewish people in all its ancient splendor could only happen in relation to a renewing their relationship to *Eretz Yisrael*.

In 1914 Rav Kook went to Switzerland to participate in a conference of Agudat Yisrael and was unable to return to Palestine because of the outbreak of World War I. He therefore took a temporary post as rabbi of *Mahzikei ha-Dat* in London. Rav Kook began to wield great influence during these years, and upon his return to Palestine, he was named Chief Rabbi of Jerusalem. And when the Chief Rabbinate was formed in 1921, he was named the first Ashkenazic Chief Rabbi of Palestine.

In 1924 Rav Kook established a unique *yeshiva* in Jerusalem called *Merkaz HaRav*. He died in 1935. His motto was, "Let the old be renewed, and let the new be hallowed." His mantle was assumed by his son, Rabbi Yehudah Tzvi Kook, and two of his students, Rabbi Charlap and Rabbi David Cohen, the latter known as the Nazir.

The Sacred and the Secular

> *We see people everywhere holding on to objectives that are focused on the physical or the secular, such as endeavors that aim at building up the nation or the world. We, on the other hand, feel that the foundation of our lives and our source of fulfillment lies in more elevated objectives—not in building up the material but rather the spiritual dimension of life, and not a spirituality seeking to mold the secular but the higher part that is purified in the Holy of Holies. Do not be distressed by all these activities. Do not forget that the Soul of Souls, to function, needs the soul and the body, properly harmonized. In other*

words, the higher holiness, the ideal that emanates from the
Divine Source, must be focused on a spirituality that acts
in the secular sphere, and this must be focused on the physical
in all variedness. When these forces are unified,
the Great Structure is complete.

—Abraham Isaac Kook, *Orot HaKodesh II*

The consciousness that sees the world as unfinished, as a process
of continual becoming, ascending, evolving, changes a person
from being "under the sun" to being "above the sun," from
a worldview where there is nothing new to one where
there is nothing old, where everything is forming into something
new. The joy of Heaven and Earth lives in him, as they were
on the day they were created.
This luminosity sees all the worlds—the universal
and the human evolution, the destiny of every creation,
and phenomena of all times.
This undisturbed Shabbat on which peace shines eternally is
the day when, by the nature of its creating, there pounds
a continual push for newness. It needs no endpoint,
no conclusion. It is the most exquisite of days,
a beautiful ornament, the origin of all blessing.

—Abraham Isaac Kook, *Orot HaKodesh VII*

Outstanding among the rabbis between the two world wars was the first Rabbi of Yaffa and later the Chief Rabbi of Palestine, Reb Abraham Isaac Kook. He was a very wonderful mystic—a mystical poet. The kind of expression that you find in Sri Aurobindo, Rabindranath Tagore, and Walt Whitman can also be found in Rav Kook.[1] Sri Aurobindo's writing is so lofty, threatening to waft you into in the air, that at times you may wonder, "Does it have any feet to it?" Well, Rav Kook did the same kind of thing in Judaism. His writings fly, looking constantly for the light. And all the books that he wrote had something to do with lights, *orot*—*Orot HaT'shuvah, Lights of Repentance, Lights of Holiness.* But he also had his feet on the ground.

Whatever you would say about Reb Levi Yitzhak of Berditchev, one thing remains clear, he was a great lover of Israel. And people often spoke of Rav Kook as a second Levi Yitzhak of Berditchev. His love for the people of Israel, as well as for the land, was overwhelming. In Rav Kook's time, among the ultra-Orthodox, those who were exceptionally pious with regard to ritual, there was much maligning of the *Halutzim,* and Rav

Kook defended them, saying, "Let's see how religious you are. There is the commandment of settling in the Holy Land, and look at what they are doing, and look at yourselves sitting around in Europe. How could you accuse them of being irreligious? You fulfill some *mitzvot* and they fulfill others. They fulfill the *mitzvah* of *Yeshivat Eretz Yisrael,* to live in the Holy Land."

He had another powerful teaching that defended the secular settlers. He said, "Only once a year, on Yom Kippur, was the high priest permitted to go into the Holy of Holies. But if a carpenter had to go in and fix something in the Holy of Holies, he could go in on any day of the week. He didn't have to purify himself; he could go in with his hammer, nails, and everything else." So, he said, "these people on the *kibbutzim* are like the carpenter in the Holy of Holies."

So even though he was not officially a Hasid, Rav Kook nevertheless had the characteristics of a Rebbe. His creative approach was Hasidic. People came to him for advice as if he were a Rebbe. And the compassion he felt for them was so great that he was able to realize that besides advice, they sometimes needed some money too. So with Rav Kook there was a tremendous openness to individuals and their needs. And his openness to the seriousness of an individual soul's quest for God was most strongly manifested in the way in which he dealt with his disciples. For instance, there was his disciple, Reb David Cohen,[2] who was known as the Nazir.

A *nazir* is a person who has made a vow to abstain from wine and the cutting of one's hair. And Rav Kook gave him all the space he needed to follow his soul with this vow. And it is a vow that is not very common and rankles some. That, in some ways, is very different from the way in which many Hasidic masters have dealt with their Hasidim. Often they wanted everyone to follow only their specific way. Since the Maggid of Mezritch, we haven't had too many Rebbes who have allowed leeway for an individual's own soul-path. But Rav Kook encouraged this.

The statement that is so often quoted from Rav Kook is "*Ha'yashon yitchadesh,* What is old will be renewed, *v'hechadash yitkadesh,* and what is new will be sanctified." This is a very powerful teaching, embracing the maximum of tradition while acknowledging the evolving uniqueness of modern times, waiting expectantly to be made holy. May this thought be a light before us always!

YEA, THOUGH I WALK THROUGH THE SHADOW OF DEATH

REB KALONYMOUS KALMISCH OF PIASETZNA

(1889–4 CHESHVAN 1944)

KALONYMOUS KALMISCH SHAPIRA was the son of Rabbi Elimelekh of Grodzisk. He married Chayyah Miriam, the daughter of Yerahmiel Moses Hofstein of Koznitz. He spent four years with his father-in-law in Koznitz until the latter's death in 1909.

After this, he became the rabbi of a small town near Warsaw called Piasetzna. He also had a home in Warsaw and commuted back and forth between the two communities. In 1923 he established a *yeshiva* that soon became a well-known institution of learning. In 1932 he published a small tract called *Chovat HaTalmidim* that would become a guide for *yeshiva* students throughout Eastern Europe.

He was tireless in his efforts to raise the morale of the downtrodden among his followers and sought fervently to encourage Sabbath observance among the businessmen of Warsaw. Though he never studied medicine, he often amazed the doctors of Warsaw with the efficacious medicines that he prescribed for his Hasidim.

In just five days, January 22 through 27, 1941, the Jewish community of Piasetzna was liquidated. Followers urged him to flee to Stolin, but Reb Kalonymous Kalmisch refused, saying, "I am not one to desert my followers at a time like this. My place is surely with them."[1] He worked in the Warsaw ghetto in the Shultz shoe factory. Later he was deported to the Lublin area, where he was murdered by the Nazis. His son and daughter-in-law were also killed. After the war, some of his works were recovered and have since been published and are growing in influence.

———○———

Stilling the Mind

As once I heard from my Master, when one pays attention
to the flow of one's thoughts for an entire day, one can see
that there is no difference between oneself and a madman.
What makes one a madman is that the meshuggener *immediately*
brings his thoughts to actual expression, but in the process
of witnessing one's thought, one can see that one thinks
exactly like a madman.
He then gave us practical advice on how to calm the thoughts.
He said then that a person is to look at his thoughts
for a small amount of time—say, a few minutes—and then
he begins to see how slowly his mind is emptying,
and his thoughts stop rushing in their usual manner, and then
let him begin to say one phrase, such as, "Ribono Shel Olam."
This is in order to connect his now emptied mind with one
thought of holiness; then after that, he can begin to request
in prayer what he needs; which mode he needs to be made
whole in, strengthened Faith, Love, or Awe.

—Letter from Rabbi N. Gescheid

The Piasetzner Rebbe lived in Poland in this time of change. His writings are full of wonderful talk of meditation and stilling the mind. One of my students translated his book *Conscious Community,* and another wrote a book on his teachings called *The Holy Fire.* Here is someone who already knew that if Hasidism were going to continue to work, it had to be restructured. You can't follow the old patterns; you must set up something new for being a Hasid in the cities.

Reb Kalmischel of Piasetzna was left an orphan at a very early age, and he was raised by relatives who were all involved in great and holy *Hasidut,* but there was one thing that he could not learn from them and had to find out for himself. That was, "How do you do it on the inside?" And although we don't have any journals or personal reminiscences of his explaining how he discovered these things, he was psychologically very astute and aware. I almost want to say shrewd because he had a sense of psychodynamics far beyond "you ought to do this, or you ought to do that," because many people see the religious and spiritual matters in terms of dos and don'ts, but very seldom do they say *how* to do and *how* not to do. It was the Piasetzner who pointed to this.

For instance, you have a situation where you haven't been able to reconcile with someone in your life and there is a great deal of anger in you. He says, "Write that person a letter with all the vituperation that you feel; then read that letter while imaging that this person is sitting in a chair in front of you. Do this for about forty days, and see what happens as a result of that." Now I can't see Fritz Perls having done any better than the Piasetzner with Gestalt therapy, and the Piasetzner did it first, before Perls was even a psychologist. And it was about this time that Moreno started psychodrama. And the Piasetzner had a very rich way of moving the psychodrama from the outside to the inside, so that people might experience the imaginal greatly and strongly.

It was also at the same time that the question came about recognizing that an agitated mind is not capable of steering clearly—to place oneself in the Presence of God in such a way that I don't try to second-guess what God is going to say to me. And in order to be able to do this, I have to do some quieting of the mind. The Piasetzner suggests a number of ways, including looking at a watch and paying attention to the minute hand to see how to slow down mind processes and calm oneself.

Many of the Hasidic masters have spoken about these things and then talk too much about them. The people heard that the Rebbe had said a great deal about the power of silence—and then went on to talk some more. In contrast, the invitation that comes from the Piasetzner is to actually move into that silence.

It is a great pity that we did not merit to have him live unto old age so that he might have written more about the how of these things or that we might have had the report of his training of his son in these matters. It would be wonderful to have a record of the lab work, the experiential-empirical testing, as it were.

THE MYSTIC PROLETARIAN

REB HILLEL ZEITLIN

(1871–29 ELUL 1942)

REB HILLEL ZEITLIN was born in Korma, Belorussia, to Shterne Brakha and Rabbi Aaron-Eliezer, who brought the Mitnagged and the Chabad Hasidic traditions together under one roof. For a time they also lived in Homel. Zeitlin was a prodigy who was well versed in Talmud, Kabbalah, the teachings of Maimonides and Judah Halevi, and Hasidism, especially Chabad Hasidism. Later he would come to imbibe and master Western ideas and literature, especially of Hegel, Schopenhauer, and Nietzsche. And like many Jews of the time, he left traditional Judaism.

However, in 1903 he returned to the tradition of his forbears. That was the year of the terrifying pogroms in Kishinev. After this, Reb Hillel became a tireless servant of the Zionist cause. At that time he was among those who supported the idea of seeking an autonomous homeland for Jews, whether it be in Palestine or elsewhere.

After having lived in Vilna for some time, he made his way in 1906 to Warsaw, which would be his home until 1942. It was here in 1919 that he seems to have undergone a "spiritual transformation" of lasting effect. His home at 60 Slizka Street was a gathering place of ideas and people of ideas—Hasidim, Mitnaggedim, authors, and activists of every hue. Even his son, Aaron, would become a celebrated Yiddish author.

Reb Hillel was often a visitor to the Sabbath discourses of Reb Alter Israel Shimon Perlow, the Novominsker Rebbe. There he could be observed slipping in at twilight in his cape and broad-brimmed hat, with his flowing black hair and reddish beard. The Rebbe's children later reported that he took particular interest in the Rebbe's comments on Kabbalah and the Zohar and listened intently to the distinctive Novominsk *niggunim*. Then, just as quietly as he had entered, he would disappear from the room.[1] He himself would say, "Whenever I felt depressed and needed to repent, I visited the Rabbi of Novominsk."[2]

Reb Hillel translated the Zohar into Hebrew and wrote a commentary on it. This was also done independently by his contemporary, Rabbi Yehudah Ashlag. However, only Reb Hillel's introduction was ever published. He did publish works on both the Ba'al Shem Tov and Reb Nachman of Bratzlav and numerous articles on Kabbalah and Chabad Hasidism. He wrote for the Yiddish paper *Der Moment* for thirty-six years, publishing controversial and stirring articles on Reb Shneur Zalman of Liadi and Reb Nachman to socialism and Zionism. From that platform he also, and often, foretold the end of European Jewry.

On September 12, 1942, the Jewish Hospital in which he was living was liquidated. He was murdered on the road to Treblinka, wrapped in *tallit* and *t'fillin* and with a volume of the Zohar under his arm, on the eve of Rosh HaShanah.

Yavneh

> *What does Yavneh want?*
> *Yavneh wants to revive the early Hasidism of the Ba'al Shem*
> *Tov, to base it on foundations closer in consonance with*
> *the needs of our era, it being the moment of the approaching*
> *footsteps of the Messiah.*
>
> —Hillel Zeitlin, *The Ark*

> *. . . Hasidism today has become a social affair to most Hasidim.*
> *They study without enjoyment, they pray without joy, seek glory*
> *and riches just like anyone else, and perhaps they seek it even*
> *more than those who are not Hasidim. They are too absorbed*
> *in praising their own Rebbe and demeaning Rebbes of other*
> *Hasidim. Courts of rabbis and dynasties arose, always involved*
> *in politics about rabbis,* shochtim, *and other religious officials.*
> *Only themselves do they count as proper Jews. All other Jews*
> *seem like naught to them. All of Hasidism has become, to them,*
> *external signs, garments, and other such externals.*
>
> —Hillel Zeitlin, *The Ark*

I have seen some pictures of Reb Hillel Zeitlin when he was young. At that time, Nietzsche was his great idol, as it were. You have to understand what he stood for—the sense that a person is most alive while in rebellion. He was a person of wide interests. He wrote a column for the newspaper and was interested in socialism and teachings about the afterlife. His two great Hasidic influences were Reb Nachman of Bratzlav and the teachings of Chabad Hasidism.

However, he felt somehow, though, that the Hasidic way had become tame and domesticated. It wasn't anymore in the service of radical God-seeking the way it had been in the early days. Instead, it was very much about being a good householder. There was a Hasid, a fishmonger, in a video documentary on Hasidism I have seen, who said, "Listen, what do the *Goyim* have that I don't have? I finish a day's work. I come home. I have a schnapps,"[3] and he describes an ordinary life. I didn't hear from this man that he was storming Heaven to get anywhere. He was quite happy where he was.

I remember what my grandmother said to me when she first heard that I was becoming a Hasid: *Oy, Chasidish, negiddish und ba'aley batish,* 'Hasidic, well to do, a good householder." Then she heard that I had become a *Chabadnik,* "*Oy vey!*" So I asked her, "*Bubbishee,* Grandma, what is so wrong about *Chabadnikes?*" So she tells me, "In our *shtetl,* in Zolkiew, there was a *Chabadnik.* And he would hang out in the synagogue day in and day out, all day long in silence." In other words, he was meditating. And the worst thing was, not only did he do his meditating, but he used to snare the young men. He persuaded them to come and meditate with him, and he would teach them those teachings, and everybody in Zolkiew hated him—because he was not "Hasidic, well to do, a good householder."

So here was Reb Hillel Zeitlin getting more and more disappointed with the modern world, and even the socialism that he had embraced, after seeing what had happened in Russia. I have a book that was published in 1915 called *Otzar Dinim Uminhaggim,* an encyclopedia of Jewish laws and customs, dedicated to "the wonderful new regime in Russia." You see, there was a great hope, now that the tsar was out, that there would be freedom and equality for all people. So the new regime was welcomed with open arms. But later, when its defects became manifest, people became disenchanted with socialism, and communism didn't quite work out the way they had hoped. Hillel Zeitlin was one of the disenchanted.

More and more he was becoming convinced that what Jews needed was to start Yavneh groups. When the Temple was destroyed, Rabban Yochanan ben Zakkai, who, instead of trying to hang on to the past, took a few of his disciples into a small town called Yavneh and from there rebuilt Jewish culture and Jewish religion. So Reb Hillel Zeitlin was say-ing, "It is time to have Yavneh again," which meant a radical reforming of the tradition as it then existed. He said, "Let us go back to the Hasidism of the Ba'al Shem Tov. It has gotten off track. Let's find that great spark again." And this is when he wrote his manifesto (it was a time of manifestos) for Hasidism. To my knowledge, it didn't get much beyond the manifesto; just a few meetings were held. But I have found his writings to be very helpful in Jewish Renewal work.

To Serve God Together

> In the era of the Ba'al Shem Tov, it sufficed to illumine Yisrael alone. However, in our days, in a time when worlds are ruined and worlds arise, it is the task of Yisrael to make light both for themselves and for all the nations, as it is written: "It was easy being My servant to establish the tribes of Jacob and to claim the treasure of Yisrael. Now I will set you as a light unto the nations, to be my salvation to the ends of the earth." And as it is also said, "Then I will change the nation to speak with a clear tongue, so that you can all call in the name of God and serve Him together."
>
> —Hillel Zeitlin, The Ark

Reb Hillel Zeitlin is trying to find a way in which he can say that the con-cerns that we have must extend past the bounds of the Jewish people. Now, in the time of the Ba'al Shem Tov, we were suffering so much from Chmielnicki and the aftermath of Shabbetai Tzvi and Jacob Frank that the sense was, "How could we possibly worry about what is happening to the non-Jews? We are in such bad shape, we have to pull ourselves together." In our day, after the Holocaust, it was almost the same situa-tion. When the Lubavitcher Rebbe, Yosef Yitzhak, and the Satmarer Rebbe came to America, everything was so bent on restoration that there wasn't any time to think about non-Jews.

How amazing it is now that Chabad has a Web site for the *Noachides*, Gentiles who follow the seven Mitzvot of Noah. And I remember the Lubavitcher Rebbe said once to his *shlichim* (emissaries), "When you are sitting on an airplane next to a non-Jew, start a conversation with him. And talk to him about the seven commandments of the Children of Noah and about faith in God." But that kind of outreach couldn't have hap-pened at that time, when we were just emerging from deep trauma.

Well, between the two world wars, Reb Hillel Zeitlin was trying to say something to people who had sanctified the high degree of surface tension between us and non-Jews. In so many of the stories on both sides of the divide, the other people were always expendable. For non-Jews, for Christians, Jews were expendable. For Jews, Christians were expendable. Often they were seen only as useful expedients—as *Shabbos Goyim*—and the rest were superfluous. That was the attitude that they took. We are finally emerging from that attitude. But there he was in his time, and how was he going to say that? Zeitlin reached into what people have called Second Isaiah and that universal vision, and he realized that nobody can be redeemed without everybody else being redeemed. When a person becomes fully aware of that, it ushers in a whole new way of thinking.

This sort of begins in a funny way with Reb Levi Yitzhak of Berditchev, who says, "Dear God, if you don't want to redeem us, then redeem the *Goyim* already!" There was a feeling that redemption has to happen, and the best way for that to happen is if the world as a whole is redeemed. So Reb Hillel Zeitlin starts out as a socialist, as a Nietzschean, and he never shakes this, despite the fact that he embraces Chabad (the Kopust branch) and Bratzlav. So when he begins his work for Yavneh, this Noah's ark for survival, it is enriched by all of these things. There was the Judaism from before the destruction of the second Temple, and what came afterward was Yavneh and its wise people. So he was trying to create another Yavneh.

The word *Yavneh* contains the letters of the word *bonoh*, "to build," and has a sense of "he shall build, he will build." And so he wants to create a situation where he can build a new kind of Judaism. It was a time of manifestos for the proletariat—"Workers, unite!"—and this one too wanted to create a change built on people power. And for a while it worked because he did have some groups in Warsaw and other Polish cities that followed the way of Yavneh. But the time wasn't quite ripe. Zeitlin's visions were daring and profound; unfortunately, they were also ahead of their time.

Reb Hillel Zeitlin was concerned for the non-Jewish world, but he did not leave us with a program for outreach to them. It may be that he had an idea of the second phase of the work, but that has not come down to us. Still, one must admire his foresight and courage, because this was dangerous talk and might have led to his being ostracized—or worse. But there is another reason that might have delayed a program of outreach. Many a spiritual teacher will say, "Before we try to fix society, let's make sure we have fixed ourselves." And that is where he begins.

Redeeming the Muses

Thus in the generation of the final winnowing of the holy Sparks,
we must search for the light of the Torah in the best works
of art and literature, as well as in the sciences of the world.
This one must approach with a special care and insight, with the
"candle of God, the soul of man searching all inner recesses,"
interpreting, searching, and seeking, throwing piles
of deceit away, and revealing the grain of truth.

—Hillel Zeitlin, The Ark

Sanctify your sex life. The preservation and sanctification
of the covenant, these are the exalted bases of both the interior
and the exterior holiness. Concerning this, we are charged:
"Be holy," and, "He who sanctifies himself a little here below
will be greatly sanctified from above." "The foundation is
the extremity of the body. It is a sign of the holy covenant."

—Hillel Zeitlin, *The Ark*

Just as he was concerned about what others in his generation and generations before were not concerned about—namely, outreach to the world—it was also clear that he was someone who saw himself in the creative role of an artist and thus would want to say something about the arts.

In the past, the attitude was, *Yaft'Elohim le yefet v'yishkon b'chaley shem,* "Let beauty be for the children of Japhet," meaning for the Greeks and all the people who belong to the Aryan races, "and the things that have to do with God's dwelling, those belong to the Semites." However, with the understanding that he had, his concern for the people in Warsaw, and the understanding of the media that were emerging at that time, he also realized that a sense of beauty is also somehow necessary. And this comes from Reb Nachman, too, in his wonderful stories. Reb Nachman said, "Why are our prayers spurned? Because they don't come with gracefulness." They don't come with *hain,* with that *je ne sais quoi* quality of delightful engagement and aesthetic presentation. So he felt that he had to open the arts up.

Once, when a young man confided in the Rebbe, Reb Menachem Mendel of Lubavitch, that he wanted to become a painter, the Rebbe told him, "Talk it over with Zalman." So the young Baruch Nachshon, who went on to become one of the good painters of Chabad, came and we talked, and I asked him, "What did the Rebbe say to you?" And he said,

"That the muses, too, have to be redeemed." So when I look now at what has been created on the Web sites of the various Torah folk, the amount of programming that is available, and the aesthetic appeal of that, it makes it clear that this is a precursor for the Messianic situation.

In subsequent conversations, we discussed symbols and the way in which we see, how the eyes take in simultaneously much more than comes through the mouth and the ear, and how important it is to express all that in form, shape, and color. Now, when you open up to visual aesthetics, I want to say, what the eye appreciates most are those rounded feminine shapes—those beautiful curves. More than other animals, horses have those rounded shapes that are so pleasing to the eye, and so many of the great artists have spent their time painting nudes of women and those beautiful lines. Even in Michelangelo's *David,* though a male figure, the elegant curve of the beautiful form is still the major emphasis. But with this sensitive appreciation of the round aesthetic there is also a danger that comes with the arts and with the artist's life.

Artists often tend to see themselves as more liberated than other people in the area of sexuality. And they almost feel that for the sake of the arts, anything and everything is permitted. That leads into the fallacy of Nero, who fiddles while Rome is burning. Here you can have a situation in which aesthetics is so totally divorced from ethics that people may suffer while someone else plays music. And closer to our own day, there were the orchestras that the Nazis set up in the concentration camps that played while the people were arriving. This was a misuse and a desecration of aesthetics in relation to ethics and morality. So Reb Hillel has to warn his people about that, even while endorsing the arts and sexuality.

The truth is also that one of the most powerful drugs is already in us, in our hormonal system. And when this is active, it may dominate the thought processes, the inner processes, and what happens in the reticular formation system, what we pay attention to or ignore. All this has a lot to do with how we deal with our sexuality. So he wants to be able to warn people about that—to sacralize sexuality.

I can also see this in the *Sidra* of the week, when we come to the end of *Balak,* where the Israelite and the Moabite daughters began to have congress with one another, and this was considered an abomination. It has something to do with the fact that the words are being used for idolatry, "going a-whoring after other gods," and the sense of what was that sexuality that the Moabite women brought in, which was, "If you want to have me, you have to do a libation to my god." So there is a sense of the overpowering urge at that time. It was also a feeling that the people don't want to have this for animal expression alone. They want to attach to it some kind of spirituality. And Jewish spirituality, by and large, has not given as much space for attaching sexuality, on the exoteric level, to God. So it feels that is a "no-no." It took the Zohar and Kabbalah to open up that area for us—to be able to say that we "act" in the Divine Image and that on *Shabbat,* sexuality is a Mitzvah. But that still implied that during the week a certain kind of control had to be exercised. Thus Reb Hillel Zeitlin was very conscious of the complexities and possibilities of living in the city and having a rich spiritual life and awakens us to all of these in his *shtikele* (little) "ark."

THE MASTER
OF VIRTUOUS REALITY

REB SHLOMO CARLEBACH

(1925–16 ROM-CHESHVAN 1994)

SHLOMO CARLEBACH, one of the twin sons of Paula Cohn and Rabbi Naftali Carlebach, was born on January 14, 1925, in Berlin. During the difficult birth of the twins, Paula prayed fervently that if the children were born safely, they would be consecrated to God and raised in the life of Torah;[1] she delivered safely. And from an early age, both boys seemed destined to live lives of piety.

Shlomo was a scion of one of the most distinguished rabbinic (though not Hasidic) families of Europe. The Carlebach family traced its lineage back to King David and to the great commentator, TaZ,[2] and Shlomo was himself named after his famous grandfather, Rabbi Dr. Solomon Carlebach of Lübeck, whose sons were among the most highly regarded rabbis of Europe. His mother, Paula, was the daughter of the Chief Rabbi of Basel in Switzerland.[3]

Almost immediately, Shlomo became known for his irrepressible joy and inexorable loving energy. But there was also an innate piety in him, coupled with a prodigious ability in Torah study. Once, when he was but four years old, he disappeared from the synagogue, only to be found later hiding in the ark, adoringly holding and kissing the Torah scroll. And none of these unusual qualities went unnoticed. Very soon his father was having him tutored privately and exposing him to the great halakhic minds of the time. Even at the tender age of four, he had begun his study of *Chumash*—and Talmud but a year later.[4]

In 1931 Naftali Carlebach became the Rabbi of Baden bei Wien in Austria, through which passed numerous Torah scholars of note, many of whom pronounced young Shlomo an *illui*, a Torah prodigy. In 1938

Shlomo was enrolled in the famed Ponovezher Yeshiva in Lithuania and was introduced to the analytical Lithuanian method of Talmud study. But in 1939 Shlomo and family left for New York, where they settled in Manhattan, and Reb Naftali opened Congregation Kehilat Jacob, later to be widely known as "the Carlebach Shul."

In America, Shlomo learned from some of the greatest Torah sages of the time—first in Rabbi Isaac Hutner's Chayyim Berlin Yeshiva, then in Yeshiva Torah Voda'at of Brooklyn with Rabbi Shlomo Heiman. Finally, he received an invitation from the legendary Rabbi Aaron Kotler to study at Lakewood Yeshiva, the most prestigious Talmudic institution in the country. He became the pride of the *yeshiva* and the personal protégé of Rabbi Kotler, who also recognized Shlomo as an *illui*.[5]

However, in the 1940s Reb Shlomo, along with his brother, Eliya Chayyim, became increasingly interested in Hasidism. He began to frequent the Bobover Shul of the late Reb Shlomo Halberstam and the previous Lubavitcher Rebbe, Reb Yosef Yitzhak Schneersohn. Eventually, and much to the dismay of Rabbi Kotler, he transferred his allegiance to Lubavitch and became a Hasid of Reb Yosef Yitzhak. And in 1949, he and I were asked by the Rebbe to begin visiting college campuses, an activity that would radically alter the lives of both men. Armed with a guitar, stories, and irrepressible zeal, they set out.

In 1959 Reb Shlomo released his first music album, *HaNeshomah Loch*, "Songs of My Soul," which was an instant hit in Jewish music circles. Reb Shlomo's fame as a Hasidic folksinger was beginning to grow. He began appearing in concerts all over the world, from Berkeley to the Soviet Union.

By this time, the Lubavitcher Rebbe was the dynamic Reb Menachem Mendel Schneerson, but Reb Shlomo was outgrowing the role of a Lubavitch outreach worker and was really coming into his own. In 1966 he founded the House of Love and Prayer in San Francisco, which reached out to estranged and discontented youth. The country, the world, was in social upheaval—old values were falling away, and a radical attempt had to be made to reach the youth of this generation. The House of Love and Prayer was one such attempt. Reb Shlomo embraced every "holy sister" and "holy brother" he met right where they were and gently coaxed them toward God. It was not his way to coerce anyone.

In 1972 he married Neilah Gluck of Toronto, who to this day continues the work that he began. And over the next two decades he continued to reinfuse the Jewish world with fervor. Faces and places changed, but the tireless work went on. In 1977 he closed the House of Love and Prayer in

San Francisco and relocated to Moshav Modiin, a settlement near Tel Aviv. After the death of his father, he and his brother became joint rabbis of the Carlebach Shul on West Seventy-Ninth Street in New York, which became a haven for Jews of all backgrounds. He continued to crisscross the globe, giving concerts, teaching, and telling stories just as he had begun. He ordained a number of students, including two women, and made a way where none existed before. In addition to all of this, he gave *tzedakhah*, charity, perhaps like none other of his generation. Reb Shlomo's giving was prodigious, like most of his other activities. He gave of time, money, and talent, to the very limits of possibility, to anyone who was in need.

In 1994, the same year that saw the loss of Reb Menachem Mendel Schneerson, Reb Shlomo passed on. He was a rare person who recognized the God-spark in everyone. May the mention of the righteous be a blessing.

———————— o ————————

A Vision of Peace and Harmony

> Thank G-d that the world's religions are coming together
> more and more, as people are coming together. However,
> I don't mean to suggest that they are just to be mixed
> like a gefilte fish of religions. Indeed, the very idea of that makes
> me feel a bit hurt. And sadly, there are a number of people trying
> to make this "gefilte" of religions: "Everybody put an ingredient
> in, and let's make a new soup!" This is not what I am talking
> about, at all. What is happening in the world today is
> that everyone really wants to know: What is it about?
> What do you believe in? . . .
> There is a very important teaching from one of the more
> contemporary holy rabbis, Reb Zadok HaKohen of Lublin.
> Although he lived one hundred fifty years ago, he was centuries
> ahead of his time. He was one of the greatest scholars and
> Kabbalists in the history of the Jewish people. He had only fifty
> disciples, but this was because his teachings were so deep that
> if you didn't know every word of the Kabbalistic teaching
> by heart, you just didn't have a clue as to what he was talking
> about. And he had a teaching that went something like this:
> "The world says, 'The world is becoming less and less religious,'
> but I say, 'On the contrary, the souls of people are becoming

more and more refined.' Perhaps on the outside it looks
as if they are breaking away from G-d, but on the inside,
they are getting closer and closer."

—Shlomo Carlebach, "A Vision of Peace and Unity," *Connections Magazine.* © 1988,
The Inner Foundation. Used with the permission of Rebbetzin Neilah Carlebach.

What can I say about Reb Shlomo, my buddy? I was ten or eleven years old when I first met him in Baden, near Vienna. I had to go and ask his father, Reb Naftali, a question about a chicken that I had brought along with me on the trolley from a neighboring town called Voeslau.

He and his brother, Reb Eliya Chayyim,[6] were twins. And Eliya Chayyim was a wonderful person in his own right who sought to be close to Hasidic Rebbes and Hasidim in both his demeanor and his garb. And if Reb Shlomo was like buckshot, then Reb Eliya Chayyim was a sharpshooter. He would pick individual students and would train them to become rabbis and scholars. He also traveled around to collect money for Zekher Naftali, which printed wonderful volumes of Hasidic materials that had gone unpublished or fallen out of print.

When I met Reb Shlomo again, in the United States, I urged him to come join us in the Hasidic *yeshiva.* He refused at that time. He was studying under Reb Aaron Kotler, of blessed memory, who was one of those amazing *geonim,* prodigies of Talmud, the commentaries, and the codes. So I asked him then, "Why do you stay there?" And he told me, with a tear in his voice, "The reason I stay is that if I go, there won't be anyone to take over where Reb Aaron left off."

I think to his dying day, Reb Shlomo kept with him little notebooks in which he would record, while on the plane, going from place to place, beautiful Torah *novellae* that he didn't have customers for. Several times he had tried to open up something like a *yeshiva* in Brooklyn, but never with great success. And shortly before he died, he had organized a gathering of descendants of Hasidic Rebbes and wanted to reinfuse them with the fervor and the light so that they might be able to carry out the chain of transmission. That meeting never happened. Reb Shlomo passed on.

On another occasion, later, after Reb Shlomo had left the Lakewood Yeshiva for the Lubavitcher Yeshiva, I asked him a similar question. By now Shlomo was considered one of the most promising young Talmudists in the country and pronounced an *illui,* a Torah genius, by Reb Aaron Kotler. So this time I asked him, "Shlomo, Reb Aaron treated you as his own son, your future was sure—how could you leave that?" And he looked at me penetratingly and said, "Don't you see, the Jewish world has been destroyed! The leaders of our people are gone—who will guide us?

Somebody has to take their place. From Lakewood come scholars, but from Lubavitch come outreach workers. At Lakewood I could expand my own soul, but at Lubavitch I'll learn to expand the souls of thousands! I did it, Zalman, for the six million."[7] He was an amazing being.

But that was also part of his music. He designed that into his melodies. He wanted to have melodies that would go so quick that people would learn them with great ease and then join in the harmony and in the sharing. Singing with Reb Shlomo would open up the heart for his teaching. But if you asked people later on, "What did he say?" hardly anybody remembered. It was a quality that was experienced.

Recently, on Reb Shlomo's *yahrzeit* (the anniversary of his death), we had a meeting at my home, and people brought some of Shlomo's melodies that they had transcribed. One melody is from the *Kedusha,* from the *Sanctus* of the *Shabbos* morning liturgy, which is so complex and beautiful (very different from Reb Shlomo's later melodies). One person sat down at the piano, another was at the clarinet, and I sang along with them. And we made that old melody live, that melody which will probably fade into obscurity. Most people don't sing it anymore because it isn't easy to learn like the later ones. And what we then discussed is how Reb Shlomo gave up even his genius for making more complex music, much as he had given up his genius for Torah scholarship, in order to be able to make the music that people would be able to get very fast and to sing along with.

Shlomo was also known as a great storyteller, and I like to say of him that he was a "genius of virtuous reality." Not virtual but *virtuous* reality. When he would tell the stories, they would come out in such a way that they would give you a great longing to live the life of the person whose great virtues were being talked about. You aspired to that holiness. He always told stories about the hidden ones, despised by people on the outside who were unaware of their real value and true saintliness. And I think that was also a description of Reb Shlomo himself. For it happened that on the thirtieth day after his passing, there was a meeting at the synagogue, and when the people came out, they found some homeless people standing there crying. And the people said, "What are you crying about?" And they answered, "Who will come to us now that Reb Shlomo is gone?" It turned out that there was a place where many of the homeless would go "bunk out" (before Mayor Giuliani drove them away), and Shlomo would come to them laden with food and with his guitar, and he would sing to them and tell them stories. They said, "Even if you will give us the food, who will come in the middle of the night and tell us stories and sing and help us?"

One Saturday, Reb Shlomo was walking on Broadway, and a young man came up to him and said, "Give me your money!" Reb Shlomo turned to him and said, "Brother, it's *Shabbos* today. I don't have any money on me. But if I see you during the week, I'll give you a five, OK?" And the man let him go. And during the following week, he actually saw the man who tried to stick him up and called, "Hey, brother!" and ran after him. And the guy ran away, probably figuring that Shlomo wants to get even with him or something, but Shlomo caught up with him and with hand outstretched said, "Here's the five that I promised you." He really had a beautiful sense of compassion.

Reb Shlomo was on a bus in Jerusalem when a woman came up to him and said, "You're Shlomo Carlebach, aren't you?" And he said, "Yes." And she said, "You know, when I was in prison, one of the things that kept us going was recordings of your songs. It would be such a *mitzvah* if you could see your way to visit and perform at that women's prison." Shlomo immediately wrote down the name of the prison and where to go and made inquiries and appeared at the prison. The wardens were also glad that they would get a break and would get entertained by Reb Shlomo. So they brought everybody into a hall and had them seated there and set up Reb Shlomo to start.

Then Reb Shlomo asked, "Are all the prisoners here?" And they said, "All the *Jewish* prisoners are here." "Are there other prisoners?" "Yes, there are also Palestinian prisoners." He said, "Why are they not here?" "They didn't want to come." Reb Shlomo said, "How could that be? Show me where they are." And they walked him into that wing of the prison, and there was a Palestinian woman sitting there and wailing on the floor. Her son had just been killed. And Shlomo took his shoes off, which is a sign of grieving and mourning, and sat down and wept with her. And there was another young woman in the cell across the corridor who had been a great security risk, she had planted a bomb. And Shlomo said to her, "Please come to the concert." And she said, "Why should we?" He said, "There are some people who are prisoners outside the prison walls, and some who are prisoners within. We're all prisoners in a way, of our habits and our ways. Come." And she had seen how he had shared with the grieving woman, and so she hollered to the other women, "All right. Let's go!"

They came, and Shlomo gave his concert and told stories, and in the end, as he was chanting and singing, they were all together dancing and singing along with him—Jewish women, Palestinian women, and even the wardens! These are the kinds of things that made Reb Shlomo's life important.

One of the great teachings of Reb Shlomo was the teaching of the "Torah of the Nine Months." The Talmud states that there is an angel who teaches the fetus while in its mother's womb. A candle is burning at the fetus's head (obviously, this is not to be understood as a physical candle), and there the angel instructs the fetus in the Torah that she or he will need throughout life. At birth, that same angel touches the child under the nose, creating the cleft, and all the teaching that was learned in the womb is forgotten. And so the question is raised, "What is the point of the teaching if it is only going to be forgotten?" And the answer is that the teaching is indeed forgotten, but it gets restored, resurrected. This is the source of the *déjà vu* phenomenon. Someone teaches us something, and we feel as if we knew it all along. Reb Shlomo was fond of saying, "How do you know that you have met your true teacher? Whatever this person teaches you, you knew it all along." And it is the Torah of the other three months that gives us trouble; other people have to handle that for us. And when Shlomo and I were discussing this teaching, my daughter Shalvi was in the womb, and so was his daughter Neshamah. So you can imagine how excited we were about this teaching of the "Torah of the Nine Months" at this time. And both of us were eagerly awaiting these babies to make their appearance, thinking, could they possibly remember?

That is an example of one of Shlomo's popular teachings. They are fun and helpful, but he could also teach in such a way that he could penetrate to the core of one's heart with great skill. And in a way, I have been leading up to the teaching with this long introduction so that you will get a sense of what a complex and magical person has given this teaching based on the words of Reb Zadok HaKohen, one of the great students of Reb Mordecai Yosef of Ishbitz. Shlomo glossed these teachings with a depth of insight all his own.

So in the text, when the world says that the "world is getting less and less religious," Reb Shlomo via Reb Zadok says, "On the contrary, the souls are becoming more and more refined." And notice that he doesn't make the distinction between religion and spirituality. When we look at the issue of spirituality, which many people are into as opposed to religion, we have to ask, what is it that they don't like about religion? One thing is the hierarchical and patriarchal language, the antifeminist sentiment that goes all the way through the Vatican to the Taliban, *Meah Shearim* to the Laws of Manu, and that is a big part of the problem.

The other thing is that most of the religious traditions have wanted to draw a distinction saying that nature is tainted, nature is fallen, and spirit is elevated. *Hasidut* always makes the claim for the supranatural, saying that the name *YHVH* represents the supranatural while the name *Elohim* represents the natural and that we see ourselves as being in a supranatural situation. The Church has done the same thing, and I think that when orthodox Islam looks at itself, it can see the same trend. There is a sharp vision that comes with monotheism that wants to say there is good, which is Divinely ordained, and there is evil, which is all that is against the good. And this is what people who are into spirituality don't like so much and why philosophies that come from the "export East," which is very monistic and shorn of its obligations and cultural attachments, are embraced so quickly.

However, this dissatisfaction is quite natural when our worldview, our paradigm, has shifted to an organismic way of looking at the universe. Because then it looks to us as if all those other paths, which create that sharp surface tension between good and evil, are definitely not where we want to go. The *Tanya* of Reb Shneur Zalman of Liadi talks about the "middle domain," which he calls the *K'lipah* of *Nogah*—Venus is the way we translate that—and this comes close to Freud's libido theory. *Nogah* is basically neutral in and of itself but can go either toward the holy or in the other direction. If an action is done selfishly and for one's own sake, it tends to go for the evil side, but it can also be raised to the holy because it is basically translucent—light passes through it—which is why Venus, *Nogah,* also means "shining."

So Reb Shlomo keeps the definition of *religious* even when he means *spiritual* so that there is not an unnecessary divorce. And maybe, he says, on the outside it looks like many people are breaking away from God, meaning that they are breaking away from formal religion, but on the inside they are becoming increasingly holy. On the exoteric level, there seems to be a shriveling up, but on the esoteric level, a lot of strengthening is going on. People are getting some distance so as to be able to discern the chaff, which is necessary periodically.

Some years ago, Pir Vilayat Khan[8] organized a meeting in San Francisco that was held on a weekend, including *Shabbos.* And for Sunday, since so many other people were going to be at that meeting, we organized a special meeting of Jews that we called "Torah and Dharma" (while a protester walked around outside with a placard that said, "Torah *versus* Dharma"). It was at the Paulie Ballroom, and some wonderful things happened at that meeting. First, we walked the room before the meeting, dedicating the space, because the Paulie Ballroom was used for secular activities previously, and we had to make it a sacred space. On the platform there were about ten panelists and a moderator, Murshid Moineddin Jablonski, the only non-Jew. All the rest were of Jewish birth. One wore a Sikh turban, another was the prior of a Zen monastery, and others were Sufis, but each had a different kind of belief, and I turned out to be the only "Jewish Jew" on the panel. And we had come together to deal with the relationship between Torah and Dharma. So I asked Reb Shlomo if he could come and join me on the panel. And he said he couldn't because he was already committed on that date. But we were in my car during this conversation, and since I had a tape recorder with me, I asked if he could record something for the meeting. And here is how he began:

The Torah spells out that a *kohen,* a priest, is not to defile himself unto the dead. He must not be in a place where a corpse is and must not be under the same roof with a corpse and so on. Elsewhere it says, *Siftey kohen yishm'ru da'at v'torah yevakshu mipihu,* "The lips of the *kohen* guard knowledge, and teaching you will seek from his mouth."

So it is clear that one of the functions of the *kohen* is to teach people. Thus the Ishbitzer, Reb Mordecai Yosef, in his *Mei HaShiloach,* points out that the reason why a *kohen* must not defile himself unto the dead is not so much for reasons of physical purity and impurity as for reasons of emotional response, for the existential feeling of the situation. Often a person who is confronted by a corpse cannot help but be angry at God— "Why did you do this? You give people life and then they have to die. Why do you take that life away from them?" And this anger turns people off from being able to say a good word about God. So since the *kohen* is supposed to be speaking to people about the knowledge of God, and you are supposed to seek Torah from his mouth, he must not defile himself unto the dead in order to avoid that anger.

After the Holocaust, Shlomo said, we all became defiled by death. We all were in touch with so much death that even the teachers who were supposed to be teaching us, like the *kohen,* were in some way angry at God. The anger wasn't even conscious with many people. It was unconscious, and therefore it even contaminated the teaching that they gave. And so the souls of people weren't quite able to absorb the teachings, nor were they quite open. It was as if people had been impregnated—and this is my interpretation of what Shlomo was saying—by an attitude that was "doing Judaism" in an angry, reaction-formation way, doing the *halakha* as if saying, "See God, we keep our word. Where were you?" That is the unconscious motivation. So what did God do at that time? Since there were some people in the Far East, in India, Japan, and Tibet, who could teach us about God Most High and were not then contaminated, they came to America and many Jews turned to them in order to have a connection with God.

That was a wonderful teaching, and it touched us all a great deal to hear that little bit of tape from Reb Shlomo. Many of the people who were on the panel spoke afterward of how their souls had taken them to spiritual paths and what a pity it was that they didn't have anyone in Judaism to teach them at that time. Now this was in 1974 or 1975, and you figure that fifteen to twenty-five years before, many of them were around bar mitzvah age in the 1950s and 1960s. And that way had been closed to them after the Holocaust. They didn't have a sense of juicy spirituality in Judaism then because at that time everything spiritual was considered to be an aberration of mind or superstitious in the normative traditions.

When I came to Manitoba in 1956, another rabbi there called my board and said, "You must fire him!" Why? "Because he's teaching the kids how to meditate, and don't you know you can go crazy from meditation?" That is where we stood at that time. But from the place in which we now stand, it looks quite different, and some things have come full circle. My wonderful compensation after all these years is that one of my students is now the rabbi of that congregation. So now they have someone who is an expert meditator.

PRECOCIOUS MYSTICAL FEMINISM

REB CHANNAH ROCHEL OF LUDMIR

(C.1814–C.1905)

REB CHANNAH ROCHEL was born in Ludmir, on the Lug River, around 1814.[1] Her father, Monesh Werbermacher, was a shopkeeper whose wife had been childless for many years. Indeed, he was continually counseled to divorce his wife in favor of another who would be able to bear him children. However, Monesh was very much in love with his wife and would not hear of it. So like many of the time, he sought the help of the man known as the Seer of Lublin, Reb Ya'akov Yitzhak. The Seer prayed that the devoted couple would have a child born of love, and one year later, Channah Rochel was born.

Because at that time only men could support the world with their study of Torah, a male child was much desired. However, Monesh wished for his "miraculous" daughter to imbue the world with the Divine also, as he had received her only by the grace of God. And while he knew that she could never participate in the community as a man, he nevertheless wanted her to reach her fullest potential. So as soon as she was able to go to school, ignoring the doubts and instruction of his wife and a prominent rabbi, he enrolled her in the most exclusive *cheder* in Ludmir. The only female student in the class, she learned Torah from behind a screen.

Young Channah Rochel proved to be a precocious and distinguished student of Talmud, moving well beyond the expectations of even her proud parents. But now with her successes, even her determined father began to question the wisdom of his choice. For although her intellectual horizons seemed to be without limit, he knew that eventually she would

meet the small enclosure of her worldly horizon. And her parents' mis-
givings were not without foundation. Channah Rochel had begun to
avoid the company of other children and even that of her parents. She sat
with rapt attention over her books, moodily ignoring everything else.

It was during this period that her mother died. Saddened by the death
of his wife and perplexed at the turn of his vow, he sought release from it
and removed Channah Rochel from the *cheder*. But this only made the situation worse. The young girl withdrew into her room for days and days,
swaying over the huge tomes of Talmud. Eventually, Monesh sought to
marry the girl off. But when he mentioned the prospect to Channah
Rochel, she said that she had no wish to be like other females.

Since the Seer was dead by now, Monesh sought the counsel of Rabbi
Mordecai of Chernobyl. He put Channah Rochel in the wagon and drove
the girl fifty-five miles to the north for an interview with the Chernobyler.
Rabbi Mordecai promptly reprimanded Monesh for exposing the girl to
the wisdom of the holy works. But before he was finished speaking, the
girl interrupted the sage and began to debate him on the role of women
in Jewish life. Shocked at the impudence of this outburst, the Chernobyler
angrily scolded the girl and her father for interfering with God's will. The
Chernobyler was resolved that the girl should marry and bear children,
as her role in life demanded. However, the Rebbe was no fool and did not
push the point with Channah Rochel. He called Monesh aside and counseled him to arrange a situation of advantage.

This was a sad time in Jewish history when many Jewish boys were
forcibly recruited into the Russian army and effectively cut off from
Judaism. So Monesh used the situation to his purposes. He went to the
local military post and bribed a Russian official to release a certain
promising young man into his custody every *Shabbos*. Channah Rochel,
seeing the comely young man, soon told her father that it was her duty to
instruct this unfortunate one in the ways of piety that he was cut off from
during the week. Monesh soon noticed that his usually antisocial daughter was becoming talkative, attentive, and even concerned with her
appearance before the young man, eight years her senior. Even more
amazing was the fact that the young conscript didn't seem to be threatened by Channah Rochel's learning and unusual devotion to God. Sadly,
fate soon intervened, and the young soldier was abruptly shipped out for
a tour of twenty-five years!

Channah Rochel was heartbroken and distraught. She began to frequent her mother's grave, finding a devotion to the woman in death that
she had not known in life. It was as if a bond had formed between them,
and Channah felt a certain sadness for the counsel missed. One night she

fell asleep at the tombstone and awoke frightened in the dark and began to run. In her haste, Channah Rochel tripped and fell to the ground, unconscious. In the morning her quivering body was discovered, and she was taken home. For days afterward, she lay as though in a trance. Finally, she awakened to the sound of her father quietly praying in her room. She said to him that she had just returned from the Heavenly Assembly, where an oversoul had been bestowed on her. She rose from the bed and retrieved the *tallit* and *t'fillin* she had given to her lost Sabbath companion and put them on. Monesh looked on in silent wonder.

When she was nineteen, Monesh joined his wife, and Channah Rochel disposed of the family property, which left her with a small measure of independence. This was the beginning of her rabbinical career. Word began to spread about the Holy Virgin of Ludmir, living in isolation and observing the Mitzvot as the men of the time did. Pious women and even men began to gather to hear her teaching and receive her counsel. Soon her reputation began to spread even outside of Ludmir, and travelers from far and wide began to arrive at the "green hut" of Channah Rochel. Because of the presence of men among her Hasidim, she gave teachings through a small window into the anteroom of her hut while she remained secluded in her bedchamber and study.

However, with fame came condemnation. Missives began to arrive from irate rabbinical authorities throughout Europe. These she simply refuted, citing sanctions for her behavior from the Talmud. Hearing the refutations, the rabbis threatened excommunication. This war of words persisted until finally a riot broke about before the green hut and rocks were even thrown through her window. Many of Channah Rochel's followers were hurt in the melee. Things had come to a head.

When the rabbinical authorities heard of the counsel of the late Chernobyler, a *bet din* (court) was convened, and the three judges were admitted to Reb Channah Rochel's inner sanctum. In behavior, they honored her rabbinical status but eventually convinced her that a marriage was necessary. So she married her elder attendant.

But the next morning she threw her husband out of the green hut, demanding a divorce. She had intended it to be a marriage in name only. The husband protested, but the authorities were frustrated and saw nothing left to do but excommunicate her. This enforced, she was shunned and finally resolved to leave Ludmir and go to the Holy Land.

Once there, she held court in *Meah Shearim* in the manner of a Rebbe with a small and devoted group of Hasidim. Preceding each blessing of the New Moon, Reb Channah Rochel would conduct her devotees to the tomb of Rachel and deposit petitions for matriarchal intercession. For the

Yarzheit of Rachel the Matriarch, Reb Channah Rochel and her disciples would hold vigil all day and spend the night in public prayer and reading from the Psalms.

It is said that the Maid of Ludmir finally went to her rest in the year 1905. Her legacy of disciples and teaching is shrouded in mystery, and it is still anxiously sought by many hungry hearts.

A Buried Legacy

It needs to be said that there were a great many Hasidic women of note whose names are no longer known but should be. There was the wife of Reb Avrohom of Trisk, known as Malke the Triskerin, to whom people came and gave *kvittel* (the small notes you give to a Rebbe), and treated her like a Rebbe. But it was easier for her because her husband was a Rebbe. She was legitimized through him. In other words, she shared Rebbedom with her husband. It was a similar situation with Malke, the Rebbetzin of Reb Sholom of Belz. And still others were gifted daughters of Rebbes, who found a measure of legitimacy that way. There was Rachel, the daughter of Abraham Joshua Heschel of Apt, and the daughter of the Maggid of Koznitz, who actually donned *tallit* and *t'fillin*![2]

Even in the time of the Ba'al Shem Tov, there was a model for these women: Udel, the Ba'al Shem Tov's daughter. It was she who was the inheritor and apprentice to his knowledge of herbs. She was also the keeper of his pharmacopoeia. And there are some letters extant in which he writes to her, saying, "Udel, my daughter, I'm to be in such and such a town, and I need such and such herbs. You will know which ones to give, and so on." And even before the birth of Hasidism, there were other important examples of prominent women. The daughters of Rashi, the great commentator on the Pentateuch, were women in leadership and teaching situations. And if you go back further, there was the wife of Rabbi Meir, Beruriah. A number of times when the Rabbis in the Talmud were having arguments, she was the one who showed them up.

However, the most famous was Channah Rochel, the Maiden of Ludmir. But right there in her name was the source of many of her difficulties. She was known as the Betulah of Ludmir, the Virgin of Ludmir. That conveys something that draws little sympathy in the Jewish community. That she had no desire to marry, in addition to acting as a Rebbe, upset a big apple cart. Here was a woman who felt a great spiritual urge and she had something to teach, and they forced her into a marriage that she refused to consummate, and then they didn't leave her any peace until she finally fled to the Holy Land.

Many people are upset at her fate, and some lament how she might have affected Judaism and all of Jewish culture if she had stuck around and fought it out. But I don't think so. People say, "Pick the fights that you have a chance of winning." I'm not certain there was any possibility for her to win that fight, not at that time. I am sad that she wasn't able to break through. That is why I have been so interested in finding something she has written, because I believe that this would not be merely "run of the mill" teaching. I have been trying for years to arrange to locate her grave and stake it out to see who comes to pray there because I'd like to know if she actually left any writings. I have such a wonderful suspicion that her teachings must have been very important *Shekhinah* teachings, teachings about the feminine aspect of God. Such writings have not yet come to light. I hope that one day they will be found.

In my book of stories, *The Dream Assembly*,[3] I have a piece on Channah Rochel of Ludmir. It is an intuited story and teaching born from a meditation on the kind of teachings she might have given. I reproduce it here as a dim reflection of what might have been and as a light to those who may tread where she was not able.

The Torah of the Menorah

When Reb Zalman of Zholkiew had first heard of Channah Rochel, the Maid of Ludmir, he wondered why the blessed *Shekhinah* did not have more such holy representatives. It seemed to him right that there should be female Rebbes as well as male ones—after all, were not many of the judges and prophets of old also women?

But when he later heard how the other Rebbes in her neighborhood of the tsar's country had strongly disapproved and heaped indignities upon her, Reb Zalman was gravely troubled. In his deeper meditations he had learned that she was indeed a great *Tzaddik,* a very holy soul who had undertaken to prepare the way for other female *Tzaddikim* yet to come. Because all beginnings are difficult, she had knowingly taken this task as her own—fully aware that she would meet with opposition. For her courage Reb Zalman respected her greatly, but he also knew that his own mission would be jeopardized if he openly stood at her side.

Oy, there was now so much bickering, so much fighting among the Hasidim. Disputes between the Sanzer and the Sadigorer, between the followers of the Strelisker and the Premishlaner. Where now was the joyous path of the Ba'al Shem Tov? Some persons, devoid of the holy light, had chosen to be particularly strict in observing the *mitzvot* of judgment, and now, alas, these overzealous Rebbes had decreed on the Maid of Ludmir to marry. As if that restriction could quench her burning light! But after a brief, unconsummated marriage, she was divorced, and the painful suffering of all this made her decide to leave Europe and travel to the Holy Land. There, in solitude, she would be able to devote herself fully to the service of the *Shekhinah*.

Reb Zalman was now filled with a longing to meet her face to face. He summoned Feivel the Dark and Feivel the Light to accompany him, without first telling them of his intention. Only after they had gone some miles from Zholkiew did Reb Zalman reveal his quest. Now they understood why their Rebbe had not dressed like a rabbi, and he pledged them to conceal his identity. He would pose as a merchant, traveling with two apprentices to buy goods in a distant city.

Reb Zalman trusted that God would lead them to the encounter, for he knew not where to go, since Channah Rochel, too, had veiled herself and was traveling in disguise. He knew only that she was going through the Kaiser's country to the Holy Land, accompanied by a devoted widow who served as her personal attendant. Beyond that he could only follow the road wherever it might lead.

It was mid-November, that change-of-seasons time between the gathering of the harvest and the arrival of winter. The air was cold and crisp, with frosty winds that long ago had blown the leaves to the forest floor. Reb Zalman and his companions watched the last flights of birds wing their way southward over the stark bare branches of the sleeping trees. The sharp contrast of the dark tree trunks against the sky reminded them of ink on paper, like a kind of primal script written by the hand of God in a language long forgotten, a script that moved and danced, swirling and blurring into the white-on-white nothingness of precreation.

It was no vision but a sudden blizzard that had come upon them while they were dozing. Now the snow covered the road, growing deeper and deeper, making travel impossible. Reb Zalman wanted to leave the wagon and proceed on foot, but Feivel the Light, wise in the ways of the Northland, counseled against it. One could freeze to death in a matter of hours. Better to pull off into that grove of evergreens, unhitch the horse so he could turn his back to the wind, and wait out the storm together. Good idea. But as they turned, it seemed as if the wagon had begun to spin, as if they were carried by the storm into the timeless void. How long? Who knows? But when the storm ended, they did not recognize the little town in the valley below.

Barukh HaShem—there was an inn, with warmth and food and a stable for the horse. Inside they met two women, also lost in the storm, and yes, it was Channah Rochel and her companion. Reb Zalman was overjoyed, and as it would not become them to have a private conversation behind closed doors, they sat at one table in the corner of the room, in full view but out of earshot of the others.

They spoke of the souls of women and their service to God, about the time-bound commandments from which women are exempt, about the prayers in *Tehinnah* books and the travail of the *Shekhinah* in exile. And it was to Reb Zalman as if she herself was a personification of the teachings, a hidden light veiled from the world and unable to reveal herself to the people.

"Do you know, Reb Zalman," she said, "how great is the pain of the engorgement due to the untaught Torah that is in my being? How, like the milk from a mother's breast, it wants to flow out in blessing and light?"

Reb Zalman nodded and replied, "It is true. Torah needs the giving as well as the receiving, in order that it may be 'teaching like rain,' as Moses spoke of it in his last song. So please, Channah Rochel, will you share some of your Torah? Tell me, whom do you see as the seven holy guests in the *sukkah*? We men speak of Avraham, Yitzhak, Ya'akov, Yosef, Moshe, Aharon, and David—but who are the retinue of the Holy *Shekhinah*?"

Channah Rochel began to chant:

"This has not been revealed in fullness
except that Leah is the second
and Rachel is the last
for *Gevurah* and *Malkhut,*
but the total of the seven
are not yet revealed to the world.
As you are the first to ever ask this—
a vessel open to receive—
then you are given to understand
that Miriam is the well of Grace (*Chesed*)
and Leah weeps for the wrath of severity.
Channah is the Beauty-heart of the praying woman,
and Rebekah is the victory of enduring,
while Sarah is the shining of *Hod*
and Tamar is the womb-man of *YeHU-daH* in *Yesod*
and Rachel our Mother *Malkhut.*"

Then she spoke further to Reb Zalman, saying, "Tell me, do you know the mystery of the station of the High Priest, of the clothes he wore and the rituals he performed? He was the groomsman of the *Matronita*—the female side of God—and in that was his greatness. He ministered in the way of the woman, serving the food of the Holy One and keeping His House as the Divine Presence would have him do. In holiness and beauty he tended the fire and the sacred vessels, the golden pots and pans in the House of God."

Reb Zalman now replied, "The sages once said not to 'make much talk with the women,' and I understand now that they meant we should transcend gender. So we cannot really continue this conversation until you cease to see me as 'a man' and I cease to see you as 'a woman.'"

She agreed and said, "Since I am aware that I have in former lives been a man, and since no doubt you have lived before as a woman, let us both reach the balance of the *androgynos* within ourselves and converse as we might do between earth lives."

"But," said Reb Zalman, "does not the Mishnah teach that the *androgynos* is a 'lesser person' and ought not to rise in our conversation?"

She replied in the chant of inner teachings. "Is it not taught in the Kabbalah that when the primal vessels burst in the first moments of creation, the highest sparks fell the furthest? Thus this lower level of the *androgynos* is only until the *Mashiach* comes, since we cannot yet fully appreciate that perfection. But when we will be redeemed, this balance will be the center of our inner being, no matter what gender the body we wear. For then the split will be healed in us, as it will have been between Him and Her, when YH joins VH, for on that day YHVH will be One, and One too will be the Name."

So he said to her, "Hear, O Channah Rochel!, YHVH, our God, is One."

And she, in turn, said, "Hear, O Zalman, YHVH, our God, is One."

And they both chanted *Echad* long and in harmony.

Then she said, "With you I can remove the veil of the physical world, to share with you the teaching of the menorah. Is it not written, 'The soul is the candle of God'? Every person is a menorah, for there are seven lights in the human face: two eyes, two ears, two nostrils, and a mouth. The menorah of women had to be hidden, as mine was hidden all my life, or else the ignorant ones would have harmed the light. But since you said the *Echad* with me and put your *kavanah* to the One of the Ending, I feel free to let my menorah shine, for I trust that you will not harm it." And once again she intoned the teaching chant:

> "The holy Apter taught:
> The anointing oil
> used to anoint the tent
> and the holy vessels
> in the sanctuary
> had the property
> to bring the tabernacle to life.
> So I say that
> the Menorah, too, was anointed
> and it, too, came to life,
> and when it was lit
> the sanctuary awakened to awareness.
>
> Soon will be the Feast of Hanukkah,
> and with the hemp wool
> in which the *etrog* was packed,
> you will spin the wicks
> and you will fill the lamp with oil
> and light the wicks.
> And we have been taught
> that if one had no lamp base,

it could even be made from potatoes.
For you have learned about the wick—the body;
and you have learned about the oil—the soul;
and you have learned about the flame,
but you have not learned the secret of the Menorah.

For it is, *nur mah,*
the "light of forty-five"—
and what is forty-five? *Mah?*
It stands for *Adam.*
Now tell me, Reb Zalman,
is Adam male or female?
Is it not the number
of the Holy Name
as being the world of *Atzilut*—
yud-heh-vav-heh—
and this is the *mah*
which joins the *nur*
and forms the *Menorah.*

Now why do we choose
to have a silver Menorah
if we can?
Because the secret of the Menorah
is that She is Woman,
silver like the moon.

For the real miracle
why the lights burned
for eight days
is because of the Menorah,
for it was the Menorah herself
that stretched the oil
to burn for eight days."

Channah Rochel then veiled her face again and prepared to leave, but even then, Reb Zalman saw only the menorah. He sat for what seemed like hours, contemplating the menorah in all things, creating the vessel that contains the light. Over and over he kept repeating, "*Menorah, Mah Norah, Mah Nur.*"

Before his eyes, the menorah turned to a fiery seraph, and that again to the letter *aleph.* He saw the image of the letter *yud* on top and the *yud* below, with the *vav* on an angle, joining them together. Then the *aleph* began to dance and spin with both the *yuds* in balance on either side, and he knew that the *aleph* was *androgynos,* the balance of Wholeness. And alas, he also understood that we today are in a world that began with the *bet* of twoness.

He had been given a glimpse of how the earth is *Adamah—HaAdam*, not forty-five but fifty, and in his heart he thanked the Creator that the fifty gates of Understanding had been opened to Channah Rochel. As the sages said, "Extra Understanding was given to Woman more than Man." *Ishah*—Woman = 306 and *HaMenorah* = 306, and he had been given a glimpse of that.

The two Feivels came over and roused Reb Zalman from his thoughts. Feivel the Dark handed him a note that Channah Rochel had left before she departed. What it said was this:

"All my life, people sought to change me, to stifle my Torah and extinguish my light. But what I have revealed to you cannot be hidden forever. You have received it in secret, but there will come a time when this Menorah will shine for all to see. As it is written in the Holy Zohar in the story of Noach, when you see the rainbow shining in its fullest splendor, then will the Messiah come. The rainbow—a seven-rayed Menorah—will be the sign of the Holy Light."

Reb Zalman looked up and saw that the blizzard was over and the sky was clear. But before returning to Zholkiew, he took out his Hanukkah menorah and some polishing powder—and began to weep. The tears mixed with the powder and polished the menorah until it shone like the holy light in Channah Rochel's eyes.

NOTES

PAGES 1–26   A RENAISSANCE OF PIETY: THE TEACHINGS
OF HASIDISM AND THE SHIFTING PARADIGM

1. The material in this first section is largely derived from an earlier essay titled "Seven Generations of Chabad Leaders" I wrote in 1962.

2. In 1648–1649, Hetman Bogdan Chmielnicki led a band of Cossacks allied with Crimean Tartars in a series of pogroms against Eastern European Jews in an attempt to spread the Christian doctrine. These raids were distinguished by the almost unparalleled cruelty of the Cossacks.

3. Shabbetai Tzvi (1626–1676), a Jew of Smyrna, claimed to be the Messiah but subsequently converted to Islam under threat of death in 1666. Many faithful Jews were disappointed and desolated when he failed to live up to the Messianic claim. Jacob Frank (1726–1791) saw himself as an incarnation of Shabbetai Tzvi and, claiming to be the Messiah, led his followers astray.

4. Though the authenticity of many of the extant letters of the Ba'al Shem Tov is in doubt, they have nevertheless been of immense importance to many Hasidim and reflect the oral Hasidic tradition.

5. The source of this account is a letter from the Ba'al Shem Tov to his brother-in-law, Reb Gershon, in the Holy Land. This letter is believed to be authentic.

6. Martin Buber (1878–1965), the German-Jewish philosopher, was one of the preeminent ambassadors of Hasidism to the Western world through his retellings of Hasidic stories and interpretive essays. Abraham Joshua Heschel (1907–1972), Jewish philosopher and poet, was the scion of many "royal" Hasidic lines and brought an air of authenticity to his explication of Hasidic piety and the Hasidic approach to life.

7. Jean-Paul Sartre (1905–1980) was a French existentialist philosopher and novelist.

8. Albert Camus (1913–1960) was a French novelist whose books are characterized by existential themes.

9. Martin Buber's dialogical philosophy stressed the difference between relationships of genuine reciprocity and those that were not reciprocal, expressed in the word pairs *I-Thou* and *I-It*. See his books *I and Thou, Between Man and Man,* and *Knowledge of Man.*

10. Reconstructionism was a movement started by Rabbi Mordecai M. Kaplan (1881–1983). Its aim is to recognize the evolving nature of Judaism as a civilization and to "reconstruct" particular forms of Judaism in terms of their function in the modern world. Rabbi Milton Steinberg (1903–1950) was seen as a possible successor to Kaplan but later went his own way as a congregational rabbi. He was the author of *Basic Judaism* and the novel *As a Driven Leaf.* Richard Rubenstein is best known for his active debate on the "death of God" issue.

11. This section is derived almost entirely from my article "Hasidism and Neo-Hasidism," written for the Summer 1960 issue of *Judaism: A Quarterly Journal of Jewish Life and Thought,* which reflected my views at that time. The limitations of those views will be borne out as the reader progresses through this introductory text.

12. A good portion of this section are notes excerpted and edited from Andrea Cohen-Kiener's transcription of the initial talk I gave at the course on spiritual leadership at Elat Chayyim in the summer of 1996. In it, I deal with the nature of Rebbe in the Renewal tradition.

13. The idea of paradigm shift is also discussed in my book *Paradigm Shift: From the Jewish Renewal Teachings of Reb Zalman Schachter-Shalomi.*

14. Ganesha is an elephant-headed god from the Hindu pantheon who is called the "remover of obstacles." Hanuman is a Hindu deity with simian features who is considered the model of a devotee. Sekhmet is a lion-headed goddess in Egyptian religion. Anubis is the dog-headed god of Egypt. Nandi the bull is the mount of the Hindu god Shiva. In Greek mythology, the Minotaur was a monster, with the body of a human and the head of a bull, who required a yearly human sacrifice.

15. This is not to be confused with the rationalist notion of deism that believes God created the world and its laws and then withdrew from history.

16. To this very day, people go on pilgrimages to holy places. Catholics would go, just before the terrible war broke out in Yugoslavia, to a place where there was a sighting of the Virgin Mary in Medjegorzhia.

17. Ugaritic is an extinct Semitic language related to classical Hebrew. The inscribed clay tablets from the ancient city of Ugarit (c. 1300 B.C.E.) are

probably the most important source of information about the prepatriarchal forerunners of Israel available today. They have also played an enormous part in our current understanding of ancient Israelite religion as Israel's original matrix.

18. Rabbi Moses ben Maimon (1135–1204), called Maimonides, was a great codifier of the law and a philosopher of major importance.

19. Santeria is a religion transported from the Yoruba peoples of West Africa, and various related forms are practiced today mainly in Cuba, Brazil, Haiti, and Trinidad.

20. Onkelos the Proselyte translated the Hebrew Bible into Aramaic, *Targum Onkelos*.

21. Mircea Eliade (1907–1986) was a Rumanian-born scholar of comparative religion and a respected novelist.

22. In the Christian tradition, forty weekdays from Ash Wednesday to Easter Sunday are maintained as days of fasting and penitence in remembrance of Jesus' forty days in the wilderness.

23. In Islam, a *muezzin*, "one who causes hearing," is the person who makes the call to prayer from a tower called a *minaret*.

24. One of the things Werner Erhard was doing in his "forum" was to try to give us back the power of the word.

25. *Mantra* is Sanskrit for a sacred word formula of spiritual significance or particular power. It is sometimes said to be God as word.

26. Francis Bacon (1561–1626) was an English philosopher and essayist.

27. The parable of the Good Samaritan is found in Luke 10:30–36.

28. *Star Trek* was a popular television science fiction series created by Gene Roddenberry in the 1960s and revived in the 1980s. It also gave rise to a series of motion pictures.

PAGES 27–44   A HIDDEN FIRE REVEALED: THE BA'AL SHEM TOV

1. Some authorities give the date of his birth as 1700.

2. Aryeh Kaplan, *Chasidic Masters: History, Biography, and Thought*, rev. 2nd ed. (New York: Moznaim, 1989), p. 9. Other information on the life of the Ba'al Shem Tov is taken from Tzvi M. Rabinowicz and Jacob Benard Agus, "Israel Baal Shem Tov," in Tzvi M. Rabinowicz (ed.), *The Encyclopedia of Hasidism* (Northvale, N.J.: Aronson, 1996), pp. 234–236.

3. The Zohar is the preeminent book of Jewish mysticism, traditionally held to have been written by Shimon bar Yochai. Kabbalah scholar Gershom

Scholem suggests that it is the work of the thirteenth-century Spanish Kabbalist Moshe de Leon; Gershom Scholem, *Major Trends in Jewish Mysticism* (New York: Schocken Books, 1946), pp. 190–191.

4. *Ari* is an acronym for *HaElohi Rabbi Yitzhak.* This was Rabbi Yitzhak Luria (1534–1572), the great Kabbalist of S'fat.

5. Kaplan, *Chasidic Masters,* p. 9.

6. *Tzava'at HaRivat* was translated into English by Jacob Immanuel Schochet as *Tzava'at HaRivat: Testament of Rabbi Israel Baal Shem Tov* (Brooklyn, N.Y.: Kehot Publication Society, 1998).

7. Menachem Boraisha, *Der Gayer: Kapitlen fun a Lebn* (New York: Komitet "Der Gayer," 1943).

8. Franz Rosenzweig (1886–1929) was a German Jewish philosopher and translator known for his seminal work *Star of Redemption.*

9. Ya'akov Yosef of Polonoyc, *Toldot Ya'akov Yosef,* "*Yitro.*"

10. Maimonides' Commentary on *Mishnah,* end of "*Makkot.*"

11. This story is found in a letter of disputed authenticity that is purported to have been written by Reb Adam Ba'al Shem to Reb Israel Ba'al Shem Tov.

12. Sogyal Rinpoche is a reincarnate Tibetan Buddhist lama of the Nyingma school. He is the author of the *Tibetan Book of Death and Dying.*

13. Geshe Wangyal (1901–1983) was a monk of the Gelukpa school of Tibetan Buddhism and one of the most influential of the Tibetan Buddhists who first came to teach in the West. He is the author of the now-classic *Door to Liberation.*

14. This parable is found in Reb Yaakov Yosef of Polonoye's *Toldot Ya'akov Yosef,* "*Devarim.*"

15. Ya'akov Yosef of Polonoye, *Toldot Ya'akov Yosef,* "*Bo.*"

16. Matthew 7:29. In the King James version it reads: "For he taught them as one having authority, and not as the scribes." The use of the word *parable* in place of *authority* is based on a Hebrew approach to the text. The word in Hebrew for *authority, mashal,* also means "parable." Thus those statements that the church fathers took to be of a legal nature were actually parables introducing an approach to life, not law.

17. Chaim Potok, *The Chosen: A Novel* (New York: Simon & Schuster, 1967).

18. Peter I (1672–1725), tsar of Russia from 1682 to 1725.

1. Jacob Immanuel Schochet, *The Great Maggid: The Life and Teachings of Rabbi Dov Baer of Mezhirech,* Vol. 1: *Rabbi Dov Baer of Mezhirech and His Leadership of Chassidism: A Biography* (Brooklyn, N.Y.: Kehot Publication Society, 1990), p. 19.

2. Tzvi M. Rabinowicz, "Dov Baer (the Maggid) of Mezhirech," in Rabinowicz, *Encyclopedia of Hasidism,* p. 92.

3. Kaplan, *Chasidic Masters,* p. 34.

4. Tzvi M. Rabinowicz, "Koretz, Pinhas, of Korezec," in Rabinowicz, *Encyclopedia of Hasidism,* p. 268.

5. Harry Rabinowicz, *World of Hasidism* (Hartford, Conn.: Hartmore House, 1970), p. 48.

6. J. B. Phillips, *Your God Is Too Small* (Old Tappan, N.J.: Macmillan, 1953).

7. Sufism is a mystical branch of Islam.

8. This is from the prayers of the Sufi Order International, founded by Hazrat Inayat Khan, who was of the Chishti order of Sufism.

9. Jiddu Krishnamurti (1895–1986) was an Indian philosopher whose widely influential ideas bore some similarity to the *Advaita Vedanta* of Hinduism and the *Madhyamika* of Buddhism, but in a nonspecific language.

10. In Buddhism, a bodhisattva is a being who has vowed not to leave the cycle of birth and rebirth until all sentient beings have attained enlightenment. Technically, a bodhisattva is anyone who has taken the bodhisattva vow of Buddhism but ideally is an enlightened being who actually measures up to the profundity of the vow.

11. Sri Ramakrishna liked to talk about two kinds of religious approaches. One he called "the cat" and the other "the monkey." The cat picks up a kitten and takes it from one place to the other, and the kitten just lets mama do it. And there are some people who so beautifully abandon themselves to Divine Providence that they are willing to say, "Let go and let God." By contrast, the mama monkey is climbing a tree, but her baby is holding on for dear life to mama's neck. That is how we understand attachment, *d'vekut.* Very much in monkey fashion, whatever I can do to stick with God, I want to do. It's as if God had said, "Stick with me, and you'll be all right." That kind of persistence, stick-to-it-iveness, is what the word *d'vekut* stands for. It is the glue (*devek* in Hebrew). Both the monkey and the cat are forms of transparency. It is as if the cat becomes transparent to God when we say, "Do with me whatever you want." The monkey goes

and grabs at the food and grabs at mama when it is hungry. There seems to be a lot more monkey in Judaism than there is cat.

PAGES 55–60   THE ASCETIC SAINT: REB ELIMELECH OF LIZHENSK

1. Rabinowicz, *World of Hasidism,* p. 87.

2. Story told to Nataniel Miles-Yepez by Rabbi Mordecai Twersky of Denver, head of the Talmudic Research Institute. He is the son of Rabbi Shlomo and grandson of Rabbi Jacob Israel, the Rebbe of Milwaukee.

3. Do Jews hear confession? Reb Nachman said it is really important that a person should do *Viduy d'varim lifney talmid chakham,* and it is very much like the fourth step in Alcoholics Anonymous, where you take a very straightforward accounting of who you are and what you have done. The reasoning is that you can't really fix anything until you have done that.

PAGES 61–70   THE PASSIONATE DEFENDER: REB LEVI YITZHAK OF BERDITCHEV

1. Kaplan, *Chasidic Masters,* p. 71.

2. Let us look at Elijah's Hebrew name, *Eliyahu.* If you understand a little Hebrew, you know that *El* is "God" and *Yahu* is also a name of God. So *Eliyahu* is sort of "God-God." Sometimes you simply have *Yahu* added to a name, as in *Netanyahu.* So this is like saying that even in *Natan* there is *Yahu,* God. There is also *Natan-el* or *El-natan.* These are called *theophoric* names, and they exist in many languages. For example, Theodore in Greek means "God's gift," and Timothy means "one who fears God." Philotea is "she who loves God." In Arabic, you have names like Allah-uddin (Aladdin) and Abd-allah (Abdullah). *Eliyahu* is rare in that it is a double theophoric.

3. Hermes is the god in Greek mythology who serves as the herald of the gods. His counterpart in Roman mythology is Mercury.

4. Babaji is an eternally youthful yogi in the Himalayas who appears periodically to certain practitioners of Kriya yoga.

5. Enoch, the son of Jared (Genesis 5:21–24), and Achiya HaShiloni are two others.

6. Elisha was the first jogger mentioned in the Bible. While other people are riding on horses or donkeys, he was running. He ran ahead of them. Apparently, he was a "baldy" and didn't wear a *yarmulke,* so he didn't have to worry about it falling off.

7. See 2 Kings 3:4–16.

8. Hillel and Shammai, two great scholars of the second or first century B.C.E, are usually discussed together and contrasted with each other. The Talmud records over three hundred differences of opinion between *Beit Hillel* and *Beit Shammai*. Hillel's opinion usually prevailed.

9. Rolfing Structural Integration was developed by Dr. Ida P. Rolf. It is a technique of soft tissue manipulation and movement education. She discovered that great changes in posture and structure could be effected through manipulating the body's myofacial system.

10. *Pranayama* is Sanskrit for the "control of breath" and refers to yogic techniques of regulating the breath in meditation.

11. Term made popular by the Tibetan Buddhist teacher Chogyam Trungpa Rinpoche. It refers to a level of awareness free of the usual layers of conceptual imputation.

PAGES 71–78   HEAVEN IS HERE! REB MOSHE LEIB OF SASSOV

1. Rudolph Otto, *The Idea of the Holy (Das Heilige)*, trans. John W. Harvey (Oxford: Oxford University Press, 1923).

2. William Blake (1757–1827) was an English artist, poet, and mystic.

3. Authors who have written several popular books on the topic of pain and the process of dying.

4. Larry Dossey is the author of such books as *Healing Words: The Power of Prayer and the Practice of Medicine* (New York: HarperCollins, 1993), *Prayer Is Good Medicine: How to Reap the Healing Benefits of Prayer* (San Francisco: HarperSanFrancisco, 1996), and *Be Careful What You Pray For . . . You Just Might Get It* (San Francisco: HarperSanFrancisco, 1997).

PAGES 79–87   DANCING FROM THE INFIRMARY:
THE MAGGID OF KOZNITZ

1. The biographical material is drawn from Kaplan, *Chasidic Masters*, pp. 133–135, and Tzvi M. Rabinowicz, "Kozienice, Israel Hofstein," in Rabinowicz, *Encyclopedia of Hasidism*, pp. 270–271.

2. The letters of Hebrew also double as numbers. *Gematria* is a Kabbalistic interpretive technique using the numerical value of the letters in Hebrew words to find correlations with other words with the same numerical value.

3. Sam Keen, *The Passionate Life: Stages of Loving* (San Francisco: HarperSanFrancisco, 1992).

1. The material in this discussion is largely derived from an earlier essay titled "Seven Generations of Chabad Rebbes" I wrote in 1962.

2. Elijah ben Solomon Zalman (1720–1797), the Ga'on of Vilna, thought by many to be the preeminent Talmudist, Kabbalist, and legal authority of his generation. He was the leader of the opposition to Hasidism.

3. To be called "Rebbe Reb" is a mark of exceptional respect and authority.

4. The word *Chabad* is an acronym for the Hebrew words *Chokhmah* (wisdom), *Binah* (understanding), and *Da'at* (knowledge).

5. The succession of the seven Rebbes of Chabad is often repeated as a very clear process of investiture in one chosen leader from generation to generation; however, in truth, the succession has had a very colorful history. When Reb Shneur Zalman died, his most brilliant disciple, Reb Aaron of Starosselje (1766–22 Tishri 1828), who at one time was a very great friend of Reb Dov Baer of Lubavitch, actually took over the leadership of a sizable portion of the Chabad Hasidim. The others followed Reb Dov Baer, who differed slightly with Reb Aaron as to the correct interpretation of certain of the master's teachings. When Reb Aaron died, his son took over his role, but eventually his line died out and most of that group rejoined the major portion then under the dynamic leadership of Reb Menachem Mendel I. But even within the Schneersohn family, there have been numerous valid candidates for the leadership of the movement. Often in this situation, one son would inherit the major portion of Chabad Hasidim while others became Rebbes of satellite groups until eventually most merged to form one solid movement. The inheritors of the main portion of Hasidim are those highlighted in the usual recitation of the lineage.

6. Louis Jacobs's English translation of this work, titled *On Ecstasy: A Tract,* was published in 1982, and portions have been translated by Aryeh Kaplan in his *Chasidic Masters.*

7. Saadiah ibn Joseph al-Fayyumi, called Saadiah Ga'on (892–942), was a North African rabbi and philosopher who was the head of the Babylonian Academy at Sura.

8. The Kabbalist Chayyim Vital (1542–1620) was the foremost disciple and expositor of the teachings of his master, Rabbi Yitzhak Luria.

9. Reb Yitzhak Meir of Ger (1789–23 Adar 1866) was one of the chief disciples of Reb Menachem Mendel of Kotzk. He carried on the teachings of his master and formed a very influential Hasidic dynasty of his own.

10. *Kuntres HaT'fillah* has been published in English as *Tract on Prayer* (Brooklyn, N.Y.: Kehot Publication Society, 1992).

11. This story is found in the *Likkutey Dibburim* of Yosef Yitzhak Schneersohn and is also reproduced in Herbert Weiner, *9½ Mystics: The Kabbala Today* (New York: Henry Holt, 1969).

12. "It is like the trump suit in cards. The suits can be likened to seasons. A year has four seasons; a deck of cards has four suits. A season has thirteen weeks; a card suit has thirteen cards. And if you lead a winter card in the summer, a deuce of summer trumps an ace of winter, as it were. The idea is what is in its time is best." Now, if I'm paying attention at this point to thought, and I go deep into the power that thought has, and by this I do not mean just discursive thought but the full-blown imagination of something, and I can see how if I spend time "juicing up" an evil thought, sooner or later this is going to energize some kind of action. Then, there is a lot more power in the thought to do that than in the act if it is done thoughtlessly. So that is the point he wants to make. Especially because he is also Chabad, focused on—wisdom, understanding, and knowledge. So he wants to say it is all this technology of mind. "I'm here to teach you how to use your mind in such a way that it should beget emotions." He said, *HaMiddot hen toldot Chabad,* the attitudes, the feelings, are the result of how he thinks, or "as a man thinketh in his heart, so is he." It is the same thing. Therefore, the way of Chabad is to spend time in a meditation so that you can straighten out your thought system and get from conceptual thought into situational thought so you would actually have something that you would do as a result.

13. From 1903 to 1911 he was arrested four times in Moscow and St. Petersburg. When they wanted to get rid of the father of Reb Menachem Mendel II, the last Lubavitcher Rebbe, Reb Levi Yitzhak Schneerson of Yekaterinoslav, from his post as chief rabbi of that town in the Ukraine, they claimed that he came from a family of "jailbirds." And this was true—most of the Lubavitcher Rebbes spent some time in jail.

14. Even from American presidential candidate Herbert Hoover.

15. Rabbi Chayyim Soloveitchik (1853–1918) of Brest-Litovsk, called Chayyim Brisker, was a brilliant Talmudist and originator of the Brisker method of Talmudic study. The famous Rabbi Joseph Baer Soloveitchik (1903–1993) of Isaac Elchanan Seminary of Yeshiva University was his grandson.

16. The same name as the wife of his own namesake.

17. It is often stated in various Lubavitch materials that Reb Menachem Mendel II holds numerous degrees and studied at the Sorbonne in Paris.

However, in a two-volume biography, *Larger Than Life,* Rabbi Shimon Deutsch argues that while the Rebbe did study at the University of Berlin, he never actually attended the Sorbonne but rather was a student at the Polytechnic. Rabbi Deutsch, in the absence of a successor to Reb Menachem Mendel, has broken off from the main branch of Lubavitch to form a Chabad group of his own.

PAGES 105–116   BETWEEN PERFECTION AND EVIL

1. From the title page of the *Tanya.* An English translation with facing Hebrew was published by Kehot Publications in 1969.

2. Reb Dov Baer's book *Likkutey Amarim* was first printed in Koretz in 1871.

3. The *Bardo* in the Tibetan Buddhist tradition refers to an intermediary state, specifically the intermediary states after death and before rebirth.

4. Shneur Zalman of Liadi, *Likkutey Amarim—Tanya, Sefer Shel Beynonim,* ch. 1.

5. Shneur Zalman of Liadi, *Likkutey Amarim—Tanya, Sefer Shel Beynonim,* ch. 14.

6. Descriptions of Reb Chaim Mottle Yisrael Hodakov can be found in Weiner, *9 1/2 Mystics* and in Deutsch, *Larger Than Life.*

7. John Dewey (1859–1952) and William Heard Kilpatrick (1871–1965) were important American thinkers who put forward influential philosophies of education.

8. Rabbi David Zeller, a student of Reb Shlomo Carlebach, is a singer and teacher.

PAGES 117–128   SOUL MATTERS

1. Shneur Zalman of Liadi, *Likkutey Amarim—Tanya, Sefer Shel Beynonim,* ch. 1.

2. Eligio Gallegos also relates these totem animals to the chakras.

3. Shneur Zalman of Liadi, *Likkutey Amarim—Tanya, Sefer Shel Beynonim,* ch. 9.

4. Shneur Zalman of Liadi, *Likkutey Amarim—Tanya, Sefer Shel Beynonim,* ch. 42.

5. Saul Bellow, *Henderson the Rain King* (New York: Penguin, 1996).

6. Shneur Zalman of Liadi, *Likkutey Amarim—Tanya, Sefer Shel Beynonim,* ch. 2.

7. Sometimes I envy Catholics for having these expressions. The closest we have is when we have the *t'fillin* on and kiss the *t'fillin*. That is like an "Oh, wow," exclamation point.

8. Shneur Zalman of Liadi, *Likkutey Amarim—Tanya, Sefer Shel Beynonim*, ch. 2.

9. *Patah Eliyahu* from the *Tikuney Zohar*. This is my translation and can be found in the appendixes of Zalman Schachter-Shalomi, *Fragments of a Future Scroll: Hassidism for the Aquarian Age,* ed. Philip Mandelkorn and Stephen Gerstman (Germantown, Pa.: Leaves of Grass Press, 1975). The full stanza is as follows:

> You are wise
> yet not in wisdom known
> You are understanding
> yet not in understanding known
> In You there is no place
> for knowledge
> (to hold on).

10. Ram Dass, formerly known as Richard Alpert, is a popular exponent of Hindu philosophy and was early associated with Timothy Leary and his experiments with the "mind-expanding" possibilities of LSD. A well-known book by Ram Dass is *Be Here Now* (New York: Crown, 1971).

11. Shneur Zalman of Liadi, *Likkutey Amarim—Tanya, Sefer Shel Beynonim*, ch. 2.

12. *Sushumna nadi* is the central channel through which the *kundalini* energy rises in the subtle-body in the *kundalini* yoga of the Hindu traditions.

13. Jalaluddin Rumi (1207–1273) was an important Sufi mystic and poet.

14. Shneur Zalman of Liadi, *Likkutey Amarim—Tanya, Sefer Shel Beynonim*, ch. 2.

15. The *Targum* is the translation of the five books of Moses into Aramaic by Onkelos the Proselyte in which most of the anthropomorphisms relating to God were reinterpreted.

16. In the thought of Ken Wilber, as expressed in his monumental *Sex, Ecology, Spirituality: The Spirit of Evolution* (Boston: Shambhala, 1995), the reptilian brain refers to that part of the brain that is primarily instinctual and acts according to reflex. The limbic brain processes information primarily in terms of feelings and emotions. And the neocortex is the place where information is processed self-reflexively.

PAGES 129–141 ATTRIBUTES AND GARMENTS OF THE SOUL

1. Shneur Zalman of Liadi, *Likkutey Amarim—Tanya, Sefer Shel Beynonim,* ch. 3.

2. Baruch Spinoza (1632–1677) was a Dutch philosopher of Jewish descent.

3. The Langley Porter Institute does research on psychology and the brain.

4. Shneur Zalman of Liadi, *Likkutey Amarim—Tanya, Sefer Shel Beynonim,* ch. 18.

5. The *Sefer Yetzirah* is one of the primary texts of Kabbalah.

6. This was said by Rashbatz, the teacher and mentor in adolescence of Rabbi Yosef Yitzhak Schneersohn.

7. William James, *Varieties of Religious Experience: A Study in Human Nature* (New York: Longman, 1925).

8. A major portion of this section was written in 1954.

9. Shneur Zalman of Liadi, *Likkutey Amarim—Tanya, Sefer Shel Beynonim,* ch. 4.

10. Spiritual eldering is discussed in Zalman Schachter-Shalomi and Ronald S. Miller, *From Age-ing to Sage-ing: A Profound New Vision of Growing Older* (New York: Warner Books, 1997).

11. In 1954, I submitted a version of the following material to the Lubavitch organ *Di Yiddishe Heim.* It is orthodox Chabad in both language and content.

12. *Chazal* is an acronym for *chakhmenu zichronam levaracha,* "our sages of blessed memory." This refers to the Rabbis of the Talmud.

PAGES 143–147 THE VICTORY OF THE RATIONAL SOUL

1. Much of this material was presented at an Amana conference in 1959. I was invited by a mentor, Professor Hugo Bergman, to contribute something on Chabad thought. Bergman was part of a group, which also included President Zalman Shazar of Israel, who studied Chabad thought under the guidance of a young Adin Steinsaltz, currently one of the most celebrated rabbis in the world.

PAGES 149–160 DUALITY OF GOOD AND EVIL

1. Shneur Zalman of Liadi, *Likkutey Amarim—Tanya, Sefer Shel Beynonim,* ch. 9.

2. Matthew Fox is an innovative Anglican priest whose work deals with the renewal of the Christian tradition in the light of an emerging paradigm. He is the author of numerous books, including *Original Blessing* and *Sheer Joy*.

3. Shneur Zalman of Liadi, *Likkutey Amarim—Tanya, Sefer Shel Beynonim*, ch. 10.

4. *Sangha* is Sanskrit for a unit of a Buddhist spiritual community.

5. Shneur Zalman of Liadi, *Likkutey Amarim—Tanya, Sefer Shel Beynonim*, ch. 13.

6. Zoroastrianism was the religious tradition of the Persians before the rise of Islam. It was a dualistic system of opposing forces of good and evil. Its founder was Zoroaster, and its holy book was the Zend-Avesta. Parsianism is an Indian sect of Zoroastrianism founded by Persians fleeing the Muslim dominance in the seventh and eighth centuries.

7. Franz Kafka (1883–1924), Jewish-Czech author. This tale can be found in Kafka's *Parables and Paradoxes* (New York: Schocken Books, 1961).

8. Bosnian-Serb soldiers are known to have committed atrocities in the 1992 war in Bosnia-Herzegovina against the Muslim civilian population. In addition to mass killings, it was reported that Bosnian Serb soldiers engaged in the systematic use of rape and other sexual abuses against women, men, and children.

9. Shneur Zalman of Liadi, *Likkutey Amarim—Tanya, Sefer Shel Beynonim*.

10. Sometimes this phenomenon can last all day and sometimes for only a few minutes.

11. In Buddhism, the concept of emptiness, *shunyata*, shows that there is nothing in the world of our experience that is permanent, eternal, or inherently existent.

12. *Tikkun* means kissing the frog and turning it into a prince. In a sense you are killing the frog when you kiss it. And some might say, "He was a good frog. What do you think you are doing, making a prince out of him?" There is a story something like that. A princess said to Rabbi Akiva, "Your God is a thief. He put Adam to sleep, stole one of his ribs, and made woman out of the rib. He is a thief." So Rabbi Akiva said, "Let me explain it to you. Imagine you fell asleep, and beside you there were a few pieces of iron, and when you woke up, you found some pieces of gold in their place. Would you call him a thief who stole the iron from you?" Rabbi Akiva is saying the same thing as kissing a frog to create a prince: He took a rib and gave a woman in its place; isn't that a better exchange?

PAGES 161–164   WOMAN AND THE DIVINE FEMININE

1. Shneur Zalman of Liadi, *Likkutey Amarim—Tanya, Sefer Shel Beynonim*, ch. 14.

2. Saint Augustine (354–430) was the bishop of Hippo and perhaps the first great theologian of Christianity. His major writings are *Confessions* and *City of God*.

3. Sri Ramakrishna (1836–1886) was a modern Hindu saint whose teachings were spread far and wide by his disciple Swami Vivekananda (1863–1902).

4. Georges Ivanovitch Gurdjieff (1877–1949) was the founder of a spiritual discipline called The Work.

5. Shneur Zalman of Liadi, *Likkutey Amarim—Tanya, Sefer Shel Beynonim*, ch. 52.

6. The *I-Ching* is an ancient Chinese divinatory practice.

7. Yitzhak Luria/Chayyim Vital, *Kitvey Ha-Ari*.

PAGES 165–170   FEAR AND LOVE

1. Shneur Zalman of Liadi, *Likkutey Amarim—Tanya, Sefer Shel Beynonim*, ch. 19.

2. Shneur Zalman of Liadi, *Likkutey Amarim—Tanya, Sefer Shel Beynonim*, ch. 43.

3. Shneur Zalman of Liadi, *Likkutey Amarim—Tanya, Sefer Shel Beynonim*, ch. 1.

4. This was in 1975. Allen Ginsburg (1926–1997) was a famous poet and former director of the poetry program at the Naropa Institute. He was of Jewish parentage but was a student of Buddhism under Chogyam Trungpa, Rinpoche. Jack Kornfield, also of Jewish parentage, is a Buddhist and an influential teacher of Theravadin Insight Meditation.

5. Yehudah Halevi (1075–1144) was a famous Sefardic poet and author of the *Sefer al-Kuzari*.

PAGES 171–180   ANNIHILATION OF EXISTENCE AND BROKENHEARTEDNESS

1. Shneur Zalman of Liadi, *Likkutey Amarim—Tanya, Sefer Shel Beynonim*, ch. 34.

2. Flagellants were a heretical Christian sect that originated in the thirteenth century and were known for large processional gatherings where members, stripped to the waist and with covered faces, scourged themselves with leather thongs until blood ran, all while chanting hymns. Today, sporadic flagellant processions take place under the authority of the Catholic Church and are said to have no connection with the heretical flagellants of the past.

3. Shneur Zalman of Liadi, *Likkutey Amarim—Tanya, Sefer Shel Beynonim,* chs. 28, 29, and 26.

4. Defragmenting your hard drive is a procedure whereby all the files on a hard disk are rewritten such that all parts of each file are contained in contiguous sectors.

PAGES 171–184   THE END OF THE JOURNEY

1. *Avidya* is Sanskrit for "ignorance." It is the opposite of *vidya,* "knowledge."

2. Shneur Zalman of Liadi, *Likkutey Amarim—Tanya, Sefer Shel Beynonim,* ch. 35.

3. David Bohm is an influential physicist and is known for his theory of implicate order and a series of fascinating dialogues with Krishnamurti.

4. Shneur Zalman of Liadi, *Likkutey Amarim—Tanya, Sefer Shel Beynonim,* ch. 35.

PAGES 185–200   THE WORD THAT CREATES: *sha'ar hayichud vehaemunah* AND THE REST OF THE *tanya*

1. Shneur Zalman of Liady, *Likkutey Amarim—Tanya, Sha'ar HaYichud VeHaEmunah,* ch. 1.

2. Julian Jaynes (1920–1997), U.S.-born author writing on psychology and ethnology. He is known primarily for his provocative book on the evolution of human consciousness, *The Origin of Consciousness in the Breakdown of the Bicameral Mind.*

Jaynes briefly discusses that there are three speech areas of the brain, for most people located in the left hemisphere. Jaynes focuses mainly on Wernicke's area, which is roughly the posterior part of the left temporal lobe. It is this area that is crucial for human speech.

The theory of the bicameral mind focuses on the corpus callosum, the major interconnector between the brain's hemispheres. And it was this interconnector that served as the means by which what was assumed to be the voice of "gods" (who actually dwelt in one hemisphere of the human brain) were able to give "directions" to the other hemisphere. Thus the two hemispheres at the period in human evolution functioned almost as two individuals.

3. George M. Lamsa is the author of an Aramaic-based Bible called the *Abundant Life Edition of the Holy Bible,* published by the Aramaic Bible Society.

4. Satya Sai Baba is the second Sai Baba ("incarnation"). The first was Shirdi Sai Baba. Satya Sai Baba is a venerated Hindu teacher known for his miraculous materialization of objects and more commonly of a sacred tree called *Vibhuti.*

5. Rabbi Yehudah Loew of Prague (1525–1609) was a Kabbalist who was Chief Rabbi of Prague. He is famous in the popular mind as the creator of the Golem.

6. "The Sorcerer's Apprentice" is a segment of the 1942 animated Disney film *Fantasia,* in which brooms are accidentally brought to life and proceed to fetch endless buckets of water.

7. Shneur Zalman of Liadi, *Likkutey Amarim—Tanya, Sha'ar HaYichud VeHaEmunah,* ch. 4.

8. Aldous Huxley (1894–1963) was a novelist, philosopher, and exponent of the Perennial Philosophy.

9. Shneur Zalman of Liadi, *Likkutey Amarim—Tanya, Sha'ar HaYichud VeHaEmunah,* ch. 6.

10. Schachter-Shalomi, *Fragments of a Future Scroll,* pp. 149–154.

11. Paul Tillich (1886–1965) was an influential German-Christian theologian and existentialist philosopher and the author of *The Courage to Be.*

12. *Neti neti* is a Sanskrit expression meaning "not this, not this."

13. Johann Wolfgang Goethe (1749–1832) was a German romantic poet and philosopher and the author of *Faust.*

14. You might enjoy reading the works of Alan Watts. *Joyous Cosmology* and *Beyond Theology* are both about that which hides and wants to manifest itself.

15. Shneur Zalman of Liadi, *Likkutey Amarim—Tanya, Igeret HaT'shuvah,* ch. 8.

16. Adolf Eichmann was a Nazi war criminal put on trial in Israel. Tensions ran high as the issue of his punishment was discussed. This trial was the subject of a book by the philosopher Hannah Arendt, *Eichmann in Jerusalem: A Report on the Banality of Evil* (New York: Penguin, 1994).

17. Shneur Zalman of Liadi, *Likkutey Amarim—Tanya, Igeret HaKodesh,* ch. 9.

PAGES 201–204 RADICAL HASIDISM AND THE CHALLENGE OF CHANGING PARADIGMS

1. Zionism was a movement initiated by Theodor Herzl (1860–1904) to found an independent state for Jews in the Holy Land as a homeland and a refuge.

PAGES 205–244 DREAMER OF ARCHETYPES: REB NACHMAN OF BRATZLAV

1. Most of the material in this chapter, except that on Reb Gedaliah, came from a lecture and discussion of Reb Nachman and his teachings from Philadelphia in the 1980s called "Reb Nachman of Bratzlav and His Stories" and a lecture titled "Of Three Rebbes and Four" given in 1961. The Reb Nachman tapes from the lectures on the Hasidic masters given at the Naropa Institute in 1998 were lost.

2. This sketch was written by Rabbi Avraham Yitzhak (Arthur) Green, based on conversations with Zalman Schachter-Shalomi.

3. Shankara (788–820) was the main expositor of the Hindu philosophy known as *advaita* (nondualism). Chaitanya (1486–1533) was an ecstatic mystic from the Hindu Vaisnava tradition. Akiva ben Yosef (c.15–135) was a *tanna* and foremost expositor of the Mishnaic material. Yitzhak Luria (1534–1572) was the great Kabbalist of S'fat. Saint Augustine of Hippo (354–430) was a Christian bishop and theologian. Teresa of Avila (1515–1582) was a well-known Spanish nun and mystic.

4. Mahayana Buddhism is a type of Buddhism that puts a special emphasis on the concepts of emptiness (*shunyata*) and the *bodhisattva*.

5. Rabbi Moshe Heschel was the son of Yitzhak Meir Heschel of Kopiczinitz (1862–1 Tishri 1936); a brother of the Kopiczinitzer Rebbe, Abraham Joshua Heschel (1888–16 Tammuz 1967); and a cousin of Professor Abraham Joshua Heschel (1907–1972).

6. This comment was made by his cousin the Kopiczinitzer Rebbe, Abraham Joshua Heschel.

7. Norman Vincent Peale (1898–1993) was a popular Protestant clergyman who applied Christian teachings to everyday problems. He was known for his book *The Power of Positive Thinking*.

8. Bishop Fulton Sheen used to have a radio program and wrote the popular book *The Greatest Story Ever Told*.

9. Arthur Green, *Tormented Master: The Life and Spiritual Quest of Rabbi Nahman of Bratslav,* reprint ed. (Woodstock, Vt.: Jewish Lights, 1992).

A more traditional hagiography of Reb Nachman was written by Reb Natan of Nemirov.

10. Saint John of the Cross (1542–1591) (*Juan de la Cruz*) was a Christian mystic and poet known especially for his "dark night of the soul."

11. Martin Buber says, "Most of the tales (especially those not included in this collection) were recorded in a garbled and fragmentary manner." Martin Buber, *The Tales of Rabbi Nachman,* trans. Maurice Friedman (New York: Horizon, 1956), p. 45 (originally published 1906).

12. "The Seven Beggars" (*"Die Ma'asseh mit die Zib'n Bettler"*) is translated and commented on in Aryeh Kaplan, *Rabbi Nachman's Stories* (Monsey, N.Y.: Breslov Research Institute, 1985); Adin Steinsaltz, *Beggars and Prayers* (New York: Basic Books, 1985); and Martin Buber, *Tales of Rabbi Nachman*; among other places.

13. The material for this biography was largely gathered from "Rav Gedaliah Aharon Kenig," *Tzaddik,* Erev Rosh HaShanah 5760, pp. 4–5. This is a small publication of the S'fat Bratzlav community now under the leadership of Gedaliah Kenig's son, Reb Elazar Kenig.

14. Saint Francis of Assisi (1181–1226) was a Christian mystic who experienced the *stigmata,* the wounds of Jesus, upon his own body.

15. Devanagari script of the Marathi language spoken in the Indian state of Maharashtra.

PAGES 245–250 WHO WALKS ON THE EDGE OF THE SWORD: REB MENACHEM MENDEL OF KOTZK

1. Some of this material was taken from the lecture "Of Three Rebbes and Four" (1961).

2. Søren Abbaye Kierkegaard (1813–1855) was a Danish philosopher and precursor of existentialism and dialogical philosophy.

3. Oral fragments of the Kotzker's teachings have been compiled and translated into English by Rabbi Ephraim Oratz in the book . . . *And Nothing but the Truth* (Brooklyn, N.Y.: Judaica Press, 1989).

PAGES 251–261 DEPLOYED BY GOD: REB MORDECAI YOSEF OF ISHBITZ

1. Morris M. Faierstein, *All Is in the Hands of Heaven* (Hoboken, N.J.: Ktav, 1989), p. 12.

2. Faierstein, *Hands of Heaven,* p. 12.

3. The *Mei HaShiloach* has recently been translated into English by Betsalel Philip Edwards under the title *Living Waters* (Northvale, N.J.: Aronson, 2001).

4. Bratzlavers wear two.

5. Betar was a youth movement associated with Revisionist Zionists who were advocates of a more forceful action to establish a Jewish homeland than most conventional Zionists favored. Haganah was an underground military organization of the *Yishuv* in Palestine from 1920 to 1948. It evolved from a loose organization of defense groups to a finely disciplined military organization. The Irgun was a right-wing underground terrorist organization operating until 1948. The Stern Group or Stern Gang was a Zionist terrorist organization in Palestine founded by Avraham Stern after he split from the Irgun. It was suppressed in 1948.

PAGES 271–274   LOVING THE LAND AND ITS PEOPLE IS LOVING GOD: REB ABRAHAM ISAAC KOOK

1. Sri Aurobindo (1872–1950) was an influential and somewhat nontraditional Hindu thinker whose works focused on a vast synthesis of ideas. Some of his great works are *The Life Divine* and *Synthesis of Yoga*. Rabindranath Tagore (1861–1941) was the "poet laureate," so to speak, of modern India. He was the author of *Gitanjali*. Walt Whitman (1819–1892) was an American poet whose blank verse was revolutionary in form and content. He was the author of *Leaves of Grass*, which contained his epic, "Song of Myself."

2. Rabbi David Cohen edited some of Rav Kook's writings and figures prominently in Herbert Weiner's classic, *9 1/2 Mystics*.

PAGES 275–277   YEA, THOUGH I WALK THROUGH THE SHADOW OF DEATH: REB KALONYMOUS KALMISCH OF PIASETZNA

1. Tzvi M. Rabinowicz, "Shapira, Kalonymus Kalmish, of Piaseczno," in Rabinowicz, *Encyclopedia of Hasidism*, p. 448.

PAGES 279–286   THE MYSTIC PROLETARIAN: REB HILLEL ZEITLIN

1. Edward K. Kaplan and Samuel H. Dresner, *Abraham Joshua Heschel: Prophetic Witness* (New Haven, Conn.: Yale University Press, 1998), vol. 1, p. 62.

2. Rabinowicz, *World of Hasidism*, p. 165. An insightful study of Reb Hillel Zeitlin up to 1919 is the doctoral thesis by Moshe Waldoks, "Hillel Zeitlin: The Early Years, 1894–1919," Brandeis University, 1982.

3. Menachem Daum and Oren Rudavsky (prods.), *A Life Apart: Hasidism in America*, film broadcast on PBS (Oren Rudavsky Productions, 1997).

PAGES 287–296   THE MASTER OF VIRTUOUS REALITY:
REB SHLOMO CARLEBACH

1. Yitta Halberstam Mandelbaum, *Holy Brother: Inspiring Stories and Enchanted Tales About Rabbi Shlomo Carlebach* (Northvale, N.J.: Aronson, 1997), p. xxvi.

2. Rabbi David Halevy (c. 1586–1667), called TaZ, an acronym for *Turei Zahav*, his commentary on the *Shulhan Arukh*.

3. Mandelbaum, *Holy Brother*, pp. xxv–xxvi.

4. Mandelbaum, *Holy Brother*, p. xxvii.

5. Reuven Alpert, *God's Middlemen: A Habad Retrospective: Stories of Mystical Rabbis* (Ashland, Ore.: White Cloud Press, 1998), p. 72.

6. Rabbi Eliya Chayyim Carlebach (1925–1990) was a Bobover Hasid, a scholar of excellent reputation, and founder of the Hasidic Research Center, *Zekher Naftali*.

7. This story is also told in Mandelbaum, *Holy Brother*, pp. 51–52.

8. Pir Vilayat Khan is the son of Hazrat Inayat Khan, who brought the *Chishti* teachings of Sufism to the West and is the present spiritual leader of the Sufi Order International.

PAGES 297–306   PRECOCIOUS MYSTICAL FEMINISM:
REB CHANNAH ROCHEL OF LUDMIR

1. The biographical material is taken almost entirely from Charles Raddok's short biography, "Channah, the 'Rebbe' of Lodomeria (A Hasidic True Story)," *American Judaism*, Spring 1965.

2. For more on these Hasidic women, see Harry M. Rabinowicz, *Hasidism: The Movement and Its Masters* (Northdale, N.J.: Aronson, 1994), or the entry for "Women" in Rabinowicz, *Encyclopedia of Hasidism*.

3. *The Dream Assembly: Tales of Rabbi Zalman Schachter-Shalomi, Collected and Retold by Howard Schwartz* (Nevada City, Calif.: Gateways/IDHHB, 1989). The story of Channah Rochel was written by Zalman Schachter-Shalomi with an introductory passage by Yonasson Gershon, pp. 176–184. It has been adapted slightly for this volume, and some of the spellings have been changed.

GLOSSARY

Ada'ata d'nafshey ("minding one's own soul") Situational thinking and feeling in prayer.

Ain Sof ("endless") The Infinite Nothing. The Kabbalistic designation for the absolute Godhead.

Assiyah ("deed") The World of Action according to Kabbalistic teachings; the lowest world just below *Yetzirah*.

Atzilut ("emanation") The World of Emanation. The highest of the Four Worlds. In the Kabbalistic cosmogony, the archetypal world.

Avodah ("service") Often used as a synonym for *prayer*, as in *avodah sh'b'lev*, "heart service."

Barukh HaShem ("Praised be the Name") "Name" refers to the unpronounceable four-lettered name of God, *YHVH*.

Beynoni ("intermediate one," pl. *Beynonim*) One who does not transgress but is still inclined to transgression. The man in-between the *tzaddik* and *rasha*. A key concept in the *Chabad* philosophical system.

Binah ("understanding") The second (or third)* of the *Sefirot* (divine emanations).

Bittul ha'yesh ("annhilation of existence") Effacing, or making the ego transparent.

B'riyah ("creation") According to the Kabbalah, the World of Creation, produced from the World of *Atzilut*.

Chabad (Acronym for *Chokhmah, Binah, Da'at*) The name of a mystical and intellectual group within Hasidism.

Chayyah In Kabbalistic terminology, the transmental state of the soul.

Chesed ("lovingkindness") One of the ten *Sefirot*. Also known as *Gedulah*.

Chokhmah ("wisdom") The first (or second)* of the *Sefirot*.

---

*In some systems the *Sefirot* are ordered *Keter, Chokhmah, Binah, Chesed, Gevurah, Tiferet, Netzach, Hod, Yesod, Malkhut*. In another system the order is *Chokhmah, Binah, Da'at, Chesed, Gevurah, Tiferet, Netzach, Hod, Yesod, Malkhut*. Hence "second (or third)."

Da'at ("knowledge") An intermediary *Sefirah* very important in the *Chabad* system.

Davvenen Praying, worshiping, living the liturgy. (Possibly derived from the Latin *divinum*.)

Dibbur ("word," speech) The middle garment of the soul. The inner one is Thought, the outer one is Action.

D'vekut ("clinging," absorption) Sticking or cleaving to God.

Etzah ("counsel," pl. *etzot*) Points of advice with which you can make a change and a difference.

Gemillut chasadim ("Deeds of lovingkindness") One of the three pillars the world stands on.

Gevurah ("strength," severity) One of the ten *Sefirot*.

Halakha ("way to walk," the process) Jewish law.

Hasid ("one who is pious") A member of the Hasidic movement.

Hasidim ("pious ones") Followers of the third religious movement known as Hasidism, founded by Reb Israel, the Ba'al Shem Tov, in the seventeenth century. The earlier ones were the desert Hasidim mentioned in the Talmud and the Hasidim of medieval Germany, followers of Judah the Pious.

Hasidut Teachings of the Hasidim.

Hitbodedut ("aloneness," "solitude") A term for extemporaneous prayer among the Bratzlaver Hasidim, which finds them "alone with God."

Hitbonenut ("self-inspection") Looking deeply into oneself or into a sublime idea. A general term for meditation in the Jewish tradition, and a technical term in *Chabad* Hasidism.

Hitkal'lut ("blending") Merging, harmonizing of all things; integration.

Hod ("glory" beauty, elegance) One of the ten *Sefirot*.

It'hapkha ("convert") Making something into its opposite. The transformative process making bitter into sweet, evil into good, darkness into light. A technical term in the *Chabad* philosophy.

It'kaffia ("self-enforcing," "bending," "subduing") The process of denial. A technical term in the *Chabad* philosophy, referring to the *Beynoni*'s working with a process in which the *Nefesh HaBehamit* is deconditioned from addictive habits and virtually replaced by the assertion of a more humane, more Godly identity.

Kavanah ("intention," "aiming") The spiritual concentration invested in the service of God.

Keli ("vessel," pl. *kelim*) A vessel.

Kiddush ("sanctification") The prayer of sanctification recited on the Sabbath and festivals.

K'lipah ("shell," "husk," pl. *K'lipot*)   A synonym for the energy system of evil.

K'lipat Nogah ("translucent shell")   The rind of Venus; a shell containing some good and distinguished from the more obscuring, opaque *k'lipot*.

Kohen ("priest")   A Jewish priest.

Kuntres ("treatise")   A tract or pamphlet.

L'vush ("garment")   A technical term for the cloak in which one becomes invested in the *Chabad* philosophy.

Ma'aseh ("deed")   The outermost garment of the soul.

Machshavah ("thought")   The innermost garment of the soul.

Maggid ("preacher")   One who tells the *Aggadah,* the tale.

Makom ("space")   A synonym for God.

Mal'ach ("angel," "messenger," pl. *mal'achim*)   An angel.

Malkhut ("kingdom," "majesty")   One of the ten *Sefirot,* specifically representing the feminine, the *Shekhinah.*

Mamash (Yiddish, "so-beingness," "palpability")   The feeling that something "is really so," immediately evident as if felt bodily.

Mashal   An analogue or parable.

Mashiach ("anointed")   The Messiah.

Menorah ("candelabra")   Ceremonial candelabra.

Mentsch (Yiddish, "man")   An exemplary human being.

Middah ("attribute," pl. *middot*)   Each *middah*, or emotional attribute, is a consequence of a *sekhel*, an intelligence, thought sequence, or idea syndrome, consisting of *chokhmah, binah,* and *da'at.* The *middot* correspond to the lower seven *Sefirot.*

Minyan   Quorum; the minimum number of ten Jews required for communal prayer.

Mitnagged ("opponent")   An opponent of the Hasidim.

Mitzvah ("connection," pl. *mitzvot*)   A "commandment" in the Jewish tradition, popularly equated with a good deed.

M'malleh Kol Almin ("fills all worlds")   The immanent light of God in creation.

Mochin ("brains")   The energies of the mind or reason.

Nachus   A feeling of deep satisfaction.

Nebukh ("alas!")   Poor, pitiful; an expression of alarm.

Nefesh   The lowest soul level. The animative function of the soul.

Nefesh HaBehamit ("Animal Soul")   The animal aspect of the soul; the habits of the body.

Nefesh HaElokit ("Divine Soul")   The Divine aspect of the soul.

Neshamah ("soul," pl. *neshamot*)   The level of the soul coming between *Ruach* and *Chayyah*. The intellectual manifestation of the soul.

Netzach ("victory")   One of the ten *Sefirot*.

Niggun ("melody," pl. *niggunim*)   Dr. Abraham Joshua Heschel described the Hasidic melody as "a tune in search of its own unattainable end."

Olam ("world")   World.

Rasha ("evil one")   A person whose and actions and intentions are wicked.

Reb   A term of respect and friendly admiration.

Rebbe   The spiritual leader of a Hasidic sect; the religious leader of a Hasidic community.

Reshayim sh'aynam gemurim   People who are not altogether wicked.

Ribono Shel Olam ("Master of the Universe")   One of the many names for God.

Rosh HaShanah ("new year")   The Jewish New Year.

Ruach   In Kabbalistic terminology, the spirit in human beings. The emotive function of the soul.

Sefirah ("emanation," pl. *Sefirot*)   Any of the ten divine emanations or attributes that manifest themselves in the Four Worlds.

Sekhel   An intelligence or thought sequence consisting of *Chokhmah*, *Binah*, and *Da'at*.

Shabbat   Hebrew name for the Sabbath.

Shabbos   Yiddish name for the Sabbath.

Shavuot   The holiday commemorating the receiving of the Torah on Mount Sinai.

Sh'ma ("hear")   The prayer, "Hear O Israel, the Lord is our God, the Lord is One."

Shochet   A ritual slaughterer.

Shofar   Ram's horn blown on Rosh HaShanah as part of the ritual.

Shtetl   A small Jewish town or village in Eastern Europe.

Shul   A Jewish house of worship; synagogue.

Siddur   A prayer book.

Sitra Achra ("the side of the otherness")   The evil aspect of the universe.

Sovev Kol Almin ("surrounds all worlds")   The light of God that transcendently encompasses the world.

Sukkot   The harvest festival, celebrated by dwelling in temporary shelters.

Tallit   A prayer shawl.

Talmud   A collection of commentarial literature on the primary work known as the Mishnah, the oral Torah.

T'fillah   Prayer.

T'fillin   Small leather boxes containing particular scriptures attached to the head and arm for prayer.

T'hillim   Psalms.

Tiferet ("beauty")   One of the ten *Sefirot*.

Tikkun ("ordering," "repairing")   Making reparation and restitution.

Tohu ("chaos")   Chaos.

Torah ("instruction")   Specifically, the five books of Moses, but generally any Jewish teaching.

T'shuvah ("repentance")   Repentance.

Tzaddik ("the righteous one," pl. *Tzaddikim*)   A saintly, righteous person; a charismatic leader; the leader of a Hasidic sect, a Rebbe.

Tzaddik gamur ("the complete righteous one")   A perfect *Tzaddik* in the system of *Chabad* who no longer feels even the slightest urge to sin.

Tzimtzum ("contraction")   The self-concealment of God.

Tzitzit   The ritual threads hanging from the *tallit* to signify the 613 *mitzvot* (commandments) in the Torah and to remind one to observe them.

Yahrzeit   A death anniversary, usually celebrated in memory of saints or special persons.

Yechidah   In Kabbalistic terminology, the highest state of the soul.

Yeshiva   An advanced academy for studying Torah, especially for the training of rabbis.

Yesh m'Ayin ("something from nothing")   An expression of how God created the universe. The same as *creatio ex nihilo* in Latin.

Yesod ("foundation")   One of the ten *Sefirot*.

Yetzer ha'ra ("evil inclination")   The impulse to negativity in thought, word, or deed that arises in a person.

Yetzirah   According to Kabbalistic teachings, the world of angels, formed from emanations from *B'riyah*.

Yir'ah   Respect.

Yom Kippur ("day of atonement")   The Day of Atonement.

Zohar   The central work of Jewish mysticism.

BIOGRAPHIES

RABBI ZALMAN SCHACHTER-SHALOMI, better known as Reb Zalman, was born in Zholkiew, Poland, in 1924. Raised largely in Vienna, his family fled the Nazi oppression in 1938 and finally landed in New York City in 1941 and settled in Brooklyn, where he enrolled in the *yeshiva* of the Lubavitcher Hasidim. He was ordained by Lubavitch in 1947. He received his master of arts degree in the psychology of religion (pastoral counseling) in 1956 from Boston University and a Doctor of Hebrew Letters degree from Hebrew Union College in 1968.

He taught at the University of Manitoba, Canada, from 1956 to 1975 and was professor of Jewish mysticism and psychology of religion at Temple University until his early retirement in 1987, when he was named professor emeritus. In 1995 he accepted the World Wisdom Chair at Naropa University, where he is currently a professor in the Department of Religion.

Throughout his long career, Reb Zalman has been an unending resource for the world religious community. He is the grandfather of the Jewish Renewal movement, the founder of the Spiritual Eldering Institute, an active teacher of Jewish mysticism, and a participant in ecumenical dialogues, including the widely influential dialogue with the Dalai Lama documented in the book *The Jew in the Lotus*. He is the author of *Paradigm Shift, Spiritual Intimacy,* and *From Age-ing to Sage-ing*. Reb Zalman currently lives in Boulder, Colorado, and continues to be active in mentoring the next generation of Jewish Renewal.

NATANIEL M. MILES-YEPEZ was born in Battle Creek, Michigan. He studied history of religions and comparative religion at Michigan State University, contemplative religion at Naropa University, and contemplative traditions at Naropa University. He is ordained in the Sufi tradition and currently lives with his wife, Jennifer, in Boulder, Colorado, where he is a painter of religious icons, writer, and the editor of print and Web site publishing for the Spiritual Paths Foundation.

INDEX

A

Aaron-Eliezer, 279

Aaron of Starosselje, 314n5

Abraham, 8, 16, 62, 166, 242–243

Abraham, Reb ("the Angel"), 90, 92, 214

Abraham Abba, 47

Abraham David of Klimovitch, 99

Abraham Gershon of Kuty, 28, 30

Abraham of Pzhysha, 79

Achiya the Shilonite, 28–29, 33–34, 228, 312n5

Adam Ba'al Shem, 310n11

Agudat Israel, 202, 272

Ain Sof, 5, 7, 48, 194

Akavya ben M'hallallel, 248

Akiva, Rabbi, 52, 179, 212, 319n12, 323n3

All Is in the Hands of Heaven (Fairstein), 253

Amalek, 81–87; love and, 86–87; the Maggid of Koznitz and, 81–87; personal struggle and, 81–83; redemption of, 83; and renewal, 85; strength and, 83–84; yetzer ha'ra and, 81, 83, 84, 87

Angels with Dirty Faces (film), 155–156

Animal Soul (Nefesh HaBehamit): the absolute Rasha and, 109; the body and, 109, 118–120; Divine Soul and, 109, 118, 143; as dwelling in the left side of heart, 149; God's creation of Man's, 9; and maintenance of Beynoni, 145–146; and Nefesh/Nafs, 119, 126; Rational Soul and, 143–146; and self-image and identity, 143; Shneur Zalman's

teachings on, 109, 117–120, 135, 143; totem animals and, 118, 316n2; in a Tzaddik, 118

Animals: Neshamah of, 127; Ruach of, 127–128. See also Animal Soul (Nefesh HaBehamit)

Anubis, 16, 308n14

Ari. See Luria, Yitzhak

Asherah, 162

Ashlag, Yehudah, 280

Assiyah ("deed"), 155, 194

Atzilut ("emanation"), 7, 8, 155, 194, 200

Augustine, Saint, 10, 161, 212, 320n2, 323n3

The Autobiography of a Yogi (Yogananda), 64

Avidya ("ignorance"), 181, 321n1

Avodah ("service"), 8, 144

Awe: Heschel on, 191; love for God and, 165–168, 181–184; Moshe Leib of Sassov on love and, 72–73; Otto and idea of holy, 72–73; in prayer, 182–183; and relationship between YHVH and Elohim, 190–192; Shneur Zalman and, 165–168, 181–184, 190–192. See also Fear

B

Ba'al, 16, 162

Ba'al Shem Tov, 27–44; daughter Udel, 300; death of, 30, 46, 47; disciples of, 29–30, 36–38, 46, 47, 114; early enemies, 29; early study of Zohar, 28; first teacher, Achiya the Shilonite, 28–29, 33–34, 228; letters of, 1, 307nn4, 5; and Levi

M